VOLUME II OF
NORTHWEST PASSAGES

by Bruce Calhoun

A collection of Northwest cruising stories.
Some of these articles have appeared under this title
in recent issues of *Sea and Pacific Motor Boat*.

Published by the Book Division of
Miller Freeman Publications Inc.
San Francisco, California 94105

Dedicated
to Aletha E. Smith

who has been invaluable
in the preparation of this book.
Her constructive criticism,
editing, typing, and encouragement have made the task easier.

Library of Congress Catalog Card Number 75-8887.
Standard Book Number 0-87930-002-7.

Copyright © 1972
by MILLER FREEMAN PUBLICATIONS INC.

First impression, March, 1972.
Printed in the United States of America.

About this book

Acceptance of *Northwest Passages* (Volume 1) by both cruising yachtsmen and armchair skippers, not only in the Pacific Northwest but along the entire Pacific Coast, has been so enthusiastic that it seems fitting to continue the publishing of these articles in book form. The first volume was primarily concerned with the waters from Olympia up to, and including, Desolation Sound. Volume II revisits some of the same areas and continues northward and northeastward with more detailed treatment from Desolation Sound to southeastern Alaska. While most of the material has appeared in recent issues of *Sea and Pacific Motor Boat,* new information has also been included.

Although most of the cruising areas in Northwest waters remain much the same today as when Captain Vancouver first saw them, some things do change, particularly the more civilized aspects. With this in mind and to keep good cruising information up-to-date, a series of "Rediscovery" cruises was taken. Thus Section I is an updating and extension of material covered in Volume I, not so much in a cruising story format but as an informational and factual presentation for help and guidance to the skipper.

Again, since the publication of Volume 1, *Sea and Pacific Motor Boat* has carried Northwest cruising stories by other authors. Their work adds much to the enjoyment of cruising in this area and certainly has a proper place in a book of this kind. We are most grateful to those authors and photographers who so generously gave permission to include their material. We also appreciate contributions of photographs by other individuals and organizations: Fred Belcher, Austin Seth, Stearns of Seattle, Bob and Ira Spring, Alaska Airlines, State of Alaska Travel Division, and the U.S. Coast Guard.

It is the sincere hope of the author and the publisher that this book will be as well received as was Volume 1, and that it may prove valuable to Northwest yachtsmen, their families and guests by increasing their enjoyment of these "greatest cruising waters in the world."

Bruce Calhoun

Contents

Charts and Maps

Charts and maps in Northwest Passages II are not to be used for navigation.

Cruising in the Pacific Northwest: an Overview

"Nothing can be more striking than the beauty of these waters without a shoal or a rock or any danger whatever for the whole length of this internal navigation, the finest in the world. Nothing can exceed the beauty of these waters and their safety. I venture nothing in saying that there is no country in the world that possesses waters equal to these." So said Capt. George Vancouver in describing Puget Sound.

Vancouver, with the typical British Navy tradition for understatement in most of his original journal, waxed enthusiastic about these waters. He further wrote, "To describe the beauties of this region will, on some future occasion, be a very grateful task to the pen of a skillful panegyrist. The serenity of the climate, the innumerable pleasing landscapes, and the abundant fertility that unassisted nature puts forth, require only to be enriched by the industry of man with villages, mansions, cottages, and other buildings, to render it the most lovely country that can be imagined."

This is the area with which we are concerned, and today, nearly 200 years after Vancouver's exploration, his assessment is still valid with one exception. Knowledgeable skippers are aware that the statement, "without a shoal or a rock or any danger whatever," cannot be accepted. Compared to other waters of the world, these are relatively safe but we do have shoals and rocks and dangers. While there are hazards and opportunities for an occasional misadventure, it is well to remember that only the skipper who does nothing never makes a mistake. Most boatmen in this area "do things," and there aren't too many mistakes made.

The name Puget Sound, given by Vancouver to honor his lieutenant, Peter Puget, who did the exploring of the southern part of this inland sea, actually applies only to those waters south of Tacoma's Point Defiance and the Narrows. Today official charts show Admiralty Inlet and Saratoga Passage as the two inlets to the north, while Puget Sound extends to Foulweather Bluff.

The San Juan Islands, along with another set of straits, passages, sounds and inlets, lie in Washington Sound, a name which, unfortunately, has been little used and is almost forgotten. Even most charts fail to use it.

By popular usage the entire area from Georgia Strait to Olympia has become loosely known as Puget Sound, and it includes nearly 1800 miles of shoreline. It encompasses so many bays, coves and harbors that the boatman hardly needs to drop his anchor in the same place twice, unless he has found a favorite spot to which he enjoys returning.

We've mentioned only Puget Sound thus far but these same words can be used over again for the enchanting waters of British Columbia and southeastern Alaska. True, Vancouver wasn't enthusiastic about Desolation Sound, as evidenced by the name with which he graced it, but anyone who has cruised there will be quick to argue that a lovelier area would be hard to find.

As the cities become more congested, as life becomes increasingly more tense with man's competition for the almighty dollar, as high-speed freeways take their toll of lives and nerves, the peace and solitude of our blessed Northwest waterways become more and more desirable. Here the boatman can travel as he wishes, go where he wants when he wants, and be relaxed as he leaves a bustling civilization behind. Waterways with inexpressible beauty and an infinite variety of physical attributes stretch from Olympia to Skagway. It is small wonder that Seattle, largest city of the area, has come to be known as the "Boating Capital of the World," with the largest boat registration per capita.

Emerald-clothed islands, unspoiled and uncluttered, pleasant quiet beaches, hospitable harbors and anchorages, solitary campsites and peaceful retreats — all offer escape from the cares and noise of the city. Boatmen take full advantage of this. They cruise the solitary passages, picnic or camp on the beaches, fish off the points or where the tides meet, hike to tidelands to beachcomb, gather interesting and fantastically shaped pieces of silver driftwood and study marine life in the tidal pools.

The state of Washington and the Province of British Columbia, recognizing the need of boatmen for an access to shore with cooking, camping and sanitary facilities, have established marine parks. Some of these have additional facilities, while others are strictly unimproved wilderness areas which permit the boatman to get ashore and enjoy the unspoiled heritage of nature on publicly owned land.

Boats in these waters come in all sizes and shapes, the selection depending on each skipper's tastes, ideas, dreams and pocketbook. With the coming of the outboard motor and mass production of fiber-glass boats, along with easy credit financing, almost anyone can become the master of his own ship. Boating is no longer only for the wealthy.

Whether "rag picker" (sailor) or "stinkpotter" (power-boater), the small boatman is by far in the majority. Powerful outboards or the ever-more-popular inboard/outdrive boats have given a mobility to the small boatman. By trailering his boat and by virtue of speed, he can cover plenty of land and water in a short time. A large number of these are in the 20- to 25-foot cabin-type class. They may offer a minimum of space and comfort to the cruising family, compared to the larger yachts, yet both skippers and mates use remarkable ingenuity in utilizing every bit of room and devising methods of living, eating and cooking to the best advantage. The larger boats, of course, offer more "livability" and are more self-sufficient, but they cost more.

Whatever the boat size, when the sun sends its glistening jewels to dance on the rippling water, or the green of forested islands is reflected in the mirror of a bay, the boatman is beckoned to board his craft and take off for the weekend, a vacation or the summer. Some may set a course for a favorite solitary anchorage, while others will head for a marine resort. It all depends upon likes and dislikes.

Another area of Northwest cruising waters lies in Oregon, along its coast and up the many miles of the Columbia and Snake Rivers. Here boating conditions are a little different but, for those using these waters, they are equally enjoyable.

Let's not forget the possibility of winter cruising in the Northwest. Warmed by the tempering influence of the Pacific Ocean and the Japanese Current, the region boasts a considerably milder winter climate than the same latitudes across the rest of the country.

True, some boat owners, perhaps with origins in other parts of the country, virtually put their craft in wraps some time after Labor Day and don't break them out until April or May. Many others, more and more each year, have discovered the joys of winter cruising. It's somewhat different than in the warm summer months, but it can be just as enjoyable for the skipper and his family.

With a wary eye on the weather and storm forecasts, there are many periods when cruising can be a delight. The waters, passages, coves and bays take on a different aspect, and fishing, clamming, oystering or crabbing are still good. There is a coziness aboard the boat, with the stove or small fireplace exuding a comforting warmth, although rain may be pocking the water surface outside and playing a little symphony on the deck overhead. Even at rare times when the crisp air will condense atmospheric moisture to form a coating of ice on outer decks, there is an exhilaration as you step out of the warm cabin to savor the clear, pine-scented breeze mixed with the wood smoke from fireplace or range. It makes that steaming cup of coffee or other hot drink taste doubly good.

Place-names add fascination to cruising anywhere but particularly in the Northwest. Many of our names have historical backgrounds, honoring people and events of the past which take us back to the early days of exploration. Others whet our imaginations or lend an aura of color to our cruising. Places such as Massacre Bay with its Skull Island, Smugglers Cove, Horsehead Bay, Mosquito Pass, Active Cove, Mystery Bay, Hole in the Wall, Apple Tree Cove, Buccaneer Bay, Secret Cove and many others intrigue as we seek them out, explore them and add them to our logbooks.

In considering the vastness of these Northwest cruising waters, we find a tendency to catalogue them into separate natural areas. Depending on the location of one's home port, any given area may be utilized for short overnight or weekend trips or perhaps those winter-month cruises. Others will be an objective for that annual vacation cruise, while the more remote ones will be saved for the time when several weeks or even months can be found in saved-up vacations or retirement to enjoy them.

Although the nature of this volume does not permit a clear-cut designation of areas, we have divided the chapters into six parts. Five of them deal with cruising waters from Olympia to areas in southeast Alaska. While there will be overlapping and inclusion of waters outside the designated areas, the chapters within each section will deal primarily with the main points of interest within that area.

Starting in the south and moving north, Part 1 includes waters from Olympia to Johnstone Strait. This area we have divided roughly into eight chapters. They include waters from Olympia to Tacoma, embracing Captain Vancouver's intended Puget Sound and correctly called Upper Puget Sound; the mid-sound section from Tacoma north to Foulweather Bluff; and farther north and west, Admiralty Inlet, Saratoga Passage and Hood Canal, since its entrance is in this area.

Part 1 also includes Washington Sound and the San Juan Islands; the Canadian Gulf Islands; and the area around the Gulf of Georgia, embracing everything from a line between Nanaimo and Vancouver northwest to the 50° parallel on the top of the gulf. We use the term "Gulf" rather than the officially charted "Strait of Georgia," because that was the original name given by Vancouver before he knew it connected with the Pacific to the north, and because of common local usage by Canadians. Also in this "Gulf" area are

Sechelt and Jervis Inlets with their very attractive appendages.

Still in the waters covered in Part 1, are those we call the Desolation Sound area, although Desolation Sound is actually only a small part of it. This area takes in waters from Campbell River east to Malaspina Inlet, north to Stuart Island at the Yucultas and Toba and Bute Inlet.

Moving still farther northwestward, or mostly westward, Part 2 runs to the 51° parallel to include the myriad of inlets, arms, straits and sounds to the northern tip of Vancouver Island. This area has been explored by a small minority of Northwest skippers but is still remote, quiet and lonesome, just waiting to share its beauty and charms with those having the time and inclination to cruise a bit farther.

Vancouver Island's west side, with a wealth of beautiful and fascinating inlets and sounds, takes up much of Part 3.

Now we come to the northern part of British Columbia's west coast, a vast area, all somewhat similar. It contains the famous Inland Passage to Alaska, but there are innumerable waterways of all kinds, islands, bays and coves of incredible beauty, offering the cruising yachtsman a lifetime of exploration. This area is included in Part 4, which also takes in parts of southeast Alaska, where still another lifetime could be spent in seeing and enjoying all that is available.

Part 5, whose chapters are all by other authors, is also devoted to Alaskan cruises. However, there is much of interest about other areas along the way from home ports, on journeys covering many miles.

Towering snow-covered mountains spawning glistening glaciers are a highlight of Alaskan cruises, although history, spectacular scenery, interesting towns and tranquil anchorages must be given their due in the list of attractions.

Part 6, dealing with the Northwest maritime scene, gives information on parks for boating families, and light stations that may be visited. It also describes Seattle's Opening Day pageant and includes a couple of chapters showing that some of these waters can be turbulent during the winter. Ports of call, with points of interest, end the section.

It is small wonder that Northwest boatmen feel they have been many times blessed with a rare heritage in their cruising waters. This meandering inland sea, with its many enthralling charms, captivates and soothes the boatman's mind, renews his body and transports him from a demanding civilization to a realm of quiet peace and relaxation. Best of all, he can never run out of places to go. If he were to cruise all of his life, he could never fully cover all that these waters have to offer.

Captain Vancouver's description and projection are true, and this corner of the world must certainly be set apart as one of the most scenic and enjoyable on earth. The Pacific Northwest definitely offers the finest cruising waters to be found anywhere in the world.

Views such as this one at Wahshihlas Bay in British Columbia await the yachtsman who cruises in the Pacific Northwest.

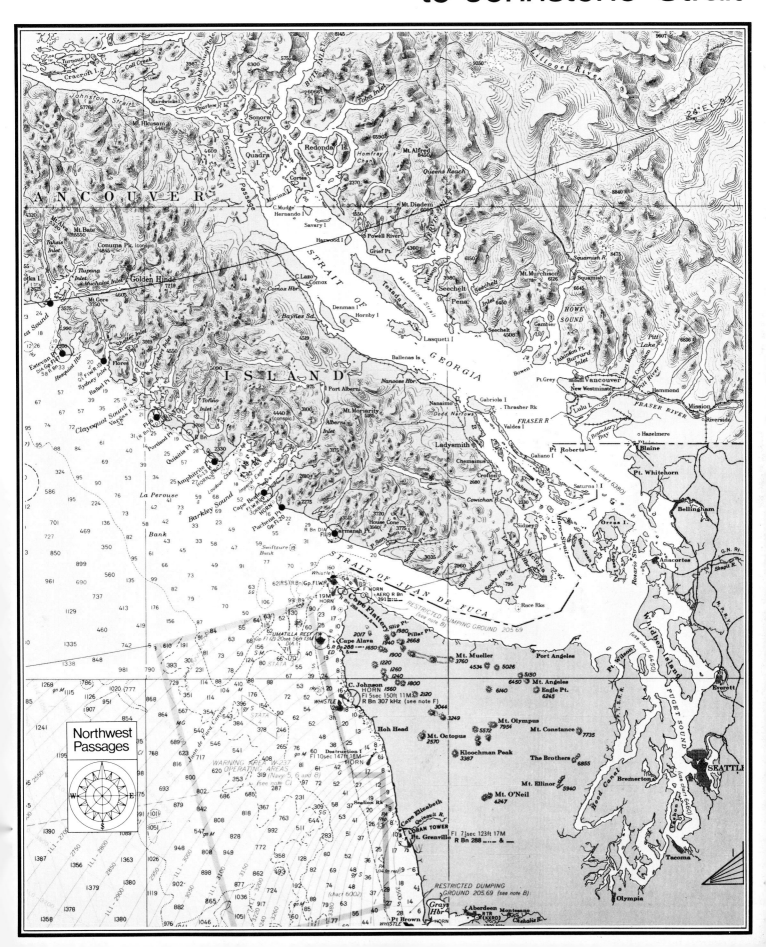

Northwest
Passages

1

Peter Puget's Discovery

A dank, chilly blanket of fog greeted us as we arose after a night spent at the Olympia Yacht Club guest floats. The shoreside buildings behind us assumed ghostly shapes, while the beautiful Capitol dome in the distance was completely hidden. The waters of Budd Inlet to the north were entirely enshrouded so that even the first marker buoys were not visible. The fog blanket seemed to be hanging fairly low, however, and we hoped that the sun, which we could see trying to break through up above, would burn off the fog by the time we had finished breakfast and made a shopping tour uptown. We only had a few days for our mid-October rediscovery of Puget Sound.

What we call South Sound is, in reality, Puget Sound.

When Captain Vancouver dispatched his lieutenant of the *Discovery*, Peter Puget, to explore the southern regions of the inlet he had found taking off from the Strait of Juan de Fuca, he sent him "upsound" from Point Defiance. As mentioned earlier, to honor his lieutenant for his labors, Vancouver named these waters Puget's Sound. In later years the more northerly waters as far up as Foulweather Bluff have been included as part of Puget Sound on official charts. The Indians called these waters the Whulge.

Skippers of old sailing ships apparently found prevailing winds behind them when they coasted easily to the north from Olympia to the strait; so it was always "downsound" in this direction and "upsound" when they headed south.

Then there is that other seeming contradiction by which the southern end of the sound is called the "upper sound," while it would logically seem it should be "lower sound." This, of course, is the same as the "head" of a bay being the innermost part regardless of its compass direction.

Upper Puget Sound or, as we call it, South Sound, is a delightful cruising area. Much used by boating families whose home ports are nearby, it doesn't get the attention deserved from those in Seattle and to the north. It offers many attractions any time of the year, but is particularly interesting for winter cruising. Protected waters, a wealth of cozy harbors and convenient facilities make the South Sound an appealing area for not-too-far-away trips.

The southwest portion of these waters consists of five fairly narrow fingers. Olympia, the state capital, lies at the head of Budd Inlet. For trailerboat owners from the south, this is a popular entrance to Puget Sound and more northerly waters, with several marinas and launching facilities. The Olympia Yacht Club guest floats are available to members of other clubs with reciprocal privileges. From there it is only a short walk to stores and restaurants, and a visit to the State Capitol, with its beautiful landscaping and gardens, is a rewarding experience.

By the time we were ready to leave, the fog had lightened considerably and we were able to pick up the channel to the north. This narrow channel runs between shoal waters on both sides, but it is well marked with buoys, lights and ranges. However, careful attention should be paid to these markers. The recommended course leads northwestward and north after leaving the narrow, marked channel, to run between two lights westward of the Olympia Shoal Light. With care, however, one can head north after clearing black buoy "C1" on Spoilbank Shoal and leave Olympia Shoal Light to port.

After clearing Olympia Shoal, we swung over to the west shore and headed up toward Cooper Point. Rounding Cooper Point, we entered Eld Inlet which almost parallels Budd Inlet. On a beachcombing course that skirted both shores of the inlet, we enjoyed the many beautiful subur-

Looking toward the entrance of Taylor Bay at the southern end of Case Inlet, a quiet bit of water for high-tide enjoyment.

ban homes which line the shores. As is the case with all these southern inlets, the heads are very shoal and are used for log storage and oyster beds. Most of them dry at low tide and so care should be used not to go in too far.

These are some of the finest oyster-growing waters to be found but *Yachtsman Beware!* The oyster beds are all private or commercially farmed; so taking the oysters is a definite "no no." If you just must have some oysters, it's usually possible to find an oyster farmer who will sell you some.

A turn to the left around Hunter Point took us through Squaxin Passage, with Hope Island to our starboard and Carlyon Beach and little Steamboat Island to our left, to enter Totten Inlet. Skookum Inlet, a small arm taking off from Totten, is comfortably navigable for only about a mile but offers good anchorage just inside the entrance. There are several small bights in these inlets which offer a cozy anchorage, but be sure to check depths and watch the tide conditions carefully.

Leaving Totten Inlet, another left turn about a mile to the north took us into Hammersley Inlet, a very narrow arm, which runs westerly into Shelton with Oakland Bay continuing this waterway for about four miles to the northeast. Although some skippers hesitate to try this six-mile-long narrow passage to Shelton, which shoals in some parts of its 0.2-mile average width, it can be successfully negotiated by an able boatman. In entering it is best to avoid the middle and to favor the north shore from Hungerford Point to Cape Horn. Then cut to the south shore until Cannery Point is passed. From there a mid-channel course can be steered, but don't get too far right into the bulge east of Church Point. Then after passing Skookum Point, favor the north shore to Church Point and hold to mid channel the

rest of the way in. Shoals are charted and some are marked. Large-scale chart #6461 is comforting to have along.

The logging-lumbering town of Shelton has all facilities to meet most of the needs of the cruising family. Our stop here and a later exploration of Oakland Bay, with interesting Chapman Cove, proved to be a rewarding experience.

Coming out of Hammersley Inlet, we swung down between Hope Island and Squaxin Island and around Unsal Point to pass between Squaxin Island and Hartstene Island through Peale Passage. It was time for some leg stretching and so we landed at the floats for the Squaxin Island State Marine Park on Coon Cove, not far from the southern tip of the island on the eastern shore. There we found good anchorage with mooring buoys, moorage floats and picnic and camping areas. There are clams available on the beach, and this is one of the popular spots for those cruising in this area.

The run up Peale Passage and later into Pickering Passage, with Hartstene Island on our starboard, reminded us that the South Sound is not entirely populated. We found many stretches here where the shoreline, sometimes with fairly steep banks, presented a forest of massed colors with stately firs, hemlocks, cedars and madronas forming a green background for the brilliant yellows, oranges and reds of the deciduous trees. This riot of autumn colors, together with the crispness in the air and the sparkle of the retreating sun on the still waters, created a mood of cool quietude and proved that cruising in the fall can be just as enjoyable as in the summer.

As the passage bends to the right, we swung into Jarrell Cove which indents the north shore of Hartstene Island. Here is another state marine park high on most cruising skippers' list of favorites. Originally called Bay of Despond,

11

South Sound, a delightful cruising area at any time of the year, offers cozy harbors and convenient facilities for the yachtsman and his family. Here (from top) are views of Tacoma Yacht Club's floats in Wollochet Bay; Pitt Passage, where the water is a bit "thin"; and Pitt Island.

and later, erroneously charted as Gerald Cove, it is small but offers protected anchorage and moorage floats with picnicking and camping sites available. The Jarrell's Cove Marina has gas, groceries, ice, fishing supplies and laundry facilities.

As we prepared to snug down for the night, the sky became pale with the moon coming up full while the afternoon sun was still tracing shadows. The oil range exuded a comforting warmth, and later the night sky glowed with the confetti of constellations.

The next morning we rounded Harstene Island's Dougall Point, where Pickering Passage runs into Case Inlet with little Stretch Island and smaller Reach Island nestled against the west shore. Reach Island, known locally as Treasure Island, is reserved for private-property owners. Between the island's southern portion and the mainland is Fair Harbor, a cozy, protected, though shallow anchorage. The Fair Harbor Marina has moorage, gas, water, ice, fishing supplies, camping and launching facilities. We regretted the closing of Stretch Island's St. Charles Winery where it was always a pleasure to stop for a visit, a sample of the wine and an inspection of the interesting museum. We were told that, although the winery is closed, grapes are still grown there.

Up near the northern tip of Case Inlet, the town of Allyn has a public dock with access to groceries, meats, drugs, and so forth. Heading back to the south, we found two bays indenting the northeast shore of Case Inlet. Rocky Bay is aptly named with its rocks, shoals and shallow water. It is scenic and attractive but offers no protection. Below and around Windy Bluff is the entrance to mile-long Vaughn Bay. This attractive, landlocked harbor is protected by a spit. Entrance around the northern tip of the spit has only two feet at low tide, but there is ample depth inside for good anchorage. The village of Vaughn has some supplies, and there is a launching ramp.

On the east side of Case Inlet, we poked our bow into several little coves which are delightful for small boats or dinghy exploration. Dutcher Cove, Herron Bay, Whiteman Cove and Taylor Bay are quiet little bits of scenic charm for high-tide enjoyment. Herron Island is another "for residents only" island which can be passed on either side.

Rounding Devils Head at the tip of the long peninsula separating Case and Carr Inlets, Anderson Island came into view. This southernmost island in the sound has two bays. We swung into Amsterdam Bay, which pokes into the west side of the island, and found it quite shallow. However, anchorage can be found in a pool about in the middle but depths and tide levels should be closely checked and watched both within and on entering.

On the southeastern part of the Island, Oro Bay is split into two parts. The northerly section is open, with two fathoms at zero tide shoaling toward the head. The westerly section provides protected anchorages at two fathoms. Care should be used on entering to avoid the shoaling point to the left. The settlement of Vega is on the west shore of this part of the bay. Protected anchorage can be found in both the north and the south portions of this section, but the south section provides a bit more depth.

To get the historical background as well as catch the mood and atmosphere of Anderson Island, we highly recommend Hazel Heckman's book *Island in the Sound*.

Swinging around the north end of Anderson Island through Balch Passage, we passed between Anderson and McNeil Islands. In the center of the passage between the two islands is Eagle Island, which is a state marine park although unimproved. McNeil Island, site of the federal penitentiary, is completely restricted and no landing is permitted.

By midafternoon the sun had ducked behind a cover of heavy dark clouds, and a brisk wind sprung up. We decided to call it a day and swung into Filucy Bay, one of the most popular and used coves in South Sound waters. It is on the mainland just off the western tip of McNeil Island. The village of Longbranch dominates the bay in the middle of the inside shoreland where most boating needs are readily available. Two to two and a half fathoms provide good protected anchorage in both ends of the bay. We chose to drop the hook in the northern part of the bay. An abandoned old lighthouse tower on the tip of McDermott Point added charm to the setting before it burned down in 1970.

It wasn't long before the rain came, cold and slanting, painting the sides of the cabin, as well as the houses and trees and hills, and gargling down the scuppers. In our protected anchorage we were warm and cozy and enjoyed the symphony of rain drops pattering on the decks above us.

By morning the rain had quit, although there was a heavy overcast in the sky. Leaving Filucy Bay, we headed north into Carr Inlet on a course between McNeil Island and the mainland through Pitt Passage. Plenty of caution is needed here for, as one of the Seattle Yacht Club's promi-nent sailors says, "the water is a bit thin," especially at low tide, with a minimum of 10 feet in mid channel at zero tide. Going north, the shore of McNeil Island should be favored to avoid a rock in mid channel. About 0.3 mile after leaving Pitt Island to port, a swing closer to the west shore will clear Wyckoff Shoal and its marker buoy.

Around South Head is Delano Beach and back of Penrose Point is another popular state park, Penrose Point Park, which has docking facilities, camp and picnic sites, swimming beach and many other conveniences. Two bays here, charted as Mayo Cove and Von Geldern Cove, take on local names among residents. Mayo Cove is frequently known as Lakebay, the name of the little settlement at its head. No one seems to know why, but Von Geldern Cove is locally called Joe's Bay and is the site of the village of Home. Both of these offer some anchoring possibilities but shoal toward the heads.

Farther up along the west shore of Carr Inlet, we found a couple of friendly little coves which are particularly attractive to the small and shallow-draft boats. Both Glen Cove and Huge Creek are delightful, protected bights at or near high tide. The settlement of Elgin is on the eastern side of Huge Creek. Henderson Bay forms the upper end of Carr Inlet with Wauna and Purdy at the head.

Coming down the east shore of the inlet, we find two excellent bays featured. In behind Raft Island is good anchorage for boats of any size. Lay Inlet and the town of Rosedale add interest and a quiet majesty to this very scenic harbor. Larger cruisers and sailboats should go around Raft Island, but those needing a vertical clearance of less than 17 feet can go under the connecting bridge between the island and the mainland.

Abandoned lighthouse on the tip of McDermott Point was a landmark before it was destroyed by fire in 1970.

13

Floats at Jarrell Cove State Marine Park, a popular spot with cruising families.

A couple of miles south is the entrance to Horsehead Bay, another favorite of ours as well as many other yachtsmen. Here is a peaceful harbor, well sheltered from all winds and offering a restful anchorage. Around the peninsula forming Horsehead Bay and Green Point is a popular fishing area.

In cruising Carr Inlet, it is well to remember that the Navy conducts sonic tests in these waters and attention should be paid to the warning light system which has been set up.

South of the mainland is Fox Island, connected by a bridge across Hale Passage with vertical clearance of 31 feet. Along the northern shore of Fox Island are two bays, one large and open, the other a small cove. In the center of the larger one is Tanglewood Island, formerly called Grave Island. Good anchorage is found on either side of the island. Beware of a shoal extending some 200 yards eastward of the island, usually marked by kelp. Gas, oil, ice, groceries and some moorage are available at Fox Island Marina. The village of Sylvan is on the east side of the bight.

There is a legend of Fox Island about an Indian Princess, daughter of an important Nisqually chief who lived on the mainland across the channel from the island. She was beautiful and desirable, with flashing dark eyes, her long black hair braided with bright ornaments or fresh flowers. Many a young brave tried to woo her with gifts and stories of their feats, but, while she was kind and gentle to them, she wasn't more than a friendly companion to any of them.

One day a handsome stranger came to the island. Tall and strong, with a rich voice, keen eyes and a regal bearing, he entertained the tribe around the campfire with stories of his adventures in a strange country from which he came.

The chief's daughter listened intently, a new emotion surging in her heart. She and the stranger were drawn together. They sat on the shore, watching the tide race through the channel, walked hand in hand through the forest on winding trails, and often paddled a canoe to the lovely island across from the village. Through the days their love for each other grew.

One day she sat on the shore looking across to the island and watching the wavelets following each other up the beach. Her lover paced nervously up and down the beach. Suddenly her reverie was broken as she missed the sound of his steps. Looking up, she saw him walking out over the water toward the island. She was dismayed to see him disappear in a shroud of mist that rolled along the island's shore and then drifted away.

There was no comforting her empty heart. Her friends did their best to raise her spirits and interest her in things she formerly enjoyed, but nothing moved her. Her only happiness came in recalling the time she had spent with her love. The island seemed to offer solace with a strange charm that drew her there, and she was less lonely. He seemed near and she fancied she heard his voice, recalling the joys of the enchanting days of the past. Sitting on the beach, she scooped up sand in her hands. As it trickled between her fingers, it fell on the beach forming small figures of animals, birds, fish, a tiny hand or foot. They remained on the beach as pebbles formed by the action of the water.

One day, on her way to the island, her canoe was stopped as if by an unseen hand. Looking over the side to see what was holding the craft, she saw below the surface of the water the smiling face of her lost lover. She stretched her arms toward him in a supplication to return to her. This he could not do, he told her, for he could return to earth no more.

They talked together for a long time as he described his beautiful home and urged her to join him. Although his familiar voice warmed her, she grew cold with fear when he pleaded with her to join him. Love, however, brought a new strength and overcame fear.

After ordering those paddling her canoe to return to the mainland and tell her father she would return in a few days, she dove into the water and disappeared.

For five days the entire tribe mourned the loss of their lovely princess. Then their mourning turned to wild joy as the sea gave up the missing girl to return to her people. She lived as before but divided her time between her father's lodge and her beloved's mysterious home below the water.

As the years passed some strange enchantment kept her young and beautiful with a vibrant freshness, while her companions aged and died. As her generation passed into memory, she spent less and less time among her people, although she did not forget them. She returned as something half human, appearing as a lovely vision above the sea, enshrouded in a misty cloud, to warn them of coming storms. She did not always appear in a cloud, but her phantom seen on a clear, bright day would foretell the death of some of the tribe by drowning.

With the coming of the white man, she appeared no more but the legend remains, and some Fox Islanders claim authenticity for it by the stones still found there.

Across Hale Passage from Fox Island a two-mile-long finger of Wollochet Bay pokes into the peninsula. Here the Tacoma Yacht Club maintains an outstation with floats for members only. There is good anchorage off the floats in about nine feet, or anywhere in the bay inside the entrance in deeper water. The settlement of Wollochet is on the eastern point at the entrance.

Along the eastern shore of these southern waters opposite Anderson Island is Ketron Island. Here we found an extensive real estate development with the Ketron Island Marina providing gas, diesel, groceries, ice, water, moorage and laundry facilities. Fishing is sometimes good south of the island and in Nisqually Reach, south of Anderson Island.

At the southern end of the Narrows is Day Island, charted as Days Island. In reality a finger peninsula rather than an island, it is the home of the Day Island Yacht Club, and there are marinas offering moorage and all facilities and services to meet the needs of the boating family.

The Narrows, sometimes called Tacoma Narrows, run from Day Island to Point Defiance. Through this passage the tides pour into the entire South Sound and back out again, moving a tremendous volume of water through this narrow passage. Although it has a three-quarter-mile average width, currents up to six knots cause many skippers, particularly those with slower boats, to plan passage near slack-water periods. Huge boils and whirlpools sometimes develop as far south as the tip of McNeil Island, and the meeting tidal waters can cause sharp tide rips around Point Defiance. These are not considered particularly dangerous. The Point Defiance rips are a favorite fishing area where many good-sized salmon have been caught.

As we ended our rediscovery cruise of the real Puget Sound, or South Sound, as we call it, we found that it has much for the cruising family. Whether the craft is large or small, the skipper, family and guests will find quiet, protected waters, good anchorages in a host of bays and coves and a wide variety of scenic beauty. Although most of the shoreline is privately owned, there are enough state marine parks, towns, villages, and marinas with shoreside access to satisfy the needs of those with pleasure boats. Supplies and services are readily available and the people are friendly.

After completing this portion of our cruise and heading into Gig Harbor for the night, we had reconfirmed our previous conviction that the South Sound area is an attractive portion of our Northwest "greatest cruising waters in the world" at any time of the year.

Olympia Yacht Club headquarters, with the Capitol dome in the background.

2

Playground in Busy Water

There was a typical early-morning haze softening the silhouettes of the trees along the horizon surrounding little Gig Harbor as we awakened for another day of our cruise to reexplore Puget Sound. The autumn sun, which was sleeping in a little longer each day, already appeared bright enough to forecast a beautiful day.

This charming little landlocked harbor has much to offer the yachtsman. Coming in, it's very easy to miss the entrance as it is almost hidden by a sandy finger which nearly closes it. On entering, keep well to the left till past the point, then swing to the right and favor the curving shore until well into the bay.

In 1841, when members of Capt. Charles Wilkes' crew were doing some exploring in the captain's gig, a sudden storm sent them scurrying for shelter. They found it in this little bay and it was only natural to call it Gig Harbor.

The first white settlers didn't come until 1867. Founding fathers were Sam Jerisich, John Farugo and Peter Goldsmith who came to homestead. As more settlers came, they found fishing to be a profitable pursuit, thus forming the foundation for a fishing fleet that consisted of some 50 boats by 1915.

With a growing demand for boats, it followed that some of them should be built in Gig Harbor. Many of the purse seiners fishing in Northwest waters today were built here by the Skansie Shipbuilding Company. Although it is no longer in business, some of the boats it built still have Gig Harbor as their home port.

Boats are still built here but they are mostly pleasure boats. The Eddon Boat Works turns out everything from salty little sailing dinghies to a 44-foot racing/cruising sloop. The fishing fleet may have shrunk a bit as the years have passed, but Gig Harbor maintains a nautical atmo-sphere with several new large marinas for pleasure boats and plenty of anchorage space.

The town itself has changed, too. Instead of a bawdy haven for fishermen, seamen, loggers and farmers, it has now gone cultural. Boutiques, a candle and wine shop, an antique nautical shop, art galleries, the famous farm-museum, Scandia Gaard, and many specialty shops do much to change the mood of the place. An excellent restaurant provides moorage floats for its waterborne patrons.

A new festival, Harbor Holidays, was started in 1970. In addition to the permanent attractions already mentioned, the main street becomes a midway with all kinds of fun booths, bands and other entertainment as well as food. An authentic San Francisco cable car runs the length of the town for those too weary to walk from end to end. Parades, a Leaky Teaky boat race and free boat tours of the harbor add to the carnival spirit.

Highlight of the two-day event in early June is the Blessing of the Fleet. Purse seiners, gill netters and trollers raft side by side facing the shore. A band concert, introduction of boats in the fishing fleet and patriotic ceremonies are followed by a blessing of all the boats by clergymen of different faiths and then, as the boats peel off to parade by the official barge, they are individually blessed. The success of Harbor Holidays seems assured, and it no doubt will continue to grow through the years.

Leaving the friendly shores of Gig Harbor, we set out on the second portion of our cruise to cover the mid-sound section from the Narrows to Foulweather Bluff. Puget Sound in general, and the mid-sound section particularly, is one of the busiest waterways in America, yet it is the center of Washington's famed Evergreen Playground. The rugged Olympic Range to the west and the snow-crested Cascades

Miller Bay, now part of a development, has no shore access but is a pleasant spot to drop anchor for lunch or overnight.

to the east belie the fact that this landlocked sea is a great tidal arm of the Pacific Ocean.

Across the entrance to the Narrows and around the end of Point Defiance is Tacoma, the state's third largest city. Its fine harbor, Commencement Bay, not only is famous as a commercial port but has several marinas and facilities serving the yachtsmen of the Northwest. The Tacoma Yacht Club, with its moorages and boathouses protected by the Tacoma Smelter slag peninsula, has its beautiful new clubhouse on the tip of the peninsula at the outer entrance to the moorage basin.

Tacoma has several boat yards, a wide selection of fine restaurants, several of them with moorage facilities, and many points of interest throughout the city.

After a stop to inspect the Tacoma Yacht Club's new facility and an excellent lunch at Johnny's Dock, we headed north out of Commencement Bay. Here one has a choice of two routes. With Vashon and Maury Islands lying in mid sound, Colvos Passage runs up on the west side and East Passage on the east side. Although named separately, these two are actually one island joined by a narrow strip of sand. Tramp Harbor, where the two islands join, in East Passage, is fairly open but old-timers say it offers more protection than appears.

On the inside the two islands form Quartermaster Harbor. Both the inner and outer harbors provide excellent, sheltered anchorage. Watch it in the inner portion, however, on minus tides for it is quite shallow. The village of Burton, Larsen's Marina and the Quartermaster Yacht Club occupy the neck of the peninsula separating the two parts of the harbor. Dockton County Park on Maury Island has floats, picnic areas, playgrounds and bathhouses.

Other than Quartermaster, Vashon Island has little in the way of protected bays. A couple of little bights can be used but are not protected in some winds.

On the east shore of East Passage, a breakwater and new boat basin have been built at Des Moines, almost across from Point Robinson. This is also the home of the Des Moines Yacht Club, formerly the Vagabond Yacht Club. Some three miles farther north is Point Pully, known locally as Three Tree Point and home of the Three Tree Point Yacht Club.

We chose the Colvos Passage route and enjoyed the cruise on quiet waters between the wooded shores, with both summer cottages and permanent homes peeking down at us through the trees from the bluffs above, or set along the shore at water level. This is an interesting waterway in that local experts claim the tidal currents always run north, regardless of whether the tide is ebbing or flooding.

At the north end of Colvos Passage, we swung to the left around the south end of Blake Island. This entire 475-acre island is a state marine park with sandy beaches, clams, campsites and trails. Tillicum Village, with an authentic Indian longhouse, serves salmon barbecued Indian fashion over an open fire, and has dock and floats for its patrons on the northeast point of the island. Some protection can be found on the west side, and the beach is a favorite spot for small-boat owners. We understand that plans are in the making for a breakwater to be built just below Tillicum Village dock with floats and buoys to provide a protected moorage here.

Swinging to the northwest, we entered Rich Passage which separates Bainbridge Island's southern end from the mainland. A mid-channel course here clears all hazards, but keep an eye open for ferry boats and watch for currents, particularly at Point White at the western end.

Here we emerged into Sinclair Inlet, which stabs inland to the west and southwest, with the town of Port Orchard, county seat for Kitsap County, on the south shore and Bremerton with its Puget Sound Naval Shipyard on the north shore. We stopped at the public moorage just east of the ferry slip and went uptown for some shopping. Bremerton has several marinas, and a tour through the shipyards and the Japanese surrender ship U.S.S. *Missouri* is available.

As the afternoon sun dropped toward the horizon, we headed into Port Washington Narrows, which separate Bremerton and East Bremerton and lead to some very interesting waters. Our objective for the night was Oyster Bay but we swung into Phinney Bay to pick up some friends at the Bremerton Yacht Club. This bay has good anchorage and the Bremerton Yacht Club guest float is along the southern edge of its covered moorages.

The Narrows continue into Dyes Inlet, a fair-sized body of water with the town of Silverdale at its northern head. Since there are no docks, floats or shore access to Silverdale, it is of little interest to the yachtsman.

The southern portion of Dyes Inlet turns into Ostrich Bay with Oyster Bay beyond it. Here are a couple of delightful, sheltered retreats with a sylvan peacefulness unexpected so close to metropolitan activity. Oyster Bay, be-

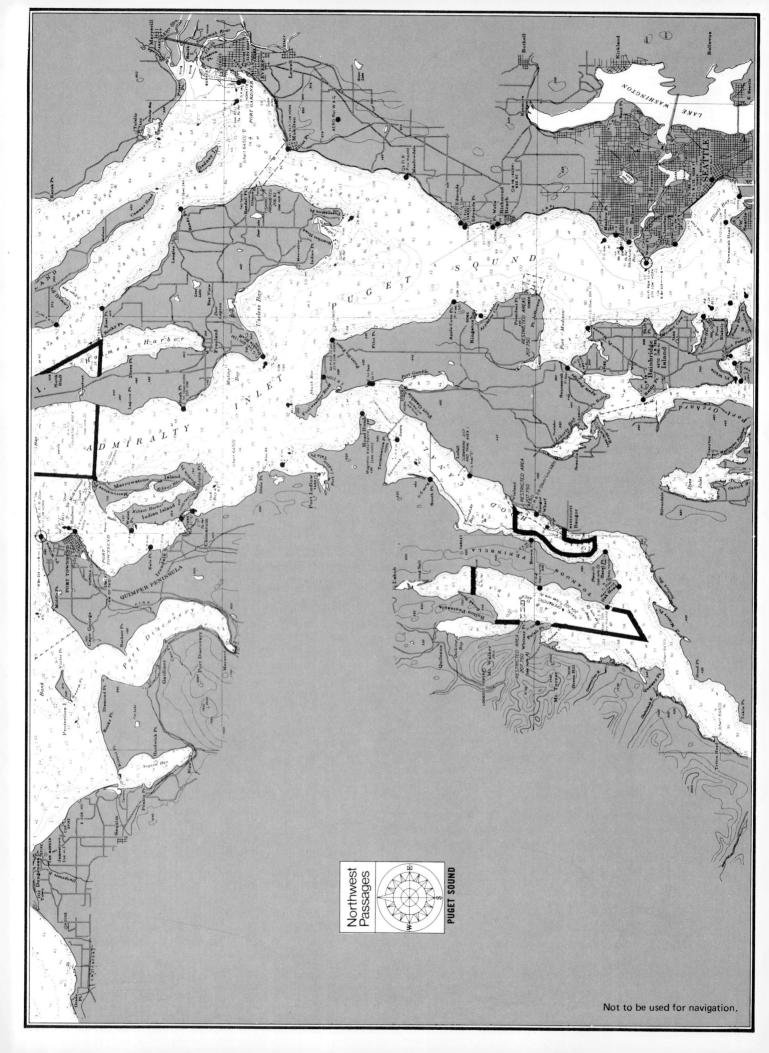

Northwest
Passages

PUGET SOUND

Not to be used for navigation.

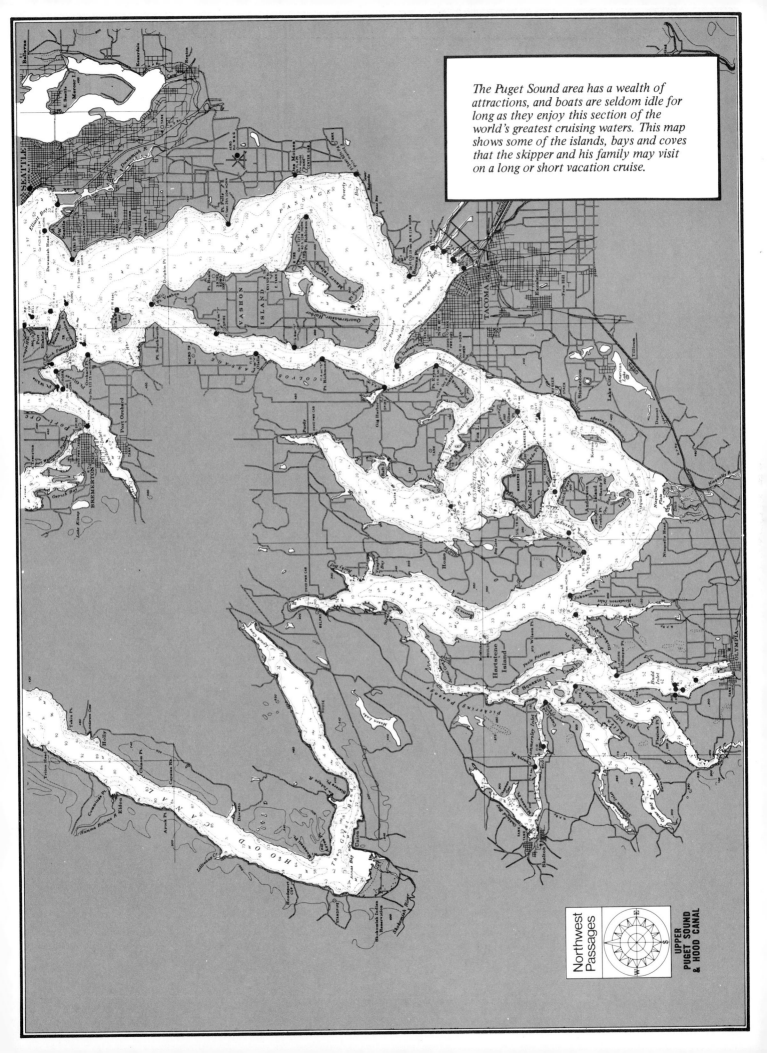

The Puget Sound area has a wealth of attractions, and boats are seldom idle for long as they enjoy this section of the world's greatest cruising waters. This map shows some of the islands, bays and coves that the skipper and his family may visit on a long or short vacation cruise.

Northwest Passages

UPPER PUGET SOUND & HOOD CANAL

Poulsbo, known as Little Norway, was settled in the 1880s.

cause of its long entrance channel and a peculiar action of the tidal flow, has warmer-than-average water; so is a favorite swimming and water-skiing spot. A small island in the northern cove of the bay adds to the scenic beauty. It is one of our favorite close-by or off-season anchorages.

With private residences lining the shores of these two bays, there is no access to land. One exception is a street end near the Hearthstone restaurant on the south end of Oyster Bay, where the dinghy can be run ashore for those wishing to enjoy the excellent food to be found at the Hearthstone. We were the only occupants of the bay this night except for a small, lonesome little outboard anchored near the island. After a luscious dinner of charcoal-broiled steak, we sat in the darkened cabin for a time enjoying the play of the moon on the mirror-smooth water. Peeking out from behind patchy clouds, it would alternately paint a white path between our boat and the shore or hide its face to send spotlight rays between the breaks in the clouds. We were visited by a flotilla of ducks and couldn't decide what they were doing out that time of night. It was either the bright moonlight, which kept them from their slumber, or the smell of our barbecue with hope for a free handout of food. Their hopes were rewarded and the iridescence of their bright plumage in the moonlit waters painted a never-to-be forgotten picture.

Heading northward again the next morning, we ran up the west side of Bainbridge Island. This waterway is charted, not as Port Orchard Passage or Port Orchard Channel, but merely as Port Orchard. Vancouver named it after H. M. Orchard, a clerk on the *Discovery*. It separates north of Battle Point to become Agate Passage, continuing along the west shore of the island, and into Liberty Bay to the northwest.

About a mile and a half up Port Orchard, we repassed Point White on the west shore of Bainbridge Island and, a little farther up, Illahee State Marine Park on our left. This park has floats, full facilities for picnicking, camping, swimming, clamming and boat launching. Two miles north, still on the west shore, is the Brownsville Marina with most of the usual marina facilities to serve the yachtsman.

Bainbridge Island's west side has two bays. Little Fletcher Bay, about a half mile in length, is nearly shut in by a sandbar across the entrance and should be negotiated on half tide or better. There is deeper water inside but

caution should be used by the skipper in these waters.

Nearly three miles to the north and around Battle Point is Manzanita Bay. Larger and deeper, it is a favorite anchorage for Seattle area skippers. Here again, shoreside access is not available, and it should be remembered that oyster beds and clam beaches are all private in these waters. Manzanita Bay is protected from most winds but can rough up in a northwesterly.

Approaching Liberty Bay, formerly called Dogfish Bay, we swung in to pass the Keyport Naval Torpedo Station on the left at the entrance. Liberty Bay has good anchorage in 8 to 52 feet of water but shoals and dries at the head. The bay at one time harbored a fleet of codfishing sailing schooners, but today its fishing fleet concentrates on salmon and halibut.

Up near the head of the bay, we pulled into the floats at the town of Poulsbo, familiarly known as Little Norway because of its many Scandinavian residents. Originally settled in the 1880s with Jorgen Eliason as one of its first homesteaders, it was intended to be named Paulsbo. The first postmaster, I. B. Moe, wanted that name (meaning "Paul's Place") to honor a small place near his home in Norway. The Post Office Department made a mistake in the spelling and it has been Poulsbo ever since.

With the emphasis on the older generation's commercial fishing changing to their descendant's interest in pleasure boating, the facilities are now more oriented toward the yachtsman, although a fair portion of the fine moorage floats still serve some fishing boats. Modern stores and shops line the main street while the homes are clean and neat, typical of Scandinavian people. Another long-time community industry is the oyster-packing plant on the shore of the bay.

Like Gig Harbor, Poulsbo has been invaded by culture. The annual North Kitsap Arts and Crafts Show is held there as part of the Velkomen Festival each May. Northwest painters are featured, along with craftsmen in action demonstrating their skills. These include macrame, stitchery and needlepoint, miniature watercolors, wood plaques, candy and cake decorating, silhouette cutting, pottery, sculpture and many others. The artisans come from all over the area.

Coming out of Liberty Bay, we swung around Point Bolin to head northeastward through Agate Passage. This waterway, connecting Port Orchard with Port Madison, is only about a mile in length and less than a quarter of a mile wide. Considerable tidal water pours through at times, which isn't particularly dangerous but can slow a boat down or speed it up, depending on direction. A fixed bridge with vertical clearance of 75 feet connects Bainbridge Island to the Kitsap Peninsula.

Port Madison is charted as the large bay with Point Jefferson and Indianola on the north, Suquamish on the west and the top of Bainbridge Island over to Point Monroe on the south. In local usage, however, Inner Port Madison, the bay indenting the north end of Bainbridge Island, is generally referred to as Port Madison.

The larger Port Madison, named after President Madison, has several features interesting to the boater. The little

Left: Boats anchored to watch the Daffodil Festival Marine Parade at Tacoma. Right: The Persis, a home-built boat, is launched at Winslow in Eagle Harbor. The 54-foot ketch is the result of five years of hard weekend work.

town of Suquamish is on the western shore. Here Chief Sealth, after whom Seattle was named, was born and his grave is located up behind the village. This was also the location of Old Man House, an Indian version of a condominium which was 900 feet long and 60 feet wide. Chief Sealth and his second-in-command, Chief Kitsap, lived there along with many other families of the tribe.

At the turn of the century, Allan A. Bartow was Indian agent at the Port Madison Reservation, which encompassed much of the land west of Port Madison. Mrs. Bartow became the first postmistress and called the post office Bartow. The second postmistress, Mrs. C. C. Pickrell, also the wife of an Indian agent, changed the name to Suquamish and so it has remained. The town was incorporated in 1909 and, although modern suburban-type homes can be seen around, the tall firs and cedars, as the Indians knew them, grow along the roads, and little paths lead to the same berry patches enjoyed by the red men. The same sandy beaches the Indians used to launch their canoes today invite the yachtsmen to come and inspect an area that has changed but little over a 200-year period. The town has a dock and floats.

Leaving Suquamish, we went a mile farther north into Miller Bay. This is another of those little bays in a sylvan setting, protected by a sandspit across the opening. Formerly a favorite clam beach, this sandy finger has now been "civilized" as part of a real estate development. Miller Bay, however, still attracts boating families of the Puget Sound area. The shores are all private property and so there is no shoreside access, but it is a most pleasant place to drop anchor for a Sunday lunch, afternoon snooze or an overnight stay. Watch the depths, though, as well as tide levels. There is sufficient water in several places, but one must find them among the shoal areas, by careful use of the depth sounder or lead line.

The small settlement of Indianola, with the post office called Kitsap, has a long pier extending out over the shallow

beach on the north shore of larger Port Madison. It was formerly used by the ferries when they served the smaller communities here. There is nothing in Indianola to interest the yachtsman.

Across the bay, Inner Port Madison Bay, or Port Madison, as it is usually called, is one of the finest small harbors on Puget Sound and certainly one of the most popular. Home of Seattle Yacht Club's outstation, the Fo'c's'le, it provides protected anchorage for all sizes of boats. Many skippers use it for a nearby weekend destination, or for a first-night-out stopover on a longer cruise, after clearing Seattle's locks or Shilshole Bay on a late Friday afternoon. The head of the bay is known as Hidden Cove, but don't go in too far because it is shallow at low tide.

On the northeast end of Bainbridge Island is Point Monroe on the "Sandspit." This half-moon narrow strip of sand, nearly enclosing a lagoon, is somewhat of a rarity in these waters, reminiscent of a New England beach. Formerly the site of ramshackle beach-type summer homes, it now has many artistically designed year-round residences with a charm and a setting not to be found elsewhere.

Bainbridge Island's east side has several bays, two of them excellent anchorages. Rolling Bay, about halfway down the shore, is a bay in name only, with no protection. Murden Cove is also open and too shallow to be of value to the yachtsman.

Eagle Harbor, with the island's principal town of Winslow and a ferry landing, has outstations of Queen City Yacht Club and Tyee Yacht Club. A long shoal extends southeast from Wing Point to make a dogleg entrance. Going in, follow the buoys, lights and range to stay out of trouble. There is plenty of room to anchor, but don't go too far into the head without checking depths and tide levels carefully. The head dries at low tide.

Winslow has stores, shops and an excellent restaurant which is popular with cruising families using the harbor. There is a commercial moorage just inside the state ferry

Eagle Harbor, on Bainbridge Island's east side, serves the town of Winslow, popular with cruising families.

moorage, storage and repair facility, and a marina on the south shore offers the yachtsman many facilities, services and a gas float.

A mile and a quarter south of Eagle Harbor is Blakely Harbor, another fine anchorage with plenty of water and no hazards. Former site of a large sawmill and shipyard at Port Blakely, the harbor is steeped in history. None of this remains today, however, and the shore is lined with homes.

Coming out of Port Madison, we swung to the north around Point Jefferson, President Point and into Appletree Cove to the town of Kingston. Here, behind the breakwater, is a fine new marine facility. All marine needs, services, fuel and moorage are available. Like Port Madison, this has become another popular first-night-out stopping place at the beginning of a cruise or a short-trip destination.

After replenishing our fuel and water supply, we headed north again around Apple Cove Point and along the shore of the Kitsap Peninsula on the west side of Puget Sound. As we approached the northern boundary of our arbitrary mid-sound area, we rounded Point No Point, which really is a very definite point, regardless of its name. One of Puget Sound's important lights is on the point, and changing tides produce riptides to form an excellent fishing spot where many of the big ones are taken. Several fishing resorts nestle in behind the point at Hansville.

Skunk Bay is merely a curve in the shoreline between Hansville and Foulweather Bluff, offering very little, if any, protection. Foulweather Bluff is aptly named for a combination of hills, tide rips, and meeting of tidal streams and winds, can blow up some nasty conditions here at times.

We next crossed the sound to head on the eastern shore to the town of Edmonds. Although it has no natural harbor, the Port of Edmonds has built a breakwater and a boat basin. Edmonds Yacht Club is located here, and recently another breakwater and basin has doubled the moorage capacity. We have always found Edmonds to be a particularly friendly community and the yacht club serves excellent meals. It provides a guest dock for members of clubs with reciprocal privileges.

Around Edwards Point and heading south past Point Wells and Richmond Beach, we came into Seattle's municipally owned Shilshole Bay Marina. This fine facility is protected by a rock breakwater and, with recently added floats, provides moorage for 1540 boats. A complete fuel dock is located in the center of the moorage area with visitors floats inside of the fuel dock and along Pier J, just north of the fuel dock. The offices of the marina, a fine restaurant and several shops are located in the administration building. At the north end of the harbor is a launching ramp, and a haul-out facility and dry storage area are located at the south end.

Seattle, Washington's largest city and Puget Sound's principal port, is situated on a narrow neck of land, six and a half miles across at its widest point, lying between the sound and Lake Washington. Elliott Bay, one of the world's finest deepwater ports, has few attractions for the yachtsman except for a couple of floats for temporary moorage and a scenic tour along the waterfront. Fishing inside West Seattle's Duwamish Head is usually good.

The Lake Washington Ship Canal, with the Chittenden Locks, split Seattle to join the salt water of Puget Sound with fresh water of Lakes Union and Washington. Lake Union, with primarily a commercial waterfront, has many marinas and boat yards serving the yachtsman.

Lake Washington is actually a cruising area in its own right, with several nice bays and marinas. Two floating bridges across the lake have speeded automobile traffic to the growing east side but spoiled the lake for sailboat racing except for smaller boats. Bailey Peninsula and its Andrews Bay, Rainier Beach and Mercer Island dominate the southern part of the lake, with several marinas on both shores and at Renton.

On the east shore off the tip of Mercer Island is Meydenbauer Bay. For many years this was a popular anchorage for Seattle yachtsmen. With the growth of Bellevue in late years, it is now ringed with private homes but is still the home of Meydenbauer Bay Yacht Club and a pleasant place to head for.

A bit north we find three fingers of land pointing into the lake to form Fairweather Bay, Cozy Cove and Yarrow Bay, with the Yarrow Bay Yacht Club on the latter. These are small bays with shorelands privately owned; so offer little to the yachtsman. A mile up the shore is the town of Kirkland with municipal floats providing access to stores and fine restaurants. Juanita Bay, just to the north, is another popular place for those cruising the lake. Two marinas at Kenmore and one at Bothell are at the northern tip of the lake. At Leschi Park on the west shore are a yacht basin, marina, small boat moorage and the home of the Corinthian Yacht Club. This club, for sailors only, also has quarters at Shilshole Bay for their larger sailboats.

Seattle is home port for a tremendous fleet of pleasure boats. Its skippers range far and wide in their cruises and compete in innumerable sailboat races and predicted log contests for powerboats, all of which keep them on the water as much as possible throughout the year. Many of them are avid fishermen, some of whom spend most of their time fishing the waters of the sound, while others work their fishing in with their cruising.

Looking out from Shilshole Bay, one sees a panorama of this lovely evergreen country. To the north is Possession Point, the southern tip of Whidbey Island. Slightly to the left is Scatchett Head, marking the west side of too-shallow Cultus Bay. To the west are the Kitsap Peninsula and Bainbridge Island with their many sheltered bays. A glance to the south shows us Blake and Vashon Islands with Mount Rainier lifting its great white head skyward.

Although Puget Sound boaters have access to the delights of both northern and southern waters, they also have such a wealth of attractions in their own close-in area that their boats are seldom idle for long as they enjoy this section of these "greatest cruising waters in the world."

Linking freshwater Lakes Washington and Union with Puget Sound, Chittenden Locks are used by many pleasure boats.

3

Port Madison:
A Tranquil Harbor

The chain rattles through the hawsepipe as the anchor is dropped. A dinghy is launched from the yacht and soon children are rowing around in the peaceful waters of Port Madison Bay on the north end of Bainbridge Island. The gentle remnants of the wake roll a couple of gaunt, emaciated piling stumps, which look like ghosts from the past.

A tranquil harbor for hundreds of pleasure boats, some of them weekend visitors, others owned by residents whose beautiful homes line the shore, today's Port Madison, happily, has "regressed" from its heyday of a hundred years ago. Shaped much like an old sock with the toe dropping off the end of the foot, this is one of the finest protected harbors on Puget Sound.

Once a favorite nook of the Indians, it has had several names throughout its recorded history. Local Indians in the early 1800s called it Tchoak-um-cguck. When the Hudson's Bay Company man, John Work, was touring the sound in 1824, looking for a likely site for a fur-trading post, he called it Soquamic Bay. In the Indian Treaty, Governor Stevens recorded it as Noo-sohk-um. In 1841 the Wilkes Exploring Expedition officially called it Port Madison at the time Point Monroe and Point Jefferson were named.

In the early 1850s, about the time the first settlers were landing at Alki Point to found what would later become Seattle, a young man named George Meigs was establishing a mill on the east shore of Port Madison. A blockhouse was built and, although it was never used for defense, it provided community housekeeping quarters for the first few families, until permanent homes could be built.

There was soon a company general store, carpenter shop, machine shop, blacksmithy, as well as family homes and rows of cabins for the single men. Behind the store was a warehouse, while the second floor contained the library and Masonic Hall, which was also used for other meetings, church and Sunday School, dances, shows and entertainment. "The Captain's Club," for visiting ship captains, was a bench on the sheltered side of the warehouse. It is interesting to note that a geography book published about mid century describes Seattle as "a flourishing mill town across Puget Sound from Port Madison."

Nearly halfway into the bay on the west side is a tiny island. A clamshell midden indicates that Indians used the island, and it later became an Indian burial ground. In 1861 an explosion at the mill killed six men who were buried

Port Madison Prams round the mark in a Sunday race.

Aerial view shows the well-protected anchorage at Port Madison Bay.

there and it became a community cemetery until around 1870, when it was removed to the present cemetery east of Port Madison. During this time and for some time afterwards, the island was called Dead Man's Island. Today it is known as Treasure Island. For a time it was owned by Luke S. May, prominent criminologist of the Northwest, and is now owned by Russell Gibson, well-known Northwest yachtsman.

Twice the mill was destroyed by fire, once shortly after it was started and once in 1864. Each time it was promptly rebuilt. By 1870 the Port Madison and the Port Gamble mills topped the 42 mills in the state, each with a capacity of 100,000 board feet a day. The mill was lighted by lamps of open tin receptacles with wicks floating in herring oil or dogfish oil. Burning some 2000 gallons of oil a month, they required a full-time man to keep them filled and the wicks trimmed.

Across the bay, on the west side, near the pool of John Powell's present big stone house, was the first oil refinery plant north of San Francisco. Indians, fishing from their canoes between Agate Point and the Sandspit, provided the dogfish. The products were the oil and a thick brown grease used on the skid road. There were no ecologists in those days to do anything about the heavy fish fumes in the air.

About 1870 a plant was established for the preservation of fish and manufacture of fish by-products farther in the bay on the east side. In the 1875-76 season this plant put up 5000 boxes of smoked herring, each containing six dozen fish and delivered at 30 cents.

Ships were also built on both sides of the bay. One of them was the *Wildwood*, the first full-rigged ship built on Puget Sound.

Even in those lusty days, Port Madison was a dry town. Mr. Meigs was a strong temperance man and allowed no saloons. The 300 to 400 residents were like one big family, working and playing together; and the well-whitewashed houses, shaded by maple trees against a background of stately firs and cedars, made it a beautiful picture. William Seward, of Alaska Purchase fame, called it "the most beautiful mill town I have ever seen."

In 1857 when Kitsap County was established, Port Madison became the county seat. The blockhouse was remodeled to become the courthouse and jail. One man, an Indian, was hanged there for the murder of his wife.

It may be thought that daylight saving time is a modern innovation but it was practiced at Port Madison. When the days began to get longer, the mill superintendent would order the clock to be set ahead a half hour. Since the clocks of the town were set by the mill whistle, everyone went on daylight saving.

The Fourth of July and Christmas were the only holidays observed by the mill, and so these occasions called for real celebrations. On the Fourth everyone enjoyed orations, community singing, fireworks, lemonade, a picnic for both whites and Indians, games, races and a dance. At Christmas a huge tree was set up in the Town Hall and Santa Claus arrived, mysteriously, through a second-floor window. The whole town participated in the Christmas party.

By 1892 the heyday of the lumber industry was past and the Port Madison mill was closed. The county seat was moved to Sidney (now Port Orchard) in 1893, and the town rapidly declined with the rows of nice white houses empty and deserted by 1895. Mr. Meigs, once one of the wealthiest men in the Territory, was now nearly penniless and was killed in a fall on Seattle's waterfront in 1897.

Today there are few evidences of the thriving town and businesses that once graced the shores of Port Madison. The tall masts of the ships loading lumber are gone, the whining and screeching of the saws are stilled, and fumes of fish oil are no more. The abandoned structure of the mill, the store and the wharf all burned to the water's edge, and old landmarks have been removed. The bay has returned to the quiet, dignified tranquility that the Indians once knew. Weekends, a fleet of Port Madison Prams tack around the water in family-style competition sponsored by the Port Madison Yacht Club.

Modern-day residents on the shores of the bay like it this way and the many Northwest yachtsmen who visit the Seattle Yacht Club "Fo'c's'le" or seek anchorage here also appreciate its many charms.

4
Passages to Bays and Coves

The water, blue and sparkling ahead of the bow, is an invitation. Long arms from the Pacific stretch ahead, forecasting many happy hours of beachcombing, fishing, clamming, cruising new passages and exploring unknown harbors. A slight breeze ruffles the surface of the water while bringing that invigorating, distinctive smell of a low tide. After days and nights of dreaming, planning and preparing, you are, finally, at sea with a choice of many courses leading to fun and adventure.

Our course was laid to continue our rediscovery of Puget Sound and our present objective was what we are calling Northern Puget Sound. We are using this broad term which so many use to include the waters north of the officially charted Puget Sound, continuing up to the Strait of Juan de Fuca and Rosario Strait. We include Hood Canal because its entrance is in this vicinity.

Captain Vancouver sometimes named waterways "channels" but showed them as "canals" on his charts. His journal states that he named this inlet Hood's Channel after the Right Honorable Lord Hood, but it became Hood Canal on his chart and so we know it today.

Plans to reexplore Hood Canal took us around the tip of Foulweather Bluff and between the Bluff and Tala Point which is actually the opening into the canal. After passing Twin Spits on our left, we came to Hood Head on our right about three miles in from the entrance. This comes close to being an island but a narrow strip of land connects it to the mainland. Known locally as Whiskey Spit, it is a good place for clam digging, and land has been acquired there for future development as a state park.

Another two and a quarter miles in and across the channel is the entrance to Port Gamble. This entrance is narrow with Pope and Talbot's big mill on the right. There is now no access to shore and nothing in the town to serve the yachtsman. The harbor itself, about two miles long by half a mile wide, can sometimes be a poor anchorage, particularly in the winter months. The small bight on the east side near the head offers the best protection.

Around the corner from Port Gamble, just below Salsbury Point, we came upon the Hood Canal floating bridge crossing the channel. If you need height, better use the east span with 55 feet of clearance. The west span has only 39 feet.

Coming down the west shore of the canal, we swung into Squamish Harbor and Thorndyke Bay. These are both open and we found nothing of interest in either of them. A little farther in on the east shore is the Navy's ammunition-loading facility at Bangor. Be sure to check the chart and observe the restricted area here.

We rounded Hazel Point to turn southwestward and swung into Fisherman Harbor, a half-mile-long narrow finger poking into the southern end of Toandos Peninsula. The entrance dries at low tide; so coming and going should be governed accordingly, using at least half tide or better. This is a charming little bay, favorite of many cruising families. Walls on either side are steep, and 300 yards inside the protecting sandspit there is plenty of water—3 to 17 feet—except at the head. After crossing the shoal at the entrance, turn and follow the inside of the spit and the west shore closely until deeper water is reached. It is best to enter on a flooding tide, and remember, *the oyster beds are private.*

Fisherman Harbor is one of our favorite spots and, although we had not planned to stop here for more than a quick look, we had to pause for a few moments to soak up some of its delights. It lies in a setting of thick foliage, and sunlight filtering through the deep green of the evergreens,

Floats of Alderbrook Inn, on Hood Canal just beyond Union, where moorage, food and lodging are available.

or the more delicate green of the broadleaf maple, forms a lacy scalloped reflection in the limpid waters below. We hadn't been in here for some time and we decided then and there to return soon for an overnight stay.

Rounding Oak Head at the foot of the peninsula, we turned into Dabob Bay which opens up to the north. Here is another Navy testing area; so keep an eye peeled for the traffic control lights. Near the head of Quilcene Bay on the west shore, moorage is available in a small boat basin. Gas, water and some camping facilities are also available. Our next objective was Pleasant Harbor, a delightful little bay on the west shore of the canal, just a bit below the foot of Toandos Peninsula. This is perhaps one of the most popular destinations in the area for both individual cruising and yacht club group cruising. The narrow entrance has a depth of four feet at zero tide and no hazards. Depths within the harbor are sufficient for comfortable anchoring and there are floats at the state marine park just inside the entrance on the right. Beyond is the Pleasant Harbor Marina with moorage, gas and supplies. Whether you moor or anchor, you will find this protected little cove a delightful place.

Continuing down the west shore, we found several resorts, some of them having gas available. Hoodsport and Union have marinas to serve the cruising family. On the south shore of the Great Bend where the canal swings to the east, we pulled in to the long T-shaped floats of Alderbrook Inn. This is another favorite spot of yachtsmen just beyond Union, offering moorage, gas, water, ice, excellent food, lodging and other services.

The long foot and the east shore of the canal have very little to attract the yachtsman. There are several small bights and coves, some of them where rivers enter, but we found no facilities or services except at Peck's Harbor at Seabeck where moorage, fuel, groceries and a restaurant are available. Seabeck Bay, in behind Misery Point, offers protection in some winds.

Lord Hood's Channel, or Hood Canal as we know it, is an important part of our cruising waters and a popular area with many Puget Sound skippers. It's close enough for a

weekend cruise and pleasant enough for a vacation. Green shores, inviting coves and water that seldom gets rough even when the wind blows, all combine to invite the pleasure boat owner to partake of its charms.

Back at the top of the canal and around Tala Point, we swung into historic Port Ludlow. Be sure to give this point a wide berth, at least 200 yards, to clear the shoal extending out from it. This bay has two parts, the outer and inner harbors. Site of an early lumber mill which was purchased by Pope and Talbot in 1878, this has been a favorite with cruising families for many years. The mill was closed in 1936 and the town has been replaced by an attractive resort and rustic residential development with a restaurant, a saltwater swimming pool and a marina on the north shore of the outer harbor. Better anchor out, though, as the developers are not particularly interested in the transient boater and restrict the facilities for the use of residents, unless unassigned space happens to be available. It's best to check at the fueling float.

The inner harbor is still available to boaters and we hope that the developers will see fit to leave these shores undeveloped, so that this delightful little harbor can remain one of the beauty spots in our Northwest cruising waters. This has always been a top favorite anchorage as was evidenced by the large number of boats already riding at anchor when we arrived. Entrance should be made between the Twin Islands, with a careful lookout for the rock just south of the smaller island. Zero tide depths of from 4 to 16 feet and a mud bottom make this landlocked cove a most pleasant destination for a weekend get-away-from-it-all cruise.

A midafternoon arrival, a warm sun, and the beauty of this peaceful setting with its forest-clad shores reflecting in the mirror of the deep blue water to paint a double picture around the edges—all combined to issue an invitation for some socializing. As our dinghy wove in and out among the anchored boats, we found many with whom we were acquainted, and we spent a pleasant afternoon renewing friendships and exchanging cruising experiences. As the sun sank behind the trees, the air was laden with the smell of barbecuing steaks and seafood mixed with the delicate scent of fir, pine and cedar from the shore.

Good anchorage can also be had in most of the outer harbor, but don't go too far into the head. Frequently logs are stored in this area. Port Ludlow is the home of Meydenbauer Bay Yacht Club's outstation, located not far from the entrance to the inner harbor.

Two and a half miles north of Port Ludlow is another landlocked cove called Mats Mats Bay. It is small, shallow and formerly had a tricky entrance, but it has long been popular with Puget Sound skippers and families. The entrance channel has now been blasted and dredged out and is well marked with a range and lights for safe passage. Large-scale chart #6421 is a good one to have aboard in this area. Not shown on the chart is a sandbar just inside the entrance opposite the stone quarry. Local residents told us this bar was formed by the tugs bringing barges into the stone quarry. When entering or leaving at low tide, better stay close to the quarry side of the channel. Anchorage at Mats Mats should not be made too close to shore as there are some shallow areas. Without local knowledge or careful check of the depths, it is probably better to anchor toward the center of the bay. A small marina offers mooring, gas, water and small boat launching facilities are nearby. The Edmonds Yacht Club has property here for a proposed outstation.

In running between Port Ludlow and Mats Mats Bay, careful attention should be paid to the chart to avoid Snake Rock, Colvos Rocks and Klas Rocks.

A swing around Olele Point, north of Mats Mats Bay, brought us into Oak Bay at the southern end of Marrowstone and Indian Islands. This leads into the Port Townsend Canal, a narrow three-quarter-mile channel between Indian Island and Quimper Peninsula. The fixed bridge over the canal has a vertical clearance of 58 feet.

Once through the canal, it is three miles to the entrance of Kilisut Harbor which lies between Indian and Marrowstone Islands. These two islands are connected at the south by a narrow isthmus, and Scow Bay forms the southern part of Kilisut Harbor. The entire harbor is sometimes called Scow Bay.

After rounding Whalen Point, we picked up buoy "N2," the first in a long series of red nun buoys and black can buoys marking the rather tricky channel into the harbor. By following the buoys closely, and keeping a careful check on their numbers, the inverted S channel can be easily followed into deeper water. Fort Flagler State Marine Park, on the sandspit just inside the entrance, provides floats, mooring buoys, camp and picnic sites and other facilities. Clams can be found on the spit.

Mystery Bay is a charming little cove indenting Marrowstone Island from about the middle of Kilisut Harbor and is one of the most popular bays in the area, the end goal of many a yacht club group cruise. With depths from 3 to 25 feet over a muddy bottom and good protection, it provides a fine anchorage. A county dock and float maintained by the Port of Port Townsend is just inside the entrance to Mystery Bay, on the left side and near the head of the bay is a small store with landing floats.

From Kilisut Harbor entrance it is only two miles to Port Townsend's Point Hudson Boat Harbor. Named after the marquis of Townshend by Captain Vancouver, Port Townsend, as it is now called, was first sighted in 1792. Actual beginning of the town dates back to 1851. By the 1880s the town had grown to provide capabilities for a population of 20,000. The historic and picturesque city contains the best collection of Victorian architecture north of San Francisco. A rapidly growing center for art and culture, it is the home of the Summer School of the Arts, Summer Arts Festival, the Pacific Northwest Music Festival and Rhododendron Festival. Old Fort Townsend and the Historical Museum portray the history of one of the Northwest's oldest cities. On surrounding beaches are found oysters, clams, crabs and shrimp. There is good salmon fishing as well as stream fishing for trout and steelhead. The many activities and the low rainfall, mild year-round climate make this a favorite area for the cruising yachtsman.

Mats Mats Bay, a landlocked cove north of Port Ludlow, now has a well-marked entrance channel.

Although Port Townsend never achieved its dream of total greatness, it has maintained a charm and friendliness that annually attracts many visitors who enjoy its attributes and climate. Point Hudson, with its marina, restaurant, motel, many services and attractions, has become a mecca for cruising boats. The special arrangements for Customs provided by the port have added to the appeal of Point Hudson as a clearing place for boats coming from Canadian waters.

Around Point Hudson and a couple of miles north is Point Wilson, marking the meeting of Admiralty Inlet with the Strait of Juan de Fuca. Here the yachtsman runs out of protected waters, frequently encountering tide rips, sometimes violent. Short, steep waves stand on end, vying with each other to confuse the pilot by their complete lack of direction or pattern and slapping the boat from every side.

We crossed the three and a half miles from Point Wilson to Admiralty Head to where we could sight the abandoned lighthouse on Whidbey Island. Here tucked in behind it is Keystone Harbor, a small cove bypassed by many skippers but well worth a visit. Here is good anchorage, protected from prevailing westerly winds. It is the eastern terminus for the Keystone-Port Townsend ferry; so in anchoring, leave room for it to come and go.

There are no shore-access facilities and so the dinghy is required, but we found rewards in a visit to the Fort Casey State Park, the old guns and emplacements, the abandoned lighthouse and museum. Fort Casey, set up in 1856 as a coast defense point, was named for its first commander, Col. Silas Casey.

We next swung down Admiralty Inlet through Admiralty Bay past Bush Point and Double Bluffs across the entrance to Useless Bay and Cultus Bay and around Possession Point and into Possession Sound to explore the other entrance, or exit, to Puget Sound, which is Saratoga Passage on the inside of Whidbey Island. On the east side of Possession Sound is Mukilteo on Elliot Point, which has marinas and facilities and services for the yachtsman as well as nearby stores for the vacationing family.

Some five miles northeast are Port Gardner and the city of Everett. The beautiful Fourteenth Street Yacht Basin has guest dock, full marine services and is the site of the Everett Yacht Club. While the downtown area is some distance away, taxi service is available. The long sandspit protecting the harbor, available by dinghy or ferry, offers interesting hiking and picnicking possibilities.

The Snohomish River with its several sloughs winding around behind the town is a fascinating cruising area where several yacht clubs schedule fall and winter cruises in protected waters when winds may be kicking up outside. A little local knowledge obtained from Everett or Edmonds Yacht Club members will prove helpful in planning to run in these waters.

As we left Everett, we were careful to stay outside of the buoys marking a rather extensive shoal area which is the delta of the Snohomish River. Gedney Island, locally known as Hat Island, lying about three miles out in Everett's front yard, we passed to the north. Property on this island is all privately owned. The Hat Island Yacht Club has quarters and moorages in the boat basin on the northwestern shore.

Wishing to reacquaint ourselves with picturesque little Tulalip Bay, which is due east of Camano Head, we swung into the right. Here is a lovely, quiet little cove in which to relax or spend the night. Two resorts provide moorage, gas and other services. The bay is quite shallow with a mud bottom, but good anchorage can be found in 3 to 18 feet at zero tide. Large-scale chart #6448 is helpful in determining depths and the shoal areas. Some slower boat skippers use this bay to break the trip from Deception Pass to Seattle, Tacoma and mid-sound points. Good fishing can sometimes be found off Camano Head.

Lying between Whidbey Island and the mainland in these waters is Camano Island. Named for Spanish explorer Lt. Jacinto A. Caamano, it really is an island, although it appears to be a peninsula as Vancouver thought it was. A shallow pass with shoal areas at both ends separates the island from the mainland. Only vessels with very little draft

Inner harbor of Port Ludlow, one of the beauty spots in these waters.

29

Fort Flagler State Marine Park floats in Kilisut Harbor.

and skippers with local knowledge should attempt to go through here.

Snuggled in behind Camano Island, Port Susan has about 10 miles of navigable water but with no protection from southeasterly winds. Although there has been much speculation as to whom Vancouver was honoring with this name, Prof. Edmund Meany has no doubts. Vancouver had served under, and had great respect for, Sir Alan Gardner. He originally called the passage from Deception Pass to Everett, Port Gardner. Professor Meany says, "Therefore, when he named one port after Admiral Gardner, he named the other after the admiral's esteemed lady."

Westerly, on Whidbey Island across from Camano Head, is Langley with the Langley Marina and a municipal moorage. Here is another stopover point frequently used to break the trip from the San Juan Island area to mid Puget Sound. A couple of warnings might be in order here. Don't tie too close to the shore if a low tide is due or you'll be stranded or even grounded and, if you tie on the outside of the outer float, you'll be rocked by the wakes of the passing boats.

Around East and Rocky Points is Holmes Harbor, a five-mile-long bay cutting into Whidbey Island to the south. A popular fishing area, the bay offers little protection from summertime prevailing northwesterly winds. A bit of protection can sometimes be found in behind the little island off Rocky Point, charted as Hackney Island but known locally as Baby Island. A new marina is being built in Holmes Harbor.

Continuing up Saratoga Passage, we turned west into Penn Cove to check on the new floats at Coupeville. This cove, indenting the island westerly for about three miles, was named by Vancouver for an unidentified friend. Coupeville, on the south shore of the cove, was named after Capt. Thomas Coupe who, in 1851, sailed his full-rigged barque *Success* through Deception Pass. The new floats, recently installed, make this interesting town more readily available to the cruising family and provide additional moorage space for those wishing to stop overnight.

A bit to the north are Oak and Crescent Harbors, separated by Forbes Point. While the Navy has had restrictions on a good portion of these waters for some years, they are being relaxed in many ways. Oak Harbor has plans for a small boat basin and marina.

Across the water to the southeast on an open bay on the north end of Camano Island is the village of Utsalady. We found the bay had some good protection from southerly winds but not much from the north, with anchorage on the village side in 10 to 20 feet of water over a mud bottom. There is no shore access but the dinghy will put you on the beach, and we found a store to provide for our immediate needs.

Running on north through Skagit Bay, one is really in "thin" water and it's a good idea to follow the channel which is well marked. Many skippers, even experienced ones, sometimes have trouble locating some of these channel-marking buoys. They seem so much farther in to the east and northeast than they appear on the chart. Buoy "N2" seems particularly hard to find. When running north, we like to come in fairly close to the Strawberry Point Light and then favor the port-hand shore, where there is enough depth if you don't get too close in, until you can pick up buoy "N8" or the two lights marking either side of the channel. If you aren't well acquainted through here, take along large-scale chart #6376.

This can be a point of decision for some. Following the channel past Hope Island and around Hoypus Point is a route to Deception Pass and across Rosario Strait to the San Juan Islands. If the "time of the tide" is wrong at the pass or if indications are that the wind may be roughing up the strait more than you like, a near 90° turn to the right will put you on course for the so-called back door, easy entrance to the islands.

A narrow but well-marked channel past Goat Island leads to Swinomish (with accent on the first syllable) Channel which is often mistakenly called Swinomish Slough. Besides offering a calm water passage, this route is interesting and beautifully scenic. There are no hazards if markers and ranges are carefully followed.

Entrance to the main part of this channel is through Hole in the Wall, a spectacular passage between high rock walls. Three-quarters of a mile upchannel is the Shelter Bay development with its homesites on a series of canals and a marina and moorage for use of residents. Beyond is the Rainbow fixed bridge with vertical clearance of 75 feet in the center.

The town of La Conner, named for Louisa A. Conner, wife of its founder, is one of the oldest settlements in the state and home of the *Puget Sound Mail*, Washington's "oldest living weekly" newspaper. Editor-publisher Pat O'Leary still prints his four-page paper on an ancient Cranston flatbed press. Not having been here for some time, we toured the town to visit some museums, antique and other interesting shops, as well as some of the architecturally interesting old buildings and homes which hold fascination for history buffs. Bellingham Yacht Club's former building, towed in by barge, is now a popular dining room on the waterfront.

A new marina, recently constructed by the Port of Skagit County, has fine covered moorages and a guest float.

When coming in or landing, watch that current because its velocity can really surprise you.

We always enjoy cruising this route, perhaps because it is so peaceful, or perhaps because it is so different. While we love the forests, the rocks, the hills, and the islands in our usual cruising passages, a change is always welcome and the flat, level meadows and fields on both sides of the channel make an enjoyable picture.

We passed under the bridge at the north end of the channel and carefully checked the buoys in the two-and-a-half-mile-long dredged channel which runs through the flats of Padilla Bay to March Point. From here a choice of several routes leads to a quiet water passage among some of the eastern San Juan Islands to Peavine or Obstruction Passes and into the main group of the San Juans.

If you choose the Deception Pass route, the channel up Skagit Bay passes Hope Island, one of the area's top spots for catching those big salmon. Around Hoypus Point is Cornet Bay, a favorite place to end a day's run, either going to or coming from the islands, or to wait for favorable currents in the pass. Enter the bay to the east of Ben Ure Island. The other side is shoal but can be used at higher tides.

On the left as you enter is a part of Deception Pass State Park with pier, floats and mooring buoys. Farther in on the same side is the Cornet Bay Marina. This portion of the bay is very shallow but a channel and the basin have been dredged. Be sure to follow the marker buoys carefully. The marina has moorage, fuel, water, groceries and other facilities for the cruising family.

Deception Pass is one of the most scenic spots in Northwest waters, but many skippers consider its fast currents a serious hazard. While these currents can attain velocities up to nine knots on spring tides, most old-time skippers maintain that the fast-moving water, the whirlpools and boils aren't too dangerous. Many years ago we were negotiating the pass with a tug and log boom taking up most of the narrow passage. Far over near the shore a whirlpool caught the stern and swung it menacingly toward the straight-up rock wall. It seemed the stern must certainly be thrown against the wall but the backwash swung us safely away.

Bob Nelson of Rainier Yacht Club claims he takes his seven-knot boat *Bessie* through with the current at any stage of the tide. General concensus seems to be that, if you go with the current, even if you should lose power, and if there aren't other vessels near you, you'll make it without danger. You may be swung around or turned a few times

but you will get through with no difficulty. Personally, we want full control of the boat to avoid the possibility of hitting a log or deadhead being tossed around in the swirling waters, and will continue to run the pass in our slower boat within a half hour or so of slack water.

Paul Morris of Seattle Yacht Club likes to use little Canoe Pass, on the north side of Pass Island. He claims the currents do not run as fast through there, but local knowledge is necessary to avoid the rock right at the turn of the channel. This is a fun passage but use caution if you try it.

We've intentionally, though erroneously, called the waters in this chapter Northern Puget Sound. Whatever we call them, they are filled with fascinating and interesting bays, coves and cruising possibilities and are a vital part of our Northwest cruising waters.

Fascinating bays like this one invite exploration.

5

There's Magic
in Those Islands

"An indescribable archipelago of islands, kelp, rocks, and big and little inlets," wrote Juan Pantoja y Arriga, probably the first white man to see the San Juan Islands.

A year later, in 1792, Lt. William Broughton described them as "rocky isles, well clothed with wood."

Pantoja, commanding the *Santa Saturnina*, had been sent by Francisco Eliza to explore the islands, while Broughton had been sent on the same mission in the *Chatham* by Captain Vancouver.

The United States Coast Survey in 1853 and 1854 gave the name Washington Sound to the whole archipelago between the mainland and Vancouver Island, separating the Straits of Georgia and Juan de Fuca. As mentioned earlier, the name is seldom heard today and has unfortunately been left off of many charts in late years.

These islands are generally discovered early in a new boat owner's cruising life. They are savored and enjoyed for a year or two before he moves on to new waters, farther north, and new challenges. As the years pass, he continues to speed through them, hurrying on to ever-more-distant harbors.

The San Juans are never lonely because there are always plenty of new boat owners, but the old-timers should occasionally plan to spend some cruising time in rediscovering them. After all, they are set in one of the world's most lovely areas. Like beautiful gems in blue settings, they are full of contrasts with forested hills and smooth, green pastures, wide expanses of sandy beaches, as well as steep craggy cliffs dropping sharply to the sea below. Sleepy, quiet, old-fashioned villages reign benignly over harbors sheltering sailing yachts, cruisers and fishing boats of all types. There is still much for the old-timer to see.

Renewing our acquaintance with the San Juans is a never-ending pleasure with us, sometimes done as part of a longer cruise, sometimes as an objective itself. We like to vary our courses, one time taking the direct route via Deception Pass and Rosario Strait and another time via Swinomish Channel and through the eastern San Juans.

Rosario Strait forms a natural dividing line between the eastern and western islands of the group. The eastern group, then, includes Lummi, Eliza, Sinclair, Vendovi, Cypress, Strawberry, Towhead, Cone Islands, Jack, Guemes, Huckleberry, Saddlebag, Dot, Hat, Burrows, Allan, Young and Fidalgo. Officially, Whidbey Island is one of the San Juans which would mean that Northwest, Deception, Pass, Strawberry, Ben Ure, Skagit, Kiket, Hope, Goat and several other smaller islands should be included, but we generally don't think of anything below Deception Pass as being a part of this archipelago.

Skippers heading across Rosario Strait from Deception Pass for the western group miss these eastern islands with the possible exception of Burrows, Allan and Young. In cruising between Deception Pass and Skyline Marina, we sometimes stop at a tiny little cove called Peartree Bay, tucked into the southeast shore of Burrows Island and protected by Young Island. We like to use it for a lunch or siesta stop or for killing time while waiting for slack at the pass.

Most of the names in this vicinity were given by Capt. Charles Wilkes. Burrows Island honors Capt. William Burrows of the *Boxer*, while Allan Island was named for Capt. William Henry Allen who was mortally wounded aboard the *Argus* in 1813 during combat with the British brig *Pelican*. Some careless chart maker changed the *e* to an *a*.

Skyline, on Flounder Bay at the north end of Burrows

Scenic Hicks Bay is a pleasant spot in good weather.

Bay, is popular with Northwest yachtsmen. Facilities include moorage, groceries and supplies, ice, restaurant and lounge, complete fuel float, laundry, launching and haul-out, hull and engine repairs, camping, lodging and fishing supplies. Many boat owners, both from the Puget Sound area and east of the mountains, moor their craft here all summer in order to have quick access to the islands.

Flounder Bay, originally named Boxer Bay, after Captain Burrows' ship, is said to have been called that later because of the many flounder there before it was dredged. Popular usage has converted what was originally Argus Bay, after Captain Allen's ship, to Burrows Bay.

An all-electric sawmill was built here in the early 1920s occupying the entire area from the restaurant to the deep water of Burrows Bay. Demolition of the mill was completed in 1961 with the huge planing mill building remaining for use for dry boat storage. Many artifacts from the mill can still be seen. The back bar in the cocktail lounge is from the old hotel, wood-stave water mains are the standing lamp bases in the dining room, the chandelier and barbecue building center support are old bits of driftwood from the beach, and timbers and planks now used for boardwalks, bulkheads and structural beams were salvaged from the old mill.

The town of Anacortes on the northern tip of Fidalgo Island was named by its founder, Amos Bowman, for his wife Anna Curtis, but the spelling was changed to conform to the Spanish tone of Fidalgo. Several marinas facing on Guemes Channel and around in Capsante Waterway provide all facilities and services for the yachtsman. Anacortes is known as the "Gateway to the San Juans" and for those vacationing families who are without boats, charter boats, with or without skipper, are available.

On a recent cruise in which we entered Washington Sound from Swinomish Channel, we cruised the narrow dredged channel through shallow Padilla Bay and then headed north to leave Hat Island on our starboard. Just beyond are Saddlebag and Dot Islands, where we had to stop for a try at crabbing. The bays on both the north and south sides of Saddlebag can be good but it seems to depend on the right positioning of the trap. We've seen several boats, all with traps out, some making a good catch in a short time while others got nothing. This was our lucky day. With the trap down about an hour we got enough legal keepers to provide a good meal.

Over to the west, less than half a mile across the channel, is little Huckleberry Island with a partially protected cove behind it on Guemes Island. Farther up is a minicove called Boat Harbor. The rest of Guemes Island is of no particular interest to the yachtsman. The same holds true of Sinclair, Vendovi and Eliza Islands. They are all privately owned with no bays, harbors or facilities available to cruising boats.

Entering Bellingham Bay, we swung in to the right around Governors Point to visit friends in Chuckanut Bay with picturesque little Chuckanut Island in the middle at its entrance. If entering north of Chuckanut Island, it is best to hold close to the island or to the point as there are rocks in the middle between them. South of the island the entrance is all clear.

In Bellingham Bay there is public moorage and the Bellingham Yacht Club in the Squalicum Boat Basin with most boating needs readily available. It is a short taxi ride to the center of town. Bellingham Bay is quite shallow with 16 fathoms its greatest depth. When the wind blows, a nasty chop can kick up.

After an excellent lunch at the yacht club we crossed the bay to cruise up Hale Passage between Lummi Island and the long peninsula where the Lummi Indian Reservation is located. Lummi Island was named for the Indian tribe of that vicinity and is about eight miles long with the lower half quite high, rising to a 1740-foot peak, while the other half is relatively low and flat. A couple of marinas are on the west side.

After we had rounded Point Migley, situated on the northern end of Lummi Island, we headed south again to circle Cypress Island. Bordering on the east of Rosario Strait between Blakely and Guemes Island, Cypress has more to offer the cruising family than most of the other eastern San Juans. On the southeast shore is Deep Water Bay, about five miles of fairly open water but with little coves in behind the points forming both ends. Secret Harbor, at the southeast end of the bay, shallows to four feet at zero tide but offers good protection. The cove at the northeast end is less protected.

Just around the point is a small peninsula forming another tiny cove for small boats. Eagle Harbor, farther up the east shore of Cypress, is a somewhat open but frequently used anchorage when the tide is above the zero mark. Strawberry Bay on the west side, with little Strawberry Island across part of it, is a somewhat exposed anchorage although it served both Vancouver and his Lieutenant

Broughton. It was from the wild strawberries they found growing there that the island and bay got their names, while they called the big island Cypress because they thought the tall evergreens were cypress trees.

Across Rosario Strait we find four passes or entrances to the western group of the San Juans. Lopez Pass, the most southerly, is between an upturned tip of Lopez Island and Decatur Island. The main channel, 10 to 14 fathoms deep, runs southwesterly between that tip of Lopez and Ram Island. It's best to give the southern tip of Ram Island a wide berth to avoid the charted rocks. Skippers with local knowledge take a westerly heading through the pass running between two tiny islands north of Ram Island, but care should be used in taking this course.

Thatcher Pass, between Decatur and Blakely Islands, is wide and clear of hazards. Between the north end of Blakely Island and the southeastern tip of Orcas Island lies Obstruction Island which divides this waterway into Peavine Pass on its south and Obstruction Pass on its north. Both of these passes are clear in center channel, but currents can run up to five knots through them.

Decatur Island has a couple of anchorages. On the eastern side a long, low sand beach curves out to connect with Decatur Head. The bay thus formed offers shallow anchorage, although a southeast wind can whistle across the sandy neck. James Island, which is an unimproved state marine park, lies just off Decatur Head and has a snug little cove on its west side. We like to anchor here and take the dinghy ashore to explore the island or go out to fish the meeting tides off Fauntleroy Point. In passing between James Island and Decatur Head, steer a mid-channel course to avoid rocks on both sides.

On Decatur's west side is a peninsula forming a cozy, protected little cove known locally as Kan Kut Harbor. Although the shorelands are all privately owned, it provides a good protected anchorage for ending or beginning a day's run from or to mid Puget Sound for the slower boats.

Lopez Sound, between Lopez and Decatur Islands, has Trump and Center Islands (which may be safely passed on the inside by steering mid channel), and a few smaller ones, all of no particular interest to the yachtsman. At the head of the sound are Hunter and Mud Bays. The latter is shoal, not a very good anchorage, but good for dinghy exploration and sometimes for fishing. Hunter Bay offers good anchorage. At the north of the sound, Spencer Spit, another state marine park, pokes its sandy finger at nearby Frost Island. The spit is a favorite small boat rendezvous and picnic spot.

Lopez Island's Shoal Bay and Swifts Bay, separated by Humphrey Head, are both shallow but, with local knowledge and care, can be usable anchorages.

We have found through the years, along with many other cruising families, that Lopez Sound, with its islands, bays and coves, offers much cruising enjoyment.

Blakely Island is sometimes called the "Paradise Isle of the San Juans." Privately owned, it is being developed only as fast as its owner wishes. An excellent air strip is bordered with homes of flying enthusiasts who tie their planes down in their own yards. For the yachtsman there is the protected harbor just off Peavine Pass. A complete marina with all facilities and services makes this a favorite stopping place for those cruising these waters. The Blakely House Restaurant and Boatel offer good food and luxurious lodging.

Thatcher Bay, about midway down the west shore, has good anchorage in six- to nine-foot depths but the shore is posted against landing. Little Willow Island, lying off the southwest shore of Blakely, may be passed safely on the inside.

Orcas Island, sometimes called the "Resort Island," is U shaped like a saddlebag with East Sound nearly cutting it in two. Smaller West Sound and still smaller Deer Harbor indent the western half to help produce more waterfront than on any of the other islands. Orcas is also the largest of the group with 58 square miles, but only slightly, for San Juan Island has 57 square miles.

In circumnavigating Orcas Island, we turned up a wealth of attractive features which are of interest to the cruising family. Entering through Obstruction Pass, we found the Obstruction Pass Motel Resort with gas, groceries, mooring and launching facilities. Rounding the point, we swung into Buck Bay where the State Parks Department maintains the floats for the village of Olga with its store and post office. Two miles farther up the east shore is Cascade Bay, the site of Rosario Resort and Boatel. We, and many others, always enjoy a stop at this former home and estate of Robert Moran. Here is everything any crew could desire for a night, a day or more ashore. It is one of the finest facilities in the islands, which, of course, makes it popular with yachtsmen and calls for an early arrival or an advance reservation, as moorage is somewhat limited. When stopping here we always meet many of our boating friends and enjoy the excellent meals in the dining room, the historic mood of the place, and the friendly hospitality of the hosts, Mr. and Mrs. Gil Geiser, and their cheerful and efficient staff. Specially planned activities for children are available, and the swimming pools are attractive to all ages.

The village of Eastsound at the head of the sound has an excellent store and a fascinating museum but no good means for getting ashore. Ship Bay and Fishing Bay can be used for anchoring but are not protected against southeast winds.

Cruising down the west shore of East Sound, we found nothing of particular interest until we rounded Shag Rock where there is a cozy little cove tucked in between it and Foster Point. About three-quarters of a mile the other side of the point is snug little Grindstone Harbor, where we like to anchor in the shallow inner cove. A couple of rocks lie in the center channel of the outer entrance but these are usually marked. A mile farther west is another little cove formed by a near-island connected by a sand and gravel spit. This is a friendly little bight where we like to duck in for a lunch or an afternoon siesta.

Around the corner is the village of Orcas with the ferry landing, floats, fuel dock, excellent store and state liquor store. The floats are somewhat exposed to the wakes of passing boats; so it's a good idea, if moored on the outside, to leave someone in attendance or be sure the boat is well fendered.

We found, as we always have in the past, that West

Sound, a peaceful, quiet bit of water, has much to offer. There are at least a dozen bays and tiny coves and a scattering of wooded islands. The area hasn't always been peaceful, however, as evidenced by such names as Massacre Bay, Skull Island and Victim Island taking us back a hundred or more years when the fierce Haida Indians came to harrass the local Lummi tribe. Both Skull and Victim Islands are undeveloped state marine parks. A marina, the West Sound store and Orcas Island Yacht Club are in the bay between Sheep Island and Haida Point.

Around Caldwell Point, narrow Pole Pass cuts between Orcas and Crane Islands. It was here that the Indians stretched nets between high poles to knock down ducks flying through, which accounts for the name. While the pass isn't particularly dangerous, tidal currents can run through at fairly good velocities at times which, together with the narrow passage, can cause accidents if there is much other traffic. There are a couple of rocks on the northwest side of the pass, so it's a good idea not to cut to the west too quickly after coming through. The first-timer should study chart #6379 before negotiating the pass.

Deer Harbor with its little Fawn Island, has a good marina near the head on the east shore, and Deer Harbor Inn, a pleasant hike to the north, has long been known for good food served family style.

Steep Point is the southwestern extremity of Orcas. The northwest shore on President Channel has nothing to attract the yachtsman up to West Beach. Here we found the West Beach Resort had some mooring, groceries, ice, gas and other facilities. Around the point, Beachhaven Resort has moorage, gas and facilities for boats. In rounding the point, watch for the rocks and reef extending out from it. A little less than a mile below Point Doughty is little Freeman Island, another undeveloped state marine park property, and the YMCA's Camp Orkila is on the shore of Orcas Island here.

On the North Shore of Orcas Island, in behind the Parker Reef Light, is Bartel's Resort with full boating facilities. Although it appears from the outside that there are solid beds of kelp along the shore, there is a marked channel through the kelp into the floats.

Around Point Thompson, we found the northeast shore of Lawrence Point is almost straight, rising steeply from the water, and has nothing to offer. Around Lawrence Point is a favorite fishing area. Peapod Rocks are nesting places for sea gulls and have become particularly interesting in recent years to diving enthusiasts. Little Doe Island is also a state marine park. Doebay Village on Doe Bay has moorage, gas, groceries, ice, and other facilities.

We now returned to Obstruction Pass to complete our circle tour of Orcas Island. Each of the San Juan Islands has a charm all its own and Orcas is no exception. Away from the pressures of the big city, life begins to slow until a new mood is born and one's entire outlook is transformed to a basic serenity such as man was intended to live by. This mood is particularly evident on Orcas Island, and the visiting yachtsman will soon recognize and embrace it no matter where on the island he may stop.

We next cruised through Harney Channel to Shaw

Narrow Wasp Passage, a main channel for boats going west through the islands, was a pirate's delight in early days.

Upright Head, Lopez Island's northernmost point, is the first ferry stop after Anacortes. Shoal Bay is to the left.

Island which lies south of Orcas Island. Sometimes called the "Hub of the San Juans," it features several nice bays and a beautiful sandy beach. The Shaw store and ferry landing are about a mile southeast across Harney Channel from the Orcas landing. There is a gas float and small moorage tucked in behind the ferry slip.

We turned into Blind Bay, with Blind Island across its entrance, to find good anchorage for the night. This bay shoals out from the shore; so depths should be carefully checked. Best entrance is the east side of Blind Island favoring it on the starboard hand, but not too close, to avoid the rock about halfway between the island and the shore. Blind Island is being held for future development as a state marine park. Large-scale chart #6379 is a comfort to have aboard for this entire area.

After returning from dinner with friends on the island, we prepared to snug down for the night. A full moon had already taken over the mastery of the sky from the fast receding afterglow of the sun in the west. The lonesome, eerie call of a loon, the gentle lapping of the water against the hull, and the musical creak of the anchor rode in the chalk as the tide swung the boat, quickly produced a sound sleep.

Next morning we swung down Upright Channel to inspect Picnic Cove, Indian Cove and Squaw Bay on the southeast side of Shaw Island. The sandy beach of Indian Cove is a county park so is available for use. Squaw Bay shallows to a quarter fathom at zero tide in the middle so shouldn't be used except on the higher tides. Passage between Shaw and Canoe Islands is safe on plus tides, but at lower water favor Canoe Island to miss the three-quarter-fathom shoal in mid channel.

On the south of Shaw Island, little Hoffman Cove and Hicks Bay are exposed to southerly winds but offer protection in winds from other directions. Coming up San Juan Channel on the southwest side of Shaw Island, we swung into Parks Bay, one of our long-time favorite anchorages in

this area. Here is excellent protection in a scenic spot but the shores are privately owned and posted against landing.

Continuing northwesterly, we swung around Shaw Island's Neck Point and across Wasp Passage to the Wasp Islands. There are nine named islands and islets in the group and several small islets and rocks. We always find this an interesting group to explore, with most of the passages between the isles and islets comfortably deep enough; but chart #6379 should be carefully watched to miss the shoals and rocks that are there, although most of them are fairly well marked by kelp.

To the west of Steep Point across Spring Passage is Jones Island which is a state marine park. This 179-acre island is a favorite of many with mooring floats and buoys, campsites and picnic facilities. Hiking on several trails, clamming, fishing and swimming can be enjoyed here.

Waldron Island, northwest of Orcas, has little to attract the yachtsman although, perhaps more than any of the other islands, it still retains an idyllic old-time charm. Its Cowlitz Bay is too open to afford much protection but there is a small cove on its east side.

Across the top of Orcas are several islands popular with Northwest skippers which we always visit whenever we are in the area. Patos Island, northernmost of the San Juans, has a lighthouse which we love to visit and Active Cove offers shelter but should be entered with caution. Entirely government owned, the island provides interesting opportunities for studying marine life or picking up a fantastic bit of driftwood on its shores.

To the southeast are the Sucia Islands. Sucia, itself, was purchased by Puget Sound yachtsmen just in time to save it from becoming a development, and was donated to the state for a marine park. Sucia in Spanish means "bad" or "foul," referring to the many reefs surrounding the islands. It is noted for its unusual rock formations and is a source of interesting fossil formations. Principal harbor with floats and moorage buoys is Fossil Bay, although we also enjoy

36

Reef Point gives promise of the beauty to be found behind nearby Turn Island, a state park with picnic facilities.

anchoring in Shallow Bay on the west and Echo Bay on the east, both of which are popular anchorages, but Shallow Bay is not much used.

A stop on Sucia is always a must with us; and, no matter where we anchor or tie, we always enjoy the trails through the island to the other bays and coves. As a state park, it has picnic and camping facilities in a natural setting while, as an unspoiled island, it offers a quiet scenic beauty which can be savored and enjoyed only by the boat owner, his family and friends.

Still farther southeastward is Matia Island, properly pronounced Ma-Tee′-ah, but called by many Matey Island. This is also a state marine park with two coves on the west end and one on the southeastern end. The latter should be entered with extreme caution as there are many rocks across the entrance, but it is a particularly interesting bay. Matia means "no protection" but yachtsmen have found good anchorage and moorage in the northwestern cove.

Continuing to the southeast, we find Barnes, Clark and the Sisters Islands. Clark Island is a state marine park, unimproved but affording some nice beaches for dinghy landing and exploration.

Swinging back to the west across the top of Orcas Island, we find a few small islands and rocks including Skipjack Island, to the north of Waldron, White Rock, Gull Rock and Flattop Island, southwest of Waldron.

To the west are Spieden Island with its satellite, Sentinel Island, the Cactus Islands, Ripple Island, Johns Island and Stuart Island.

Spieden Island was recently purchased, renamed Safari Island and stocked with a variety of exotic animals. For a fee you can engage in a hunting safari. A lively exchange of pro and con editorial comments has ensued, with no results either way at this writing.

Stuart Island has two very popular harbors both of which are state marine parks. Reid Harbor and Prevost Harbor have floats, moorage buoys and are connected by a trail

across the island. Clamming, fishing, camping and picnic facilities, hiking trails, swimming, delightful scenery and a visit to the Turn Point Lighthouse are just a few of the many attractions. Both of these harbors are so delightful and provide such good anchorage that we always have trouble deciding which one we will favor. We always end up visiting both of them. Johns Pass between Stuart and Johns Island can have a four- to five-knot current, tricky in the dogleg, but not really dangerous. Other hazards are well marked by kelp in the summer months.

We had neglected the west side of Lopez Island and so we swung back down through San Juan Channel to go into Fisherman Bay, a most popular spot near the middle of the island. Here is good, protected anchorage and the Islander Lopez Resort with facilities and services for the yachtsman as well as a fine restaurant. The entrance is an inverted S, easy to miss, but with no hazards if due caution is used.

Continuing southward through Cattle Pass, we made a quick, although cautious, visit to some of the interesting little bays and coves on the southwestern side of Lopez Island. Davis Bay, Jones Bay, Mackaye Harbor, Outer Bay, Aleck Bay, Hughes Bay and McArdle Bay (all with a scattering of rocks throughout) offer exciting exploration possibilities in waters little used by yachtsmen; but, for safety, the chart should be studied carefully and plenty of caution used.

Back through Cattle Pass we set out to reexplore the shoreline of San Juan Island. This island, with its satellites, forms the southwestern boundary of the archipelago. With a historical background of political maneuvering, military sabre rattling, the bloodless Pig War and plenty of pioneer bloodshed in the last century, plus a fair quantity of interesting events in this century, the island produces a fascinating story which has been well documented and interestingly told in David Richardson's excellent book *Pig War Islands.*

The entrance to San Juan Channel through Cattle Pass can be exciting if a southeast wind is blowing against an ebbing tide. Once through the pass, however, peace and quiet can be found in Griffin Bay, with the little cove called Fish Creek indenting the toe of the island. Farther up is North Bay, too open for good protection. Around Pear and Reef Points is Turn Island, a state marine park with picnic and some camping facilities, trails, clams and a fascinating channel on its back side, which, if you haven't been through, shouldn't be left unexplored.

To the west is Friday Harbor with its Brown Island, now sometimes called Friday Island. The town of Friday Harbor, county seat of San Juan County and largest in the islands, has good moorage, stores and all needs for the yachtsman. The Oceanographic Laboratories of the University of Washington are on the north shore of the harbor.

Continuing around Point Caution and on up the northeast shore, we came to Rocky Bay which is open but has a couple of little coves providing some protection. O'Neal Island lies in the middle of the bay. Limestone Point with its Lonesome Cove forms the northeast corner of the island. A scalloped shore runs along the north end of the island to Neil Bay in behind Davison Head.

Roche Harbor, nearly landlocked by Pearl and Henry Islands, is rich in history and probably the largest and most complete yachting center in Northwest waters. Here can be found all facilities and services for the yachtsman, as well as activities of all kinds and a unique atmosphere. Although Roche Harbor is always fascinating, it cannot be enjoyed to its fullest unless one spends a little bit of time studying its background and history. This is another place where yachtsmen enjoy spending some time ashore, meeting up with boating friends, taking a hike to the mausoleum or other points of interest while the youngsters swim in the pool, and giving the first mate a break by treating her to a meal in the excellent restaurant.

Henry Island, to the west, is shaped like a rough H. One of its bays at the west end of Roche Harbor is the site of a Seattle Yacht Club outstation. Below it, Nelson Bay is quite shallow with about eight feet down the middle at zero tide. Open Bay, at the south end of the island, is deeper but is all that its name implies.

We ran south from Roche Harbor through Mosquito Pass, a curving, scenic waterway with plenty of depth in mid channel but strong currents at times. Running east from Mosquito Pass is the entrance to Westcott and Garrison Bays, two more favorite spots for Northwest cruising families. Both of these bays are shallow around the shores but provide good protected anchorage offshore a ways. Little Guss Island in Garrison Bay is an undeveloped portion of the San Juan Island National Historical Park. In entering and cruising in both Westcott and Garrison Bays, keep a close check on the depth sounder and watch the charts for reefs and shallow water.

Leaving Garrison Bay, we continued through Mosquito Pass and swung into Mitchell Bay for a visit to Snug Harbor Resort which offers a full list of boating services and facilities. While quite shallow, Mitchell Bay is navigable except for deep-draft vessels, on plus tides. Chart #6379 again is recommended here.

There is little of interest on the rest of San Juan's west coast. Smugglers Cove, Smallpox Bay, Deadman Bay, Kanaka Bay, False Bay and Eagle Cove can be used at times but aren't too desirable because of size, shallow water and rocks, and lack of protection.

After exploring this west side of the island we ran back in to Roche Harbor. As the sun slipped toward the horizon to the west, we enjoyed the flag lowering ceremonies which are held each night at sunset. In these days when patriotism is so easily forgotten or ignored by many and where we frequently see the national ensign left flying at the stern staff of yachts all night long, it is inspiring to watch the flags being lowered, to suitable music and then, a short time later, to marvel at the spectacular afterglow across the water in the western sky.

The San Juan Islands, all 172 of them, seem specially designed for the cruising yachtsmen's enjoyment. Near enough to be easily reached yet far enough away so that the cares of everyday life can be left behind and quickly forgotten, they are a prime favorite in the Northwest's cruising waters. A word of warning, however—they will likely "take you over"—but it will be pleasant.

This old barracks on the site of the English camp in Garrison Bay, is a relic of Pig War days.

6
Evergreen Gems in an Inland Sea

A fleet of beautiful islands lying anchored off the southeast coast of Vancouver Island is generally known as the Gulf Islands. Don't dare to call them the Canadian San Juans as a few unknowledgeable people have done from time to time.

These evergreen gems, set in an azure-blue inland sea, form another well defined section of the Northwest's "greatest cruising waters in the world." Geographically they are one with the San Juans, separated only by that imaginary line called the international boundary. Much the same, yet subtly different, they have charmed those who have known them from the earliest pioneers to the present residents and particularly the cruising yachtsmen who ply the placid channels between them.

In reacquainting ourselves with the islands in this charming group, we made two separate cruises, one through the western channels along the shores of Vancouver Island and the other through the more easterly passages. Starting in Haro Strait, we first visited the group nestled around the northeastern tip of the Saanich Peninsula. Although most of the smaller islands in this group are surrounded by rocks and reefs, there are features here of interest to the yachtsman. Sidney Island's long sandy finger pointing northwestward is a provincial marine park and affords mooring buoys and anchorage. Whenever time permits, we like to stop here as it is a spot well-known for good crabbing.

Across Cordova Channel from James Island, we have found anchorage in Saanichton Bay behind Cordova Spit. Three miles to the north, the town of Sidney is a port of entry with stores, an excellent bakery and supplies and services for all boating needs.

After a shopping stop at Sidney, we swung around Roberts Point into Roberts Bay, which is separated from Tsehum Harbor by Armstrong Point. Several complete marinas, the Philbrook Shipyard, a hospital and Royal Victoria and Capital City Yacht Clubs' outstations are located in Tsehum Harbor. Be sure to watch the depth sounder, markers and chart in here, especially at low tide, for it is shallow with rocks and shoals.

Just north, between Coal Island and the peninsula, is a maze of little passes winding between as pretty a group of small islands and islets as can be found. Large numbers of Northwest skippers who have been cruising through here for years have mistakenly thought they were using Canoe Pass. Close inspection of a large-scale chart will show that Canoe Pass runs southeast from Canoe Bay, between the shore of the peninsula and Kolb Island and Harlock Islet. With only a foot of water in some places, this pass lives up to its name and definitely is not recommended except for a canoe or those with local knowledge, and then only at high tide.

Most used route through here is Iroquois Pass. Going north, leave Fernie Island to port and run between Fernie and Goudge Islands, keeping in mid channel and leaving Musclo Islet to port. A mid-channel course the rest of the way past Swartz Head will give clear passage into Colburne Passage.

Passage can also be made between Goudge and Coal Islands if close watch is kept for a couple of rocks. Some skippers use Page Pass to the west of Fernie Island and Johnson Islet. On straight runs we usually prefer Iroquois Pass but, if time is available, we love to explore through these other passes among the islands.

Canoe Cove, below Swartz Head, is a finger of Canoe Bay and harbors the Canoe Cove Marina. Full marine facilities and services, groceries and restaurant are found here.

Although this area is full of rocks, shoals and reefs, the water is clear and so they are easily seen. With slow speed and attention to chart and depth sounder, safe passage can be made. Large-scale chart #3455, covering from Sidney to Satellite Channel, gives full details, adds confidence and opens up some wonderful exploration possibilities in this delightfully different scenic section of the Gulf Islands.

A trip that shouldn't be, but frequently is, missed while in this area is a cruise down Saanich Inlet with its Squally Reach and Finlayson Arm. This waterway has many attractions, including beautiful little Tod Inlet, several bays and coves, marinas, fishing and the back door to world-famous Butchart's Gardens.

Heading north through the Gulf Islands, there are several courses that can be taken. Big Saltspring Island, largest of the group, lies somewhat in the center with principal passages on both sides. On this trip we chose the western passage going through the Sansum Narrows along the west side of Saltspring Island and Stuart Channel, skirting Vancouver Island's east shore.

Off the southern entrance to Sansum Narrows is Cowichan Bay, famed for its good fishing. The town of Cowichan Bay, marinas, moorage, fuel, stores, and so forth, are on the south shore. The shallow head of the bay is used for a booming ground. Indenting the north shore is Genoa Bay, a popular spot with yachtsmen for many years. Although Captain Morgan's Lodge is no longer operating, a marina is located inside the hook. On entering, be sure to stay between the marker and the point, with the marker to starboard as the other side of the marker is shoal. It's also a good idea to go around the black buoy.

We found currents through Sansum Narrows up to three knots but these are not enough to cause trouble; however, the channel around Burial Islet can be filled with boats fishing. Burgoyne Bay and Booth Bay indent Saltspring Island. On the Vancouver Island side, Maple Bay and its Birdseye Cove have long been popular. The Maple Bay Yacht Club has recently moved from up near the top of the bay down into Birdseye Cove, and two marinas provide all facilities and services. This has long been one of our favorite stopover bays.

Across from Booth Bay, the village of Crofton in Osborn Bay has the big B.C. Forest Products mill with a government wharf, post office, marina and store. Just to the north are the Shoal Islands and their unusual rock formations, but the water here is very shallow, so use care. Back across the channel above Booth Bay are Vesuvius Bay and an unnamed little cove in behind Dock Point.

Northwest from the Shoal Islands, a long peninsula ending in Bare Point protects Chemainus Bay. A government wharf, fuel, stores, customs office, another excellent bakery and a hospital in the town of Chemainus make it a popular stopping point for cruising families.

Still more to the northwest is Ladysmith Harbor. The town of Ladysmith has a government wharf and everything to meet boating needs. There are several good anchorages here in coves or behind islands. On the north shore, just beyond the larger of the Woods Islands is Mañana Lodge, a favorite with Northwest skippers, providing full marina facilities and services. Canadian large-scale chart #3471 has good harbor plans for Osborn Bay, Chemainus Bay and Ladysmith Harbor.

Across Stuart Channel from Ladysmith are Thetis and Kuper Islands, with Telegraph Harbor nestled in between them. This has long been a favorite spot for those cruising in the Gulf Islands. Two marinas provide moorages and excellent facilities and there is good protected anchorage. Little Boat Pass, separating the two islands, has been dredged and, with care, can be negotiated to Clam Bay on the other side of the islands. In entering Boat Pass from Clam Bay, be sure to leave the marker at the entrance to starboard.

Preedy Harbor, around Foster Point from Telegraph Harbor, also has good anchorage. Entrance can be made between Crescent Point and Dayman Island or between Dayman and Hudson Islands, but watch chart, markers and depth sounder carefully for rocks and reefs. With local knowledge and care, entrance can also be made at higher tides between Hudson Island and Foster Point, but this isn't recommended for the novice.

Off the southern tip of Kuper Island is Tent Island. For some time this has been maintained as a provincial marine park on land owned by Indians. Although this is one of the most popular spots in the islands, it is not known how long this arrangement can be maintained. While the bay isn't too well protected, it is only a short run into Preedy or Telegraph Harbors, and the sandy beaches, swimming, clamming, exploring possibilities and picnic facilities make it a favorite of many skippers.

In heading north from these islands up Stuart Channel or coming into them from the north, be sure to check the chart and give a wide berth around False Reef. There is a beacon here but it is easy to get on the wrong side.

We always like to swing into a couple of interesting coves on the north end of Thetis Island, and across Stuart Channel we have found anchorage in Kulleet Bay, although it is fairly open. For years it has been reported that the rock off Yellow Point is not in the charted position. We are not sure if this has been corrected; so it is a good idea to keep well off.

We continued up the Vancouver Island shore some four miles to Boat Harbor and into Kenary Cove, tucked in behind Flewett Point. If you are not a spit-and-polish, white-pants type of yachtsman, you might enjoy a visit with Ken and Mary Kendall. These are interesting people who have a fascinating place with private floats, but if you are of the stuffed-shirt variety, beware — you may get a cannonball across the bow from one of Ken's collection of ancient artillery.

Dodd Narrows, connecting Stuart and Northumberland Channels, were named for Capt. Charles Dodd who was in the service of the Hudson's Bay Company for 25 years. Less than 200 yards wide, the narrows should be run at or near slack current or with local knowledge. Currents of 8 to 10 knots can cause an overfall and can be dangerous for small and slow boats.

On the other side of Mudge Island are False Narrows, connecting Pylades Channel with Northumberland Channel

This point at one end of the bay at Tent Island is popular with boaters who take advantage of the provincial park there.

through Percy Anchorage. Shallow and full of shoals, they should only be run at high tide with local knowledge or by the very adventurous. There are two ranges for guidance in the proper channel and large-scale chart #3471 should be used. It's interesting to note that current in Northumberland Channel always sets eastward, regardless of flood or ebb tide.

Nanaimo, at the top of the Gulf Islands, is usually included in a cruising itinerary of these waters. It is an interesting and historic town, providing just about all boating needs. A good public boat basin is in Commercial Inlet behind the C.P.R. Dock with easy access to the downtown area, while the Nanaimo Yacht Club is near the north end of town. Because of many shoals and much shallow water, Nanaimo Harbor chart #3558 should be aboard.

In Nanaimo's front yard are Newcastle and Protection Islands, the former a provincial marine park with moorage and many attractions. When at Nanaimo, if time permits, or if the commercial moorages should happen to be full, we like to run over to Newcastle Island and tie up at the floats or at one of the moorage buoys and walk along the island trails, some of which lead to the other side of the island and present a magnificent view. Narrow, but well-marked Newcastle Island Channel leads to Departure Bay, used by many skippers to await good weather for a crossing of the Gulf. Be sure to run through here at slow speed and pay careful attention to the markers.

On the west end of Gabriola Island are several little

coves, Descanso Bay and the famous rock formations known as Malaspina Gallery.

On our cruise through the easterly channels of the Gulf Islands, we started from Prevost Harbor, crossed Haro Strait to Bedwell Harbor on South Pender Island. Canadian entrance and customs clearance can be made here, and there is a complete marina, one in the chain of excellent facilities of the B.C. Coastal Marine Resorts Ltd. At the entrance to the harbor is Peter Cove, a snug little anchorage with a couple of sandy beaches. This is a favorite spot of ours, and if you're looking for a quiet little cove for a bit of relaxation this is it; but be sure to use large-scale chart #3474 and watch the depths.

Half a mile up the north shore in Bedwell Harbor are the Skull Islets, protecting a little bay with a delightful sandy beach and a provincial marine park in behind them. Again, check chart #3474 and watch the depths.

A mile farther up the shore, a narrow passage with a minimum of six feet of water at zero tide separates North and South Pender Islands. This is a scenic little pass providing a shortcut to Port Browning and Plumper Sound. A bridge between the two islands has 26 feet of clearance at high tide. At the north end of the passage is Shark Cove, a cozy anchorage for an afternoon or a night. It's a good idea to put out a stern anchor here or a stern line ashore to keep from swinging into the channel. Chart #3474 is valuable here, too.

At the head of Port Browning, Scot's Lair Marina has

Top: Bedwell Harbor, South Pender Island, where visitors may clear Canadian customs and find a complete marina and excellent facilities. Bottom: Coming into Boat Harbor's Kenary Cove, behind Flewett Point.

mooring, fuel, a restaurant and other boating facilities.

Across Plumper Sound, Saturna Island has Narvaez Bay on its eastern end, Lyall Harbor and popular Boot Cove on its western end. Boat Pass, between Saturna's Winter Point and Samuel Island, has rocks through and on both sides and shouldn't be used except with extreme caution or local knowledge.

There is a nice little bay on Samuel Island and, to the northwest, Curlew Island gives protection to Horton Bay on Mayne Island. Farther up on the outside of Mayne is Campbell Bay, exposed to the southeast but otherwise a good anchorage.

Mayne Island is separated from North Pender Island by Navy Channel, and we crossed here to Hope Bay's post office and store in behind Fane Island on North Pender. We then continued to round North Pender's northern tip to the east side and into Port Washington, Otter Bay and a couple of little bights where we found anchorage possibilities.

To the northwest, Prevost Island, with its seven scenic bays, coves and inlets, offers tremendous anchoring variety with good clams and oysters, and is one of our favorite islands. Be sure to watch the chart and markers carefully for rocks and reefs, particularly off the long finger points between the bays and inlets.

On the west is Saltspring Island, the name originally having been given by Hudson's Bay Company officers because of the numerous salt springs on the island. In 1854 Sir James Douglas named it Chuan Island and in 1859 Capt. George Richards, in his surveying, named it Admiral Island to honor Pacific Station Commander Rear Adm. Robert Lambert Baynes, but local usage and pressures caused the Geographic Board of Canada to readopt Saltspring as the name in 1910.

Fulford Harbor on the southern shore has a government wharf, store and a couple of marinas. It is well-known to northwest yachtsmen as the principal reference station for Canadian Tide Tables for the area.

We rounded Beaver Point and cruised up Ganges Harbor to the head, where the town of Ganges has two good boat basins, stores and facilities for all boating needs. Anchorage can be found in several small coves in Ganges Harbor and in Welbury Bay. To the north around Scott Point is Long Harbor with an inviting protected little cove at its head where we have anchored on many an occasion. Anchorage can also be found in the main harbor, and the Scott Point Marina, with good facilities, is on the south shore.

Saturna, Mayne, Galiano, Valdes and Gabriola Islands form the buffer for the other Gulf Islands, protecting them from the Strait, or (as it is locally called) the Gulf of Georgia, which at times can blow up some good storms. Three principal passes lead from the islands to the Gulf—Active, Porlier and Gabriola. Active Pass, between Mayne and Galiano Islands, is the main thoroughfare but that isn't the reason for its name. It was named for the U.S. revenue and surveying vessel *Active*, the first naval steamer to use the pass.

Just outside of Active Pass, to the north, is Sturdies Bay with well-known Galiano Lodge and, beyond, protected by Gossip Island, Whaler Bay with good anchorage. Fishing is usually good at both ends of the pass but be alert for the traffic. It is well to remember that the tidal currents, running to and from the Strait of Juan de Fuca, flood outward through these passes from the islands and ebb in toward the islands.

Up the inside shore of Galiano Island from Active Pass is Montague Harbor, in behind Parker Island. Here is another favorite spot for those cruising these waters, with several good anchoring areas, clams, oysters and a provincial marine park providing moorage buoys, a float, picnicking and camping facilities. A short distance across the peninsula is a beautiful sand beach. Montague Harbor is a favorite rendezvous spot for both Canadians and Americans, as well as the destination for many a yacht club's group cruises.

Trincomali Channel is the waterway in the Gulf Islands running from Active Pass northwesterly to about the middle of Valdes Island where it joins with Pylades Channel. Some five miles up this channel from Montague Harbor is a snug little anchorage on Galiano Island called Retreat Cove. This is one of our favorite spots and usually it isn't too crowded. Entrance should be made to the east of Retreat Island and careful soundings made before anchoring as parts of the cove are quite shallow. There is a government wharf, and a hike up the road will, in season, be rewarded with luscious wild blackberries. Farther up the shore Spotlight Cove and an unnamed little bay offer some protection.

We crossed Trincomali Channel and came back down to reexplore Wallace Island, the two Secretary Islands, Mowgli, Norway, Hall and Reid Islands. Running between them and around the northern tip of Saltspring Island, Houstoun Passage leads over to Stuart Channel. As in the past, we found the cove formed by Panther Point on the southern end of Wallace and Conover Cove on the west side are ideal places to visit, and there are several other small bights in this group of islands; but be sure to use caution in avoiding the rocks, reefs and shallow water. These are excellent places for the skipper with a touch of adventure in his nature to explore. If those rocks and reefs look mean to you instead of scenic, perhaps it is better to anchor the boat and use the dinghy in this exploration. We have found, however, that running on a slow bell and keeping a sharp lookout through the clear water will avoid any trouble and reward the explorer with much of interest and beauty.

Porlier Pass between Galiano and Valdes Islands is full of rocks and reefs, as evidenced by the wreck in about the middle. By favoring the Galiano side, there is no difficulty in getting through. Currents can run up to eight knots.

There is nothing on the inside shore of Valdes Island but rocky cliffs 100 to 450 feet high. Running parallel to the west is the DeCourcy Group of Islands, separated from Valdes by Pylades Channel. Whaleboat Passage, between Pylades Island and Ruxton Island, can be negotiated with caution, while Ruxton Passage, between Ruxton and DeCourcy Islands, is clear with the only hazard marked by a beacon.

We next headed for one of the top favorites in the Gulf Islands—Pirates Cove on the east side of DeCourcy Island. Formerly called Gospel Cove, this well-protected bay is now a provincial marine park. Good anchorage, clams,

Top: Rocks off Mowgli Island, a place to reexplore. Bottom: Pirate's Cove, a well-protected bay on the east side of DeCourcy Island. It is a provincial marine park and a popular stopping place for Northwest yachtsmen.

Porlier Pass, one of the three principle passes leading from the Gulf Islands to the Strait of Georgia.

oysters and delightful scenery are some of its attributes but, for the first-timer, it is difficult to find and tricky to enter.

A long rocky finger pointing northwestward forms the outer protection of the entrance and is submerged, or nearly so, at high water. The skipper should run northwestward to about the middle of the little island where paint splotches on the rocks mark the turning point. Then turn south between the island and the reef, keeping in center channel or a bit to right of center channel to avoid rocks on both sides. The water is generally clear and so with slow speed and a careful lookout no trouble should be experienced. The hike from the southeastern end of the cove to Ruxton Passage is a rewarding one through interesting rock formations, but mosquitoes can be thick through here in season.

DeCourcy Island was a part of a communal type of "kingdom" presided over by the notorious Brother XII. He developed a religious cult and attracted people from all over the world to his rustic islands hideaway. His operation achieved a shady reputation and, as the law began to close in on him, he disappeared. Most of the available information makes him out a villainous charlatan, but Ken Kendall of Boat Harbor says he has known several former members of the cult and that it is his impression Brother XII wasn't as bad as history paints him.

Gabriola Pass, between Valdes and Gabriola Islands, is a narrow pass, more scenic than the others, with currents up to eight knots and sometimes a bit of overfall on the ebb. Inside the pass, Degnen Bay on Gabriola Island has a government wharf and good anchorage. On the other side of the channel, a small unnamed cove and Wakes Cove are frequently used while waiting for slack water in the pass.

Outside Gabriola Pass, a bit to the north, are the Flat Top Islands and Silva Bay. Many Northwest skippers consider this bay and group of islands unsurpassed in the area for beauty and cruising pleasure. Although local usage has put different names on some of these islands, we will use the names as shown on the charts.

Leaving Gabriola Pass, an easterly course should be steered for the beacon on Breakwater Island until well past Rogers Reef on the port hand. After a 90° turn to port, the Breakwater Island side of the channel should be favored. The recommended entrance to Silva Bay continues this course until nearly to the southern tip of Acorn Island, then makes a 90° port turn to run between Tugboat and Vance Islands, watching for markers. With local knowledge and care, entrance can be made west of Sear Island. This entrance is easy to miss and the island side of the channel should be favored until about halfway in, then mid channel. It's probably best not to use this entrance on minus tides but it can save some time over the other route.

Silva Bay has about all a yachtsman could ask for. Clams and oysters are abundant; there are a shipyard, several stores and marinas, and another in the B.C. Coastal Marine Resort chain providing just about all facilities and services, as well as excellent meals and lodging. The Royal Vancouver Yacht Club has an outstation on Tugboat Island, reserved for their members exclusively.

With facilities and attractions such as these, in a sylvan setting where the blue water mirrors the green clothing of the islands and the peaceful quietness drives away the tensions of city life, it's easy to understand the popularity of Silva Bay and the Flat Tops, and they should definitely be included in the itinerary of any cruise to the Gulf Islands.

That evening we sat in the cockpit following a meal of food taken from the sea. The deepening orange rays of the departing sun and the kiss of a light breeze made the mind wander back to memories of cruising on enchanted waters with colors rich and warm, green in the shoal areas, blending into royal blue in the deeper places and sprinkled with islands, alike in many respects, yet each with its own special charm and distinguishing characteristics. As darkness came a yellow moon blushed behind the trees, and lights on the shore looked like the embers of a dying fire.

Each area in these Northwest cruising waters has its own special features, attributes and attractions and the devotees of each swear it is the best. The only answer, of course, is to try them all, if you can live long enough, but it's a certainty the Gulf Islands will be high on many skippers' lists of favorites to be revisited again and again.

7

Let's Go Skookum

Its correct name is the Strait of Georgia but Captain Vancouver, not knowing it had a connection with the Pacific to the north, named it the Gulf of Georgia in honor of King George III. The Spaniards had called it Gran Canal de Nuestra Senora del Rosario la Marinera and we can be glad that name didn't stick. Canadian skippers as well as many from the United States side of the line still nostalgically refer to it as "the gulf."

Whatever it's called, it is a large body of water, not to be taken lightly by the yachtsman. Northwesterly and southeasterly storms can whip it into a furious sea and, even in good weather, the prevailing afternoon westerly can make it uncomfortable. On the other hand it can be as smooth as a mirror.

One can hear a variety of suggestions as to the best time to cross the 15 to 30 miles of open water, depending on destination. Some recommend early morning but one of the roughest crossings we have ever experienced followed a 5:00 A.M. departure from Gabriola Pass with a southeast wind of 25 to 30 knots coming up about halfway across. Others say late afternoon or early evening is better. Best advice is to pay strict attention to the local weather forecasts, perhaps talk with fishermen or tugboat skippers, poke your bow out for a look and then decide, according to your boat's speed, whether to give it a try. Averaging our total experiences, we find the late afternoon or early evening crossing to be the best if there is any wind blowing.

For the timid skipper or one with a nervous first mate, heading north, there is an "out." Leaving Nanaimo's Departure Bay, turn around Horswell Bluff and head for Nanoose Harbor. If it's too rough, hole up there. If not, proceed on a heading for the southerly tip of Lasqueti Island. If it's too rough, duck into the Ballenas Islands. If

not, go on to Lasqueti Island. The final leg is from the southern tip of Texada Island to the Thormanby Islands. Although this route is a little longer, you are never exposed to open water for more than six miles in any one leg without a chance to get protection.

It's a shame Captain Vancouver never knew of the city which was named for him. In one of the most beautiful settings imaginable, this metropolis has many attractions, including everything for the yachtsman. The Royal Vancouver Yacht Club has its clubhouse and some mooring on the south shore of English Bay and its main moorage in Coal Harbor, with Burrard Yacht Club just beyond.

In considering the gulf and its adjoining waters, we are pooling experiences from several different cruises in this area. Leaving Vancouver and heading out of English Bay we turned to the north and northwest into Howe Sound, a favorite nearby cruising area of Vancouver yachtsmen. Dotted with both large and small islands and surrounded by snow-capped mountains, this sound has much to offer both in scenic beauty and boating facilities. We rounded Point Atkinson and headed up Queen Charlotte Channel where we turned into several small bays, including Fisherman Cove, home of the West Vancouver Yacht Club and several marinas. Around several points is Horseshoe Bay with more marinas, ferry landing, stores and restaurants. Across the channel on Bowen Island, we found Snug Harbor and Deep Bay, both of which are very popular places with yachtsmen.

Howe Sound features Gambier Island, about in the middle of the sound, with its four bays on its south side and several interesting attractions. Up Montague Channel past Anvil Island and up to the head of the sound is Squamish Landing. On the west side of the sound are several small settlements with a couple of landing places.

Boats wait in cove for slack tide at Skookumchuck Rapids.

Plumper Cove, on the west side of Keats Island, has a provincial marine park and provides protected anchorages. Across the water is a town formerly called Gibsons Landing but now shortened to Gibsons. Mooring and all boating needs can be found here.

The cruising family will find much to interest and enchant them in Howe Sound. It certainly should be included on some summer's cruise itinerary.

Coming out through Shoal Channel, which can be negotiated with care, we rounded Gower Point to head up the mainland coast some 16 or 17 miles to the Welcome Pass area with several popular bays and coves. This distance is about the same as that across the gulf from Nanaimo. Some of the names in this area have an interesting source but they have all been documented in *Northwest Passages, Volume I,* and so we won't repeat them here.

We headed next into Frenchman's Cove on Half Moon Bay, a very popular spot. Local knowledge, or careful attention to chart and depths, is required here, as it is shallow and full of rocks but very rewarding for those interested in making the visit. The beautiful labyrinth of channels among the rocks is well worth dinghy exploration.

Making a sharp turn around the point and running through Welcome Pass and Grant Island, we went into Smuggler Cove, another favorite of Northwest yachtsmen. The rock in the middle of the entrance should be left on the starboard going in, with the port-hand shore favored. Good anchorage can be found in several parts of the cove. The far end, in behind the little island, is our favorite and also popular with many skippers.

Across the pass, the two Thormanby Islands meet to form Buccaneer Bay. Here is another popular destination. The sandy neck joining them is a favorite picnicking and swimming beach at low tide. Unless the weather is right, overnight anchorage isn't recommended here, although Water Bay to the east near the head offers some protection as well as a chance for clams.

Sticking up to the north from South Thormanby Island is Tattenham Ledge. A break in the reef allows passage but, unless you know where it is, better be safe and go around the buoy at the northern end. Large-scale chart #3509 is excellent for the entire Welcome Pass area, including all of the above mentioned bays and coves.

Just a bit to the north of Smuggler Cove, tucked in behind Turnagain Island, is Secret Cove, still another favorite, with three arms, several good anchoring areas and another of the B.C. Coastal Marine Resorts chain of marinas. They have good mooring, a fine store, fuel, water, ice, laundry, showers and other facilities. Here, again, a rock lies in mid channel of the entrance. Leave it to starboard coming in and favor the Turnagain Island shore. Clams and oysters can be found in several parts of the cove.

Fishing is usually good to the north and west of Thormanby Islands. Bargain Bay, about six miles up the coast, is also a popular and productive fishing area.

Rounding Francis Point and Beaver Island, we turned into Pender Harbor with its wealth of bays, coves, anchorages, moorages, marinas, stores and other facilities for the yachtsman. If you have large-scale chart #3510, you will be able to locate many of the attractions. Excellent fishing is usually found outside the entrance; there are clams and oysters and, if you drop your shrimp trap in better than 50 fathoms, you could get a nice mess of those delicious little ones.

Best entrance to Pender Harbor is north of Williams Island, leaving the Skardon Islands to starboard, but entrance can also be made between Williams and Charles Islands and, at higher tides, through the Gap, between the little islands south of Charles Island and Beaver Island. One should have local knowledge or the large-scale chart and plenty of caution when using the Gap.

Just inside the entrance around in back of Henry Point, we turned into Irvine's Landing Marina which has full facilities. A mile farther in on the north shore at the east end of Hospital Bay are government floats and Lloyds store, marina and fuel dock. This store has long been known for its large stock of general merchandise, groceries and excellent meat. There is also a post office here. Around the Garden Peninsula, Garden Bay has two marinas with mooring and full facilities, a hotel with cafe, and protected anchorage. A short trail leads from the head of the bay over to Lloyds store. At the east end of the bay is a complete boat works with marine ways.

At the head of Pender Harbor is Gunboat Bay with a shallow narrow entrance which should be run only at high slack or, better yet, in the dinghy. We like to go in here for clams and it is an interesting place to explore. The oyster beds at the far end are private.

In Wellbourn Cove on the south shore is a government wharf leading to Madeira Park stores and post office. A bit to the west is Larson's Resort with lodging, moorage and launching facilities. Anchorage can be made in the small cove to the west. Still farther to the west, Gerrans Bay is formed by Beaver Island with Bargain Narrows, locally known as Whiskey Slough, connecting to Bargain Bay. This isn't recommended for passage as it dries at about half tide but some smaller boats can go through at high tide. The bridge over the narrows has a clearance of 13 feet. The hazards in the bay are marked. Haddock's Marina in the eastern part of the bay has mooring and full marine facilities and services including a marine ways.

On the north side of Beaver Island, southeast of Charles Island just inside the Gap, is the Indian Island Marina with mooring and complete marine facilities.

About a mile to the northwest of Pender Harbor's entrance, we swung into Agamemnon Channel which takes off to join Jervis Inlet with Nelson Island lying to the west. The only point of real interest in this channel is charming little Green Bay, right where the channel makes a slight turn. This small cove has a sylvan character all its own but its head has some flat rocks which dry at about half tide; so extreme caution must be used. For a bit of real enchantment, poke your bow in for a look sometime when passing.

At the junction of Agamemnon Channel and Jervis Inlet, Sechelt Inlet runs to the southeast. This is an interesting waterway worthy of some of any skipper's cruising time. A mile or so within the entrance on the south shore, Johnny and Dorothy Bosch operate the Egmont Marina and Resort with moorage, fuel, groceries, ice, lodging and marina facilities and services. This is the last chance for fuel and supplies when cruising up Jervis Inlet to Princess Louisa Inlet.

A little farther along is the settlement of Egmont in Secret Bay with store, post office and marina. Supplies, fuel and marine services are available here.

A mile beyond Egmont are the Sechelt Rapids, called by most yachtsmen the Skookumchuck Rapids. In the Chinook jargon skookum means "strong, mighty," and chuck means "water." Thus Skookumchuck is an apt name for these rapids which can attain a velocity of 12 to 14 knots. A tremendous flow of water through this narrow passage can create overfalls of 8 to 10 feet; so passage

should be made within 15 minutes either side of the nine-minute slack period. *Northwest Passages, Volume 1,* as well as the official current tables, give complete instructions for figuring the time of slack periods.

Any visit to this area should include a close-hand observation of the Skookumchuck Rapids at full flood. From above, take the trail from Egmont. From below, anchor in the little cove behind Rapid Islet and take the dinghy to the little point 0.2 mile up the shore. It's an awesome experience that will not soon be forgotten. The roar of this tremendous volume of water fighting its way through this narrow passage can be heard a mile away. Although we have watched the rapids several times, we go again each time there are new guests aboard and always enjoy the repeat visit.

Sechelt Inlet runs south-southeasterly for about 18 miles, where it comes within three-quarters of a mile of making the Sechelt Peninsula into an island. The village of Sechelt is on the joining neck. Two long arms—Narrows Inlet and Salmon Inlet—take off to the east and provide some excellent cruising enjoyment. We found all three of these inlets water-carpeted canyons between steep cliffs terminating in snow-crowned peaks. Depths right up to the shore are too great for anchoring, but the heads of the inlets and a few small bights offer limited anchorage possibilities and, on occasion, moorage can be found alongside a log boom. Narrows Inlet has been called a junior Princess Louisa.

Best anchorage in the area is in Storm Bay, in behind Cawley Point. Here is as delightful a haven as can be found, with an indescribable peaceful beauty that will capture your heart. The whole of Sechelt, Narrows and Salmon

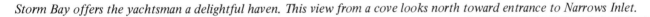

Storm Bay offers the yachtsman a delightful haven. This view from a cove looks north toward entrance to Narrows Inlet.

Princess Louisa Inlet, with lovely Chatterbox Falls at its head, is visited by more than 1200 boats each season. Its walls rise to mile-high snow-capped peaks.

Inlets should certainly be on any Northwest cruising itinerary. Chart #3589 should be used for this area.

On the charts Jervis (usually given the English pronunciation "Jarvis") Inlet is shown only as that body of water north of Nelson Island between Malaspina Strait and the bottom of Hotham Sound, but it is obvious in his journal that Vancouver intended the name to cover the entire 47 miles to the head.

Leaving Sechelt Inlet, we passed between Nelson Island and Captain Island and headed north into Hotham Sound. Here we found several bays and coves and a spectacular waterfall offering some interesting cruising. Most popular here are the Harmony Islands on the east shore. There are several delightful anchorages here but their popularity calls for an early arrival if you want to get in. A couple of times when we didn't make it, we rounded Foley Head and went into Dark Cove for a comfortable and enjoyable anchorage.

The rest of Jervis Inlet is a reversed letter S and consists of three reaches—Prince of Wales, Princess Royal and Queens. With the channel curving through towering mountains which rise almost perpendicularly from the water's edge and cascading waterfalls dashing down their sides, each turn opens up a new vista of spectacular beauty that will never be forgotten.

Cruising up these reaches, the blue water seemed to open up the mountains for us. Looking back, the way we had come was hidden; the peaks closed in, and the nearer mountains merged with the higher ones behind.

Because of the great depths (over 300 fathoms in some places), there are few overnight anchorages. Protection can sometimes be found in Vancouver Bay, at the mouth of the Brittain River, in Deserted Bay and in a couple of other small bights, depending on the wind direction. It's best, however, to plan to make the full run to Princess Louisa Inlet. Although we often tend to think of Jervis Inlet as a sort of freeway to get to our destination, it is actually one of the world's most scenic waterways, and every mile of it should be thoroughly appreciated and enjoyed.

Princess Louisa Inlet has probably been the destination for more yachtsmen than any other single spot. Over 1200 boats and some 4000 to 5000 people visit here each season. It has been called the "Yosemite of the North." Its steep walls rising to mile-high snow-capped peaks, lovely Chatterbox Falls at its head, and a quiet intoxicating beauty create a total scene that is considered by most who have been here to be one of the most beautiful places in the world.

While most of our Northwest cruising waters are still fairly remote and untouched by man's "civilizing," it is inevitable that, in time, many of our favorite cruising areas will not remain as we know and love them today. Not so with Princess Louisa. Through his deep love for the place and with great foresight, James F. ("Mac") Macdonald, who acquired the property in 1926, made a gift of it to the yachtsmen of the Northwest. He stipulated that it must never be commercialized in any way. It is now a provincial marine park and anyone can tie up to the floats, use the mooring buoys, camp or picnic ashore and enjoy hiking the trails without the expenditure of a cent. The British Columbia Parks Department, assisted by the Princess Louisa Inter-

Malibu Lodge, a summer camp for young people, may be visited on a tour.

national Society, is pledged to maintain this policy in perpetuity so, as Mac said, "your children and their children can continue to enjoy it as God made it."

If you should arrive to find the floats full and the mooring buoys all taken, you can anchor at the head. Go in toward the falls and drop the hook on the ledge which runs out a ways. You can then let out enough scope to be in deeper water and the current from the falls will keep you headed toward them. Anchorage and oysters may also be found behind Hamilton Island.

Malibu Rapids, at the entrance to the inlet, can run up to nine knots on full tides; so it's a good idea to plan time of arrival at or near slack. High-water slack is from 0 to 15 minutes after high tide at Point Atkinson and low-water slack is 20 to 50 minutes after low tide at Point Atkinson. The rapids are clear of any hazards but entrance can be tricky for the first-timer. Approaching the entrance, head on, and go almost to, the light on the rock outside. Then steer a mid-channel course toward the Malibu Club until you can see the channel open up. Do not attempt to go to the right of the islets in the entrance.

The Malibu Club was originally built as a plush and elite resort for a wealthy clientele, particularly those in the movie industry, but it was never successful. In 1954 it was acquired by the Young Life Organization and is now operated as a summer camp for young people. Yachtsmen are welcome to tie to their floats for an hour and will be given a conducted tour of the resort. They reserve the right to tell you where to tie up at their floats and request no smoking while ashore. You may also visit the snack bar, Totem Inn and Totem Trader when they are open.

Princess Louisa Inlet is one of those places one never tires of revisiting. Although we have been there many times through the years, we always return whenever possible for it is indeed, as many have said, one of the top beauty spots in the world.

A trip to the head of Jervis Inlet is worthwhile. There are some Indian pictographs on the rocks about two miles north of the Princess Louisa entrance on the east side. They can be seen just above the high-tide line. There is a deserted Indian village at the head of the inlet but not much protection for anchoring can be found.

Captain Vancouver missed Princess Louisa, thinking that the entrance was the mouth of a river. It's probably a good thing he did for, if he had gone in, he might have liked it enough to stay and give up any further exploration.

In the lower part of Jervis Inlet, on the north shore of Nelson Island, is Vanguard Bay. We have found anchorage in several parts of the bay, but the principal attraction here is a short hike over the hill for a swim in West Lake. For a small fee, moorage can be had at the floats in the bay while you make the trek over the hill to swim.

To the west, in behind Hardy Island, Blind Bay has several beautiful little coves. Best entrance from the west is south of the small islands west of Fox Island. A turn to the left, leaving Fox Island to starboard, opens up several delightful coves with good protection. On the other side, behind a group of islands, is Ballet Bay, another favorite of many cruising families. There are also several other small bights on both sides of Blind Bay where good anchorage can be found. Entrance can also be made at the northeast end of the bay through Telescope Passage, but be sure to favor the Nelson Island side of this narrow channel to avoid a couple of rocks that have damaged a number of boats and propellers.

Below Blind Bay is Billings Bay which doesn't receive too much attention from the yachtsman. Entering and clearing this bay should be only at high tide of 11 feet or more as the channel dries at low tide. The island in the entrance should be passed to the south. Anchorage can be made in the bight at the extreme head of the bay. This is an interesting bay to explore, clamming is good and it's fun to watch the tide run out of the entrance.

Inside the entrance to Jervis Inlet, behind Thunder Point, is Thunder Bay where anchorage may be found.

Across Malaspina Strait are big 27-mile-long Texada Island and its smaller partner, Lasqueti Island. In spite of its size, Texada Island has little to offer the yachtsman. Little Anderson Bay on the east side near the southern tip, Sturt Bay and Vananda Cove on the east side near the northern end, Mouat Bay and Gillies Bay on the west side, and Blubber Bay on the northern tip are the only places offering any protection. Good fishing can be found between Favada Point and Kiddie Point.

Lasqueti Island is another story. With its two dozen or more satellite islands, a host of fascinating bays and small coves, an abundance of clams and oysters and good fishing, the yachtsman can find plenty of interest here for several days. Although we have enjoyed anchoring in several of the bays in this area, one of our favorites is little Squitty Bay, near the southeastern tip of Lasqueti Island. Although it is small, it has good protection, and we enjoy the rugged beauty of its rocky shores.

We have run between Nanaimo and Discovery Passage several times, but it is a long stretch and one with very few places to duck into in case of winds or bad weather; so not too many skippers choose this side of the gulf, particularly those with slow boats. Northwest Bay, just above Nanoose Harbor, Tribune Bay on Hornby Island, a couple of coves in Baynes Sound, behind Denman Island, and Comox Harbor are the only places affording any protection.

Back across the gulf, off the northern tip of Taxada Island, are Powell River and Westview. Actually they are one town but Westview is important to the yachtsman because of moorage there. There are two small boat basins behind rock breakwaters. The northerly one is the yacht harbor, while fishing and commercial boats use the southerly one. We usually find the yacht harbor quite crowded but the harbor master will raft the boats out. Many skippers, including ourselves, prefer to try for a floatside berth in the commercial side. This is the last town of any size on a trip farther north; so it is a good place to replenish ship's stores of all kinds.

We always enjoy a stop at Savary Island, some eleven and a half miles northwest of Westview. Somehow it still seems to maintain a good share of that old-time resort island atmosphere of another era. It is in this area that the tidal streams from the north meet those from the south. Consequently there is very little movement of the water and bath-water temperatures usually prevail on Savary

Island's sandy beaches. Skipper beware, though, of the large shoals extending well out from the island in most directions and almost connecting Savary with Hernando Island. We've been told that you can wade across between the two islands at low tide.

For a warm welcome, a good family-style dinner and an interesting visit, we recommend a stop to see Bill Ashworth at his Royal Savary Hotel near the northwestern tip of the island. The South Seas atmosphere and old-world charm will enchant you.

The little settlement of Lund on the Malaspina Peninsula is the end of the road coming up the coast from Vancouver, although there is talk of extending it to Bliss Landing for a new marina development there. Lund has good moorage behind a breakwater, marina, store and most facilities and services for the yachtsman. It is a popular spot for skippers cruising the Desolation Sound area to pick up or exchange guests.

About a mile and a half up from Lund, the Copeland Islands lie off the coast of the peninsula to form Thulin Passage. Locally called the Ragged Islands, the group has several intriguing little anchorages among them. It would be difficult to identify them accurately and so each skipper will have to search them out for himself. Use extreme caution, however, or do the original exploration by dinghy until you have found the spot you like, for the water is shallow in places and there are plenty of rocks. It's all worth the effort, for when you have found a spot to your liking, you will be well rewarded and will no doubt return again and again. A marina and fuel float are located in Thulin Passage.

When we talk or think about the Gulf of Georgia, we generally tend to think only of a huge body of water, but there are enough attractions both within it and in adjoining waters to keep a cruising yachtsman, his family and guests happily occupied for a long time. Best of all, some of the finest places in these Northwest cruising waters are here.

Blind Bay, in behind Hardy Island, has several beautiful little coves, where yachtsmen can find good protection.

8

Happy Waters with an Unhappy Name

It is always a pleasure to round Sarah Point, or Cape Mudge to enter one of the finest cruising areas in all of our Northwest waters, one that is probably an actual, or dreamed of, destination more than any other.

Desolation Sound is probably the most ineptly named area of any in the Northwest cruising waters. Captain Vancouver called it that because he experienced bad weather here, had poor fishing, and could find nothing edible growing on the islands.

Present-day yachtsmen, however, find it a most blessed area, many of them referring to it as the "Banana Belt of the North Pacific." Situated so close to where the tides from the north and south meet, waters are generally warm, frequently 70° or more. Located in a pocket surrounded by the mountains of Vancouver Island and the mainland, it averages more sunshine and less cool wind than any other place, even much farther south. Because of the warm waters, there is an abundance of oysters, shrimp, crabs and clams.

Today's charts designate Desolation Sound as only a small area east of Cortes Island and south of the Redonda Islands. It's reasonable to assume, however, from Vancouver's journal that he intended the name to apply generally to all waters between Vancouver Island and the continental shore north of the Strait of Georgia, at about 50° north latitude and south of a latitude line north of Stuart Island. Right or wrong, in considering these waters, we have adopted these boundaries to designate Desolation Sound.

On a recent cruise, we took the western channels first, starting up Discovery Passage past Cape Mudge. The entrance here from the gulf can be rough. On a flood tide from the north with southerly or southeasterly winds, strong tide rips develop that can be dangerous to small boats. The same thing can happen farther up, off Race Point, just below Seymour Narrows.

Campbell River and Discovery Passage, up as far as Seymour Narrows, are world famous as salmon-fishing areas. We stopped in at the town of Campbell River for shopping, and found several new stores and also new facilities and services for the yachtsman, in addition to those that have been here for many years. There are both public and private moorages which, at times, are quite crowded.

We crossed the channel to reexplore several bays a little farther up, offering excellent anchorage possibilities. Quathiaski Cove, with Grouse Island in its middle, has a government wharf and floats, post office, store and fuel wharf. Although this is a busy harbor, anchorage can be found in several parts of it.

April Point has a popular fishing resort with moorage and all marina facilities and services. The cove behind the point also has a float for moorage and is a good place to anchor.

More to the north, Gowlland Harbor, protected by Gowlland Island, is an interesting and scenic bay. Although there is a government float shown on the charts at the southern end of the harbor, as near as we could tell it has been abandoned. We were told that, with local knowledge or great care, entrance to the harbor can be made from April Point around the south end of Gowlland Island, but the recommended entrance is to the north of the island, with plenty of caution for the charted rocks and reefs. We found several good anchoring spots in the harbor.

Time out for fishing took us across the channel to Duncan Bay, which has some protection from southerly winds and is supposed to be a good fishing area. If the tide rips aren't too violent off Race Point, fishing can be good

Cortes Bay, below Squirrel Cove, is one of the many picturesque spots in the Desolation Sound area. Moorage, lodging, groceries, and fishing supplies are available.

in this area, too, but this just wasn't our lucky day.

Seymour Narrows, less than a mile wide, should be run at or near slack water. The tremendous volume of water that must pass through this narrow channel to fill or empty a good part of the gulf causes currents up to 15 knots. Although the faster and more powerful boats can sometimes successfully challenge the dashing currents, boils and whirlpools, complete control is reduced so that it may be impossible to avoid a telephone-pole-sized log spewed up by the madly boiling water. We like to wait for something close to slack water.

Nymphe Cove and Menzies Bay, below the narrows, and Deepwater, Brown and Plumper Bays, above, can be used while awaiting a favorable time for passage. Chart #3565 should be used for the Discovery Passage area.

Continuing north, we turned into Kanish Bay, just below the entrance to Okisollo Channel. This is a fairly large bay with several islands in it and anchorage can be found in behind the islands. At the head are two fingers pointing eastward—Granite Bay to the south and Small Inlet to the north. We went into little Granite Bay to find good, protected anchorage in three to seven fathoms. We have never personally investigated Small Inlet in the northeastern corner but have been told that it is an interesting bay, if entrance and exit are made at the higher stages of the tide. Otherwise, it looks like a good place to explore by dinghy, and we hope to get in here on our next trip.

Rounding Granite Point, we turned into Okisollo Channel, which bends around the north and part of the east side of Quadra Island and is one of the most enchanting waterways to be found. In the western portion from Discovery Passage to where it turns southward, we found three principal bays and several smaller coves. Chonat Bay is open to the west but is protected from other directions. Barnes Bay is open to the south, but protection can be found in behind the hook. Owen Bay is well protected, with several good anchorage spots and a couple of floats. The former store and post office, still shown on some charts, have been closed and the latest reports do not show any fuel available here.

Around the bend, the Hole in the Wall joins the channel. This four-mile passage, running between steep rock walls, joins Okisollo Channel with Calm Channel and is a very scenic waterway, with possible anchorage in Florence Cove about halfway through.

A bit to the south we came to the Octopus Islands, a favorite area of ours as well as many other yachtsmen who have discovered its charms. Bodega Anchorage and at least a dozen little coves and hideaways are scattered among the islands and in Waiatt Bay, providing a variety of intriguing spots to drop anchor. Exploring possibilities are unlimited, with clams, oysters, crabs and good fishing available.

Three and a half miles to the southeast, Okisollo Channel ends at Surge Narrows and the Settlers Group of islands as it joins Hoskyn Channel. Yeatman Bay can be used for anchorage or while waiting for slack at the narrows.

There are three sets of rapids to contend with in this channel, which is perhaps one reason more yachtsmen don't cruise here. The Lower Rapids are east of Pulton Bay, south of the Okis Islands. An average velocity of 6.5 knots runs through here but can get up to 10 knots on a full tide. We can more or less ignore these rapids in our calculations, because they can be avoided by running north of the Okis Islands. There are some currents here but not enough to cause concern.

The Upper Rapids extend south of Cooper Point, below Owen Bay. Then there are rapids where Hole in the Wall enters the channel. This joining together of waters-on-the-go, plus velocities as high as 12 knots on bull tides, can cause dangerous eddies and sometimes heavy overfalls; so this part of the channel should be run at slack or close to it. Surge Narrows and Beazley Pass between Sturt and Peck Islands, with velocities up to 12 knots, should also be run at or near slack. With only 10 minutes between the slack at these two points, which are five to six miles apart, the question is, how is it to be done.

If a stop is planned at the Octopus Islands there is no problem but, if it is desired to run both rapids, the only answer is to do some careful figuring with the current tables and plan to hit one a little ahead of slack and the other a bit after slack. The faster boats will have no trouble with this plan and, running south, even an eight-knotter can hit the Upper Rapids 18 minutes before slack and Surge Narrows 17 minutes after slack to find no difficulty. It's a little tighter going in the other direction. With a start at Surge Narrows, this same eight-knotter will have to leave 27 minutes before slack to arrive through Upper Narrows 28 minutes past slack. Probably a decision on this will depend on the range of the tide and the velocities on any given day.

With local knowledge or caution, passage can also be made around to the north of the Settlers Group, but watch for those charted rocks. Chart #3521 should be aboard for cruising in Okisollo Channel.

After coming through Surge Narrows and Beazley Pass, we turned north to do some fishing in the head of Hoskyn Channel. Our luck was better here and, in less than an hour, we had boated a couple of nice silvers—a 9 pounder and a 13 pounder.

Whiterock Passage connects Hoskyn Channel with Calm Channel. Boat Passage, the narrow portion of this waterway, has now been dredged to a least depth of six feet. There are two sets of ranges in here to mark the channel. It is navigable but caution should be used. About a mile south is the Surge Narrows store with moorage, fuel, water and groceries.

Running down Hoskyn Channel, we poked our bow into several little bights and bays looking for suitable anchorages. We found protection in the bight behind Sheer Point, Hjorth Bay, the bay behind Bold Island, Village Bay and Hyacinthe Bay. Heriot Bay has a government wharf and floats, post office and store. A road runs from here to Quathiaski Cove where the ferry crosses to Campbell River. Good anchorage can also be had in Drew Harbor, and moorage and most marine needs are available at the Taku Resort. We took a swing around the harbor and went ashore on Rebecca Spit, a provincial marine park, a delightful place for a picnic or driftwood gathering.

Our next course took us around Viner Point on the southern tip of Read Island and up Sutil Channel, which runs northerly from the gulf between Quadra and Read Islands on the west and Cortes Island on the east. The attractions in this area alone are so numerous that a cruising family could spend an entire vacation here. Four and a half miles north of the bell buoy off the southern tip of Cortes Island, there is a lovely anchorage in Manson Bay. At Manson's Landing, mooring, fuel, water, groceries and full marine facilities and services are available. As we always do when calling here, we took the three-quarter-mile hike down the quiet country road to enjoy a swim in lovely Hague Lake with its warm blue water and white sand beach.

Leaving Manson's Landing, we cruised easterly a mile and a half to the Guide Islets, marking the narrow but spectacular entrance to Gorge Harbor, a bit of enchantment to which yachtsmen return year after year. Picturesque islands, a teahouse, a complete marina, plenty of clams and oysters, and good fishing are a few of its charms. Besides moorage at the marina in the northeast corner of the harbor, we found several good anchoring spots. There are a lot of rocks, too, scattered around the harbor; so better have a large-scale chart available and pay close attention to it. Chart #3563 is a good one for this area.

Isabel Bay, behind Madge Island, invites exploration.

Leaving Gorge Harbor, we went through Uganda Passage to get to Whaletown Bay. Here, again, pay close attention to the chart for there are rocks throughout. Shark Spit extends northeastward from Marina Island with the end of it marked by a beacon and a light on Channel Rock. Passage should be made between the beacon and the rock.

Entrance to Whaletown Bay can be made on either side of the red spar buoy marking a rock near center channel. A white beacon on another rock just to the north should be left to port, and another beacon off the point on the right should be left to starboard. Whaletown, with fuel, groceries and ice, is an interesting historical place where we found local people glad to point out the site of a former whaling station and tell more of the history of the bay.

We found both sides of Sutil Channel lined with picturesque bays, coves and islands just awaiting exploration. While some of these are exposed to certain winds, others are completely protected and provide good anchorage. Plea-

Refuge Cove is a good place to rendezvous, or to use as home base when exploring this cruising area.

sure craft skippers will find enough of interest here to keep them busy for a long time.

We next headed for Hill Island, lying near the middle of the channel, where Chuck and Hazel Mitchell have established their island paradise in a small cove on the north of the island. Fuel, ice, moorage, fishing supplies and showers are available; availability of water depends on the season. There are also cabins and small fishing boats for rent. A large deck overlooking the bay offers picnic and barbecue facilities, and we have spent many a fascinating evening in the Chart Loft with fireplace and player piano, singing or listening to stories. There are scenic trails across the island, with many good view points opening an expanse of picturesque beauty. This is not just another resort or marina. A stop is more like a visit to a private summer place and is highlighted by the cordial and friendly hospitality of the Mitchells, together with the good-fellowship of their other guests. A visit to Hill Island is an enjoyable experience but, better get there early, as there are accommodations for only 12 to 14 boats.

After a night on Hill Island, we crossed over to Birdwood Bay on Read Island for a visit with our friends the Les Stubleys and a quick turn around Evans Bay to investigate Bird Cove and the several other little coves which can offer good anchorage.

Crossing Sutil Channel again, we turned into Von Donop Inlet. This interesting waterway nearly cuts through Cortes Island. Here is another favorite of many cruising families; it has several good anchorages as well as clams, oysters and other attractions.

We continued north in Sutil Channel to where it joins Calm Channel, and cruised through Drew Passage to the southwest of the Rendezvous Islands. Here, also, is the other end of Whiterock Passage. A little farther up is the easterly end of Hole in the Wall. Calm Channel ends at Stuart Island, with the Yuculta Rapids on its west side and the entrance to Bute Inlet on its east side.

Bute Inlet pokes its exploring finger some 39 miles to the north to become a carpet of water in a canyon between mountain peaks. Its cruising attractions among yachtsmen are controversial. While some mark it off as of no particular interest, others are impressed with the primitive grandeur of its steep rock cliffs, climbing to snow-crowned mountains supporting the cloud-flecked sky, and many waterfalls.

It is an inlet of extreme depths and heights with water depths as much as 356 fathoms and peaks up to 8770 feet. The biggest problem is a near lack of anchoring possibilities. We found very few bays or coves, and water right up to the shore is too deep. Oxford Bay on the east side and a small bight around Alpha Point are the only protected spots with water shallow enough for anchoring. Waddington Harbor, at the head, has a few spots where the anchor can be dropped.

Raza Passage, north of Raza Island, leads to Frances Bay, with anchorage at its head, and Ramsay Arm, a six-and-a-half-mile-long arm. There used to be good shrimping here, but the area was cleaned out by commercial shrimpers and we haven't heard whether it has yet recovered. It, too, is deep and offers no anchorage.

Pryce Channel runs across the top of the Redonda Islands to separate into Toba Inlet and Homfray Channel. Toba is 19 miles long with more spectacular scenery, waterfalls, and good fishing, sometimes, at the head. Brem Bay is the only anchoring possibility, but moorage can be found on a log boom at the head. The rest of the inlet is deep right up to the shore. We enjoyed a trip by dinghy up the delta to the mouth of the Tahumming River, where we found an old Indian cemetery almost buried in the weeds.

Homfray Channel makes a half circle around the east side of East Redonda Island. We found anchorage in seven and a half fathoms in Attwood Bay, but Forbes Bay is too open and too deep to provide a very satisfactory anchorage.

The Redonda Islands and adjacent channels, passages, inlets, bays and coves are the final objectives for a tremendous number of cruising families. This is the area officially designated on the charts as Desolation Sound, offering, perhaps more than any other area, everything a cruising yachtsman's heart could desire.

Lewis Channel, separating Cortes and West Redonda Islands, has Squirrel Cove, Refuge Cove, and Teakerne Arm as the principal attractions. Up at its northern entrance, in Deer Passage, is Redonda Bay.

Refuge Cove is a good place to use as a home base for cruising in this area. Another in the chain of B.C. Coastal Marine Resorts offers moorage, fuel, a good store, ice, water, showers and laundry facilities. If you want to know where the fish are biting, check in with either Mr. or Mrs. Norm Hope on the hillside behind the floats. Former operators of the store there before it burned down a few years

Walsh Cove, below Butler Point and behind the Gorges Islands, is a favorite anchorage of many yachtsmen.

ago, they are now enjoying their retirement, with plenty of fishing included.

Across the channel, Squirrel Cove is one of our favorites. Here is a landlocked harbor in a peaceful sylvan setting where all the pressures and cares of civilization must disappear. Entrance is made by leaving Protection Island to starboard, and there are several good places for anchoring. We like to use the head of the bay, in behind the largest of the several small islands. In the northeast corner is a reversing rapids leading to a saltwater lagoon. There is fun here exploring in the dinghy, and the youngsters enjoy shooting the rapids.

Teakerne Arm has two bays at its head. The lower one is used for a booming ground and is usually full of logs. At the head of the northeastern bay, a float has a large hose with good water coming down from Cassel Lake above. Talbot Cove is a lovely, well-protected haven, but be sure your anchor is well hooked. The bottom is rocky and it's sometimes hard to get a bite.

Below Squirrel Cove, around Mary Point, is Cortes Bay where there is good anchorage. The Cortes Bay Marine Resort has moorage, fuel, groceries, ice, water, fishing supplies and lodging.

At the bottom of Desolation Sound is a favorite of many yachtsmen. Malaspina Inlet is actually only the upper left portion of the entire Y-shaped waterway but common usage has given the name to its entirety. Lancelot Inlet is the upper right portion of the Y and Okeover Inlet is the base.

A hurried glance at the chart may discourage the first-timer but it isn't as bad as it may look. Large-scale chart #3573 will show the way between islands, rocks and reefs to a complete cruising paradise by itself. In entering, we use either side of Josephine Island and have found plenty of depth in mid channel on both routes. Check the chart carefully and steer to miss Cavendish Rock, Rosetta Rock and the reef extending from it, the rock to the southeast of Thorpe Island and the reef extending north from the Cochrane Islands. There's plenty of channel but it's well to be aware of these dangers.

These inlets have too many bays, coves, bights and nooks for anchoring to list them all here, and part of the fun of cruising is for the skipper to search them out for himself. Grace Harbor itself has several good anchoring spots, with the inner harbor a favorite of many. Our favorite is in behind Madge Island in Isabel Bay. There are many others and enough of cruising interest so that several days or a whole vacation can well be spent in this section.

Around Zephine Head from Malaspina Inlet is Galley Bay, formerly a popular place but infested during the last few years with hippies. It's been reported they now have left.

To the north-northeast is Mink Island, still shown on some charts as Repulse Island. A finger peninsula and small island on the south shore combine to make a little cove which has become so popular that it is frequently filled up. East about two miles is Tenedos Bay, not as well-known by many, yet offering a scenic harbor with several good anchorages. Outside and around the tip of the peninsula, Otter Island can be passed on either side on a plus tide. Although the inside passage is narrow, it can save a few minutes over going around the island, and it's a picturesque little passage which you'll be sure to enjoy.

More interesting cruising and lovely coves are found between the West and East Redonda Islands. We started up Waddington Channel, which separates the two islands, and turned into the little finger bay that pokes into the west at the southern entrance of the channel. Some charts show this as Marylebone Bay but it's better known, and listed on later charts, as Roscoe Bay. It's best to enter on a half tide or better to be sure to get across the reef that crosses the channel about 600 yards inside the entrance. Once inside, there is a delightful quiet anchorage in three to five fathoms. Fishing is reported good in Black Lake, just beyond, but we've never had the opportunity to try it.

Pendrell Sound takes off to the north-northeast from Waddington Channel to nearly cut East Redonda Island in two. Here are more oysters than will probably ever be found in any other one location. The shores are literally solid with them from the low-tide to high-tide marks. An oyster-harvesting operation is located on the west shore. Depths in the sound are too great for good anchoring.

Continuing up Waddington Channel a bit is a favorite anchorage of ours on the inside of Allies Island (formerly Prussian Island) and its little satellite. Watch depths and check the tide tables closely here. Still farther up, behind Bishop Point, is Doctor Bay, not as picturesque as some yet a good protected anchorage.

Prideaux Haven, a bay in behind Eveleigh Island, has given its name to a complex of coves and small passages, all popular with boatmen. Top: A view of Prideaux Haven. Bottom: Melanie Cove, one of the pleasing anchorages.

We continued up the channel to Walsh Cove, below Butler Point and behind the Gorges Islands, a favorite of ours and of many others. A good anchorage, swimming, oysters and spectacular scenery make this one of the most delightful coves in the area. Be sure to enter south of the Gorges Islands as False Passage, to the north of them, is full of rocks and dangerous without local knowledge. Waddington Channel continues northward for about a mile and a quarter to join Pryce Channel.

Leaving the best until last, we came back to one of the top favorites of them all. Across Homfray Channel from the southern tip of East Redonda Island is Prideaux Haven. Actually this is a single bay tucked in behind Eveleigh Island, but the name has come to be applied generally to the entire complex including Melanie Cove, Laura Cove and the small passages among the islands between them.

Here are anchorages so beautiful that they are almost unbelievable. Landlocked, its rocky shores covered with oysters, with clams available on several beaches, warm water for swimming, and a quiet peacefulness, this area is a paradise for the cruising family.

Entrance to Prideaux Haven proper and Melanie Cove can be made from the south by passing Otter Island on either side, leaving Morgan Island to port and Eveleigh Island to starboard. Don't try to go south of Eveleigh Island. From the north, leave Mary Island and the Grass Islets off its northeast point to starboard. Come in fairly close to Lucy Point, but not too close, to miss the rocks on the port side. There are also rocks on the starboard near shore. The course as shown in the Marine Atlas Harbor Chart is incorrect and should be moved closer to Lucy Point, not through the rocks and islets as shown.

In going into Melanie Cove, beware of the rocks charted outside the entrance and the two rocks inside the cove.

Anchorage can be found to the north of Melanie Point and passage can be made on half tide or better to Laura Cove, south of Copplestone Island, but it's tricky and shouldn't be tried without local knowledge or an exploration first by dinghy. In entering Laura Cove from the north, run between the charted rock and Copplestone Point, *not* to the west of the rock as shown in the Marine Atlas course. There is *no* clear passage between this rock and the easterly tip of Copplestone Island.

Whether you choose Prideaux Haven, Melanie Cove, Laura Cove or one of the other spots to drop your hook, you'll find the ultimate in pleasing anchorages. A composite of turquoise-blue sparkling water, emerald-clad islands, rocky shores, sand and gravel beaches against the backdrop of mighty mountains with their snow-crowned heads playing hide-and-seek among the cotton-candy clouds, paints a picture we never tire of viewing. We, and others who have been there, will return again and again.

Regardless of the unhappy name hung on this area by Captain Vancouver, Desolation Sound surely is one of the brightest jewels in the crown of these "greatest cruising waters in the world."

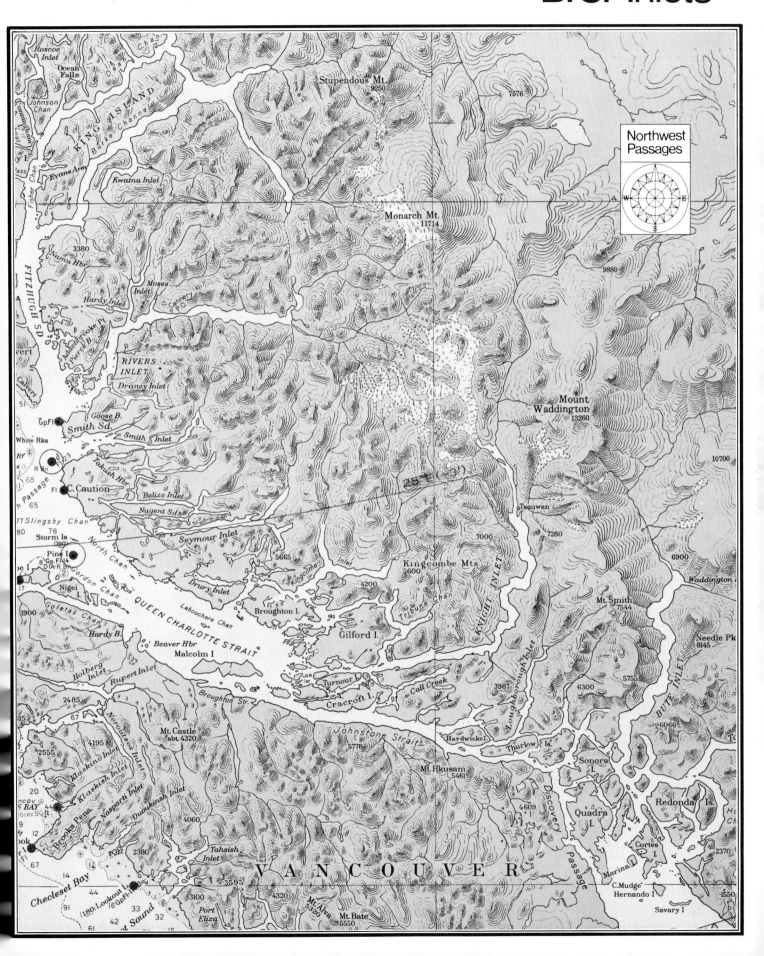

Northwest Passages

W · E
N · S

Roscoe Inlet
Ocean Falls
Johnson Chan.
KING ISLAND
Burke Channel
Evans Arm
Kwatna Inlet
Stupendous Mt. 9250
7576
Monarch Mt. 11714
9880
FISHER CHAN.
FITZHUGH SD.
Nanu Hbr.
3380
Moses Inlet
Cannery P.O.
Hardy Inlet
Addenbrooke Pt.
Pierce B.
RIVERS INLET
Draney Inlet
Calvert
Mount Waddington 13260
Gp.Fl.
Goose B.
Smith Sd.
Smith Inlet
White Rks
Rf.
R Bn.
10700
Takush Hbr.
C. Caution
Belize Inlet
Nugent Sd.
Tsauwan
Slingsby Chan.
Storm Is. (190)
Pine I.
Gp.Fl.4
DIA·R·Bn.
Seymour Inlet
North Chan.
5665
Kingcombe Mts. 5600
7000
7280
6900
Waddington
Nigei I.
Goletas Chan.
QUEEN CHARLOTTE STRAIT
Gordon Chan.
Drury Inlet
Labouchere Chan.
Broughton I.
4200
Tribune Chan.
Mt. Smith 7544
KNIGHT INLET
Needle Pk 8145
Hardy B.
Beaver Hbr
Malcolm I.
Gilford I.
Turnour I.
Call Creek
3987
6300
5755
BUTE INLET
Holberg Inlet
Rupert Inlet
Broughton Str.
Cracroft I.
Loughborough Inlet
6066
Mt. Castle abt. 4320
Johnstone Strait
5778
Hardwicke I.
Thurlow Is.
Sonora I.
2485
Neroutsos Inlet
Mt. Hkusam 5461
Discovery Passage
4195
Klaskino Inlet
4609
Quadra I.
Redonda Is.
2555
Klaskish Inlet
Nasparti Inlet
Ououkinsh Inlet
4060
BAY
Brooks Pena.
Cortes I.
2380
2370
Tahsish Inlet
VANCOUVER
C. Mudge
Hernando I.
1550
Checleset Bay
Lookout I. Gp.Fl.1
3595
3100
4320
Mt. Alva
Mt. Bate 5550
Port Eliza
Savary I.
Sound

9

Ever Nor'westward

It gets better the farther you go. There are faster rapids, greener trees, higher hills and snow-capped mountains, a wealth of seafood, birds, shoreside wildlife, majestic scenery, and more channels, passages, islands, bays and coves than can be explored in a lifetime.

"Ever Nor'westward" is becoming the byword for more and more Northwest cruising skippers as they continue to search for new and different waters each year. The San Juans are magic, the Gulf Islands are enchanting, the arms off the Strait of Georgia are enthralling, Desolation Sound is magnificent, and you run out of adjectives long before the farther reaches of British Columbia and southeast Alaska inland waters have been mentioned.

Although it's a small price to pay for such a gorgeous adventure, it might be well to warn that one is leaving behind some of the conveniences of civilization and taking on more responsibilities in piloting and navigating. Well-stocked grocery stores are few and far between, and supply ships service them only once a week. Water can be a problem, particularly if the season is a dry one. Ice becomes more and more difficult to obtain, and showers and laundromats are practically nonexistent.

The crew learns rapidly to ration the water carefully and to get along without ice, to do laundry in salt water and to take sponge baths. More care must be taken to figure slack water in the numerous narrows and rapids, and close attention to charts is a must if one is to avoid the generous scattering of rocks and reefs.

In spite of all this, each year finds more boats — ranging from 16-foot, partially canvas topped outboards to palatial yachts—tasting of the delights offered in these remote areas.

There are two gateways to these waters, Seymour Narrows and the Yuculta Rapids. Both are narrow passages through which must pour all the tidal waters entering and leaving the northern half of the Strait of Georgia and its inlets, straits, arms, channels, bays and coves. With a tidal range of about 18 feet, the emptying and filling process runs a tremendous amount of water through them four times each lunar day.

We chose the Yuculta Rapids as our gateway this time. As with many Indian words, there are various spellings encountered, most of which do not match the pronunciation. One may find Yuculta, Yaculta, Yucalta or Yucluetaw. However, Yuculta seems to be the more generally used spelling and Yoo'-cla-taw, the pronunciation. The U.S. Tidal Current Tables use both Yuculta and Yucluetaw, the former for the portion of the rapids along Stuart Island and the latter for those in Cordero Channel by Dent Island.

There are those who run the rapids at any stage of the tide, but the judicious boatman will wait for the slack. Four miles in length, the channel has two rather sharp turns, is obstructed with rocks, reefs and islands, narrows in three places and attains up to 10-knot speeds. Overfalls occur over underwater ledges, giant boils and whirlpools foam and eddy, while mad currents sweep along the shore as the resistless power of the rushing mass of water throws the entire channel into a wild confusion.

At slack it's hard to believe such a maelstrom can occur, yet there never seems to be any *real* slack. The water appears always impatient, never quite settling down after its wild surge in one direction before it turns for a repeat performance the other way. A half hour either side of slack is considered safe enough and we've run at an hour before slack without difficulty, although the boils and whirlpools swung the boat and made the engine groan. Of course the

Loughborough Inlet presents a series of scenic beauties, climaxed by a vista of snow-capped mountains at its head.

faster and more powerful boats and those with twin motors may want to gamble even further but, when one considers what the rapids have done to some large and powerful boats, it can be cause for careful decisions.

The Yucultas are also known as an excellent salmon-fishing spot, particularly the section along Stuart Island. Many yachtsmen make their headquarters at the Stuart Island Resort on the southwestern tip of the island, while others work out of the bay farther up the island. This is charted as Asman Bay but is locally known as Big Bay.

The Stuart Island Resort has been improved and enlarged. With full facilities for yachtsmen and a set of neat cabins, it is also becoming a popular spot for winter fishing as well as hunting. Boats and professional guides are available for those who do not wish to fish from their own boats or who want an expert to help them work the boils and whirlpools.

Man isn't the only fisherman in the rapids. At all stages of the tide the birds are there, too. Black-trimmed little terns dive deep into the boiling water for a fish, while flocks of gulls do their fishing accompanied by raucous screams of happiness as the turbulent water throws herring to surface. Frequently an eagle or two will soar high over-head ready for a power dive if something turns up to suit their fancy.

The Yucultas are a never-ending show. The massive power of water on the move tosses huge tree trunks around, stands them on end and then sucks them under, only to spew them out hundreds of yards farther along the channel. The sight somehow exalts the spirit and reactivates an in-herent respect for nature and her power which may have been dulled from too much civilized living. The Yucultas are an experience!

Leaving the rapids, Cordero Channel continues north-westward along the north shores of Sonora, East and West Thurlow Islands, with Frederick and Phillips Arms taking off to the north. Frederick Arm, about three miles long, is a favorite fishing area for some but generally is overshadowed by its neighboring arm. With depths of 173 fathoms shallowing to six and eight fathoms at the very head, and deep water right up to the steep shores, it offers no good anchor-ing facilities and not much protection. A few buildings at the head appear to be a logging settlement.

Phillips Arm, nearly five miles in length, has long been noted as a good salmon-fishing area, particularly around Hewitt Point at the entrance to Fanny Bay. We remember some tries in here that have been fruitless, while other times have been excellent. One year we brought up about 100 pounds of halibut. Good anchorage can be found in Fanny Bay and at the head of the arm in six to eight fathoms. There is a small settlement at the head of the arm as well as some signs of habitation in Fanny Bay.

Opposite the entrance to Phillips Arm across Cordero Channel, on the north tip of East Thurlow Island, is Shoal Bay, the northernmost of the B.C. Coastal Marine Resorts chain. All facilities and services are available here. A good cruising tip would be to take advantage of the showers and laundromat. They are the last of these facilities to be found in some distance. The Thurlow post office is also located here.

Just around the corner from Shoal Bay is Bickley Bay, which offers good anchorage at the head. Watch for Peel Rocks at the right of the entrance going in. One lone cabin is the only sign of civilization.

Continuing a westerly course in Cordero Channel, Blind Channel and Mayne Passage soon take off to the

Top: Floating houses and docks are found in Heydon Bay.
Bottom: Little Edith Cove, in Beaver Inlet, offers
a charming anchorage in which to snug down for the night.

south between East and West Thurlow Islands to connect with Johnstone Strait. Off the northeast corner of West Thurlow Island are the Greene Point Rapids. Currents here run up to seven knots with slack water before both flood and ebb approximately an hour and a half before the slack at Seymour Narrows. We came through about an hour after slack before ebb and found almost no appreciable current, although there were a few boils showing. We didn't check out the anchorage shown on large-scale chart #3555 in behind the Cordero Islands, but it looks interesting.

About three miles beyond Greene Point is the entrance to Loughborough Inlet. In naming this inlet, Captain Vancouver departed from his usual practice of using naval names and selected a lord chancellor to be honored. Alexander Wedderburn was of Scottish birth and became the first baron of Loughborough. The Thurlow Islands were also named for a chancellor and perhaps this accounts for the later naming of Chancellor Channel, which runs between West Thurlow Island and Loughborough Inlet. One hears several pronunciations for the inlet (including Lockboro, Loffboro and Lowboro) but, with the Scottish heritage of the man for whom it was named, it would seem that Lockboro would be only proper.

The inlet has several moods and, at times, the wind can blow up a fair sea. We were fortunate to have chosen a fine sunny day and the trip up the inlet was delightful, with just a few powder-puff clouds decorating the sky behind the hills and mountains. A short way up we encountered some tide rips and a current which actually was stronger than that found in Greene Point Rapids.

A good-sized logging camp is located just below Statham Point on the east side and farther up are several deserted cabins and groups of cabins which appear to have been logging camps in the past. The chart shows a government float in Heydon Bay, but the floats in there seemed to be private and several people have told us they didn't think there was a government float there now.

A trip up Loughborough presents an ever-unfolding series of scenic beauties which become more spectacular with every mile. Although the steep hills that rise from the water's edge are not as high as in some of the inlets, they are most impressive. There are numerous waterfalls, some of them quite high, but most are fairly well hidden in the thick growth of trees, only showing themselves as they dash over a rock outcropping for a time or where they cascade the last few yards into the saltchuck. We developed quite a game, trying to discover them with binoculars. Trees growing to the water's edge have all had their bangs neatly trimmed along a straight line by the high tides.

It might be said that Loughborough presents a series of stages, each set with a new and different scene. The gently rounded tops of the forest-clad hills occasionally are broken by valleys or draws, which serve to frame a gorgeous scene of blue black mountains behind, with their variegated patterns of snow fields glittering in the sun. At times the splendor of the green blanket of trees is marred where the loggers have cut a swath down the hillside, looking like a small boy's hair after he has found a pair of scissors and attempted a barbering job on himself.

The inlet is fairly straight for about 13 of its 18-mile length with some five miles of Cooper Reach turning northeastward at the top. Towry Head, sticking out into the bend, hides the final scene until it is rounded. Then is unveiled as gorgeous a vista as can be imagined, with green valleys growing into foothills of darker green and a backdrop of rugged snow-capped mountains with their halos of wispy cotton clouds. It seemed only natural to cut the motor and drift for a few minutes of silent contemplation and admiration of the awesomeness of one of nature's masterpieces of scenic beauty. The entire inlet is striking, but the picture revealed around that final bend makes the trip well worth taking.

On the trip back down we noted at least three good-sized rocks just off Cosby Point, about two miles below Heydon Bay. These did not appear on the chart we were using.

We poked our bow into Sidney Bay on the western shore to find two or three houses at the head, with a small harbor protected by boom logs. Two boats, already inside, made us decide not to invade their privacy.

Just below and around Mary Point is Beaver Inlet, a small arm about two miles long. We encountered a fairly strong westerly wind even in here. However, good anchorage can be found near the head. Little Edith Cove in behind Hale's Point, with better than two fathoms of depth, also looked like a delightful place to drop an anchor for a night's snug berth.

Beaver Inlet is a quiet, serene little waterway and it's easy to understand why it has been chosen for homesites by the loggers or fishermen who have houses in behind the Goat Islets and along the north shore. Large-scale chart #3555 is a good one to have aboard when going into this inlet.

With depths up to 140 fathoms, Loughborough is known as an excellent place to drop a shrimp trap. It is also reported that shrimp can be bought in Heydon Bay, but we didn't hear about this until after we'd left and so unfortunately, were not able to check it out.

As we came out of Beaver Inlet and back toward the entrance of Loughborough, the afternoon westerly up Chancellor Channel was carrying what we decided must be smoke. It wasn't until we turned up Wellbore Channel that we could see the source. A forest fire was burning up on one of the ridges on the east side. The rugged hillside was too steep for any kind of equipment, and the thought that there was very little that could be done to control the fire served to emphasize the many warnings about using all due caution with fires of any kind which might set off a similar conflagration.

At Carterer Point in Wellbore Channel are the Whirlpool Rapids, very aptly named, for the channel is filled with whirlpools of all sizes. These rapids attain velocities up to seven knots on large tides, and the slacks occur about an hour and three-quarters before slack at Seymour Narrows. On some charts they are noted in rather small type and can be easily overlooked.

Just beyond and around Horace Point is Forward Harbor which we had chosen as an anchorage for the night. If we had thought of a secluded haven all to ourselves, we would have been disappointed for, as we rounded the bluff to turn into Douglas Bay, there were at least 15 boats, some at anchor singly and others rafted up together. Two beach parties were already in progress. Forward Harbor's two-and-a-half-mile length affords excellent protection, as well as another magnificent vista behind its head. A verdant valley serves as a base for more snow-covered peaks in the distance to the east. We couldn't see the sunset because of a high bluff to the west, but the glory of the setting sun with all the gorgeous coloring was reflected by the stupendous panorama to the east. Forward Harbor was indeed an inspired choice for a nightly sojourn, even if we didn't have it all to ourselves, and we suspected that we should have dropped the crab trap.

Bessborough Bay, to the northwest, separated from Forward Harbor by Thynne Peninsula, is too open to the prevailing summer westerlies to be a good anchorage, as is Topaze Harbor, still farther north. The chart shows two Jackson Bays in Topaze Harbor, one a fairly good-sized indentation to the north and the other, a small cove near the head on the south shore. We decided the duplicity was probably because the smaller bay contained the Jackson Bay post office and later found that several places have their post offices some distance removed from the bay or sound with the same name.

Read Bay on the north shore is too shallow and unprotected for good anchorage. While Topaze is a pretty harbor about five miles in length and is a busy place with quite a bit of logging activity, the westerly winds from Johnstone Strait sweep up Sunderland Channel and right on in; so there is little of interest to the yachtsman.

The deeply indented shoreline of this portion of British Columbia's inland coast could aptly be called sea country. With some of the inhabitants living on land and perhaps a larger percentage in float houses moored to the steep shore, their activities, their work and play, their every movement are geared to, and often determined by, the vagaries of the sea.

In a way it is a country apart, with its residents sometimes separated by miles yet still closely knit through the common bond of the sea. There is a nautical atmosphere pervading the entire area, which somehow seems to establish a kinship with the yachtsman; he is more often than not welcomed as a visitor.

Until you have turned your bow "Ever Nor'westward" and cruised the inlets of this area, explored its passages, bays and coves, you haven't begun to really enjoy the wonders of these cruising waters.

10

A Sea Chest of Islands and Bays

Yachtsmen find the British Columbia coast the most spectacular in the world. It is a stout sea chest full of islands, bays, channels and inlets poking their fingers in among towering mountains. And because this terrain is so rugged, there are few roads and travel and communication are nearly all sea oriented. It has been called the "Great Inland Sea Country."

We continued our exploration of the myriad waterways lying north of Johnstone Strait. Topaze Harbor (named after H.M.S. *Topaze*, 51 guns, 2659 tons, 600 horsepower, on station in this area from 1859 to 1863) lay astern as the bow pointed out Sunderland Channel. Little Seymour and Poyntz Islands, in mid stream, made a scenic front-stage setting against the backdrop of forest-clad mountains.

The usual pattern of westerly or northwesterly winds, which blow in from Queen Charlotte Strait from noon or one o'clock until four or five, had begun early this mid-July day. The 10- to 12-knot breeze didn't produce enough sea to be too uncomfortable, but there was pleasant relief as we poked into a few bays and coves to check out possible anchorages.

First of these was little McLeod Bay. Here was quiet water in a depth of one-half to five fathoms, a good spot to duck into during a blow or a pleasant place to spend a night. Around Mary Island and behind Tuna Point is more protection in a small bay, which the charts fail to honor with a name.

Around the corner Blenkinsop Bay, a much larger indentation, looked like a good spot to stop for lunch. We dropped the anchor on the three-fathom line, in behind White Bluff. In these waters, one can frequently find little "accommodation harbors" just waiting to provide surcease from a rolling deck. Wind and spray vanish, the sun is warm, the water calm, and all is peaceful in the "harbor."

As sometimes happens, there is a difference between charted names and original names. This bay was named in 1860 by Captain Richards after George Blinkinsop, a native of Cornwall who worked in the sea service of the Hudson's Bay Company and later became an Indian agent. Someplace along the line an *e* was substituted for the *i*. Large-scale chart #3571-A is good to have for these bays.

It's only about a league, as Captain Vancouver might say, or three miles, around to the entrance to Port Neville. It's probable that many skippers pass up this delightful inlet in their hurry to get farther up but they're missing an interesting and scenic bit of water.

Just inside about a half mile are floats and a post office; latest reports show the former store and fuel floats closed. Proceeding in, we chose to hug the shore to July Point. Channel Rock, near mid channel, plus a fair scattering of kelp, calls for a slow bell and a good lookout, but the water is clear and the rocks easily seen.

The inlet runs northeastward for approximately five miles past places with such interesting names as Robbers Nob and Baresides Bay, with a couple of apparently deserted logging camps adding color to an already scenic trip. In the narrow passage between Hanatsa and Collingwood Points, it is well to favor the Hanatsa Point shore to be sure to miss Cuthbert Rock. Here again large-scale chart #3571-A is valuable to check such things, as well as to keep track of water depths and shoal areas.

The inlet was named by Vancouver in July, 1792, probably after Lt. John Neville, Royal Marines, Queen's Regiment. It terminates in a double head with rivers emptying on both sides of a small mountain. Two of the three logging camps shown on the chart appear to be deserted or

Crabbing is usually good in Cutter Cove, near Minstrel.

at least inactive. The one at the head was very much operational. Unlike most of the inlets, Port Neville is shallow with 13 fathoms the greatest charted depth. With its beauty and charm and protected waters, it doesn't deserve to be bypassed.

Back in Johnstone Strait, we found the westerly still blowing but decided it wasn't so bad we couldn't go on to Port Harvey, our destination for that day's run. This main waterway, familiar to those traveling the inland passage to Alaska, was originally called Canal de Describierta ("Discovery Passage") by the Spanish explorer Lieutenant Valdez. In 1792 Vancouver gave it the present name after James Johnstone, R.N., master of the armed tender *Chatham*, who made the first examination of this channel in the *Chatham's* cutter. He was later appointed lieutenant.

Currents up to three knots run through this part of the strait with the direction turning one and a half to two hours after high and low water. When winds blow against the tide, nasty seas can develop, which can be dangerous to small boats.

About eight and a half miles from Port Neville is the entrance to Port Harvey. It's well to make a fairly wide swing around the Broken Islands to avoid the many scattered rocks and reefs. The trip in past the Mist Islets and Mist Bluff, Tide Pole Islet and Range Island is a scenic one, terminating at the government wharf at the head of the bay.

An abandoned cabin not far from the wharf had been almost taken over by the growth of underbrush and weeds, but a former raspberry patch produced a nice bowlful of the ripe red fruit for breakfast. Across the head of the bay, where a dry cut separates East and West Cracroft Islands, were some deserted cabins. These always make fascinating exploring for the cruising family.

In addition to the government wharf, there are several good anchorages to be found in the bay including Open Cove between Transit and Harvey Points at the entrance. Large-scale chart #3583 is almost a must for worry-free cruising and exploring in Port Harvey and through Havannah and Chatham Channels to Minstrel Island.

Our course took us east in Havannah Channel, past Lily Islet, the Bockett Islets and into Boughey Bay. This is indeed a charmed area. A stratum of morning mist still hung lightly a few feet above the glassy water, causing the wooded isles to appear as though standing above the water supported by pedestals which were their own reflections. Above and beyond the mist, the dark greens, blues and purples of the hills and mountains rose in serried ranks to distant peaks still wearing snow patches for hats.

Boughey Bay takes off to the southeast as the channel turns northward. A delightful anchorage is found in the southernmost head of the bay. The charts are either wrong or out-of-date. The logging camp shown at the southeastern point is not there now; it is between the two points of the bay behind the booming ground.

Heading north, we went back around Mistake Island and Hull Island for a look into a couple of interesting coves. Soderman Cove doesn't offer too much in the way of protection, but after swinging in behind Round Island and into Burial Cove, we marked this as an excellent anchorage and an altogether beautiful spot. The one house has a private float.

On the eastern shore of the channel, in behind the Indian Islands, is a deserted Matilpi Indian village. Anchorage can be found behind the northern of the two main islands.

It is interesting to note how many of the names in this area are derived from one source. When Captain Richards of the survey vessel *Plumper* was working in these waters, he was assisted by the officers of H.M. Frigate *Havannah*, stationed in the area from 1855 to 1859. The channel, of course, was named after the ship. Other names given in association are: Port Harvey and Harvey Point after the *Havannah's* Capt. Thomas Harvey, R.N.; Hull Island and Hull Rock after the master, Thomas Q. Hull. Others are Boughey Bay (first lieutenant); Mist Islets and Bluff (second lieutenant); Malone Point (marine officer); Bockett Islands and Point (assistant surgeon); Atchison Island (surgeon); Ray Point (assistant paymaster); Squire Point (third lieutenant).

We next turned northeastward into Call Inlet. This 10½-mile arm of the sea was examined and named Call Canal by Lieutenant Commander Broughton of the *Chatham* after Sir John Call, a military engineer and later baronet. Its deep waters, mostly over 100 fathoms, extend between green hills which get progressively higher toward the head. One grand peak at the head still had snow patches on it. Several picturesque islands and small islets add to the scenic beauty enjoyed on a trip up the inlet.

Although similar in some respects to Loughborough, Call Inlet is not as spectacular, lacking those cuts and draws in the hills which open up a stage for the mountains behind. Near the head on the left side is an abandoned logging

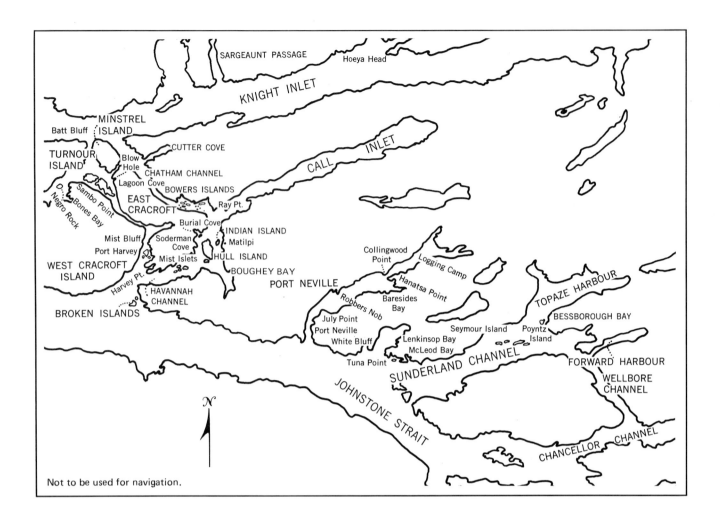

Not to be used for navigation.

camp, a couple of buildings and a float. We were told there were shrimp in the deep waters but didn't check this out. Aside from this possibility and a very scenic trip, Call Inlet hasn't too much to attract the yachtsman.

Rounding Ray Point, we turned into Chatham Channel named, of course, for Vancouver's consort vessel. In the little bay in behind Atchison Island, Bill Hadley operates a marine ways and machine shop. His ways are unusual in that the carriage is on four huge tires which run on the sand beach and can handle vessels up to 65 feet. Bill is an excellent mechanic and, with his facilities, can take care of most problems. If a needed part isn't available, he usually can make it. If the tide is low, go in slowly to the outer end of the float and keep a sharp lookout. The water in the back is shallow.

The lower portion of Chatham Channel is worthy of careful study before running it. Chart #3583 has a blowup of this area which is valuable, showing in detail where the rocks and shoals are and how the two ranges will help you to avoid them. The range in behind Ray Point should be used on the stern, when going west, until the other range comes in on the bow. The channel is narrow and shallow but, during the summer months, the danger areas to the south are well marked by kelp. There is some kelp over the

rocks and shoals surrounding the Bowers Islands but this can't be depended on. Knowledgeable skippers advise staying just out of the kelp along the south edge of the channel if you don't run the ranges exactly. Currents can run up to seven knots on spring tides.

Minstrel Island, lying at the confluence of Chatham Channel and Knight Inlet, is the main center of activity for a large surrounding area. It has a government wharf, seaplane landing, store, post office, fuel float, hotel, cabins, restaurant and radiotelephone to Campbell River. Genial Lawrence Rose presides over the store and fuel float and is a good source of information on the surrounding country, as well as on fishing, crabbing and shrimping.

In a dry year water becomes a problem at Minstrel. In such a year boats must go elsewhere to fill their tanks. Lacking here are laundry and shower facilities; however a tub bath can be obtained at the Lighthouse restaurant operated by Helen and Al Schaible and Martha McLean. Their home-cooked meals are excellent and they also have rooms. Yachtsmen find them most friendly and accommodating.

Minstrel is also a meeting spot for yachtsmen and a place where guests can join or leave a boat by flying in or out. There are nearly always a few "experts" around who are happy to give advice on fishing, crabbing, clamming or

Government wharf at Minstrel Island is a central gathering place for yachstmen, fishermen and loggers.

shrimping. We picked up valuable tips here to add to our store of knowledge from Roy Pace, Dr. Robert Manchester, Ed and Jean Niemeier, Lee Doud and Jim and Kay Arniel.

For those who have returned after cruising into some of the more remote reaches, Minstrel becomes a social center, with exchange boat-hopping between friends and acquaintances a popular pastime. Jean Niemeier had just returned from a trip to their home in Poulsbo and had brought a big supply of fresh vegetables from Ed's fine garden. An invitation to a gourmet dinner was gladly accepted and much enjoyed.

There is always something of interest to see or do at Minstrel. We spent a half hour watching a family of mink hunt and play among the rocks on the shore. This was interrupted by a commotion out on the end of one of the floats. John Harestad, a 13-year-old boy from Sechelt, had been fishing off the float. On a light line, with salmon gills for bait, he hooked a 125-pound halibut. Never was a lad prouder of his catch as the boaters, commercial fishermen, and Minstrel Islanders came to admire the huge fish.

Thursday was supply-ship day at Minstrel, when the big freighter arrived from Vancouver with supplies for the store. As the ship nosed slowly into the float, everyone gathered on the high upper deck of the dock. Large wheelbarrows and dollies were rolled out. Soon the loading boom began hoisting pallets stacked with crates, cases, sacks and packages out of the hold. While Larry Rose stood like a sergeant, checking manifests and directing whether things were to go to the store or into one or the other of two small warehouses on the dock, more of the onlookers

John Harestad with the 125-pound halibut he caught off the Minstrel Island float.

Little Seymour Island in Sunderland Channel adds scenic interest to a background of rounded hills and mountains.

turned to and helped with the unloading. It became a festive occasion. The store was closed for the rest of the day while shelves, counters, coolers, refrigerators and freezers were restocked.

One Thursday the boat failed to arrive and it was three o'clock Friday morning before it showed up. Not too many of the boaters slept as whistles, bright lights, shouts and the rumbling of winches kept the place humming. It was ten o'clock in the morning before the store opened with a tired and sleepy staff to serve the customers.

Every summer isn't the best year for salmon fishing but that shouldn't keep anyone from trying. Reported best spots in the vicinity are up Knight Inlet around Hoeya Head, in the passage between Minstrel and Turnour Island, around Sambo Point and the eastern entrance to Bones Bay in Clio Channel, and at the entrance to Sargeaunt Passage.

Besides fish, the cruising yachtsman is also interested in other seafood. Crabbing is usually good in Cutter Cove, just across the channel from Minstrel, if you drop the trap in the right place. Otherwise they can be too small to keep. Crabs are also reported in the little bight behind Dorman and Farquharson Islands off the southwest tip of Minstrel Island. Shrimp are reported available in Bones Bay and along the southwest side of Minstrel.

Larry Rose tells an interesting story about the naming of some of the places in the vicinity. We can't vouch for its accuracy but it makes a good tale. It seems that in the late 1880s or early 1890s a group of entertainers stopped at the little settlement which is now Minstrel Island to put on a Minstrel Show. That is supposed to be how Minstrel Island, Sambo Point, Bones Bay, Negro Rock and Clio Channel got their names. It may be true except for Clio Channel. It was actually named by Captain Pender in 1865 after H.M.S. *Clio*, on station in this area from 1864 to 1868. Batt Bluff on Turnour Island was named after the *Clio's* master, David Batt, R.N.

Some of the waterways in this area are of interest. If you find the floats at Minstrel Island full or if you prefer a quiet, peaceful anchorage, Cutter Cove is a lovely little bay. It has nearly a mile of usable water for anchorage and is a scenic, protected harbor for the yachtsman.

A passage called the Blow Hole runs along the southeast side of Minstrel Island to join Clio Channel. Even on the large-scale chart (#3583) one might question the advisability of going through. If caution is used to stay away from the charted shoal and a mid-channel course steered, it's most possible.

After coming through the Blow Hole, to the south is Lagoon Cove, a pleasant anchorage and the site of Ernie Rose's shipyard, boat works and marine ways. Ernie is Lawrence Rose's son and a top-notch shipwright. Although a large percentage of his work is with fishing and commercial vessels, it's good to know of such a fine facility if a cruising yachtsman has need of his services.

Some charts show a store in Bones Bay, but there is nothing there now except a large commercial net loft for fishermen. The floats may be available for a night's moorage but care should be used in entering the bay, with close attention to the beacons which mark rocks and shoals.

It's been said that the really smart skipper is a humble person who is willing to admit he doesn't know it all and is open for further learning. Our hope is that we fall in this category. We certainly learned one thing on this trip that we didn't know before. That is that oysters don't grow in the colder waters above the Yucultas. So — we forgot the oysters and substituted shrimp. According to the experts, these waters produce shrimp, not prawns, even though the shrimp in some areas grow to the size of prawns. Still they are a different breed. It really doesn't matter, however, for whether they are large shrimp or prawns, they are delectable, and anyone cruising these waters is missing something if he doesn't have a shrimp trap aboard with at least 350 feet of line.

This area is a long way from some of the more popular cruising waters of the Northwest and there may be some drawbacks to a vacation in these far reaches of British Columbia, but the rewards are great. If you want to enjoy the grandeur of the channels, inlets, bays and coves, untouched by the hand of man, with gorgeous, lovely vistas of a sea that has penetrated a mountain range, this is for you. You may have to forego such civilized amenities as laundromats, showers and ice, but it's well worth the price.

11
Between Mountains – A Finger of the Sea

You meet the nicest people while cruising. This is no doubt true anywhere in the world, but it seems particularly so in the more remote waters of British Columbia.

Yachtsmen are generally known to be friendly and helpful to fellow boatmen. It matters not whether it be bank president, corporation executive, office worker or janitor, water and boats have a leveling influence. Perhaps in the more crowded boating areas a skipper may guard his fishing secrets and favorite spots, but the farther north one goes, he finds that boaters tend to be generous in passing along knowledge, help and experience.

Exploration of Knight Inlet was our next objective. First, however, we had to find fresh water. Over a month without rain had depleted the supply at Minstrel Island and our tanks were nearly empty. Larry Rose reported that water could be obtained at Hoeya Sound, a small arm off Knight Inlet some 14 miles to the east.

The day was bright with the morning sun setting millions of diamonds to dancing from wavelet tops, and a few stray wisps of puffy clouds played tag around the mountain tops. There was very little wind and only a suggestion of a ground swell coming off Queen Charlotte Strait to the west.

After rounding Littleton Point, we saw Dr. Bob Manchester's *Trinket* bound for Hoeya Head after an early morning search for salmon at the entrance to Sargeaunt Passage. A quick turn around Protection Point convinced us that Tsakonu Cove, behind the point, would provide a good, protected anchorage in about six to eight fathoms near the head.

From here to Hoeya Sound there is very little in the way of protection. Lull Bay, just outside the sound, is too open to the prevailing westerly winds. Even Hoeya Sound itself is somewhat exposed, although toward its head the

seas do quiet down. Knight Inlet is truly a finger of the sea poking in between the mountains. Peaks up to a mile high are matched by depths of better than 260 fathoms.

In the northeast corner of Hoeya Sound is Bill Sawchuck's place. Bill is a logger, and everything – house, sheds and other buildings – is built on a mass of huge floating logs.

Although we were hesitant to invade private property, our serious need for fresh water gave us courage. Bill was away, hard at work across the inlet, but we were cordially welcomed by his lovely wife and two beautiful daughters. We were told they had plenty of water and to take all we needed. What a happy reception! These people in this country are the finest.

Leaving Hoeya Sound, we passed a sizable fleet of yachts fishing around Hoeya Head, one of the hottest spots in the area. Jim and Kay Arniel, in their *Flying Cloud*, held up a couple of beauties and invited us to join them for dinner, but we had to pass on that one. After rounding the head we called *Flying Cloud* for a radio check.

Proceeding eastward in Knight Inlet, we noticed a change in the color of the water. From the usual dark blue gray it had turned into a delicate light green. As we approached Sallie Point, where the inlet turns from an east-west to a generally northern direction, the water became increasingly milky from the many snow-fed streams which cascaded down the mountain sides to plunge into the saltchuck. At Sallie Point there was a definitely noticeable line where the milky white water from the north met the greener water from the west.

All along the south shore were deep valleys or cuts in the mountain sides, getting very little direct sun and still filled with snow. Generally these were in the higher parts, although at times we could see snow almost down to the water.

At Sallie Point the inlet turns and continues to snake generally northward through a series of S turns for about 25 miles. Opposite Sallie Point on the lower corner of the turn is Glendale Cove. On the chart it appears to be an excellent bay for anchoring with Macdonald Point offering good protection, but we were told by several skippers at Minstrel Island that winds and waves somehow manage to get in, making it a rough place to spend a night.

Knight Inlet was explored and named by Captain Vancouver's assistant, Lt. William Broughton, who was in command of the consort vessel H.M. Armed Tender *Chatham*. Originally it was called Knight's Channel for Sir John Knight, a friend of Broughton's with whom he had served on the sloop *Falcon*, while covering the attack on Bunker Hill. In 1776, the two were captured while attempting to destroy a schooner which had been driven ashore in Cape Ann Harbor.

Knight was a career navy man who served under several men whose names are familiar to us as honored by Vancouver in the naming of places in the Northwest. Sir John was made an admiral in 1813. This inlet was first named Braza de Vernaci by Valdez and Galiano after the lieutenant of the *Mexicano*.

It's also interesting to note some of the other names in this immediate vicinity and how they honor members of a family. In 1865, William Blackney was assistant surveying officer on the *Beaver*. He named Macdonald Point after William John Macdonald, a native of Inverness-shire who was with the Hudson's Bay Service and later a member of the Senate of Canada. He was one of the members of the Legislative Council instrumental in transferring the capital of the province from the mainland to Victoria on Vancouver Island.

Blackney named Mount Catherine after Macdonald's wife; Flora Peak after his eldest daughter; Mount Edith after his second daughter; and Lillian Rock in Glendale Cove after his youngest daughter. Duncan Point was named by Blackney for Macdonald's younger brother, and Murray Point after Capt. James Murray Reid of the Hudson's Bay Company, who was Mrs. Macdonald's father.

Mount Lillie was named by Blackney after Captain Reid's youngest daughter, Elizabeth ("Lillie") Reid, who later became Blackney's wife. He named Adeane Point after a pony belonging to Lillie and Kitty Cove after his own pony. Glendale Cove was named after a small residential place in Inverness-shire owned by Senator Macdonald's father, Maj. Alexander Macdonald, Yorkshire Yeomanry.

Heading northward, we continued toward the head of the inlet. Mountains grew higher, snow fields and snow caps more extensive, and the scenery became more spectacular with every mile. Around every bend was a new majestic picture. Waterfalls grew more numerous. Their ribbonlike paths of foaming froth being clearly visible for a few hundred feet, then hidden by the green forest for a bit only to break into the open again, and finally to dive with a roar and merge with waters of the inlet.

Probably the most spectacular falls in the inlet is one just below Cascade Point. We called it Cascade Falls, although Bridal Veil might be more appropriate considering its general appearance. The dashing stream of water seems to come pouring out of the rocks on the face of the cliff and hurl itself at once down the precipice, turning into a cloud of mist as it dashes on the rocks of the shore.

As in Loughborough Inlet, we found several stages, places where the sheer walls along the shoreline slope downward briefly to form a valley. The most magnificent of these stages was just a bit above Cascade Point. Here were large snow fields with one ridge actually coming to the water's edge. The backdrop was a series of higher rugged peaks with halos of refulgent clouds around their heads.

Across the inlet on the western shore is Ahnuhati Point, and just below it a small bay. Dr. Bob Manchester had told us this is a fair anchorage except in certain winds, but he recommended an even more open bay just north where the chart shows an anchorage at the water end of Ahnuhati Valley.

Continuing northward, with the water getting more milky with every mile, we remarked that Knight might be called the Lonesome Inlet. The only boat we saw on the entire upward trip was a small tug without a tow, heading south.

A northeasterly course took us around Transit Head and a few miles farther around Axe Point on a northwest heading. Here the entire gorgeous vista of the head opened up. The grandeur at the end of this longest of the fjords, which penetrates to the very heart of the majestic coastal range, together with the remoteness and solitude, produced a feeling of awe. Turreted cliffs like glistening battlements imparted their regal attitude to the entire scene, glowing in a mixture of violet, dark blues and dusky purples warmed by shades of rose. Yet the scene was cooled by a chill creeping down from the snowy heights. This was definitely a scene which will live long in our Log of Cruising Memories.

Approaching the head, a moderate southeast wind began to blow while the clouds thickened. We swung in to look at the low delta cut by several streams of Klinaklini River as it joins the inlet. To the right of Dutchman Head, the mouth of the Franklin River has also spewed a delta into the waters of the inlet. Somehow, the anchorage shown on the chart in the northwest corner at the head didn't seem too attractive. We swung back to the south around Hatchet Point and into Wahshihlas Bay.

This is where Dr. Manchester suggested we spend the night. An oval of boom logs containing a log raft appeared to offer a good tie-up, although we had been warned they can swing and cause trouble. A small boat, either a fisherman or converted cruiser, was tied near the inner perimeter of the boom. We tied near him, feeling that we were secure for the night as the wind continued to blow into the bay.

Shortly after dinner the wind did an about-face and started to blow from down the valley at the head of the bay. A close watch on the log boom showed that it was slowly changing shape. Before long we were swung around so that the boat was between the boom and a rocky south shore of the bay. With the distance to shore getting closer momentarily, we were making preparations to move when

Steep-sided mountains along the shoreline slope downward to open up a stage with backdrop of snow-capped mountains.

Trinket heads for better fishing in Hoeya Sound after a try at the entrance to Sergeaunt Passage.

the Canadian Fisheries boat *Howay* steamed into the bay, tied to the boom, and dropped anchor. Thus we were provided with a fairly solid mooring and assured of a relaxing night's rest.

With a good six hours of running back to Minstrel Island, we were off to an early start next morning to avoid having to buck the afternoon westerly coming in the inlet. Winds had died and a bright sun had dispersed most of the clouds. The trip back down the inlet was delightful as we enjoyed a retake of all the impressive scenes of the day before.

Rounding Sallie Point, our good luck ran out. A fickle weatherman had moved ahead the time schedule for the westerly and we ran into winds of 25 to 30 knots. There was nothing to do but fight it, after abandoning the thought of seeking shelter in Glendale Cove.

By quartering the waves, which seemed to grow higher the farther we went, and cutting throttle for the big ones, we managed to make fairly good headway until about 10:30 A.M. when suddenly there was no rudder response to the wheel. First thought was a broken line or connection in the hydraulic steering system, but a quick inspection showed the rudderpost responding to the wheel. We were six or seven miles west of Sallie Point.

After vainly trying to hold a forward course and quickly rejecting all of the jury-rig steering methods one could manage to recall at the moment, we decided to set a sea anchor to hold us bow into the wind and seas.

Although we were pitching and rolling considerably, a hurried survey of our situation determined we weren't in any immediate danger of loss of life or property. A review of the radio rules indicated a *Pan* rather than a *Mayday* call. A *Pan* call was sent out periodically, and we also broke out red smoke flares in case another boat or plane should appear. The complete loneliness of the trip up the inlet continued, however, as nothing came into sight.

After an hour or so we began to wonder if perhaps the *Pan* call might not be readily recognized by some skippers as a distress call and we switched to *Mayday*. Still no response.

At 3:30 P.M., after slatting around for some five hours, we noted that we were slowly drifting east and south. With depths around 200 fathoms and up to 60 and 70 right up to the shore, we couldn't see too much chance of getting an anchor down and holding. Visions of darkness setting in and the peril of drifting up on the rocks surrounding Tomakstum Island, before catching bottom with the anchor, loomed in our minds.

Suddenly the radio receiver, which had been so ominously quiet for hours, came alive with an answer to our *Mayday* signal from Jim Arniel in his *Flying Cloud*. He said he was a few miles west of Hoeya Sound. We decided he couldn't be of much help to us in his sailboat but he would try to raise someone in Hoeya Sound.

Before long we heard Lee Doud on the air saying he would come out and get us in his *Bellhaven*.

Although Lee is a dry-lander from Denver, he is an ardent yachtsman. He keeps his boat in Seattle and he, his wife and guests spend the summers cruising and fishing in these waters. He is an excellent seaman and, in spite of high seas, he did a masterful job of rescuing us and towing us into Sawchuck's place in Hoeya Sound.

It was a gala night in Hoeya Sound. Crab traps dropped off the float produced a good catch in only minutes, the Douds provided oysters and the Arniels produced luscious barbecued salmon. Everyone was happy but there was little doubt that this skipper and his crew were happiest and most relieved. Gratefulness and appreciation to the Douds and Arniels will never be adequately expressed.

Our good luck held next day when Bill Sawchuck made a trip to Minstrel Island for mail and supplies and towed us to Ernie Rose's shipyard at Lagoon Cove. He thus saved us the possibility of a long wait and the need for arranging a commercial tow. Here, again, adequate appreciation cannot be expressed.

At haul-out we discovered that four bolts through a flange holding the rudder to the rudderpost had sheared off. Fortunately the rudder was still there, hanging in the lower socket. Ernie soon had us back in the water ready to go on our way.

Being towed behind Bill Sawchuck's tug was our first trip through the Blow Hole, the narrow passage between Minstrel Island and East Cracroft Island. A look at the charts might discourage any cautious skipper from negotiating this channel, but we quickly learned it is quite possible if proper precautions are taken. A reef, baring at lower tides, is shown near the lower end. By standing well off the shallow shelf below the Minstrel Island floats, and then keeping a wary eye on the kelp, there is no problem in holding to a center channel. Bill steered a wide course around the reef northeast of the small island between Farquharson Island and Minstrel Island and swung wide around the little island marking the north part of Lagoon Cove. Careful attention to the kelp is all that is needed.

The passage between East and West Cracroft Islands is dry and not navigable. Ernie Rose told us there were no crabs in Lagoon Cove but said that they could be found in the bay behind Dorman and Farquharson Islands. We were so anxious to be on our way that we didn't take time to check this area out but had reports from others that there are crabs there and that it is a delightful and protected anchorage.

Adventuring in Knight Inlet ran the full scale from a taste of possible disaster to the glories of some of the most grandiose and spectacular beauty in the world. A skipper can't really call himself a true Northwest Yachtsman until he has tasted of the magnificent glory which is Knight Inlet.

This spectacular falls is just below Cascade Point.

12
You Can Still Find Solitude

So there was no room at the float and the moorage buoys were all in use or that favorite little cove which had always been so private was crowded with boats. You decided that even our Northwest waterways were getting too crowded and there was no more chance for solitude.

Not so! Although many favorite cruising areas do show signs of overpopulation, there are still miles and miles of inlets and passages with an abundance of forest-clad islands, where you can cruise, sometimes for days without seeing another boat. You may have to go a little farther but with today's faster boats, that's no problem.

Just how long this situation will last is anyone's guess but let's enjoy it while we can.

Continuing our exploration of British Columbia waterways north of Johnstone Strait, we left our base at Minstrel Island to follow a course very nearly that of the one Captain Vancouver sailed in this area in 1792.

After rounding Littleton Point, we crossed Knight Inlet to run through Clapp Passage into Tribune Channel. Big Gilford Island was on our left to the west while Viscount Island lay on the right to the east, separated from a tip of the mainland by Sargeaunt Passage.

Gilford Island was named by Captain Pender in 1868 after Richard James Meade, Viscount Gilford, captain of H.M.S. *Tribune*, a screw frigate from which the channel derives its name. It is probable that Gilford's title also accounts for the name of Viscount Island. He later became admiral of the fleet.

Clapp Passage was named after Edward Scobell Clapp, navigating lieutenant on H.M.S. *Scout* on this station from 1870 to 1873; Captain Pender named Sargeaunt Passage after Frederick Anthony Sargeaunt, R.N., first lieutenant of H.M.S. *Charybdis* on this station from 1868 to 1871. This

passage offered some of the best salmon fishing in the area. While it is quite navigable, shoals on both sides narrow the channel about two-thirds of the way up, and caution should be used.

Our heading took us fairly close to Bamber Point in order to give Humphrey Rock, nearly in mid channel, a wide berth. At the north end of Viscount Island, the channel turns northeastward and then forms a Y, with Tribune Channel continuing to the northwest while Thompson Sound pokes into the mountains to the northeast for about four and a half miles.

Like most of the inlets in this area, Thompson Sound is lined on both sides with steep mountain walls, which continue on down into the water producing depths up to 106 fathoms. Rather than the sharp peaks seen in some places, these are more rounded and deep green. Even in midsummer numerous waterfalls play hide-and-seek in the trees as they tumble down the cliff sides, peeking coyly out for a time, darting back to hide again, and finally dashing into the sea, sometimes quietly, sometimes with a defiant roar. Rocky cuts and valleys are visible, giving evidence of many more waterfalls in the spring.

Approaching the head, Sackville Island appears to separate the deltas of the Kakweiken River and McAllister Creek. To the left is a large house, apparently a farmhouse, while a logging camp and log dump are to the right. The green of the river delta faded into a valley leading to the mountains, shimmering in the sun behind with stringy wisps of cotton candy crowning their heads.

Going into the sound we saw on the left shore what appeared to be snow on the rocks. On the way out we swung in to investigate. It is evidently lime or some mineral deposited by the water coming down from the mountains.

Our charts, marked at Minstrel Island by helpful friends, showed shrimp in the sound but we didn't take the time to check this out. It was back to Tribune Channel for a short northwesterly course, then north for three miles to Irvine Point where it turns westerly.

In this area, on the right, we came upon what we chose to call the "Ghost Forest," a whole hillside of tall, stark white tree trunks raising their ghostly arms threateningly above the green of the shorter second-growth trees. We occasionally saw the results of a forest fire but this was different, with a deathly whiteness rather than the usual burnt brown or charred black.

The smooth beauty of hillsides of evergreens is broken here and there all through the area by the ugly scars of logging. Nature is the great healer, however, covering the wound in a very short time with a new growth of trees.

Bond Sound takes off to the northeast and north for three miles, at the corner where the channel turns west. At the entrance, large rocks on the hillside look like huge dark chunks of Dutch chocolate while, farther in, the lighter brown rocks are like milk chocolate fudge pieces.

At the head, as in most of these finger inlets, a river has carved a valley in the mountains on its way down and built a delta at its mouth. With deep water and a straight shore-line, there are no anchorage possibilities except at the extreme tip where a small bay offers good protection and shallower water. The water of the sound, reflecting the sky, is a robin's egg blue spangled with dancing diamonds.

About one and a half to two miles west in Tribune Channel are two enchanting bays sure to delight the heart of any yachtsman seeking peaceful beauty and solitude. To the left, Wahkana Bay indents the northern shore of Gilford Island for one and a half miles, with a nearly landlocked cove at its head. The walls are high and steep but there are flat places where one can get ashore.

Almost opposite is two-mile-long Kwatsi Bay. Here, too, a cove at the head offers several picturesque, quiet spots for anchorage. It was here that we saw the first boat we'd seen on this section of our journey, a fish boat sitting out the closed days of fishing.

A little farther along the north shore, Watson Cove pokes in between high hills to form a delightful little anchorage, although care must be used to avoid the reef and rock at the entrance off the point. Keeping well to port will give safe passage.

Six miles farther west, we rounded King Point to turn easterly into Viner Sound, leaving Penn Islet and its reefs to starboard. This was to be our anchorage for the night and

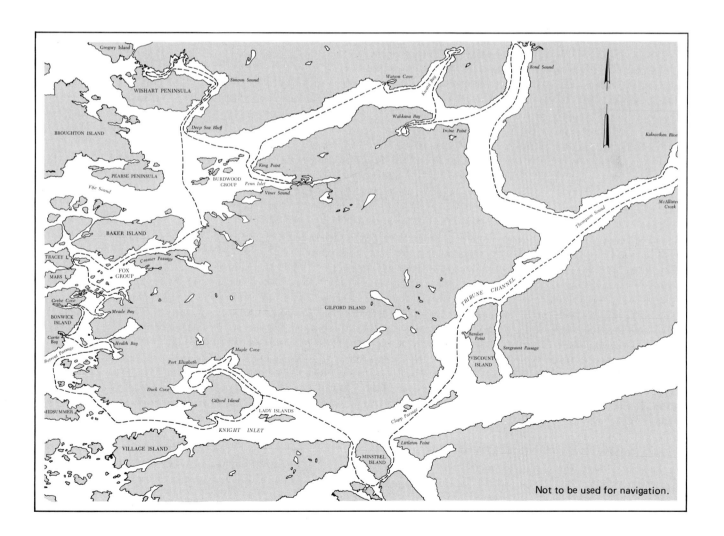

Not to be used for navigation.

we were looking forward to a promised mess of crabs. The long inner finger of the sound has several good anchorages. We chose to set the hook just east of a small island at the entrance to a shallow cove which looked as though it should be a good home for crabs.

This is another of those peaceful, beautiful bays with an engaging charm, a quiet luxurious place where the breezes whisper gently through the firs and cedars above the two-toned waters. We'd really expected to find other boats here but we had it all to ourselves. We were late for a rendezvous with the Jim Arniels in their *Flying Cloud* bringing supplies they'd picked up for us in Alert Bay. The crabs failed to materialize. Either they didn't like our bait or were all outside the cove feeding. We did manage a bucketful of lovely small steamer clams, and our California biologist crew members, John Hopper and Darrell Woods, happily collected innumerable specimens from the tidal pools.

Lying outside Viner Sound and at the western extremity of Tribune Channel are 10 larger islands and many smaller ones, as well as a host of rocks, all called the Burdwood Group. This appeared to offer fascinating exploration possibilities, but our time schedule didn't permit it and we skirted the outside and headed for Simoom Sound around the corner from Deep Sea Bluff.

It was here that Captain Vancouver's ships rendezvoused while their smaller boats explored the multitude of inlets and passages in the vicinity. In his journal he writes, "On the 26th [July], the boundary of the continent was determined to a point, which, from its appearance and situation, obtained the name Deep Sea Bluff."

Simoom Sound is a "bent elbow" sort of waterway. On the left going in is a huge bare rock cliff of many colors of striking beauty. At the elbow is a giant amphitheater with its sides showing some five different shades of green in the rise to the majestic mountains behind.

Around the bend and farther in is McIntosh Bay with islands and several coves, all offering interesting anchorage possibilities. Through a narrow opening, the sound ends in O'Brien Bay, as lovely a spot as one could hope to find. Several seals, sunning themselves on two rock islets, slid into the water before we could get close enough for pictures. We also saw many large blue herons, innumerable ducks and other waterfowl. Eagles had become almost commonplace as we continued to spot them sitting regally in the trees along the shores or soaring gracefully through the air. Simoom Sound, with all this, plus its spectacular scenery, has much to recommend it.

Leaving Simoom Sound, we headed south to Simoom Sound. No, that isn't a typographical error. Paradoxical as it may seem, the waterway called Simoom Sound and the town of Simoom Sound are some miles apart. Perhaps it's because the town (if it can be called a town) is movable, being built entirely on floating logs. It's possible it was originally located in the actual sound and moved south at some time.

The story is told that it has changed location several times. One such tale has it that the daughter of the owner became sick and needed more sunshine; so the little com-

Outboards return to Minstrel from trip to Rivers Inlet.

munity was moved across the bay. They say the weekly supply ship came in and had to search for the village.

At any rate, the village of Simoom Sound plays an important role in the area with its post office, general store, fuel float, blacksmith shop and owner's dwelling. All this is built on huge logs, tied with chains and cables to long boomsticks fastened to the shore and designed to keep the whole town from battering on the rocky beach as the tides rise and fall or as the winter storms buffet it.

To the west and southwest, between the western end of Gilford Island and Queen Charlotte Strait, lies a whole maze of islands, islets, rocks, passages, bays and coves which Captain Vancouver named the Broughton Archipelago in honor of William Robert Broughton, commander of the *Chatham*, who did much of the exploration here. This name has disappeared from the charts, leaving only Broughton Island, to the north, and Broughton Strait to commemorate the man.

Vancouver also named Fife's Passage (now Fife Sound) for the earl of Fife; Duff Point and Duff Islet, at the western end of Fife Sound, for Captain Duff of the Royal Navy; and Gordon Point, across the sound, probably for Alexander, fourth duke of Gordon.

This archipelago in itself provides enough exploration potential to last well over a week. A look at large-scale chart #3576 will show any skipper the vast number of bays

Looking toward Tribune Channel from Wahkana Bay, which indents the northern shore of Gilford Island.

and coves which invite intimate investigation. Unfortunately time didn't permit us to do any exploring here this trip, but it's on an agenda for the near future.

After leaving the civilization of Simoom Sound's floating village, we headed down Cramer Passage, took a quick run into Blunden Passage, around Innis Island and south of the Fox Group, just to get the flavor and mood of this delightful archipelago. Reluctant as we were to leave, we had to push on and so headed down Retreat Passage.

A couple of small, unnamed coves farther down Meade Bay, all on Gilford Island, offer fair anchorages, although somewhat exposed to westerlies. Waddington Bay is behind a large group of islands. On Bonwick Island to the west, as well as at Grebe Cove and Carrie Bay, are excellent places to spend the night, or duck into for lunch or an afternoon siesta. All three only whet the appetite for further exploration in the vicinity.

On a peninsula of Gilford Island, between Meade Bay and Health Bay, is a sizable Indian village with a wharf and float. Its red handrails would seem to indicate it was a government float, although it isn't so charted. Health Bay is fairly large, and open to the west, but could provide some protected anchorage either part way up the lagoon or at the southeastern head. Keep a wary eye and the depth sounder on for the rocks and reefs, however.

Rounding Seabreeze and Henrietta Islands, we turned into Spring Passage and then into the western portion of Knight Inlet. Again to the south and southwest is another fascinating archipelago of large and small islands, rocks, passages, bays and coves apparently just waiting to be explored. Here again we cruised for miles without sighting another ship, even a fishing boat, and the only other sign of civilization, the Indian village.

After entering Knight Inlet it was only five and a half miles to the Lady Islands, lying across the entrance to Port Elizabeth. This is a hooked indentation on the south side of Gilford Island with several attractions. Salmon were reported biting off Gilford Point, and both shrimp and crab can be found here.

We were looking for a quiet spot for a late lunch and Maple Cove was suggested. The usual afternoon westerly was blowing and came right over the low neck separating the bay from Knight Inlet; so Maple Cove wasn't too desirable. We found quiet water in behind one of the three islands just outside of Duck Cove at the head of the bay.

Our crab trap, dropped while we lunched, produced only females and under-limit-size babies with one legal male. He produced enough meat for a luscious crab salad for dinner.

Port Elizabeth was named by Captain Pender after Elizabeth Henrietta, daughter of Sir Arthur Edward Kennedy, G.C.M.G., C.B., governor of Vancouver Island when

This interesting formation is seen looking out from the entrance to O'Brien Bay at the head of Simoom Sound.

the frigate *Tribune* was on this station under the command of Lord Gilford. She was later married to Lord Gilford, and Pender further honored her by naming the Lady Islands after her.

Pender also named Turnour Island, to the south, after Capt. Nicholas Edward Brooke Turnour, commander of H.M. steam corvette *Clio* on this station from 1864 to 1868.

After a bit of unsuccessful fishing in the afternoon in the pass to the west of Minstrel Island, we returned via the Blow Hole to the Minstrel Island landing. Although we had cruised a number of passages and channels, explored a host of picturesque sounds, bays and coves, and enjoyed a wealth of exotic scenery, actually we had only circumnavigated Gilford Island.

This rather limited area produced a wealth of unforgettable items for our memory log and is high on a list for future attention in more detail. The scenic attractions are unrivaled, the bays and coves with good anchorage are almost innumerable, food from the sea is plentiful, and its mood and atmosphere are pleasant.

A couple of words of caution may be appropriate. Lying north of Knight Inlet, it can follow that pattern of clouds and rain. We were lucky and found good weather. Probably, like other places up the coast to Alaska, the earlier summer months are likely to be better than in later summer. Another point is to be sure and take along a full complement of charts, including all the large-scale ones. Cruising through and among the numerous rocks and shoals is easy if you have them, but can be unpleasant, unsafe and even hazardous without them.

If your favorite waters and anchorages are getting too crowded for your enjoyment, try this area. You'll find peace and solitude and be glad you came.

13

King of the Inlets

Kingcome must be the king of them all! More shrimp, largest crabs, best fishing, most spectacular scenery — these were just some of the enticements held out by Larry Norton when he told us not to miss Kingcome Inlet.

While all of the promises weren't fulfilled, the visit to this lovely finger of the sea was a highlight of our exploration of the area.

Leaving Simoom Sound (the waterway, not the village), we took a northwesterly heading through Penphrase Passage, and Shawl Bay, opening up on our starboard, invited exploration. A large float camp marked the entrance to a cove indenting the northwest end of Wishart Peninsula. This cove, as well as one on Gregory Island and a couple along the eastern shore of the bay, offered good anchoring possibilities. A very narrow strip of land is all that separates Simoom Sound's O'Brien Bay from Shawl Bay.

A narrow passage between Gregory Island and the mainland led to Moore Bay and would have cut some distance getting into Kingcome Inlet, but it didn't look too good on the chart and we didn't find out until later that it was passable. We took the caution of going around Gregory Island.

We had been told shrimping was good in Moore Bay; so we dropped anchor in a small cove on Gregory Island in behind Thief Island. The first setting of our trap produced 56 prawn-sized shrimp in 55 fathoms east of Thief Island, in a little over an hour.

Incidentally, there are several uncharted rocks lying about midway on a line from the western end of Thief Island to Thief Rocks. These can make the passage between Thief Island and Thief Rocks dangerous at low tide.

Cruising up Kingcome Inlet, it was eight miles to the entrance of Belleisle Sound, guarded by tiny Edmond Islet.

This is a charming landlocked bit of water surrounded by rounded hills, higher on the north with steep walls and more sloping on the south. With cliffs rising from the water's edge, there was very little shore except in a few small flat spots where grass and wild flowers added to the overall quiet sylvan beauty, scarred occasionally by patches of logging. The dark green of the trees on the hillsides was broken here and there by outcroppings of solid rock.

We couldn't account for the brown water, like dark coffee, in the sound. Good anchorage can be found in the little bay just inside the entrance to the left, in behind the small island along the east shore and at the far end.

It's about eight and a quarter miles from Belleisle Sound's entrance to the float near the head of Kingcome Inlet. Here is another of those spectacular reaches where nature has pulled out all the stops to impress the viewer. Cruising up the mile-wide cut between mountains, one feels a certain intimacy with the sheer cliffs rising from the water in serried ranks to the higher snow-capped peaks behind. Austerity fades and rock faces seem close enough to touch. Hundreds of streams throw themselves down the forest-clothed walls, some dashing in robust cascades over an open patch of dark rock; others, more timid, play hide-and-seek through the trees.

The closer we went to the head of the inlet, the milkier the water became. It was almost opalescent with a kaleidoscopic interchange of emerald, topaz, ruby, amethyst and turquoise, mixing the reflections from the hillsides with the creamy water.

Innumerable waterfowl scurried ahead of our bow or upended their tails to dive beneath the surface. White gulls and little Bonaparte gulls sailed gracefully overhead, while an occasional bald eagle sat regally on his tree top.

Rounding Petley Point, the gorgeous vista of the head of the inlet opens up, with the broad valley of the Kingcome River splitting the high mountains on each side. While the weather had been ideal all the way up, we were being followed by a bank of dark clouds in the west. By the time we were secured to the float and had our shrimp trap set, the storm caught up and emptied the clouds on us.

It rained hard all night. Enough water fell to increase vastly the volume of the many falls and to activate several. One falls dumping into the saltchuck just behind the float increased to a roar which was almost deafening.

Just before dusk we were joined at the float by the *Stuart Post,* a Canadian Department of Fisheries ship, and a little later by Jack Rudell, fisheries patrolman, in his tiny *T-Bay.* From them we learned that our chances of getting any shrimp were rather slim. Commercial shrimpers had been through recently and, since there are no restrictions, they had cleaned everything out. The same thing applied to crabs.

The only bit of optimism we could find in the situation was that, when we pulled up our trap, the bait and most of the mesh were literally swarming with thousands of tiny baby shrimp that looked like maggots. We sent them back to the bottom to grow up with the hope that another time we can beat the commercial boys to the catch. We were certainly in agreement with the fisheries crew that there should be some limiting regulations.

One of our top objectives on this trip was to get upriver the three and a half or four miles to Kingcome Indian Village. Several people had told us about the village and its little Episcopal church with beautiful Indian-carved altar and totems.

Next morning the crew of the *Stuart Post* busied itself making ready an 18-foot flat-bottomed aluminum boat with 65-horsepower Mercury jet outboard. Department of Fisheries officials were expected in by plane for a 9- or 10-mile trip upriver. We watched the plane land, taxi into the float, and the small boat take off.

While they were gone we discussed with Rudell how we could get up to the village. He said it would be most im-

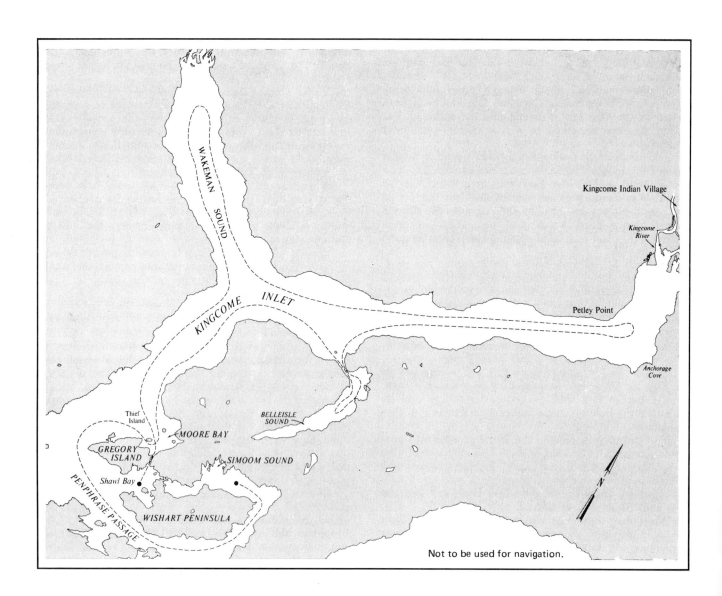

Not to be used for navigation.

practical to take our boat up the river without a pilot. Shifting sandbars, logs, snags and whole trees presented dangers that could only be coped with by someone well acquainted with the river. When asked about using our eight-foot dinghy and three-horsepower outboard, he said we would never make it against the strong current.

A road running from the head of the inlet a mile and a half up to the Halliday Ranch was reported to continue on alongside the river, but it was on the opposite side from the village. It seemed we were completely frustrated in getting to the village. Perhaps if we waited long enough, some yacht with a more powerful outboard would come in and we could hitch a ride.

When the small fisheries boat came back, Jack introduced us to Ray Kraft, an inspector for the Department of Fisheries headquartered at Alert Bay. We plied him with questions about the Indians, their history, the village and carvings in the church.

Suddenly he asked, "Do you want to go up to the village?" When we told him that was one of the main objectives on our cruise, he said he was going up that afternoon and would take us along.

After lunch, three of us, together with Kraft and Rudell, donned life jackets and started upriver in the aluminum boat. We hadn't gone far when we realized the wisdom of Jack's advice of that morning. The river was indeed full of logs, snags, deadheads, and Ray knew where the sandbars were, even under the milky water. The strength of the current was amazing. We were glad we hadn't considered the trip in either the big boat or the outboard.

We passed the Halliday Ranch with its herds of grazing cattle on the flatlands and, a little farther along, came to a sharp right-angled bend in the river. Here was a good-sized logging camp with many mobile homes and a float for seaplanes. Around another bend and three-quarters of a mile upriver was Kingcome Indian Village.

Quee (meaning "Inside Place") is the Indian name for the village. Whoop-Szo ("Noisy Mountain") towers above the village on the other side of the river, while Kingcome Mountain rises majestically behind it. Alders and cotton-

Looking out of Belleisle Sound's narrow entrance into Kingcome Inlet, one sees tiny Edmond Islet guarding the channel.

Episcopal church at Kingcome Indian Village, with the 50-foot totem alongside it.

woods line the river bank above the broad delta at its mouth.

Although the village is very old, only about 100 Indians live there at the present time. They are of the Tsawa-taineuk band of the Kwakiutl tribe. While many of the houses were modern and appeared in good repair, a few looked old, worn and uncared-for. Most of them are built on posts or piles against the time the river floods over its banks.

These are a people who have never been at war with the white man. They live where they have always lived, fish as they have always fished; they were known for their intelligence and a culture that was perhaps the most highly developed of any Indian culture in North America.

As our boat scrunched up on the sandy beach, among several 30- and 40-foot dugout canoes with outboards we were met by a dozen or so Indian children from 4 to 10 years of age. They greeted us gaily with shy smiles but were most anxious to welcome us, answer our questions and act as guides. Ray told us we had about a half hour in which to see the sights. At our request, our guides took us to the church with its 50-foot totem alongside. The Cedar-man stands at the bottom holding up the eagle, wolf and raven. On the way we passed several totem poles of varying sizes, and the charred remains of three houses.

Inside the church we were fascinated by the magnificent carvings on the front of the altar, behind the altar, the chairs on either side of the altar and, finally, the lectern,

which was a golden eagle with wings slightly spread to hold the open Bible.

Leaving the church, we returned to the village center where Ray and Jack were talking with the chief and some of the men about fishing, as they sat on a couple of overturned boats or lolled in the grass. It was here we met Jack James, well-known Northwest Indian carver. Although he has carved innumerable totem poles, his specialty is ceremonial masks and his work is recognized as the finest. He told us that one resident of the village had a large and valuable collection of masks.

Having finished their business, Ray and Jack led the way back to the beach. The children helped push the boat into the water but seemed genuinely sorry to see us go. Our visit with these proud people had been an inspiring experience which will live long in memory.

Those who might sometime visit Kingcome Village or who have an interest in knowing more about these people, their ways of life and their legends, will want to read Margaret Craven's *I Heard the Owl Call My Name*, published by Clarke, Irwin and Company Ltd. of Toronto and Vancouver. Here is a sensitive and poignant story of the Kingcome Indians, which gives a real insight into their thinking, their hopes and fears.

Going back downriver, we stopped at the logging camp where Ray had to see a man. Here we met Allen Halliday, owner of the ranch and the third generation to operate it. He told us that they presently had 109 cattle.

Interior of Episcopal church, with magnificent carvings and the golden eagle lectern.

Jack later told us the story of the original Halliday who was said to have made the trip from the ranch to Victoria each year in a rowboat, to get mail and supplies, taking two months for the journey.

Before returning to the float, Ray swung the boat in for a close look and pictures of the Indian paintings on the rock cliff just above the high-tide mark. Unlike most such paintings and petroglyphs in this area, these are not old. We heard two stories about them. One was that they depicted an Indian, his family and animals as they left this part of the country. The other was that they marked one of the last great tribal potlatches given in 1936.

Back at the float we did our best to express our appreciation to Ray and Jack for making it possible to visit the village and thus achieve our objective. That night the *Stuart Post* and *T-Bay* left for Wakeman Sound and we were soon joined at the float by the *Pamar* of Vancouver.

We were entertained that night by several seals. They would surface and come timidly toward the boat. As long as we pretended not to notice them, they would drift lazily around looking at us, but as soon as we looked at them, they would give a shy little cough and sink below the surface. Try as we might we could never get a good picture of them.

Next morning we left the head of Kingcome Inlet and headed for Wakeman Sound, a body of water which takes off north of Kingcome. It is about five and a half miles to the delta of the Wakeman River and the channel averages about a mile and a half in width. Although surrounded by high snow-capped mountains of spectacular beauty, it can become a rough body of water. Rudell told us there was a float a short way up the river but that it could be a bad place to moor. If there is any wind the float has lots of bounce and is an uncomfortable place to lie.

Again we were struck by the magnificent beauty of the sheer cliffs where the evergreens appeared growing from the solid rock face and the higher snow-covered peaks behind looked benignly down, the whole reflected in the water so perfectly that it was hard to tell where the sea ended and the hills began. Here were hundreds more waterfalls cascading from the snow fields to the saltchuck. Many were hidden until we were directly in front of them.

Instead of milky white water, Wakeman Sound was a dirty, muddy, yellow brown. The water was also full of debris — whole trees, logs and lots of small stuff. About halfway up we met the *T-Bay* coming down and as we swung around the head we could see the *Stuart Post* at the float. We decided to head back to Moore Bay for the night and another shrimp feast.

We caught up with and passed the *T-Bay* just outside Moore Bay. Jack was reading at the wheel and didn't realize we had passed him until our wake disturbed the serenity of his cruising. As we dropped anchor in our favorite little cove, we were surprised to see the *T-Bay* heading for the narrow cut we thought was impassable.

Our shrimping was again successful. Evidently the com-

These Indian paintings are on a rock face just above the high-tide mark at the head of Kingcome Inlet.

mercial shrimpers had passed up this bay. After another delicious shrimp dinner and an evening of watching the seals play in the bay, we spent a quiet night.

Next morning we were hardly out of our bunks before the *T-Bay* was alongside. Jack had come back from Shawl Bay to show us how to go through the cut. He showed us on the chart where there is a shoal just inside the pass on the left. A short distance farther in there is a rock in the middle. Neither of these is shown on the chart, but when a skipper is aware of them he can make the passage easily. We followed the *T-Bay* closely and had no trouble.

So, with the help and advice of good friends like Ray Kraft and Jack Rudell, we had made our exploration of Kingcome Inlet, Belleisle Sound, Wakeman Sound and Moore and Shawl Bays. Kingcome Inlet was named for Vice Adm. Sir John Kingcome by Captain Pender in 1865. Kingcome was commander in chief in this area on the flagship *Sutlej* from 1863 to 1864. He was also captain of H.M.S. *Belleisle* and H.M. Troopship *Simoom* which account for those names in the area. Wakeman Sound was named by Pender after Plowden Wakeman, an Englishman who was a clerk in the naval dockyard at Esquimalt.

All of the promises about Kingcome Inlet didn't come true, yet, all in all, it had been a most gratifying part of our cruise and we agree with Larry Norton that it shouldn't be missed. Its grandeur can't be surpassed, and skippers looking for pleasant cruising that's different will want to include it in an itinerary in the near future.

14
Exploration in Quiet Waters

Shawl bay was covered with a light shawl of fog but the morning sun burned it off rapidly. It was just over a mile across Penphrase Passage to the entrance of Sir Edmund Bay. In that short span of travel the day awoke to its full August glory with the emerald sea spangled in a play of gold and diamonds and the surrounding mountains shimmering in the sun.

Sir Edmund Bay and its Nicholls Island offer several pleasant anchorages in three coves. The several rocks and shoals are well charted.

Still heading northwestward in our exploration of the inlets, channels and waterways of Johnstone Strait, we next rounded Hayes and Moore Points to enter Sharp Passage with Stackhouse Island on our starboard. Here, indenting the north shore of Broughton Island, is a charming bay or group of bays and coves called Cypress Harbor. The safe entrance channel is about 500 feet wide with Fox Rock and its surrounding shoal on the right. Inside one has a choice of Miller Bay, Berry Cove or Stopford Bay for as delightful a group of anchorages as could be desired.

Into Sutlej Channel and around Walker Point, Greenway Sound opens up and, with Carter Passage, separates Broughton from North Broughton Island. This six-mile-long L-shaped sound with its islands has several coves suitable for anchoring, and Carter Passage is navigable for nearly a mile.

Farther up Sutlej Channel, little Cartwright Bay has a hooked end with two and a half fathoms of water for a nice anchorage.

Around Sullivan Point about three-quarters of a mile is Sullivan Bay, population two. A Standard Oil fuel facility, store, post office, house, several shed-type buildings and a rental cabin, making up the "village," are on float logs with long logs holding the entire assembly off the rocky shore.

Presided over by Jack and Dorothy Germaine, Sullivan Bay, like Minstrel Island and Simoom Sound, is an important center for the surrounding area and a fascinating place to visit. One catches the great sense of humor of the inhabitants, even before landing, through such signs as "Parking in the Rear," "Keep Off the Grass" and "Aquarium Rest Rooms."

The Germaines have been at Sullivan Bay for 14 years. Dorothy has a green thumb and raises many varieties of beautiful flowers, some of them rare and unusual. These grow all around the "village" but mostly around the house. Flowers aren't all, however, for in back of the house on a large float is a vegetable garden. She's happy to show you her garden of peas, beans, carrots, lettuce, onions, parsley, raspberries, strawberries and "two boatloads of potatoes" — a couple of old skiffs holding the soil for the potatoes. All of the garden soil had to be hauled from shore.

As a midway fueling stop for many planes to and from Alaska and a supply center and post office for the area, Sullivan Bay is a busy place, especially during the summer months. Jack keeps busy on the fuel float and Dorothy in the store and post office. One wonders when there is any time for gardening, yet they both are always relaxed, ready to talk and visit or exchange a good joke.

We had planned Mackenzie Sound as our next objective but, when we discovered the time was just about right for Stuart Narrows into Drury Inlet, we changed our itinerary. Someone had warned us that the rapids in these narrows should be run only at slack. A fisherman at Sullivan Bay told us one-half to three-quarters of an hour off slack was safe enough.

It was 5:35 P.M. when we entered the narrows with a

Top: Roaringhole Rapids are well named and passable only at slack tide. Bottom: Sullivan Bay, with population of two, is a float town built entirely on logs. It serves the surrounding area with supplies and post office.

slack at 6:20 P.M. We experienced no trouble, although the current was strong enough to throw us around a bit and make for difficult steering. Large-scale chart #3557 gives one a good feeling going through here.

From the chart we couldn't figure out why our fisherman friend had advised us to leave Welde Rock to port going into the inlet. There appeared to be plenty of water on either side but we followed the advice just in case some rock or reef was not charted. The unnamed island just south of the rock was difficult to recognize until we were nearly up to it.

As we continued westward the hills and mountains were noticeably lower the closer we got to Queen Charlotte Strait. Drury Inlet has several coves and bays, many of them with small islands, thus offering a host of anchoring possibilities.

We chose Jennis Bay for our overnight stop, dropping the anchor in about two fathoms in the northern cove. It wasn't long before we saw a couple of old pilings just under the surface of the water. Not wishing to have the tide drop us on one of these, we moved out from shore a bit. It seemed like a good spot for crabs, but apparently the parents sent the kids out to investigate our trap, for small ones were all we caught and we sent them back to grow up.

Drury Inlet proper ends at Sutherland Bay in behind the Muirhead Islands. The waterway itself continues, however, in a generally northerly and northeasterly direction through a most interesting series of passages, bays, sounds and lagoons. Passages are narrow, there is a wealth of rocks, and reefs, and shoals and currents can be tricky. Actually, local knowledge is desirable, but for the adventuresome skipper who uses due caution the rewards are great. The remoteness of the area and the majestic beauty of slim blue green ribbons of water — dotted with islets — winding between forest-clad hills produces a quiet peacefulness which makes one forget the rush and tensions of civilization.

Leaving Drury Inlet north of the Muirhead Islands, entrance to Actress Passage is between Dove Island and Charlotte Point with private beacons to help and a mid-channel course recommended between island and point.

The elbow past Skeene Bay is tricky but well charted. Actaeon Sound, including Creasy Bay, offers no great problems. But currents run fairly strong on the bull tides and there are rapids at the head of the sound in the narrow passage. Although the chart shows a least depth of two feet going into Tsibass Lagoon, we didn't venture into this northernmost tip. Tsibass Lagoon, as well as Bond Lagoon, with an entrance passage which dries at three feet, seemed to offer excellent opportunities for dinghy exploration.

Leaving the beauties of Drury Inlet, we ran Stuart Narrows exactly on the morning slack, rounded Pandora Head and swung in for a quick inspection of Carriden Bay. This, and Claydon Bay, a mile farther up Grappler Sound, offer good, protected anchorages.

In entering Claydon Bay, passage should be kept well toward the left shore to avoid the reef and rocks which extend over halfway across the opening.

It seems about time for another survey vessel to make a trip through this area and honor some more people by using

Blunden Harbor marked the western limit of our explorations. The derelict lying on the beach is an abandoned fishing boat.

their names. There are a number of points, several bays and innumerable islands which are unnamed, at least on our charts.

As an example, Grappler Sound runs up to a narrow passage between Watson Point and an unnamed point, and then widens into an unnamed bay. An unnamed passage runs east into another unnamed bay which may be considered a part of Kenneth Passage.

Just below Watson Point are a house and sawmill. Charlie and Ivey Kilbourn live here and always extend a welcome hand to yachtsmen. They love company, are grand people and have plenty of water if the ship's tanks are getting low.

At the head of Grappler Sound is an overflow basin with one of those interesting reversing tidal falls which flow out on an ebbing tide and reverse themselves to flow in on a flooding tide. On the west is Embley Lagoon, a very shallow but extensive bay.

Turning eastward we entered that unnamed bay. Turnbull Cove is a delightful little bay, fairly shallow and nearly landlocked, which lies off the northwest corner. Taking off to the northeast through narrow Roaringhole Rapids is Nepah Lagoon, an extensive waterway running north for some four miles.

These rapids are passable only at slack and are well named for they really roar when the tidal waters pour in or out of the lagoon. We didn't go in since it would have been necessary to stay in until the next slack.

Kenneth Passage into Mackenzie Sound provides a very scenic trip. Narrow channels thread between granite rocks and low round islands, which seem a part of the mainland shoreline until they suddenly detach themselves momentarily and then merge again with the green wooded shore, when we'd look astern to try to relate them to the islands on the chart.

The passage takes a bit of careful piloting but there's really no problem with large-scale chart #3557 on board,

and the beauty compensates for those few anxious moments when you wonder if you've swung far enough to clear that rock. Many scurrying mink along the shores were our only company.

We left Kenneth Passage and rounded Claypole Point just in time to get a fleeting glimpse of the glories that lay ahead of us in Mackenzie Sound before a dark and menacing cloud slid down the hillsides and soon drenched us with a heavy rainstorm.

Turning into Burly Bay we anchored near the head. Our quick look into Mackenzie Sound made us decide this country was too beautiful to be explored in the rain so we would wait out the weather. Our lay day was spent doing little housekeeping chores and jobs that didn't require going outside. The rain continued to pour down all that night and most of the next day.

In the late afternoon a mother bear and her cub put on a show for us. Lumbering out of the woods, they explored the low-tide beach carefully. While baby played, mother turned over rocks and logs presumably looking for little crabs and other sea life. Occasionally baby would try to help but mother didn't appreciate this and sent him sprawling with a cuff from her powerful forepaw. The show lasted for at least a half hour before they disappeared back into the woods. We also were visited by several seals who cavorted around the boat for a time but left when they apparently didn't care for our food offerings.

We were intrigued all day by the roar of a falls which was invisible behind the blanket of low clouds and fog that hid the cliff to the east. When the murky haze finally lifted we could see the straight rock-faced wall with a few scattered hardy evergreens, living a precarious life grasping for a mountain climber's toehold in tiny crevices. About halfway up the sheer cliff a bare flat rock stood out to frame a 100-foot bridal veil falls before it plunged into the trees to disappear again.

Next morning the rain clouds were gone and we continued our exploration to the head of Mackenzie Sound. The sun shone and this finger of the sea, carpeted by sparkling water and walled by forested slopes of lovely green merging with naked cliffs of warm rose, dusky browns and deep blues, was comfortable, intimate and inviting. It was a northland fairyland, seemingly placed there for our personal and private enjoyment.

A river, emptying from mile-distant Mackenzie Lake, forms a lovely valley and a delta at the head; a small falls pours into the saltchuck to the right. A mile and a quarter back from the head on the north shore is tiny Tee Bay, a pretty little one-boat basin. Three-quarters of a mile to the west, T-shaped Nimmo and Little Nimmo Bays offer sylvan anchorages. Depths are not great but sufficient except on minus tides. A waterfall in Little Nimmo Bay is noisy but almost invisible in its cloak of greenery.

Returning to Sullivan Bay for a refill of the water tanks, supplies and mail, we swung in between Watson Island and Kinnaird Island for a look into Hopetown Bay. The rocks west of Hopetown Point looked like gigantic stepping stones. The bay with its Indian settlement has several anchorage possibilities. Hopetown Passage, running into Burly Bay and Mackenzie Sound, is narrow and shallow but can be negotiated, except at low tide, if caution is used.

While we were tied up at Sullivan Bay, our good friends Les and Babe Simmers came in their beautiful *Vandal*. They were headed for Turnbull Cove to visit Owen and Clara Lane and insisted we join them. In our quick survey of the cove we had seen the rather extensive Lane spread — all on float logs. It was with real pleasure that we accepted the Simmers' invitation.

Lane is a logger with a big operation on Huaskin Lake, north of Turnbull Cove. We were fascinated by the intricate system of cables, elevators, blocks and tackles, to bring the logs from the lake down to the saltchuck. It would be impossible to describe adequately the hospitality of these wonderful people. Clara's family-style dinner was out of this world, and listening to Owen and his first lieutenant, Pepper Kilbourn, discuss the details of their logging operation was an education in itself.

While we were at the Lanes' the rains returned. We spent the next two days tied to the Lanes' floats. On the second day Les took us in his small boat over to Embley Lagoon. Here is an extensive lagoon with a river flowing into its head. Les told us that a year earlier 50,000 humpback salmon had gone up the river to spawn. We followed the bear trail upriver but didn't see a single humpy. The falls and river were beautiful and well worth the trip.

Coming out of the lagoon we met Mr. and Mrs. Bruce Collinson. He is a fisheries department patrolman and gave us considerable information about the fishing picture in this area. We found that the Collinsons live in Helen Bay in Drury Inlet, not where you'd expect to find them, in Collinson Bay. Checking back on our marked charts, we found a pencilled notation at Helen Bay: "Collinson's — Water." They formerly were the proprietors at Sullivan Bay.

Next day Les suggested we head for Blunden Harbor for a mess of crabs. With a grateful "thanks" to the Lanes for a most pleasant couple of rainy days' layover, we head-

Tree burial on Byrnes Island, an Indian tribal custom.

ed out Wells Passage into Queen Charlotte Strait. The several bays on the west side of the passage are not of much interest but there are at least six likely anchorages on the east side, in addition to Tracey Harbor with its Napier Bay and a few inviting coves.

Les and the *Vandal* led the way past James Point Light and Boyles Point into the open strait. We went well out toward the Numis Islands to avoid the Lewis Rocks where Vancouver's *Discovery* went aground.

The strait, where fog and gales are an ever-present threat, was calm and almost flat. We headed northwest through LaBouchere Passage, past the Raynor Group of islands, to the entrance to Blunden Harbor. Leaving Siwiti Rock to starboard, we rounded Shelf Head, Brandon Point and Bartlett Point, with attention to a couple of charted rocks. We anchored between Byrnes Island and the eastern end of Robinson Island.

Our first interest was Byrnes Island, a tribal burial island where some of the local Indians still put their dead in boxes in the trees. A fairly large Indian village on the shore east of Byrnes Island is unoccupied. The commercial crabbers had beat us, so legal-sized crabs were nonexistent. Clamming was excellent, however, on the sand beach between Robinson Island and the mainland peninsula.

Blunden Harbor marked the western extremity of our explorations. Our investigation of the inlets and waterways north of Johnstone Strait had resulted in an extremely interesting summer. Those searching for peace, quiet and uncluttered bays and coves, will find them in these areas. True, the weather can be cloudy, and even rainy, for days at a time, but this doesn't seem to detract from the many features of this untouched wonderland which looks the

Deserted Indian village at Blunden Harbor, left, as seen from Byrnes Island. Right: a view at the head of Mackenzie Sound.

same to the twentieth century yachtsman as it did to Vancouver and his crew nearly 200 years ago. And there are nice days, too.

If the more civilized areas are getting too crowded for you, these waters are your answer. In them you'll find the cruising of your dreams.

GLOSSARY OF PLACE-NAMES

Philip Point—By Captain Vancouver, 1792, after Sir Philip Stephens, secretary to the Admiralty at that date. (Stephens Mountain, same source.)

Pasley Passage—By Captain Pender, 1864, after Capt. Russell Graves Sabine Pasley, R.N., flag lieutenant to Rear Adm. John Kingcome.

Stackhouse Island—After Capt. Thomas Stackhouse, who was lieutenant on H.M.S. *Sutlej,* flagship of Rear Admiral Kingcome.

Sutlej Channel—After Rear Admiral Kingcome's flagship, H.M.S. *Sutlej.*

Grappler Sound—After H.M. gunboat *Grappler,* in service in this area, 1860-1868.

Watson Island—After Alexander Watson, native of Scotland. He was colonial treasurer of Vancouver Island, 1866. and general inspector of the Bank of British Columbia.

Kenneth Passage—By Captain Pender, 1865, after Kenneth Mackenzie, eldest son of Kenneth Mackenzie of Craigflower farm near Victoria. In 1866, he became clerk of the naval yard at Esquimalt and held that position for 39 years.

Mackenzie Sound—Not recorded but probably after either Kenneth Mackenzie or William Blair Mackenzie, son of Kenneth Mackenzie of Craigflower farm.

Burly Bay—By surveying staff of *Beaver,* 1865, after William Blair Mackenzie, who was generally known to his relatives and friends as "Burly."

Embley Lagoon—By Captain Pender, 1865, after Embley Park, Hampshire, the seat of William Edward Nightingale, father of Florence Nightingale.

Drury Inlet—By Captain Pender, 1865, after Adm. Byron Drury, R.N., who had last command of the *Pandora* on the Pacific.

Blunden Harbor—By Captain Pender, 1863, after Edward Raynor Blunden, R.N. He was master's assistant of the H.M. surveying vessel *Hecate,* 1861, and second master of H.M. hired surveying vessel *Beaver.*

Wells Passage—By Captain Vancouver, 1792, after Adm. Sir John Wells, R.N., in service for over 65 years.

Sir Edmund Bay (and point)—By Captain Pender, 1864, after the Right Honorable Sir Edmund Walker Head, governor of the Hudson's Bay Co., 1863-1868.

Broughton Island—By Captain Vancouver, 1792, after Lt. Comdr. William Robert Broughton, in charge of the armed tender *Chatham,* companion vessel to Vancouver's *Discovery* while exploring these waters.

Siwiti Rock—By Commander Parry, 1903, after the hereditary name of the principal chief of the Nakwak-to tribe residing in Blunden Harbor.

15
Going After Salmon

by Ronald W. Miller

For eight days each summer we have trailered our boats to Vancouver Island, launched at Campbell River or Kelsey Bay and headed down Retreat Passage toward a favorite fishing hole to catch salmon, salmon and more salmon. The "we" of these summer trips, and many others from British Columbia to Lower Baja, is a compatible group: Art Anderson, manager of a dental supply house in Yakima, Washington, Jim Houle, a dentist from Pleasanton, California, and myself, a full-time boater and part-time dentist in Yakima.

Art's crew is usually his father, a very fine smoker of salmon and small oysters and a lover of "moose milk," tasty items never in short supply aboard the Anderson boat.

Dr. Don Ainsworth from Livermore, California, and Pete, Jim's son, make a crew in the Houles' rig. Ainsworth was so enthused after a few trips that he bought a 20-foot I/O, so our cruising group is growing.

In addition to my son Mark, Tom Moore, owner of a dry cleaning business in Yakima, has been my first mate for many years. He caught the infectious disease called "owning a boat" last summer and sprung for a new 20-foot I/O. It will be hard for me to find a new ship's cook, salmon netter and filleter and expert mixer of anything liquid from coffee to Old Stump Blower. His cut of cloth is not spun very often.

In our six years of fishing this area of Johnstone Strait, Queen Charlotte Sound and Knight Inlet in small boats, some definite do and do-nots have developed. If a trailerboater has a time limit, it makes good sense to eliminate as much large water as possible — and in my book the Gulf of Georgia qualifies as large water. So we ferry our trailerboats from Horseshoe Bay at Vancouver, B.C., to Nanaimo. The cost for one of our rigs is about $20 each way.

Once on the island, an excellent paved highway leads 150 miles north to Kelsey Bay. Facilities at Kelsey are limited, but there is a hotel and a crude launching area about half a mile up the river. Launching should be within an

First mate Tom Moore shows off a couple of 30-pound fish.

Heading down Retreat Passage toward a favorite, and secret, fishing hole to catch salmon, salmon and more salmon.

hour of the high tide to insure enough water in the river to run the boats, so we pick a vacation date when high tide at Kelsey Bay and 3:00 A.M. coincide. But even on full flood the river channel must be followed accurately.

By trailing to Kelsey Bay we eliminate all but 10 to 12 miles of Johnstone Strait, a body of water with a reputation for mixing wind and tidal currents in just the correct proportions for lumps and bumps. In six years of running the strait, we have never had to hole up due to rough water, but a couple of times we traveled mighty slow. During periods of extreme tidal variation, Johnstone is filled with driftwood, logs and even whole trees, so a constant eye on the water is essential.

Johnstone Strait seems to divide the weather. Many times we have found the Knight Inlet side to be cloudy and weathered-in, while on the Vancouver Island side the sun was bright and warm. The local people refer to this area north of Johnstone as "the jungle" because of the constant clouds, fog and rain. We have learned to accept the low clouds, and even the rain, without complaint because most clear days are accompanied by wind that comes up and goes down with the sun and creates a nasty chop on the water.

By midmorning the day after we leave Yakima we are fishing in our favorite hole, the exact location of which we do not divulge. Lawrence Rose, genial owner of the Minstrel Island general store, thinks he knows where we fish and we are content to let him think so. Lawrence runs a very complete grocery (excellent meats), fishing supplies, rain gear, gas and oil — you name it and he has it. The only shortage we have ever found at Minstrel is fresh water during a dry summer. Don't ask for fresh water more than once during these periods of shortage.

Fishing in this area is an exacting challenge. For best results one must fish in just the correct location. Over the years I have observed close to 500 salmon hooked and landed in this general area, and at least 95 percent have been caught in an area 300 yards long and 50 yards wide. This narrow fishing hole borders right on the shoreline amid the kelp beds, so a large inboard cruiser is not the best boat for salmon hunting. Outboards or I/Os from 18 to 23 feet are ideal.

The first light of day and the gathering darkness of night are the productive times, with the midday hours a total waste as far as salmon catching is concerned. By midmorning we stop fishing, stow our rods and beach our boats on a pea gravel beach. We retrieve our plywood tables from the bush above the high-tide line and set up a production line for filleting and packaging our fresh-caught salmon.

This is also the time for crab catching, barbecuing, picture taking, story telling and dispensing Old Stump Blower. We are back to fishing by six o'clock and continue until darkness blots out our rod tips.

Salmon caught are mostly springs, which are kings under 30 pounds; and tyees, which are kings over 30 pounds. Coho comprise a small part of the catch. The 20- to 30-pounders are common, 40-pounders are occasional, and we once caught a 52-pounder. The daily limit is four salmon with a possession limit of eight.

Our Canadian trip last summer included our wives and children and we followed Captain Vancouver to the west side of the island and into Nootka Sound. But where he sailed around the north tip of the island, we simply took our versatile trailerboats by road to Gold River and then out Muchalat Inlet to Nootka. But that's another story.

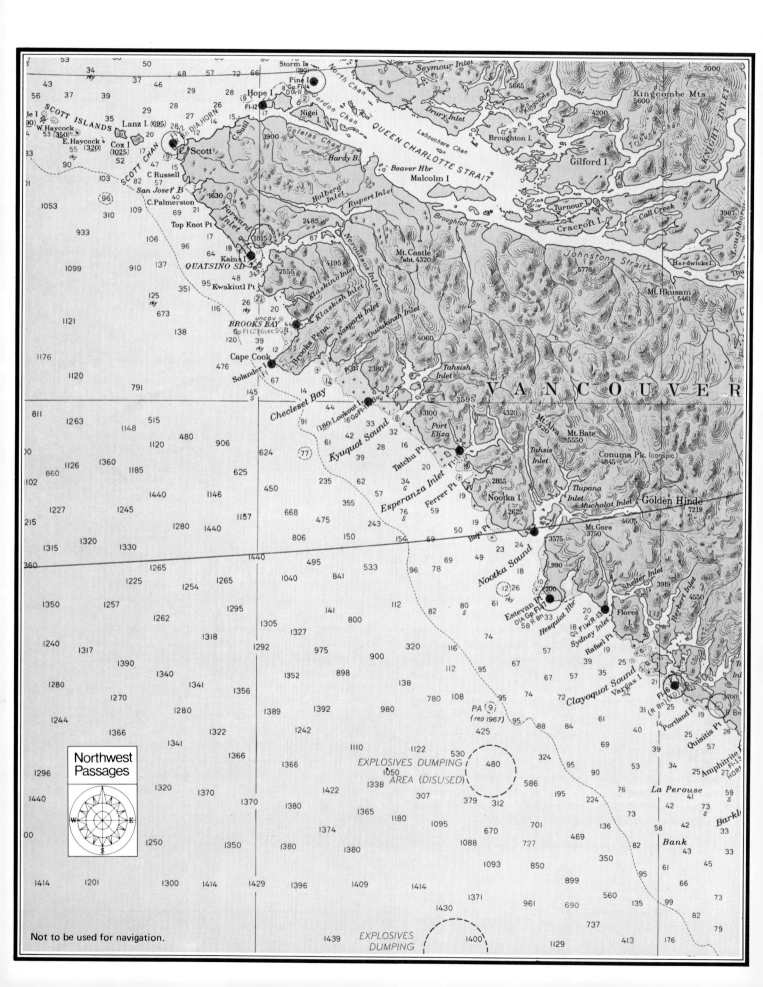

Northwest
Passages

Not to be used for navigation.

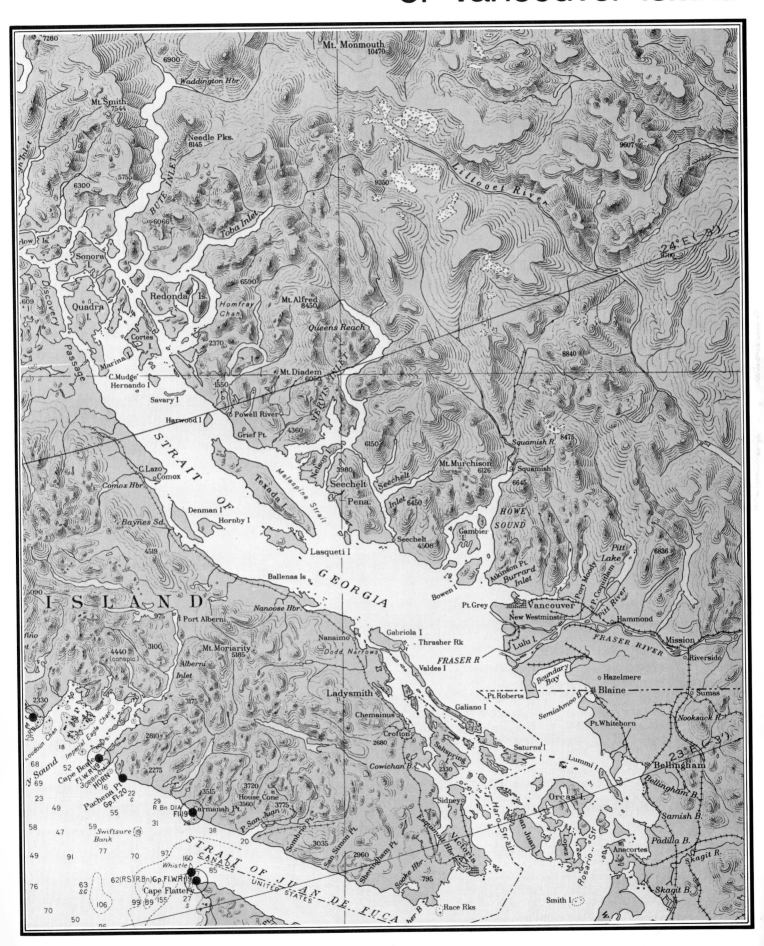

16

The Indians Called
It Wickaninnish

Wickaninnish has a musical sound which rolls easily off the tongue. Originally the name of a famous Indian chief who ruled the Clayoquots many years ago, it now names an island and a bay on Vancouver Island's western shore – the Pacific Ocean side.

The bay is the site of Long Beach, one of the most beautiful and interesting beaches on the Northwest coast. Its white sand, a quarter of a mile wide and extending some six miles, is continuously washed by the surf. When the Pacific whips into a storm, it is an awesome sight to watch as the tremendous breakers roll in.

All sorts of "loot," from Japanese glass balls to parts of wrecked ships, brought in by the tide, make the place a paradise for beachcombers. It's easy to understand why the old chief made his summer home here. The abandoned villages and burial grounds of his tribe provide an endless variety of places to explore.

Although the bay qualifies by definition, it is not a place for the yachtsman to find shelter. Lying midway between Ucluelet and Tofino, it can be reached from either place by road, the only place in British Columbia where a road actually goes to the open Pacific Ocean.

Smaller Florencia Bay, named after a ship wrecked there, and formerly called Wreck Bay, lies just to the east. Here is another sandy beach two miles long where gold has been panned. It is a fine pastime for visitors but amounts are not sufficient for profit. Large Dungeness crabs and razor clams are found at low tide on both beaches.

Quisitis Point, separating the two beaches, marked the start of our exploration of Vancouver Island's west side. We were aboard Serge and Maggie Becker's Newporter ketch *Ocean Cape.*

West of Long Beach is Schooner Cove, again offering little or no protection but containing some interesting petroglyphic carvings on a cliff of rock. From here up to the entrance to Clayoquot Sound, the coast takes on its more typical rugged, rock-strewn character.

Originally named Wickaninnish Sound by Captain Barkley in 1787, the name was changed to Clayoquot Sound by Captain Richards in 1861. The word comes from the Indian Cla-o or Tla-o (meaning "different") and aut ("people"). Legend has it that the natives, who were quiet and peaceful, later became vicious and warlike; so neighboring tribes called them Cla-o-quots (people who were different or had changed).

The sound has three main arms and four or five lesser ones with Meares Island, named by Richards for Capt. John Meares, dominating the center while Vargas Island, named by Galiano after the Spanish governor in Mexico, and the larger Flores Island, named in 1791 by Eliza after the Viceroy of Mexico, protect the inner waters from the Pacific. Smaller islands along with a goodly supply of rocks, reefs and bars dot the waters of the various inlets.

The town of Tofino is on the northern tip of Esowista Peninsula. As western terminus of the Trans-Canada Highway, it is a fishing and logging center, a good source of supplies, and has a life-saving station. Although fairly well protected, the waters surrounding the harbor are full of rocks and shallow areas, so a large-scale chart and plenty of caution are called for.

Browning Passage and Tsanee Narrows lead to Tofino Inlet and its offshoot, Tranquil Inlet, both poking their scenic way into ever-higher-and-higher mountains. Several charming coves and bays offer the yachtsman enjoyable anchorages and a pleasant reward for careful navigation in passing through the narrow and rocky channels to get there.

Skirting the east side of Meares are Dawley Passage and Fortune Channel with several more cozy anchorages, including Mosquito Harbor and Warn Bay. Directly north of Meares Island is Bedwell Sound, one of the three main arms. A little to the west and around a point are Quait Bay, Cypress Bay, with several attractive coves, and Hecate Bay. Below Saranac Island on the northwest portion of Meares Island is Ritchie Bay. All of these are popular anchorages and delightful spots for the visiting yachtsman.

Lemmens Inlet nearly cuts Meares Island in two and has several little coves, all well protected. Near the entrance and facing Tofino is the Indian town of Opitsaht.

Main entrance to Clayoquot Sound is guarded by the Lennard Island Light. It and Wickaninnish Island with its satellite, separate Templar Channel and Father Charles Channel. Lennard Island was named after Captain Barrett-Lennard; Templar Channel after his yacht; and Father Charles Channel after Father Charles Moser, the priest who succeeded the Reverend A. J. Brabant, West Vancouver Island's first missionary.

To the northwest, on the other side of Vargas Island, is another entrance to the sound leading to the western arms consisting of Herbert Inlet, Shelter Inlet and Sydney Inlet. Matilda, Holmes and Stewardson are smaller inlets off these larger arms. Bawden Bay, Whitepine Cove, Gibson Cove, Moyeha Bay and Bedingfield Bay, along with a few unnamed coves, are all lovely spots on Herbert Inlet with good anchorages and plenty of scenic cruising.

Several hundred gold claims were staked in this area during the 1930s, and when the pilchard industry was at its height, about the same time, there were six reduction plants operating in these inlets. Very little gold ore was produced, and the pilchards disappeared. Today there is no evidence of either of these activities as nature seems to have reclaimed the forested shores.

On the southeast corner of Flores Island, Matilda Inlet, named for a British trading schooner of the 1860s, is the site of Ahousat, an Indian village. The small white settlement of Ahousat is on Matilda Creek. The Ah-ous-aht tribe originally lived on the ocean-shore side of Flores Island. With 2960-foot Mount Flores behind them, they were given this name meaning "people living with their backs to the mountains."

Millar Channel and Hayden Pass, running up the east side of Flores Island, connect Herbert Inlet with Shelter Inlet. Sydney Inlet is the westernmost arm of the sound. Here again, several coves on Obstruction Island, Riley Cove, Steamer Cove, Dixon Bay and Young Bay, as well as the heads of the inlets, provide a wide variety of safe and interesting anchorages for an afternoon, a night, or a week.

At the entrance to Sydney Inlet is not only an excellent harbor but one of nature's wonders. Formerly known as Refuge Cove, the name was changed so as not to conflict with the Refuge Cove in Desolation Sound. Now known as Hot Springs Cove, it has become a well-known port in this area.

The name is authentic, too, for a mile and a half from the settlement's floats, over a winding trail, is a hot spring, one of the few in this region. With a temperature of slightly

Dominating the shoreline path, the 30-foot-high Governor-General's totem is a main attraction at Friendly Cove.

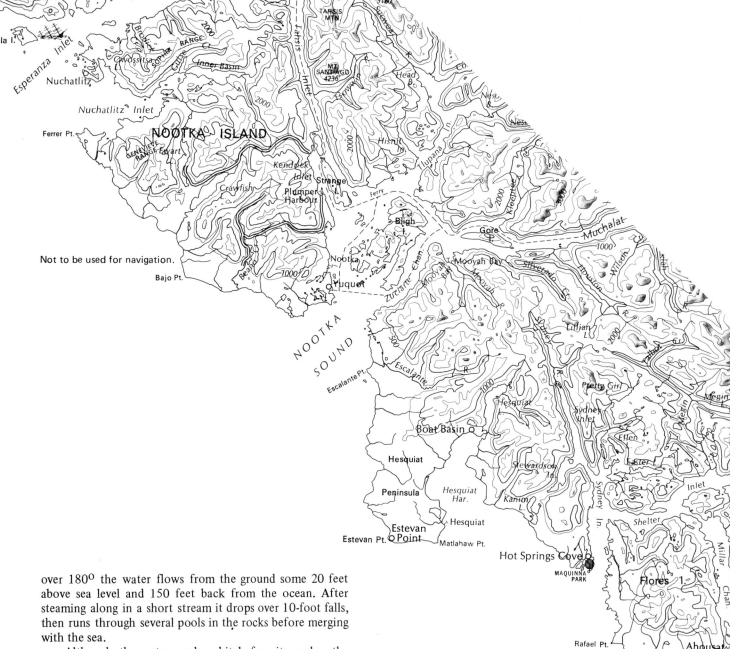

Not to be used for navigation.

over 180° the water flows from the ground some 20 feet above sea level and 150 feet back from the ocean. After steaming along in a short stream it drops over 10-foot falls, then runs through several pools in the rocks before merging with the sea.

Although the water cools a bit before it reaches the falls, it is not cool enough for a comfortable shower. By the time it reaches the pools, however, it is just right for a bath. Containing sulphur and several other curative elements, the water was used by the Indians before the white man came. Today Indians still come, along with local residents, old prospectors, fishermen and visitors from afar, to bathe and wash clothes.

The cove is about two miles long. Some 20 white and an equal number of Indian families make up the permanent population but during the fishing season this is considerably increased. Ivan H. Clarke established the original trading post in a tent and today his children continue to operate the store, fuel dock and fish-buying business. Mr. and Mrs. Clarke donated the 35 acres for undeveloped Maquinna Park through which the trail to the hot springs goes.

In addition to being a perfect vacation spot, Clayoquot Sound with its sandy beaches, coves and bays, unexcelled scenery and protected waters teeming with clams, oysters and geoducks, offers the cruising yachtsman both adventure and a challenge. The settlement of Clayoquot on Stubbs Island, across from Tofino, is the oldest permanent white community on Vancouver Island's west coast. The people of the entire area are most hospitable and extend every possible courtesy to visiting yachtsmen.

Along the coast to the northwest is famous Estevan Point named by Capt. Juan Perez, in 1774, for his second lieutenant, Estevan Jose Martinez. This point, called Breakers Point four years later by Captain Cook, was renamed Estevan on the Admiralty chart of 1849. The light is one of the most important on the Northwest coast.

It was near Estevan Point that Captain Perez in *Santiago* gave the Indians their first look at white men. Although no landing was made, it was on the basis of this contact that Spain based her claim to these lands, which were later relinquished to Britain through Captain Vancouver.

Estevan Point also achieved a measure of fame as the only place in Canada which was fired upon by an enemy in World War II. A Japanese submarine shelled the lighthouse on June 20, 1942. There was no damage to the light or radio station and only a few of the buildings were hit by fragments from the approximately 25 shells fired.

In the lee of the point is Hesquiat Bay, a good, protected bay with a rock-cluttered entrance. Here is located the Hesquiat Indian Village, which was the site for the Reverend Brabant's first mission. The Hesquiats are a subtribe of the Nootkas. Anchorage may be found here, although the entrance is a bit foul.

After rounding Estevan Point in a calm sea without enough wind to fill the sails, anticipation ran high. Nootka Sound in general, and Friendly Cove in particular, were places we had long wanted to visit. It was on March 29, 1778, that Captain Cook in the barque *Resolution* entered Nootka Sound. The next day he went ashore at Friendly Cove. The first European to land on the Northwest coast of America, he claimed this part of North America for England.

Friendly Cove, called Yuquot by the Indians, became the historical center from which the entire Northwest developed. The Spaniards came eleven years after Cook and occupied the shores around the cove until 1795. The dispute as to the sovereignty of the area having been settled in favor of the British, Captain Quadra turned possession over to Captain Vancouver in 1792.

On a rocky headland at the entrance to Friendly Cove near the Nootka Lighthouse are two stone monuments commemorating these historic events. Searching them out and reading their inscriptions is a favorite activity of visiting yachtsmen.

The Washington State University Historical Society erected a stone monument in 1903 with the inscription reading, "Vancouver and Quadra met here in August, 1792 under the treaty between Spain and Great Britain of October, 1790."

The other, a pyramid cairn of uncut stone 11 feet high, was erected by the Historical Sites and Monuments Board of Canada and dedicated in 1924. The tablet reads, "Nootka Sound, discovered by Captain Cook in March, 1778. In June, 1789, Spain took possession and established and maintained a settlement until 1795. The capture of British vessels almost led to war, which was avoided by the Nootka Convention in 1790. Vancouver and Quadra met here in August, 1792, to determine the land to be restored under the convention."

It was also here that Meares built the *Northwest America*, first ship built in the Northwest, in 1788. An inscription on the cornerstone of the new Catholic church, replacing the one which burned in 1955, records the event and marks the spot.

Chief Maquinna, ruler of the Nootka tribes, lived at Friendly Cove but also headquartered at Tahsis during certain seasons. The present Chief Maquinna still lives there. Various totem poles, including the 30-foot-high Governor-General's totem, the church and the large cemetery are other points of interest which visitors seek out in the cove.

The several thousand Indians living here in the time of the early explorers are now represented by a few hundred who are fishermen or loggers. They, with the white priest and the white lighthouse crew, make up the present population of Friendly Cove, historic birthplace of the white man's Northwest.

Bligh Island, named for Vice Adm. William Bligh of *Mutiny on the Bounty* fame, dominates the middle of Nootka Sound with three main arms extending to the east, northeast and north. Here is another cruising area of rare

Entrance to Tahsis Inlet, northernmost arm of Nootka Sound, is typical of the rugged beauty of Vancouver Island's west side.

beauty and fascinating interest to both skipper and crew.

Muchalat Inlet is the longest of the arms, extending some 20 miles eastward from Zuciarte Channel. Less than a mile wide in places, it is another of the Northwest's fjord-like waterways. Its waters, deep enough for ships of any size, lie between high mountains which rise from the shores on both sides.

Near the head of the inlet is the mouth of the Gold River and the old Indian village of Aaminkis. In recent years the modern town of Muchalat, headquarters for the Tahsis Company's Gold River operations, has been built on the flats next to Aaminkis. A road connects the town with Campbell River, some 40 miles across the island on the east side.

The inlet provides some interesting cruising possibilities amidst magnificent scenery, but the depth of the water, over 200 fathoms in places, doesn't present suitable anchorages.

Tlupana Inlet, middle of the three, is approximately eight miles long. It, too, extends into fairly high mountains, although its waters are not quite as deep. Little Hisnit Inlet, Galiano Bay, Nesook Bay, Moutcha Bay, Sucwoa Bay and the head of the inlet are all protected anchorages. An abandoned marble quarry, which furnished some of the marble for the British Columbia legislative building, is about the only indication that man has been in this area. In 1794, the Spanish governor at Nootka, Don Jose Manuel Alava, visited Tlupana Inlet and was surprised that two governments could ever dispute over such a country which he described as an "inhospitable looking inlet with stupendous precipices and gloomy ravines."

Tahsis Inlet, running north for about 15 miles, is another narrow waterway separating Nootka Island from the mainland of Vancouver Island. It was Captain Richards who named it Tahsis in 1862, although Vancouver showed it as Tahshies on his 1798 chart and the 1849 Admiralty chart carried it as Tasis. The name comes from the Indian word tashee (meaning "trail"), probably for an Indian trail from the head of the inlet across the island to the Nimpkish River.

The inlet leaves Nootka Sound proper at the southern end of Strange Island, which separates it from five-mile-long Kendrick Inlet. Good anchorages are found in Plumper Harbor and at Kendrick's head behind Bodega Island. In Tahsis Inlet the shores are mostly straight up from the water al-

though there are sandy beaches occasionally at the mouth of a river or creek.

Chief Maquinna and his followers may have livened things up at the head of the inlet when they spent summers there but later it was a lonely place until 1940, with only a couple of trappers and a prospector living there. In that year a logging camp was started, the Gibson brothers then established a sawmill which has now grown to the modern computerized mill of the Tahsis Company Ltd., a subsidiary of the East Asiatic Company Ltd. Many ships from all over the world call there regularly.

History made by the Indians, the Spanish, the British and the Canadians, added to spectacular beauty, make Nootka Sound and its inlets an altogether delightful cruising area. Perhaps one of the most lovely anchorages on the west coast is found at the head of Ewin Inlet which indents Bligh Island. Its sylvan, peaceful remoteness, set among the green-clad hills, its clams, swimming, and a full moon sneaking out from behind a mountain peak — all combined to create a picture which will remain anchored in memory for many years.

Esperanza Inlet with its main channel and four arms connects with Tahsis Inlet through Hecate Channel and Tahsis Narrows, thus forming the waterway across the top of Nootka Island. Here is another series of inlets, bays and coves, all well protected, providing another incomparable cruising area.

This might be called the Spanish inlet for most of the names were given by Capt. Alexandro Malaspina who, in 1791, explored here in the *Descubierta* and *Atrevida*. His officers for the expedition were Lt. Joseph de Espinosa and Lt. Ciriaco Cevallos.

Cruising from Tahsis Inlet through Tahsis Narrows, we first passed the settlement of Ceepeecee, a name derived from the initials C.P.C. (for Canadian Packing Corporation). This subsidiary of the California Packing Corporation built a reduction plant here in 1926 which has since burned down. The name stuck and has been officially recognized by the Post Office Department. There is also a cannery here.

A mile farther along in Hecate Channel is Esperanza with a hospital and nice hotel. Directly across the channel on Nootka Island is the settlement of Hecate, where a pilchard reduction plant formerly operated.

Zeballos Inlet, named for Lieutenant Cevallos, runs

nearly north, takes a turn to the west and then north again for a total of about six miles. The head of this inlet was the scene of a gold rush in 1935. Unemployed fishermen joined the prospectors with several of them taking out small fortunes. In 1937, there were six mines and the town of Zeballos had been established with a population of 1500. Gold worth $13 million was shipped out until 1945, when the government's setting of $35 an ounce as the price closed the mines as an unprofitable venture.

The town now has a big logging camp and is an important source of supplies for the entire region. A large deposit of high-grade iron ore nearby and a mine have added to the town's economy. Here the yachtsman will find just about anything he needs.

Next arm to the west is Espinosa Inlet, extending north about seven and a half miles with Little Espinosa Inlet taking off about midway up. The main inlet offers pleasant cruising with several little coves for anchoring. The little inlet is interesting, but watch that large-scale chart closely. The name comes from Lieutenant Espinosa.

Westernmost and shortest of the three northern arms is Port Eliza, named for Lt. Francisco Eliza, governor at Nootka for a time and an early explorer in Northwest waters. This six-mile-long inlet has several small coves and larger Queen Cove, a favorite fish boat center during the trolling season.

Years ago large shipments of oysters were made from the native oyster beds at the head of Port Eliza to Seattle and Vancouver. Subsequent establishment of beds closer to the markets killed the industry here and today the oysters are there for the taking.

Nuchalitz Inlet, the fourth arm of the Esperanza group, opens off the open ocean and indents Nootka Island for nearly 10 miles. Here is more good cruising with plenty of exploring possibilities among the several islands, in Mary Basin, Inner Basin and a variety of coves. Several shoal areas and a scattering of rocks make a large-scale chart a must for peace of mind.

The main channel of Esperanza Inlet, with Centre Island in the middle, has a wealth of bays and coves. Entrance is through Gillam Channel, named for Capt. E. Gillam, skipper of the C.P.R. steamer *Princess Maquinna* for 20 years. With a goodly scattering of rocks and reefs all around the entrance, close attention should be paid to the channel buoys.

Clayoquot, Nootka, Esperanza — three sounds within 80 miles of coastline from Ucluelet — have hundreds of miles of spectacular cruising waters set amidst some of the most magnificent scenery in the world. Add the challenge and adventure of the ocean and you have at least part of the answer to why men go down to the sea in ships. This isn't an area for the first-time boater. Knowledge, experience and preparation are necessary, but for the qualified skipper the rewards are most satisfying.

Kyuquot Sound was our next objective and we will continue up the island's west coast in the next chapter.

Top: Boats moored at Hot Springs Cove while their owners enjoy the pools. Bottom: Head of Ewin Inlet, Nootka Sound, one of the west coast's most beautiful anchorages.

17
Exploring Vancouver Island's West Coast

Water, rocks, sand and trees are the main ingredients. Add mountains and high hills, a scattering of oysters and plenty of crabs. Leaving plenty of water on the outside, roll some of it in long fingers extending into the mountains and among the rocks; sprinkle with islands and garnish with trees. Cover with blue sky and dot with puffs of white cotton-candy clouds.

Some such recipe must have been used for the creation of the west coast of Vancouver Island. Its rugged beauty, mixed with periods of storm and tranquility from the Pacific, extends to the yachtsman an awesome challenge for cruising adventure.

Continuing our clockwise circumnavigation of the island, we left Esperanza Inlet to head for Kyuquot Sound. Aboard Serge and Maggie Becker's Newporter Ketch *Ocean Cape*, we were joined by Jim and Joy Eastman in *Kimje*, Jim and Kay Arniel in *Flying Cloud* and George and Inger Heideman in their power cruiser *Vittoria*.

Although there are several shortcut passages behind and around Catala Island, they are full of rocks and reefs and local knowledge is needed for successful navigation. We had been advised to run clear out to the flashing red whistle buoy before heading for the 13-mile-distant buoy at the entrance of Kyuquot Channel.

The *Vittoria* crew elected to do a bit of beachcombing in behind the islets and rocks protecting Clear Pass but the deeper-draft sailboats kept to the open ocean. We were told by fishermen that these islets give good protection from westerly winds. Our winds weren't sufficient for sailing and so we powered all the way to Kyuquot Channel. Just inside Rugged Point is a well-protected bay, easy to duck into if the weather turns nasty.

Kyuquot Sound has two major arms, two lesser ones and several small inlets. Entering through the main channel, three islands—Whiteley, Hohoae and Moketas—dominate the middle of the sound. Cachalot Inlet takes off to the right, running about a mile and a half to the east but with only about a mile of navigable water. A whaling station was formerly located here.

About a mile north, Amai Inlet runs to the east for about three and a half miles. At the entrance, opposite Amai Point, is a lovely unnamed cove, locally known as Chief Joseph Harbor. With four fathoms in its inner basin, it's as cozy an anchorage as a yachtsman could ask for and there's a good possibility of seeing a black bear on the beach.

Heading north again, a run up Pinnace Channel opens up Tahsish Inlet to the northeast. This shouldn't be confused with Tahsis Inlet, part of Nootka Sound, although the name comes from the same source, the Indian word meaning "passage" or "trail." Depths are too great for anchoring, but two or three small bays offer good havens.

A short way in the inlet on the south side, a channel runs into Fair Harbor, a three-mile-long inlet completely landlocked except for the entrance channel. There are several good anchorages in 7 to 23 fathoms. The eastern end dries at 11 feet. The Tahsis Company logging operation is located here, and some supplies and services are available at this company town.

Eelstow Passage, across the top of Moketas Island, joins Kashutl Inlet, the longest in the sound. A bay, a cove and Easy Inlet, as well as the head, offer several good anchorages. Coming back down the inlet Chamiss Bay indents the western shore. It was here that *Princess Maquinna* and other ships unloaded supplies for Kyuquot and where the Gibson brothers established a logging camp.

Crowther Channel, returning to the ocean around the west side of Union Island, is narrow and generously scattered with rocks. Either local knowledge or close attention to a large-scale chart is required. Crowther joins Nicolaye Channel and a hard starboard turn leads to the rock cluttered-passage around Amos Island into Walters Cove, our destination for the night.

With the *Vittoria* as pilot boat and the additional help of several beacons and markers, we followed the tortuous channel into the eastern entrance to the cove. The skipper called for continuous readings from the depth sounder and all hands had a good laugh as they heard, "Ten feet—ten-eight-six-six-six-four-four-two-whoops, you're out of water —should be aground." We weren't, but it was an exciting few minutes.

Walters Cove, as picturesque a place as any we visited, is formed by V-shaped Walters Island nestling up nearly to Vancouver Island's shore with both westerly and easterly entrances. The fishing village of Kyuquot, part of it on shore and part on floats, is in the V of the island but seems to encompass the entire cove with a fleet of fishing boats moored at floats and a couple of fish-buying "camps" at anchor.

Kyuquot can lay claim to a couple of bits of fame in history. It was in 1855, when the Kyuquot tribe of Indians was the largest on the coast, and the last battle between coastal tribes was fought there between the Kyuquots and Clayoquots with the latter the victors. Kyuquot became the West Coast's first organized salmon-trolling center when the Nelson brothers set up the first fish-buying camp there.

After finding suitable moorage, it wasn't long before we were introduced to Charlie, the seal. The introduction came through Charlie's "mother," Mrs. Esko Kayra, wife of one of Kyuquot's leading fishermen. Charlie's was a Caesarian birth after the real mother was shot, and she was bottle raised in the bathtub.

No, that isn't a typographical error. It was sometime after she grew up that it was discovered that Charlie was a girl but, by then, the name was so firmly fixed that it stuck.

Charlie stays around the cove all summer during the fishing season, growing fat on a too-generous diet of salmon. When her foster parents leave for their winter home at Sidney, she fends for herself, living on herring, and returns to the cove in the spring. She's always around the Kayra float to meet visitors, jumping out of the water for a hand-out or even climbing up on the float. She was born in the summer of 1964 and her history, together with a plea that she not be harmed, is chronicled in a newspaper article posted on the door of the general store.

The people of Kyuquot are friendly and happy to share their sea-going knowledge or answer piloting questions about the area. We didn't get a chance to meet Mr. Kayra. He wasn't due in from fishing until 11:00 that night and he took off at 3:00 in the morning. The successful fisherman's hours are long.

Leaving Kyuquot, we retraced our inbound course, headed for the open sea around the Mission Group of islands and set a course for Cape Cook on the Brooks Peninsula. This meant bypassing three inlets which look interest-

ing on the chart, but we had been advised that their entrances were scattered with rocks, that they offered no protection and had nothing of interest to yachtsmen. Indeed, Vancouver Island's coastline from Kyuquot to Cape Scott is about as desolate a bit of country as can be found in the Northwest and looks the same today as it did to Captain Cook.

Forbidding high hills, from 600 to 2600 feet, slope sharply to the water's edge. Rocks and islets are strewn profusely offshore and trees are gnarled and bent from the gales sweeping in from the Pacific. With the nearest road some 80 miles away across nearly impassable mountains, the area is uninhabited, visited only by an occasional trapper or Indian.

We were told a story about one man who had lived there. He was a hermit who had settled on the southeast shore of Brooks Peninsula. Living off the animals of the land and fish from the sea, he managed to get along with only a couple of trips a year for other supplies. These trips he made by rowing in his open skiff to Kyuquot, 16 miles across the Checleset Bay, about as nasty a bit of water (with plenty of reefs and shoals) as can be found anywhere.

It's interesting to note that many of the early explor-

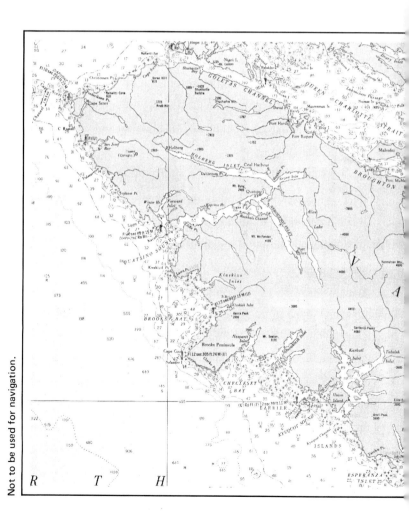

99

ers, their ships, crew members and friends have had their names perpetuated in geographical features of our Northwest waters, some of them several times. Capt. James Cook, however, who preceded them all, was nearly forgotten. It wasn't until 1860 that Captain Richards named Cape Cook after the great exploring navigator. Cook, himself, had called it Woody Point after first sighting it in 1778, shortly before his landing at Friendly Cove in Nootka Sound. Cook Inlet in Alaska was also named for him.

Oblong-shaped Brooks Peninsula, sticking further into the Pacific than any other headland on the West Coast below the top of Vancouver Island, was also named by Richards, but Brooks' identity seems to be lost. In 1788, Capt. Charles Duncan of the trading sloop *Princess Royal* named what is now known as Klaskish Inlet, Brooks Inlet, and Richards transferred the name to the peninsula.

Before we left Tahsis, Jack Christensen of the Tahsis Company, and a member of the Royal Vancouver Yacht Club, had given us a briefing and some tips on navigating this part of the coast. In describing Cape Cook, he told us that remarkable changes could be noted there. We could be sailing along in bright sunshine on calm seas and, on rounding the cape, could run into clouds, a temperature drop of 10° to 15°, fog and sudden squally winds.

Fortunately none of these dire predictions were experienced. We were enjoying a high-pressure period and, although skies were overcast, there was no wind and only a gentle ground swell disturbed the water. Rounding the cape was uneventful with the only change noted a slight increase in the misty haze along the shore.

More rocks, reefs and islets continue to line the shore all the way to Quatsino Sound. Two small inlets, Klaskish and Klaskino, run inland behind Brooks Peninsula. Although Klaskish appears to offer no protection, we were told by fishermen that it was a good harbor. Klaskino's entrance is rock strewn.

Quatsino Sound has been called the "Queen of the Sounds." With its four principal arms roughly forming a cross, the sound has over 70 miles of protected cruising waters and almost cuts off the northwest portion of the island. It is well endowed with an abundance of crabs, ducks and geese. Quatsino is named for the Indian tribe Koskimo, which had its largest village just around Cliffe Point inside the entrance to the sound.

After passing the light on Kains Island, a swing to the port opens up Forward Inlet, named after the gunboat *Forward*. Winter Harbor, Vancouver Island's westernmost settlement, is located about halfway up the inlet on the left. Here is another picturesque fishing village with a quiet harbor and friendly residents. Fuel, supplies and services are available.

Some 18 miles up the sound, Neroutsos Inlet takes off to the southeast with the town of Port Alice and its pulp mill near the head. The inlet, formerly known as Alice Arm, was named for Capt. C. D. Neroutsos, one-time manager of the B.C. Coast Steamships. Port Alice was the terminus for the seven-day round-trip runs from Victoria, which the *Princess Maquinna* and *Princess Norah* made for many years, serving the west coast of the island, hauling freight

Rock formation on Hope Island looks like a friendly bear.

and passengers. This is a favorite spot of some of the yachtsmen who have cruised around the island or participated in the biannual Van-Isle Predicted Log Race. Fishing in nearby Victoria Lake is reported good.

Drake Island lies at the entrance to the inlet and in behind it on the north shore is the village of Quatsino. Originally settled in 1894 by pioneers of Scandinavian descent from North Dakota, it is the oldest white settlement on this portion of the coast. Three of these pioneers staked the original claims and started mining copper ore, but abandoned the effort after a few years.

A short distance from the village is the entrance to Quatsino Narrows, a delightfully scenic cut leading into the other two inlets. Rupert Inlet, about five miles long, runs to the east but has no particular attractions. To the west is 20-mile-long Holberg Inlet. A few miles up from the Narrows is Stephens Bay, named for Sir Phillip Stephens, one-time secretary to the Admiralty. This is locally called Coal Harbor, the name of the post office, and it is here that a whaling station was operated until recently. Now closed down, it was long a point of interest to visiting yachtsmen, who liked to watch the processing of the great mammals.

From Coal Harbor a road some 11 miles in length runs to Port Hardy on the northeastern coast of the islands. Since the ending of ship service to Quatsino Sound, all supplies are brought to the area via Port Hardy over this road.

The village of Holberg with its logging camp and post office is at the western end of Holberg Inlet. Another big logging operation is located at Jeune Landing on Neroutsos

A number of boats in the fishing fleet were moored at Winter Harbor after unloading the day's catch.

Inlet, another area where the early Quatsino settlers located copper mining claims.

It's easy to understand why Quatsino Sound has been called "Queen of the Sounds." It is a haven for mariners who may have been fighting the wrath of the Pacific coming up the coast around Cape Cook or down from Cape Scott. And it is a beautiful waterway throughout, with its islands, bays and coves seeming to be set between shores a little lower than those of other sounds. It is also free of the "Woolies." According to the fishermen these are capricious winds prevalent in fall, winter and spring in the inlets surrounded by high mountains. They don't necessarily come with storms but can whip a protected inlet into a fury, the winds zooming down the hills to hit the water from a variety of directions, with enough force to founder small boats.

As we left Quatsino Sound the weather was still under the influence of a "high." Our passage along the forbidding coast to Cape Scott was uneventful. There wasn't enough wind to sail and only an easy swell on the water. Although the chart shows two or three bays and coves, we were advised not to depend on them for protection. We were told that, if we encountered either storm or fog and couldn't get back to Quatsino Sound, we should head for the open sea.

Luckily the advice wasn't needed. The sky was cloudy and, although there was a light haze, we had no trouble picking up the light on Cape Scott. Captains Lawrie and Guise named this point for David Scott, a Bombay merchant who helped them fit out their trading expedition in 1786. To the west of the cape, extending for about 25 miles, are the Scott Islands. Surrounded by rocks and par-

tially submerged reefs, they are a hazard to navigation. However, one fisherman told us he had found protection behind Cox Island in a bad westerly blow. A light was established on outermost Triangle Island in 1910, but wind and fog made it impracticable and it was abandoned in 1920. It was 1960 before a light was built at Cape Scott.

After rounding Cape Scott, we were unable to pick up the Nahwitti Bar Buoy in the haze and so ran on a compass course until we sighted it about halfway along the northern coast of Vancouver Island. Here again the shoreline is inhospitable with no shelter until Bull Harbor on Hope Island.

Nahwitti Bar, at the entrance to Goletas Channel, can be a hazard to a small boat. With tidal currents up to five knots, an ebbing tide, bucking a strong westerly wind, can kick up some nasty water over this bar. Even though the tide wasn't running full and there was little wind, we were still thrown about a bit as we maneuvered to miss large quantities of driftwood.

Bull Harbor was probably named by Hudson's Bay Company officers for the many bull sea lions that inhabited the area. Hope Island was named by Richards for Vice Adm. Sir James Hope. The harbor is a scenic inlet which nearly cuts through the island. During the fishing season it is alive with activity. Fish boats come and go to the fish-buying barges, to the store for supplies or to the fuel docks. There is also a marine radio station there.

We took on fuel and water here but don't recommend the water. While it tastes all right, it has a brown color which isn't very appetizing.

Next day we headed down Goletas Channel for Queen

Top of page: Shoreline caves mark the entrance to Bull Harbor off the northern tip of Vancouver Island. Bottom: The 34-foot cruiser, Vittoria, did a lot of beachcombing in waters too tricky for the deeper-draft sailboats.

Charlotte Strait and Sointula. Goletas (the Spanish name for "schooner") was given to the channel by Galiano and Valdez as they sailed around the north end of the island on their way to Nootka Sound. They also named two points for their schooners, *Sutil* and *Mexicana:* Cape Sutil on the south and Mexicana Point on the north at the western entrance of the channel.

Nigei Island, Hope's neighbor to the east, is named for the principal chief of the Nahwitti Indians who lived in the area; Bute Passage, the channel between the two islands, was named by Richards for John Stuart, earl of Bute. Another fishing village and post office is at Shushartie Bay on the south side of the channel.

So ended the portion of our trip on the "Outside" of Vancouver Island. It had been something we had looked forward to for a long time and the realization was a gratifying experience. We were extremely fortunate with the weather, experiencing neither storm nor fog. The contrast of the rugged, rock-strewn coast with the more gentle scenic beauty of the inlets added many new pictures to our memory album of these wonderful Northwest cruising waters.

The "Outside" isn't recommended for the inexperienced boater, although Barkley Sound can be enjoyed by trailerboat via Alberni. For the seasoned skipper with a dependable, seaworthy boat, however, Vancouver Island's west coast offers a challenging and rewarding experience which will be long remembered.

18
Diving for Treasure

As interest in scuba diving has grown in recent years, the west coast of Vancouver Island has attracted more attention from diving buffs. They are searching for treasure. Not gold treasure but treasure in the form of old cannons and anchors.

The stormswept, reef-dotted shore of the island's outer face has been the scene of numerous shipwrecks. Many of these ships, in an effort to keep off the rocks of the lee shore, lost their anchors. In other cases, the anchors went down with the ships when they crashed on shore, off course in the fog.

Older ships traditionally were armed and these ancient cannons are considered real treasures. Both anchors and cannons are virtually indestructible, so they outlast the hull and other parts of the ship.

First step in this kind of treasure hunting is to locate a shipwreck. A check of the provincial archives in Victoria will turn up the historical records of many of these sinkings. Indians along the coast, if properly approached with ordinary courtesy and perhaps copious amounts of candy for the youngsters, will be able to recall tribal legends of ships being sunk and describe fairly accurate locations.

Another requirement for this activity is to get the official approval of provincial and, possibly, dominion authorities.

Some of the older ships lost along the coast were the *Boston*, scuttled by Indians in Friendly Cove in 1803; the *Tonquin*, sunk in Clayoquot Sound in 1811; and the sloop *Kingfisher*, lost near the mouth of Matilda Creek on Flores Island in 1864.

In this century the *Valencia* went down between Cape Beale and Carmanah Point in January, 1906. The *Carelmapu*, after failing to locate a tug off Cape Flattery, was blown ashore on Vancouver Island's west coast in 50-foot seas on November 25, 1915. The outcroppings of Village Island in Barkley Sound caught the British freighter *Tuscan Prince* on February 15, 1923, in a snow storm. Her crew was saved, most of her cargo removed and some of her upper steel plates salvaged before she slipped off the reef and sank.

More recently, the Russian *Uzbakistan* went down near the Pachena Point Light in April, 1943; the Dutch *Schiedyk* sank off Bligh Island in January, 1968, and the Greek *Treis Ierarchai* was lost off Ferrer Point in December, 1969.

Undersea cannon hunting received quite an impetus in 1957, when ten divers from Oregon and seven from Seattle joined forces. Their principal target was John Jacob Astor's *Tonquin*, which had left New York in the fall of 1810 with supplies for a trading post to be set up inside the mouth of the Columbia River. After accomplishing that mission, she headed north to trade for furs.

The *Tonquin* was commanded by Capt. Jonathan Thorne, a tough old sea-dog type of skipper with a short temper. While bartering with the natives in Clayoquot Sound, he was shown some poor-quality furs. Angered at their craftiness, he quickly grabbed one of the mangy pelts and rubbed it in the chief's face.

This was an insult not to be taken lightly. The following day a flotilla of canoes came from shore loaded with first-class furs. It was June 16, 1811, and a husky group of Indians climbed aboard, their knives and weapons well hidden. When Chief Shewish, an experienced war leader, whooped the signal, 18 of the *Tonquin's* crew were promptly slain. The remaining five crewmen succeeded in reaching the safety of the cabin where they blockaded themselves and then swept the deck with gunfire.

Later that night, four of the survivors, trying to escape in a small boat, were captured and tortured until they died. James Lewis, the remaining crew member, guessed that his chances of survival were pretty slim; so he planned to make the Indians pay a goodly toll for such slaughter. With a cargo of some 9000 pounds of gunpowder in the hold, originally consigned to the Russian fort in Sitka, Lewis ran a fuse to the powder magazine.

His preparations completed, he tricked most of the local tribesmen into coming aboard for looting. When the ship was swarming with several hundred Indians, he set off the fuse. The resultant explosion shook Clayoquot Sound to its most remote bays and inlets and blew more than 200 Indians into eternity, as well as wounding many more.

As meager reports of the *Tonquin's* destruction filtered back to Astoria, they failed to note any exact position where the ship went down, and it has never been discovered. Members of the diving team questioned the townspeople of Tofino, natives of the beach village Ahousat on Flores Island and of Opitsat on Meares Island. They heard many stories and legends, most of them agreeing on details of the gruesome event, but varying widely as to just where the ship was scuttled.

Finally, it was decided to call on Ken Kendall, the "pirate" cannon-hunter and cannon-maker of Kenary Cove in Boat Harbor on Vancouver Island's east side. His expert knowledge and interpretation was unable to pin down an exact spot.

After experimenting with a sea sled built by the Puget Sound Mud Sharks, the divers were forced to spot dive in an effort to locate the wreck. Activity was halted for a time while Canadian authorities demanded that proper approval be obtained from dominion officials. During this time the team received a tip from some Indians about a mystery wreck (which had been fouling their fishing nets for many years) near Hot Springs Cove in Sydney Inlet.

Operations were moved and a wrecked ship was located on the first dive. Exploration turned up two barnacle-encrusted cannons, one seven feet long. The big guns were too heavy to get aboard the divers' boat but were towed to shallow water and recovered later.

Subsequent tests of wood from this vessel have fairly well established that it was not the *Tonquin*, but the divers were happy with their treasure.

A brass cannon from the sloop *Kingfisher* can be seen at Ahousat Village. Ahousat tribesmen attacked and sank the *Kingfisher* over a hundred years ago.

The ways of the sea are unpredictable as is fate. What was disaster for some, many years ago, has turned into profit and adventure in another age. There are still wrecks to be explored, cannons and anchors to be found. In fact, Captain Vancouver records in his journal that his companion ship, the *Chatham*, lost an anchor somewhere on the east side of Cypress Island in the San Juan Islands, possibly somewhere in Deepwater Bay. What a historical find that would be!

The treasure isn't gold or silver or jewels but, to modern-day divers, cannons and anchors can be as exciting.

The S.S. Beaver, the Royal Canadian Navy's replica of first steamship in Northwest waters.

19

Vancouver Island's Seaward Coves

by John C. Hill

The west coast of Vancouver Island beyond Cape Flattery is strictly sea-going country. Ninety miles out of Victoria, the first of a series of island-filled sounds with long inlets opens on the seacoast and these sounds—Barkley, Clayoquot and Nootka—are not impractical for small-boat cruising, even for short-vacation boaters. And they are an inviting variation to the Northwest's better-known cruising grounds—down-Sound, up-Sound, the San Juans, the Gulf Islands, Desolation Sound and the Inside Passage.

Although distant fields may not really be greener, it has seemed to us on our August cruises to Vancouver Island's seaward coast that the coves are more scenic, the background mountain peaks snowier, and the clams squirt higher than in inland waters.

Access for small craft is by trailer, on the ferry from Vancouver, B.C., to Nanaimo, and 53 miles of good highway to the twin towns of Port Alberni and Alberni. We launched this trip into the Somass River from Alberni's municipal ramp at 2:00 P.M. on a Friday, and fueled at one of Port Alberni's gas docks down the harbor. Checking on fishing, we heard that good results were reported from Kirby Point.

About 20 miles down the narrow channel through the mountains, Alberni Inlet meets the mouth of Uchuklesit Inlet and the upper end of Trevor Channel, at the northeast corner of Barkley Sound. Barkley is about 12 miles square, with three channels separated by two island chains. Captain Charles Barkley of the British vessel *Imperial Eagle* left his name in 1787, and named one of the channels after his ship, one Loudon Channel from his ship's former name, and

one Trevor Channel from the maiden name of his wife.

On this afternoon we continued down Trevor Channel, prowled through the narrow channel at the south end of Tzartus Island (locally known as Village Island) and beached briefly in Marble Cove. Hoping to find a pleasant anchorage for the night near Kirby Point, we continued on to Diana Island and dropped anchor in a sheltered cove at the west end.

Our boat, *El Patito Feo*, is a 23-foot Thunderbird Iroquois outdrive day cruiser, and Don and Janet Spawn were alongside with a similar Thunderbird Formula. With the elevating outdrive a shoal bay is adequate for overnight, and beaching is practical for shorter stops without launching the dinghy. We carried the rubber dinghy on the hardtop without deflating, keeping the deck and cockpit uncluttered, but giving our already rather square profile an awkward look—indeed "The Ugly Duckling." Her performance, however, is swanlike, and she rates high in comfort and utility.

We had no schedule except to get back to work in a week, and to see, as the week's weather permitted, parts of the area we had passed up previously. Being outbound, provisioned, and not equipped for stowing fish, we decided the following morning to catch only one salmon each, and head on across the sound. A salmon grabbed my wife's fly before she was really ready to fish, and thinking the line had fouled the prop, we muffed it and had to land the second one. Meanwhile, the Spawns, a mile along the shore, had also caught theirs, so we lost little cruising time in fishing.

Cruising at around 20 knots, it's a short run through the Broken Islands to Ucluelet at the west edge of the sound. Fuel and provisions are reasonably handy at any of the settlements. After lunch ashore at Ucluelet, the weather

Reprinted from Trailerboats/West, Miller Freeman Publications, 1970.

looked practical for the 20-mile offshore run from Amphitrite Point to Lennard Island at the entrance to Clayoquot Sound, and we put to sea.

We have found the late summer weather can be fairly stable, and the one fair-weather problem is to schedule the sea runs between the sounds after the morning fog moves offshore and before much afternoon sea breeze rises. Assuming the sea is not rough enough to limit cruising speed seriously, the length of time between sheltering points is reasonably short. *El Patito Feo* carries two extra 18-gallon tanks we had installed for an earlier cruise in Baja California, and dual batteries (an electric shift outdrive doesn't, without 12 volts d.c.), and our companion boat offered extra engine safety. On the Baja cruise, alone, we carried a spare 18-horsepower outboard and bracket. Sea swells don't bother a fast small boat much, so it can be fun to go outside. The thought is still there, though, that swells are no help on the rocks or the beach and we have to realize that, in case of serious trouble, fun can become disaster suddenly.

We like Clayoquot Sound particularly because white sand beaches abound on both sheltered and exposed sides of the islands, and a sandy bay on Flores Island was our stop for the evening, with salmon barbecued for dinner. We've got the razor clams spotted by now, and a future goal is to find the abalone and scallops. Crab cocktails came from dropping a fishhook over the side with a clam neck on it.

Following a lazy morning and an afternoon of prowling some of the inlets up to Pretty Girl Cove (saw none), we beached again, and took off the next morning for a run out Sydney Inlet and a short few miles at sea again into Hesquiat Harbor. The chart shows a large freshwater lake emptying into the head of the bay, and we found we could walk in to the lake up its short outlet stream. Inside the spit at the harbor entrance was the night's anchorage, and beachcombing the spit turned up our only Japanese glass net float.

By now our week had worn down to Wednesday, and with good weather we put to sea again, for about 18 miles around Estevan Point to enter Nootka Sound. In the sun along the shore, in good weather, the long history of shipwrecks on this coast seemed remote. We cruised on up to the end of Tahsis Inlet, another 20 miles or so, and lunched at the handsome new motel. It turned out Wednesday was a holiday at Tahsis, with no gas available. We had the option of continuing around Nootka Island to Zeballos, or fueling at Nootka returning. Unfortunately we felt returning was more prudent than proceeding, and we elected to reserve some time for possible weather delays.

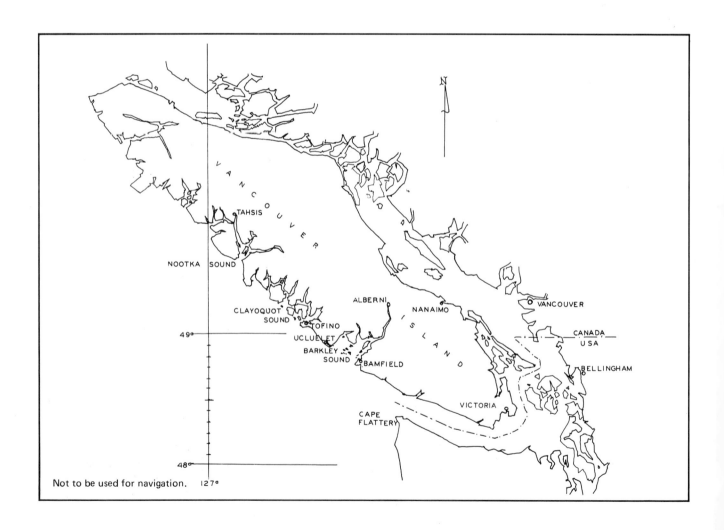

Not to be used for navigation.

Narrow channel in the Pinkerton Islands, Barkley Sound. Barkley is one of a series of island-filled sounds with long inlets opening onto the seacoast.

A Norwegian freighter pulled out of the pulp mill dock ahead of us, and we passed her on the way back down the inlet. Just ahead, at Tsowwin Narrows, bright sails appeared; the NorPac race fleet was sailing full tilt up the channel with the afternoon channel breeze astern. After several days of no company but an occasional fishing boat we found ourselves in the narrows with traffic like Sunday afternoon at Seattle's Ballard Locks.

We fueled at a store float in McKay Passage near Nootka, and headed out around Estevan Point again for the run back to Clayoquot Sound. Every trip you learn something about boating, usually something obvious you should have known already. This trip, as we hit the sea swells outbound, heavy engine knocking signaled a bad choice of fuel. Our engines are rated for regular gas, so high-octane fuel had never been a consideration. But it turns out that the fishing boat engines do better on a lower-octane fuel than regular, and fish boat gas doesn't suit our Buick V-8 outdrives. Fortunately we still had some gas in our extra tanks, and with a fresh afternoon breeze astern we traveled well back to Clayoquot Sound. Beachcombing and over-nighting at the outer islands, we went in next morning to Tofino, finding several grades of gas available at the docks.

With no weather delay, we still had a day for more exploring before heading back through Barkley Sound and up the inlet to haul out at Alberni. The overall distance from Alberni to Tahsis, excluding our exploring side trips, is about 140 nautical miles, which is not a great distance for a week's round trip if the weather cooperates. However, there would be no need to cruise that far to enjoy the area. Barkley Sound alone would be worth more than a week's cruising. Although only about 12 miles wide, it has a variety of bays, inlets and coves. I started to count the number of islands but gave up on reaching 100 on the west half of the chart alone.

The Pinkerton Islands, for instance, are a group of some two dozen islands in an area about a mile square, with narrow and somewhat navigable channels wandering between. Dead slow with a bow lookout is the rule here, so it's not so startling to see the depth finder drop from 30 feet to near zero as the boat passes over the boulders.

On the seaward side of the Broken Islands group, a sea lion colony inhabits a reef a couple of miles south of Effingham Island, and with a calm sea they can be approached closely before they slide off the rocks. Barking at them at close range through the loud hailer seemed to keep them talking back to us.

The Nootka tribes on the Vancouver Island coast saw their first white intruders when the Spanish corvette *Santiago*, under Captain Juan Perez, sailed in from Monterey in 1774, and traded briefly with the Indians near Estevan Point. Prior to that time the only water traffic the Nootkas

*Vancouver Island's west coast, an
ideal cruising ground, is not
impractical for short vacations.*

knew, other than their own canoes, were the raiding war canoes of the Haidas from Queen Charlotte Island to the north, and those of the Makahs and Clallams from across Juan de Fuca Strait.

The local canoes can still be seen in use and under construction in the Indian villages, shaped now by chain saw as well as hand tools, from cedar logs in one piece. The range of coastal voyages made under paddle and sail in these small craft is most impressive when viewed from aboard the white man's fiber-glass refinements.

20

A Queen in Green Water

by Ray H. Cooper

Skies are clear and we have a 15-mile-per-hour wind with a temperature of 68° as we leave Neah Bay, Washington, on August 22. The forecast is excellent with no storms foreseeable and the barometer is holding steady at 30.20. By 1430 the motor is off and we are moving at six knots in a good northwest wind.

We hold our speed through the evening and clear night. At 0300 the barometer reads 30.00 in the bright moonlight. At 0900 we are 107 miles out and the barometer continues to drop at 29.95. Our noon position puts us 122 miles from Neah Bay and we continue to average five knots.

By 1800 we are down to three knots and it is warm as the barometer dips to 29.00. At 1930 the wind has died and we are sloshing around in the still warmth as the sun sets. The barometer reads 29.85 at 2100 and a cloud front is building to the southeast. The storm will soon be upon us.

The waves begin building up at 2300 and we douse all sails as the winds gather pressure before the oncoming storm. At 0130 we put out the sea anchor with 200 feet of line and belay the warp at the starboard quarter. *Regina Maris* has found the big seas and is laying broadside to them. The storm is out of the southeast and colliding with the northwest swell, creating very steep, uncomfortable seas. There had been no storm warnings forecast.

Regina Maris, *Queen of the Sea, is a 38-foot trimaran incorporating lines of the Piver 35 Lodestar and including some features of the Victress 40. She is the result of dreaming, scheming, and hours of hard work by Barry and Nola Gorman of Vancouver, B.C. Constructed of three-eighths-inch plywood, with fiber glass to the waterline, she took three years to build.*

From 0300 to 0600 the seas build to 20 feet with some cresting. The wind is gusting to over 50 miles per hour. There is nothing to do but sit in the safety of the cockpit and suffer the vicious rain-filled squalls. We take some very hard bangs from waves on the starboard hull. The shudder and jerk of the hulls become nerve-racking, but *Regina Maris* rises over the seas confidently and tips 30° and more as she slants off the crests and careens into the troughs. We watch and wait, filled with emotion as the storm develops in intensity during the three-hour watch. Curling, creaming, phosphorescent waves break all around and in increasing height. The wind is a shrill whine in the rigging, and the masts shudder under the strain. Finally we go below. There is nothing to do. There are no ships in sight. We are alone. We crawl into our bunks where the shuddering and violent movements seem exaggerated, but at least in the bunks we need not hold on to survive.

At 0900 there is no letup in the torrent outside. Everyone is below and I expect many prayers are being said. The trimaran stands up well, but is not easy in its motion. The steepest waves throw us wildly up over their crests—then our angle is reversed as we slip down the other side into the trough, where the starboard float again rises high with the next oncoming wave.

We feel this teeter-totter effect of each float taking its turn to be above, and then below, the center hull is better than the very dangerous situation for a trimaran of letting it surf fore and aft down a steep wave where it could bury its bows in tons of water and be flipped or broken apart from sheer water force. Perhaps we felt a psychological comfort by believing that the vessel was less likely to flip over broadside than end-over-end, should a wild surfing set in. The fear of an end-over-end flip is prevalent among multihull sailors, and most keep the bow and stern areas of their hulls light for buoyancy, and keep all heavy gear stowed well amidships. But this bothered me: suppose a steep breaking sea astern lifted the buoyant aft sections in such a way that the underparts became well exposed to the boiling mass of breaking water—it seems there must be a point that is dangerous. Perhaps this feeling is exaggerated and would be lessened with the use of a sea anchor. However, with a fairly wide (21-foot, 6-inch) flat area to length (38-foot) ratio of relatively shallow plane, it was more comforting to weather the storm broadside, letting the seas break and pour over us, than chance getting a big sea beneath, threatening to thrust us over.

With the crest rising above the starboard windows, we can see the yellow anchor warp snaking away in the green water and we wonder if the anchor can still be attached to such a limp line. Seconds later we level in the surge of breaking water beneath us to lurch over and look down into the wide trough, white with windstreaked spume.

At 1030 our second big worry sets itself in motion. The roller-furled jib begins to flap and loosen, catching the full force of the gale. The whipping and noise is intolerable. It seems that the stays and shrouds will yank the chain plates right out of the boat. The jerking gives us a ride like a wild horse. But worse, *Regina Maris* will not stay beam-on to the seas. We start pointing away from the wind and a surfing action sets in. We can only cling to the cockpit where we now watch from, and trust the bows will not bury in the 30°-plus dives into the trough. The three girls are below and, from outward appearances, they seem to be taking the whole thing very quietly.

We have no way of getting the jib down and, in winds that we guess to be in excess of 60 miles per hour, it is not possible to unfurl and refurl the sail. Then, before we hardly have time to get excited over the development, the gale's force slits the sail to shreds and a new wild motion is set through the ship as she shudders from the violent flapping. We go below, thankful our latest danger is past.

At noon there is no letup in the wind force or size of the seas. By 1400 the seas are larger. We estimate they are as high as our main mast, which is 52 feet above the water. The boat does not get the chance to rise over every breaking crest. She is taking the full force of some of the breaking waves along her starboard side with a stunning crash, and I wonder if she can stand for long. The breaking green water pounds on board, filling the cockpit. We are soaked and we realize there is nothing we can do, but we feel less hopeless being on deck, and the noise is less frightful.

At 1430 conditions become extremely dangerous. About every tenth wave is cresting and crashing on deck, threatening the coach roofing. Green water swirls around our feet as it cascades off the deck. How can the women stand the noise and motion below!

Three bad seas are particularly frightening in that the bows leap high in the air and the huge thrusting wave beneath us literally throws the ship out of the water to crash back into the sloping wall of the water behind the crest. And the next sea rises just as menacingly above. We now seem to be in danger of flipping over sideways, float over float, rather than stern over bow as when surfing down the colossal waves. Each of us battles with his thoughts, seeking to ease the stress of the storm.

At 1800 we are all in our bunks. The motion is still violent as we are tossed wildly about and green water pounds the decks. Spray lashes at the windows. It is a long and worrying period of helplessness and still the seas outside are whipped into lines of wind-flattened white spume. I have become utterly sick with my head buried in a plastic garbage bag. I have never felt so awful on a boat and this infuriates me because normally I can keep well enough during times of rough weather.

By 2000 darkness has crept in, adding to the feeling of complete helplessness, and there is no sign of a letup. Our only consolation is that a pattern has set in and there is no worsening of the conditions.

At 2100 we try to sleep with the experience of the storm continually cramming into our minds; the noise, the wind, the cresting seas, the thud of green water, the smashing down of the hulls after a lift. It is terribly nerve-racking to all of us, but in the darkness of the bunk each of us who had spent some of the day on deck can analyze each sound and movement of the boat.

At 0300, August 25, we scramble on deck. There is an apparent lessening of the wind and some clearing. A few stars are visible. We watch and wait for an hour and then return to our bunks.

At 0700 the storm is over. The winds are down to 20 miles per hour out of the southeast. Seas are still very big. We set some sail and head back to Neah Bay with no idea of our drift. We take a noon sight and set our course with southeast and southwest winds giving us an exhilarating sail.

On August 27, the Neah Bay Coast Guard informs us we had been in an unpredicted storm with winds reaching 70 miles per hour. One tuna boat was lost and another missing. Had *Regina Maris* not been so strongly built, we might not have survived the storm.

21

Like the Wild Birds

by Betty Nunn

With mixed emotions the crew of the *Bee Jay III* watched the familiar coast line of its home port, Newport Beach, California, diminish over the widening wake, which seemed to form a farewell embrace.

One anticipatory night was spent in gay, bright Avalon; then, slipping her mooring at dawn, *Bee Jay* seemed to sense that this was the beginning of another great Pacific adventure. She became even more certain that, like the wild birds, she was heading north again, when, after passing the length of lovely Catalina in a sort of wistful good-bye, her bow was turned gently toward the Santa Barbara Channel. As her throttles advanced, she lifted easily onto her planing step, and cruised gracefully out of Southern California waters.

Santa Barbara, *Bee Jay*'s native port, was coyly hiding in fog, so she passed by this friendly harbor. Visibility was limited from there on around Point Conception, and the crew was not a little surprised to be joined by four new members. Out of the mists off the stern a quartet of tiny land birds was trying desperately to overtake the speeding craft. The helmsman throttled back and immediately the two traveling couples, apparently confused in the fog, and finding themselves out at sea, exhausted, cast off their more natural fears for the immediate crisis of landing somewhere to rest. Identified as pileolated warblers, these brilliant little birds, like flecks of sunlight in the gray afternoon, rode with the boat for more than four hours, intermittently fly-

ing away a short distance only to return, cheeping piteously, determinedly following the wake until the boat again was slowed to a stop to pick up the wee hitchhikers.

Again and again, the boat was halted to allow them to alight. They finally tamed enough to rest on our feet, under our coats and on our hands. Just before dark, the engulfing fog lifted a bit and shore was faintly visible. With gleeful chirrups they left the boat for good, heading landward in their strange swooping and surging pattern of flight.

At evening, Point Conception was her usual unreceptive self. The confusion of currents, short chop, and whitecaps made dinner simple, if not close to impossible. We were grateful for a friend's thoughtful contribution of a delicious lasagna casserole, frozen in a disposable tin to be heated in the oven. This type of frozen dinner was found to be the most satisfactory hot meal in rough water.

Point Arguello and Point Conception are close points on the chart and they deserve each other! Their sea conditions can be counted on to stay the same—nasty.

The morning mists lifted raggedly above the green hills and gold bluffs sheltering San Luis Bay. Here Port San Luis is being developed into a fine haven and salmon-fishing area with new breakwaters in the offing.

The sea had gentled in the morning hours as we rounded Point Buchon. Dusky shearwaters, gull-like seabirds, banking on stiff wings in the wave troughs, flanked our route as *Bee Jay III* neared the "Moor's Turban," which early sailors named the characteristic rock at the entrance to Morro Bay. In the shallows of the inner harbor here, the stately great blue heron seemed to have usurped the position of harbor master. This impressive blue gray bird with its large, pointed bill, stands about four feet tall on its long, slender legs, and is the coast's largest wading bird.

Bee Jay III *is a 46-foot Cedros Island Express. Ben and Betty Nunn first took her to Alaskan waters in 1966. Accounts of that Maiden voyage, and a second cruise in 1967, appeared in* Northwest Passages, Volume 1. *Here is the story of her third journey to the Northwest.*

North of Morro Bay the coastline is beautiful when it is not veiled in fog. This day the eternal fogbank lay off to port about five miles like a crouching animal, who, generously, gave us a superb day of sparkling, sun-lit sea. Onshore the dark green groves of pines near Cambria contrasted with the softer hues of the spring-fresh grass where San Simeon's castle confidently reigns over all. Here at the tiny town is a small, protected mooring which could be a welcome refuge, and the only one, on the run from Morro Bay to Monterey.

The mountains become sterner past Point Piedras Blancas, and darker, with offshore forbidding rocks, which along with the straight-front, coveless mountain shore, discourage any attempt to find respite here from the immense seas. Here, deep-blue, mammoth swells quartered at us bow and port.

Point Sur is of the same ilk in disposition, it seems, as those two terrors farther south. The *Bee Jay* really did her ups and downs here for about three hours. Finally rounding

Top: Rock formations, like this one off the Oregon coast, add to the scenic pleasures of cruising. Bottom: Bee Jay III gets a rest at fish house dock in Garibaldi.

Point Pinos and the Monterey Peninsula, the mighty swells now off her stern, she had a fast run into the hospitable marina at Monterey. One shortcoming, however, of Monterey as a stopover is the scarcity of guest slips. The marina here is crowded with commercial fish boats, and, in the wee hours, filled with loud talking, and engine pops and bangs, as the fishing fleet pulls out. As a scenic spot with local color and historic past, Monterey is one of the most interesting ports of the California coast. It is known for good restaurants, too, which suited our sea-weary crew just fine.

Leaving Monterey the next afternoon, as our boat passed the breakwater, the boisterous resident seals barked a clamorous "adios." From a jagged piling, two large bald-headed brown pelicans, patriarchs of the sea, shook their heads at the racket, swinging their tremendous bills and throat pouches, and lifting themselves effortlessly with their majestic wings, flapping and sailing in rhythm, gave us a most dignified escort out of the harbor.

We found the new marina at Santa Cruz a delightful pause for fuel and hamburgers before embarking on the surprising night ahead.

How rough is a rough sea? What's the Pacific really like? Never in my most vivid imagination could I find proper words to express the insane frenzy of wind, water, tide and current working together to wreck anything in their grip on shore or afloat. We were expecting the Pacific not to be pacific at all times, but the unexpected yawning chasms that opened frighteningly under our bow, over and over from sundown through the long night around Pigeon Point, past the Farralons to Point Reyes at dawn, gave all aboard unforgettable moments.

We had been cruising on the automatic pilot through the usual early evening pecky sea, so the helmsman didn't catch the wheel and throttles on the first unanticipated venture into space. The boat hesitated a second or two on the brink of a seemingly bottomless canyon of sunset-auburn water, and after a dizzying breathtaking descent, we crashed flatly at the bottom more like on solid rock than sea. It seemed the hull must be crushed like an eggshell by such force, but skillfully the boat was slowed and quartered to meet the next unbelievable wall of water, and up, up, up and up, poised an instant, and down, down, down.

So it continued all night with rising winds and heavy gusts, but so deftly was she handled, and so well built and functional for this type of sea, the boat met each assault resolutely, and all hands agreed she is a sea-kindly craft and kept all quite comfortable and certainly safe in the sea orgy that Neptune threw that night.

At dawn a weird, brown, suffering ocean rolled aimlessly with almond-shaped swells. The crew was spent, the sea was spent. Eerie sunlight timidly filtered through the sand-colored mist. Point Reyes Lighthouse glimmered dimly and croaked a throaty greeting as a tiny fishing boat emerged from the haze and passed by, specterlike. We righted a few objects in the cabin and galley which had orbited with the first onslaught.

Afternoon at Point Arena found the fog shroud dispelled by a brisk breeze, which embroidered the choppy cross currents with white floss. As day faded a hefty wind was lashing the sea white, ominous sign that wind and wave were building to a climax of fury by night. It was decided to let the emotional sea and her temperamental protagonist, the wind, fight their own battle for the night without the *Bee Jay III* and crew as participants. The colorful port at Noyo, near Fort Bragg, California, offered peaceful neutrality and the luxury of eating ashore.

This beautifully protected harbor and quaint fishing community follows along the winding mouth of the Noyo River. The picturesque harbor entrance, protected from the south by a natural point of land and from the north with a craggy rock jetty, is gracefully framed high overhead by the impressive steel arch of the Noyo River bridge.

The following day, leaving Noyo, the sea was calm under an overcast sky. Around Cape Vizcaino here and there a splash of sunshine would break onto shore, and, like a projected color slide, a lovely scene would come alive. Jackass Gulch, its green velvet V-cut canyon rimmed with stately evergreens, gleamed like an emerald brooch on the bosomy shoreline hills. Abeam of Bear Landing at the sea's edge, towering rocks, cathedrals of ebony, withstood stoically each violent charge of smashing breakers. At Whale Gulch, a playful rift in the low-hanging clouds spotlighted a peaceful montage of a glistening white house with red-tile roof, and sombre barn behind, nestled under eloquent eucalyptus trees.

The last shaft of the day's sun fell on the steep slope and rocky shore of Punto Gordo, gilding the wave-tossed piles of driftwood. Suddenly land was blotted out by the jealous fog, and all that was tangible rounding Cape Mendocino was the Blunt's Reef Lightship which loomed red and welcoming with its pulsating light probing the soggy gloom.

With dusk came immense swells and even before dark their intensity heightened; soon they became a series of rugged mountain ranges rushing at us in a vicious gale, snow-topped with hoary whitecaps, arched over menacingly, like shore-breaking combers. The inky blackness of night made it more terrifying, knowing that those giants were still racing savagely at the boat, endlessly, like invisible regiments hurling their unbridled strength, mercilessly, pushing and lifting and crashing in a glory of white froth against the front windows and over the flybridge.

At times like this, only the steady drone of the diesels and the eerie glow of the radar screen keep one in touch with reality. Often the scope shows no target in its sweep, so few ships pass so far at sea, and the coast is too far away to reflect. Also, over and over, the rotating radar antenna is below the horizon when the boat reels, heels and stunningly falls into blind valleys of angry water. These are lonely moments, and faith in the reliability of the boat and the experience of the skipper overrides terror.

It takes an agile helmsman to play the game of lift and drop properly to protect the hull and screws, and plan speed correctly to avoid plowing into the next oncoming devil-god rushing hungrily at the bow. Knowledgeably handled and timed, the bow does not bury itself into the wall

California's Big Sur coastline is often beset by heavy winds such as this sailor is encountering at Cypress Point.

of water, no matter how inevitable this outcome seems from the depths of the trough. The odds of the game are greater when blindfolded by night, and boat motion and sea motion are sensed rather than seen. The stakes are high enough—being life itself. Pride in holding their own against these extremes of sea, wind and temperament permeates the craft and crew.

Under better conditions, Eureka would have been the obvious haven to duck out of this nightmare, but with dense fog and darkness, too, and since the boat was well fueled and running well, the wisest move was to keep moving. Crescent City, too, is a well-protected harbor, but strict attention must be paid to the buoys and good visibility is important, especially to anyone not familiar with the bay.

Passing Point George, *Bee Jay III*'s bow soon was cleaving Oregon waters.

When the sea became tumultuous up the California coast, the incredible waves rushed monstrously open-mouthed at the bow, as though to swallow all whole. In Oregon the seas changed perceptibly. Now the behemoths nipped at the stern, boiling higher and higher, arching over, until, frothing at the top with white hissing foam, there seemed no other outcome but that they must break and engulf all. Each new building crest rushing from behind, however, found the stern lifting, and suddenly, surprisingly, smoothly and evenly, the boat was comfortably surfing at breakneck speed in the heart of the colossal wave.

The boat gradually dropped behind and seemed abandoned in an abyss of a world of water, while another enormous swell was building and threatening.

The bars at the entrance to all of the harbors of the Pacific Coast in Oregon and Washington present the most critical problems to be faced by any seafarer in these waters. Those jettied harbors mean well with their rocky arms outstretched, fending off and breaking up the fury of the sea, but they often have a heart of solid sand. The tempestuous sea deposits a barrier across the inviting harbor entrance and is aided in her construction by the rivers, depositing silt.

These underwater sandbars cause certain seas to swell large and break over—the same principle as a wave that comes from far at sea, reaches shallow water, and tends to arch higher and higher to overcome the rise of land under it, until it finally reaches a peak of arc and crashes forward onto the beach. This same action occurs when the wave hits the sandbar of these harbors. Money and time is now being spent to rectify some of this problem in individual harbors by dredging deeper channels and building better-engineered jetties in the hope of discouraging the redeposit of sand.

Under adverse sea conditions, at the bar the waves seem to squat or crouch, trying to look diminutive to lure the unsuspecting into their lair. Then one rares up and pounces at the quarry, pulling the seas out from under in the trough, leaving it fathomless; another lifts the hapless craft and drops it to an empty sea floor. The next wave can broach the boat, and it only takes one more to roll it over.

The best time to cross any of the bars, storm conditions considered, is high tide before the ebb starts to run—when the tide is neither coming in nor going out.

The first harbor above the Oregon border is Brookings at the Chetco River. Commercial and sport fishing abound here, and the weather is often better than farther north, but the bar can be bad and it bears careful watching.

Gold Beach on the Rogue River is definitely treacherous, and there is no place, once the bar is crossed, for boats to moor. The wide harbor is very shallow and no craft can move around much within the area except at high tide.

Port Orford is a pretty town, nestled in a graceful curve at one of the most scenic stretches of the Oregon coast. Here, just south of Cape Blanco, the color of the water when the sun is shining would rival Hawaii, the Bahamas, or the Mediterranean. Dark offshore rocks accent the unbelievable blue and green, and the spectacular beauty is tied up like a gift, with a silver cord of sun-spangled clouds along the distant horizon. As an anchorage, however, there is not enough protection from most any kind of sea, and most boats are hauled out in case of a blow.

Coos Bay has a bar, but it is an adequate, well-protected harbor, much like Eureka, California. Here there are facilities, but the newcomer should watch markers diligently and try to avoid entering with poor visibility.

When the *Bee Jay* approached the two widespread scraggly arms of Winchester Bay's jetties, she warily watched a tug and its tow come out across the bar before entering this snug haven on the Umpqua River. Salmon Harbor is a good mooring spot for transients, and the whole area offers excellent fishing. The nearby town is Reedsport.

Leaving Winchester Bay in the early morning at slack tide, the dour sea was so calm there was no evidence of a bar. Mists, lying on top of the tree-covered bluffs, softened

Fishing is good on the Oregon Coast. Opposite page: Fish nets take shape on the dock, and the crab boats are busy. Left: Harbor master at Garibaldi rescues a seal pup which is trying to adopt Bee Jay III.

the grim sea cliffs and demurely veiled the shoreside evergreens. While Oregon-shore mountains are less precipitous than those of the California coast, they are more heavily forested.

North of Winchester is the Siuslaw River near Florence. This and the Alsea River entrance at Waldport can be tricky bar crossings, as they break quite readily. Newport, farther north on the Yaquina River, has the same facilities as Siuslaw and offers generally better bar-crossing conditions. Depoe Bay should definitely be avoided by those not native to the area.

Along this part of the Oregon coast are miles of some of the largest sand dunes in the world. These massive golden hummocks, intricately wave carved, are crowned with sea-warped trees, their spindly, piney arms pointing landward as if to say, "Leave the sea." There are moments afloat when any mariner would like to comply.

The Yaquina Head Lighthouse near Newport, alone on its rocky promontory, was wreathed with luminous fog, a grainy fog as though browned with windblown sand. The vaporous opacity muted the stark harshness of the bleak rocky coast north toward Cape Lookout and Cape Meares.

The sheer Oregon cliffs and offshore rocks are high-rise condominiums of birds. The tenants overhead peered at our passing on the apple-green sea below, graceful necks outstretched, slender heads turning silently as one—a gallery of engrossed spectators. Here and there a flutter of wings and exchange of pecks disturbed the neighborhood peace, as did the raucous screams of a flock of elegant snowy-breasted gulls, which soared above us as we traveled north.

Most prevalent in the bird colonies along these shores are the black-frocked murres, distant cousins of the penguin family. These dark little birds swim underwater with the same wing motion as in the air added to the paddling of their stubby legs. The red-footed pigeon guillemot nests in dark, foreboding, high-ceilinged caves where the huge seas roll in hard and fast. To pass these deepmouthed caverns, a boat must navigate very close to the breaker line.

Close-in is where the crabbing is done also. The daring crab fishermen must be very cautious in placing their pots. Crab-pot floats line the sea like lanes on a freeway, and by keeping a straight compass heading, one travels for miles between two rows of colorful floats. Now and then a crabber is seen pulling his pots, deftly sorting and collecting crabs and rebaiting before casting each pot back with a splash and proceeding swiftly to the next, the plucky boat churning and rolling in the troughs.

Garibaldi on Tillamook Bay is home to a large part of the Oregon coast fishing and crabbing fleet. Here seiners, netters, and crabbers moor and sell their catch; and frequent the dock marine stores for gear and the tiny cafes for coffee and company. This is a beautifully sheltered harbor and the south jetty is expected to improve the harbor entrance and minimize the treachery of the bar situation.

When the fishing fleet is bar bound here, it is a thrilling sight. All wharf space is filled with row upon row of staunch craft, as proud as they are high in the bow, battle scarred from bouts with their demanding mistress, the intemperate Oregon sea. The sea really only bests the fleet by landlocking it in the harbors she seeks to devour—and then only by stormily and petulantly casting spume-throwing breakers across the bar she is eternally and ingeniously constructing. The boats wait in their slips, not cowering, just impatient for the moody elements to settle down so each hardy skipper with wisdom, control and good judgment can go forth to meet and master the torturous challenge that is his life on the deep.

After watchfully studying the bar situation at the entrance of the harbor at Garibaldi, and deciding it safe to cross, we found the sea one of mountainous following swells, emerald green, and dotted black with hundreds of murres which had apparently located an infinite school of tiny fish. Rounding Tillamook Head, the abandoned lighthouse on its isolated rock fortress sits like a sad, yet impregnable, castle with the entire sea for a protective moat.

All aboard became thoughtful as the water's color began to lighten, meaning that not far ahead was the "Graveyard of the Pacific," the Columbia River mouth. The Columbia River bash is generally wild, especially at ebb tide, and with a strong sou'easter meeting the outrush of this greatest of all waters spilling into the Pacific Ocean of the Northwest. The water becomes a venomous yellow and has no regularity of swell and fall—just sheer madness of the river tide pouring out and battling the normal landward surge of the sea.

As the senselessly directionless waves clashed, we were lifted precariously on ugly sulphur-colored columns of water. This maniacal, jaundiced sea shook the boat like a ravenous lion with a rabbit, and the insides of the vessel trembled with shock, and cups in the locker tinkled together like chattering teeth. The sturdiness of a boat is tested over and over in these extreme moments. The structure, design and builder are all blessed in one quick-drawn breath.

The Columbia River, however, offers the finest harbor of any between San Francisco and Cape Flattery, when due regard is given the tide and the bar and the general sea condition. Astoria, on the Columbia, has fine facilities and protection in her moorings. Under threat of storm, emergency or equipment breakdown, this would be the best harbor to enter. Markings are very explicit, but the skipper must stay alert and observe them faithfully.

Willapa, Washington, the first harbor above the Columbia River, is shallow, has a bar, offers no services to speak of and should not be used except in dire emergency. Gray's Harbor, in Washington, has the same bar problems as the Oregon harbors farther south. Once inside, though, the facilities are adequate. In almost all of these coastal harbors is a Coast Guard unit which will give advice and aid to boats requesting assistance and information on crossing the bars.

After a night on a lumpy sea, the *Bee Jay III* rounded Cape Flattery with a justifiable sense of a long course well cruised. Surprisingly, the usually cranky Straits of Juan de Fuca were so flat the off-duty members of the crew left their bunks, thinking the boat had stopped. Instead, she was smoothly skimming like a bird up the channel toward Victoria. Passing Race Rocks in the early morn, a quick stop was made at Sidney, on Vancouver Island, for inspection at Canadian Customs. Then, popping around a headland and an island, snaking down Iroquois Passage, the boat eased into her familiar slip at Canoe Cove—her home away from home.

Resting at last like a warrior after battle, the sturdy craft found no real wounds to lick. All systems were still "go." She could turn around and do it all over again—and would, going down the long coast in the fall. Meanwhile, her reward and the crews' would be a summer of frolic and fun in the lovely American San Juan and the Canadian Gulf Islands.

Landlubbers who sit at home on their beam-ends miss something of this grappling with infinity, something to learn of self and reality by coming to grips with the honesty of the elements. They do not deceive—the power of sea, wind and tide is for all to know and reckon with, and, in so doing, find in themselves a heretofore hidden strength.

Sturdy Bee Jay III finished her eventful voyage north in fit condition.

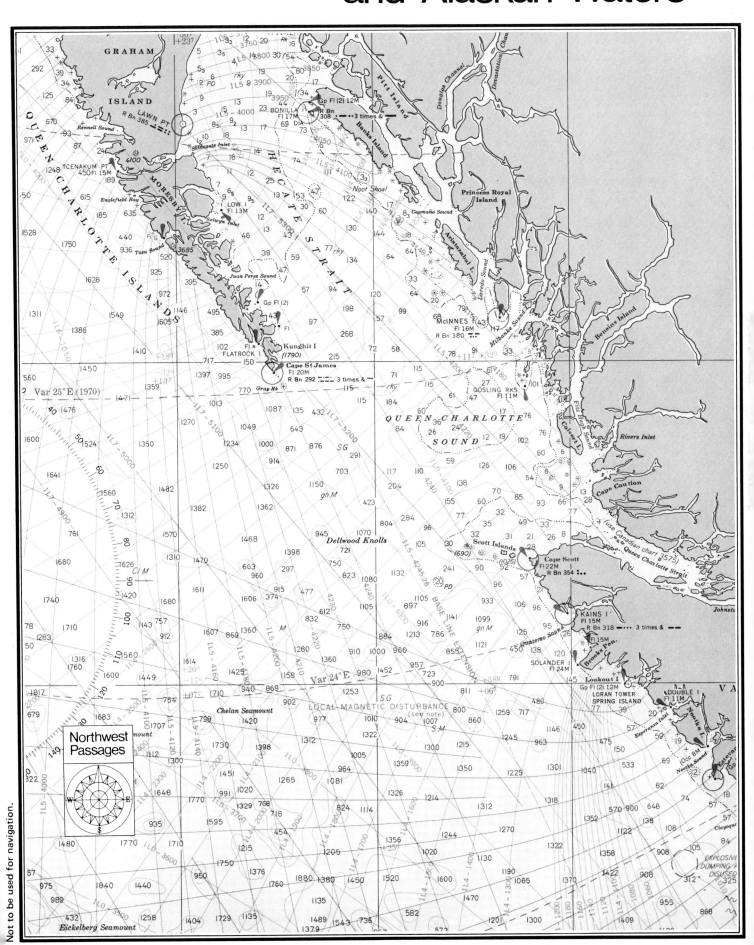

Northwest
Passages

22

Along Alaska's Inland Passage

Alaska is a land of superlatives. For the cruising yachtsman, Alaska's Inland Passage is a labyrinth of quiet channels, sparkling straits and glassy calm arms of the sea, winding among hills clothed by forests or beneath steep, naked cliffs which sometimes cradle gigantic, glistening, blue-hued glaciers.

More and more skippers, not just from the Northwest but from California and even the eastern states, are becoming interested in cruising here, investigating the warm, intimate, inviting harbors and partaking of the bold grandeur that stretches as far as the eye can see. Each year new ones come and old ones return. It's an area which could never be fully explored in a lifetime.

Yes, there is much here to attract. However, a quick look at a chart of the area, or hearing the stories of open ocean, rough water, fog and poor weather conditions can be discouraging. A boat can be a sometimes temperamental thing, subject to breakdowns and other disabling accidents in remote waterways. For such reasons most skippers prefer group cruising.

Our most recent exploration of these waters was in conjunction with the biennial Alaska Cruiser race and cruise sponsored by the International Power Boat Association. This event offers an excellent opportunity, particularly for the first-timer, to make the trip in a group under planned conditions. A very relaxed schedule and informal race rules allowed for a leisurely three-week cruise from Vancouver to Juneau. And race participation isn't required; boats "along for the ride" are accepted.

We were the guest of Harold and Ann Hovland in their beautiful new 40-foot Tollycraft, the *Gala,* on the race up to Juneau and during four delightful weeks of exploration cruising on the way back.

Racemaster Neil Armstrong of Tacoma Yacht Club planned for plenty of sightseeing with side trips and free days. Starting at Vancouver following the Seattle-to-Vancouver International Cruiser Race, the fleet cruised to Princess Louisa, then through a series of gorgeous sequestered passages and channels, with some choice of routes to and across Queen Charlotte Strait to the Noble Islets, near the top of Vancouver Island.

Since the initial leg has been covered previously, we start this account at Vancouver Island. Although our interest is primarily in the cruising, occasionally highlights of the race will appear. Such a vignette concerned our day as observer aboard Jim and Pam Clapp's *Nothing More.*

This speedy floating palace, with twin turbine motors shooting her through the water at 30 knots, hadn't yet been sufficiently tamed to establish a definite speed curve. For this reason Jim ran a test course before starting the race each day. When he was satisfied that his speed was right, he did some last-minute computing on his predicted log and we headed for the starting line off Deep Sea Bluff outside Simoom Sound.

Traces of the morning mist still hung lightly above the water like a filmy nighty that had not yet been exchanged for the brighter clothes of the day. Approaching the comparatively open water of Queen Charlotte Strait, we peered eagerly through the glasses for some clue to wind and water conditions. All looked calm.

The sea was gray except where the midmorning sun pierced the mist with searchlight shafts of gold. It wasn't long before a bright, clear day blossomed into its full glory. The strait turned a serene green with scarcely a ripple to break its mirror face. This was good, especially traveling at our speed, for there were many patches of floating drift and long curving tide lines of seaweed, broken-up kelp, chips and, occasionally, large logs.

Nothing More skimmed through the water effortlessly, leaving her ever-widening V-wake to upset the gulls which so obligingly marked the larger pieces of drift for us. In the enclosed air-conditioned pilothouse there was no sensation of speed; no feeling of flying through, or almost over, the water. Neither Jim, at the controls, snaking the boat through the patches of drift, nor Dr. Ray Marty, continually checking his navigation figures, showed any signs of tenseness. It was a most relaxing ride across a body of water that sometimes can be really nasty. Arriving at the finish line, we had run a zero-zero leg, that is, no error. To a predicted log contestant this is comparable to a golfer's hole in one. Skipper and crew naturally were elated.

Among several good harbors offering protection on the Vancouver Island side of the strait are Bauza Cove, Beaver Cove, Telegraph Cove, Port McNeill and Beaver Harbor.

Alert Bay on Cormorant Island is the major town in this area, and it has supplies and facilities to meet almost every need. About half of the population is Indian and in the middle of town is a cemetery with typical Indian graves and a large collection of totems of all sizes and shapes. The waterfront is an interesting combination of old wharves, some of them in bad repair, and new modern piers and floats. There are several public moorages, the newest and largest being at the northern end of the town. From there to the shopping area is a fair hike, but taxicabs are radio dispatched and cruise the town constantly.

Sointula, in Rough Bay on Malcolm Island, is a Finnish community with neat houses and carefully manicured yards, and even authentic Finnish sauna baths. A new breakwater protects a modern moorage basin for small boats, again at the northern end of the town's waterfront.

Port Hardy, in Hardy Bay, is a port of entry and has a public moorage, fuel, hotels, stores, telephone and medical services. The moorage is a bit south of the main part of town, but taxi service is available. Close attention should be paid to buoys, markers and beacons, coming into the bay, as a shoal extends for a considerable distance from the west shore. This puts the channel closer to the opposite shore.

In the approximately 600 miles from Alert Bay to Juneau, the Inland Passage has only three serious exposures to the open Pacific Ocean—Queen Charlotte Sound, Milbanke Sound, and Dixon Entrance. Of these, Queen Charlotte Sound's 36 miles of unprotected water can be a glassy millpond or a dangerous crossing. This is one place where it pays not to be a hero or to try to prove something. Wait until the weather and sea are right.

Port Alexander on Nigei Island and God's Pocket on Hurst Island are two popular bays frequently used as waiting or jumping-off bays for the sound crossing. Our itinerary gave us a choice of the two for the nightly anchorage, but God's Pocket was crowded with fishing boats and so we snugged down in Port Alexander.

The schedule called for a group cruise next morning to Schooner Channel, Slingsby Channel and famous Nakwakto Rapids, the fastest in North America. General confusion over standard and daylight time and delays in getting orga-

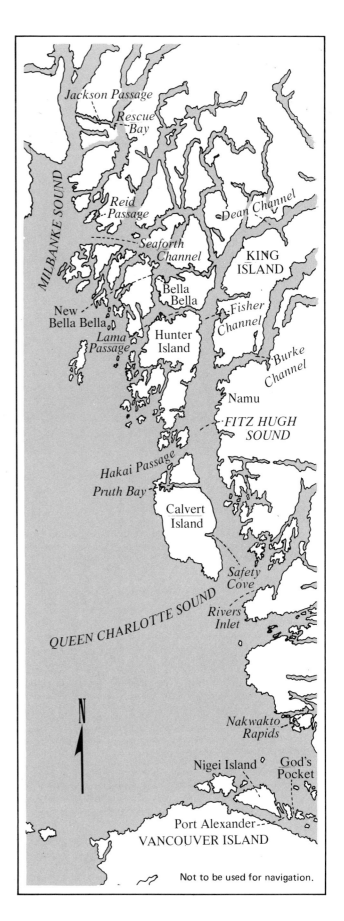

Not to be used for navigation.

On shore during the Alaskan cruise. Top: Members of the group explore a narrow fissure in the rocks leading to the sea. Bottom: In the woods between Pruth Bay and the ocean beach, a twisted tree trunk forms a pleasing frame for this picture of Karen Thayer from the Largo.

nized meant missing slack water at the rapids; so Racemaster Armstrong regretfully scrubbed this side trip.

The morning was again misty and overcast. Our observer appointment put us aboard Thol and Lillian Simonson's *Largo* for the day. It was a pleasure to ride with these pleasant people in their lovely boat. This 40-foot 1928 Matthews has been restored to mint condition by the Simonsons. Thol is a special-effects expert for Hollywood's movie and TV industry, and we never tired of hearing his answers to our questions about his work or about yachting and predicted log racing in Southern California.

A radio call from *Gala*, which had left earlier, reported good sea and wind conditions in the sound. Crossing to Christie Passage and slipping out past God's Pocket, we started our run in this bit of open ocean. There was a moderate wind, which produced a light chop but nothing serious. *Largo* was riding nicely as she passed Pine Island and headed for Egg Island.

The tang of salt-sea air was stimulating as we looked to the left at the ever-changing Pacific. On our right was the rugged, rocky coast of the mainland with Cape Caution sticking out into the sea. Trees above the rocks were olive green as they rose to a setting of lower mountains, backed in the distance by their higher white-haired brothers with their strong shoulders holding up the sky.

After we were far enough into the sound to be committed to a crossing, Queen Charlotte proved her fickleness by blowing up a wind out of the northwest. Soon long, green ocean rollers were walking in from the Pacific in slow motion while an uncomfortable chop played tag up and down their sides to produce a confused sea, not dangerous but uncomfortable. *Largo* took it nicely but her skipper had to work at the wheel. The breakers made a filigreed lace edging of foam as they crashed against the distant shore.

Under these conditions, it seemed to take a long time to pass Cape Caution and reach Egg Island and its satellites where the waves broke on sheer points, drenching the storm-stunted firs growing in rocky crevices above. Being able to see Cape Calvert and realizing that its protection was only a little over an hour away was comforting. Fortunately, this was a closed day for commercial fishing so we didn't have the usual gill-net-dodging problems in this area.

After better than four hours of an uncomfortable crossing, we were in the lee of Calvert Island. It was a relief to be cruising again in the protected waters of Fitz Hugh Sound, with Queen Charlotte Sound and her threats of gales and fog behind us. Quiet channels flanked by mountains clad in forests, friendly harbors and, we hoped, good weather lay ahead.

To our right was the entrance to Rivers Inlet. This is an interesting cruising area with a wealth of inviting bays and coves but primarily noted as a favorite salmon-fishing spot where the big ones run.

Safety Cove, poking its mile-long finger into Calvert Island nearly halfway up the east side, perhaps isn't the best anchorage in the world. Shores are steep, high and rocky except at the head where southeasterly or southwesterly gales can sneak in to produce strong gusts between

Pruth Bay proved a peaceful anchorage after choppy water on Queen Charlotte Sound. Kwakshua Channel is in background.

the 1000-foot-high walls. Vancouver used it and it offers convenient protection while awaiting a southern crossing of Queen Charlotte Sound.

Across the top of Calvert Island, Kwakshua Channel runs east-west with Hecate Island to the north. At its western end, snuggled in behind a peninsula of Calvert Island, is cross-shaped Pruth Bay, as delightful an anchorage as anyone could desire.

Ashore, a winding path twisted its way through a setting of thick foliage to the half-mile-distant ocean. Shafts of

light from the sinking sun filtered through the delicate green of firs, cedars and a scattering of deciduous trees. Suddenly the trail opened onto a scene of glittering beauty. The ocean had calmed for the evening and it was a robin's egg blue, spangled with the gold of the sun, as it gently lapped a wide half-moon spread of soft beige sand. The picturesque point presented a study of storm-torn trees twisted into tortured shapes. Huge silvery drift logs, scoured, beaten and scarred by stormy seas and tossed well back on the beach against the background of tremendous

Early morning sun lights the mountain walls of Princess Louisa Inlet, while her valley remains relatively dark. Most of the fleet tied up near Chatterbox Falls.

rocks, gave mute evidence that this ocean isn't always pacific.

Several hiking parties came through the woods to enjoy the unrivaled charm of this beach. Some brought refreshments which were enjoyed as we watched a sleek gray freighter climb up over the edge of the world, its propellers paving a glistening white road of foam behind it. Pruth Bay will not be soon forgotten as a favorite anchorage.

A channel about two and a half miles long leads north from Kwakshua Channel opposite Keith Anchorage. Running between the peninsula of Calvert Island and Hecate Island, it enters Hakai Passage, an ocean entrance to Fitz Hugh Sound. Salmon fishing was reported good to the west and northwest of the peninsula, but time didn't permit our trying it.

Proceeding up Fitz Hugh Sound the next day, we were observing aboard Allen and Faith Hill's 43-foot Tollycraft *Aukai*. This area is filled with exploration possibilities and we logged it for future attention. A look at the chart discloses the literally hundreds of bays, inlets and coves of Hunter Island and the many smaller surrounding islands and islets. On the eastern side is Namu, the cannery town of whale fame, and a half dozen coves, inlets and basins inviting anchorage or exploration.

At the foot of King Island, Fitz Hugh Sound splits into Fisher Channel, which continues northward, and Burke Channel, which leads to Bella Coola and joins Dean Channel to circle King Island. Ocean Falls is at the head of Cousins Inlet, which takes off to the north from Dean Channel.

Our course turned westward from Fisher Channel into Lama Passage. This soon swings north to Bella Bella and New Bella Bella. Some of the yachts stopped here for shopping in the general store and for fuel. New Bella Bella is the Indian village and the more impressive looking, while Bella Bella has the store.

Turning into Seaforth Channel, we ran into a fair chop with swells coming from the ocean via Milbanke Sound. It wasn't anything to worry about, but we were glad when we reached Ivory Island and turned into lovely Reid Passage behind Cecilia Island for the free run to our rendezvous at Rescue Bay.

It was here we ran into a bit of unpredicted current. The chart shows a current of 3.5 knots; however, it appeared to be considerably stronger. With fairly large rollers going with us from Milbanke Sound and an ebb current coming against us, we encountered tide rips and even some overfall. Although it threw us around a bit, there was no real problem.

There is a choice of four different routes, with Reid Passage offering the most protected and most scenic. The channel is narrow and calls for close attention to the course as shown on large-scale chart #3710. Major danger is Carne Rock, which should be left to port on the northbound course. In spite of the attention necessary to make this course good, it is impossible to ignore the spectacular beauty of enchanting islands scattered on an emerald sea. Inviting glimpses of small bays and winding arms called for more intimate exploration at another time.

If Milbanke isn't kicking up, a course can be laid directly up Mathieson Channel, up the sound to Moss Passage to get into Mathieson Channel, or farther up to Oscar Passage, or directly up into Finlayson Channel. Our course took us into Mathieson Channel to Rescue Bay at the eastern end of Jackson Passage.

The cool quiet of this anchorage is well protected, with two islands standing guard at the entrance. It was here that we found ourselves orphaned because *Gala* had found it necessary to put into Namu for engine repairs and only got as far as Bella Bella that night. The Hills were equal to the occasion, however, for their giveaway observer was aboard the *Gala*. We enjoyed a fine dinner, hot shower, even an extra toothbrush and a comfortable bunk as a guest aboard the *Aukai*.

The lower portion of the Inland Passage, from Seattle to the top of Vancouver Island, is fairly familiar to many yachtsmen. Now we had crossed the "big water" and were on our way to Alaska.

GLOSSARY OF PLACE-NAMES

Queen Charlotte Sound—After Queen Charlotte Sophia, wife of King George III.

Hardy Bay and Port Hardy—By Captain Richards, 1860, after Vice Adm. Sir Thomas Masterman Hardy, Lord Nelson's captain of the *Victory* at the battle of Trafalgar.

Malcolm Island—By Comdr. George T. Gordon, 1846, after Adm. Sir Pulteney Malcolm, R.N., who had a distinguished naval career and was especially appointed to guard Napoleon at the St. Helena station.

Alert Bay—By Captain Richards, 1860, after H.M. screw corvette *Alert*.

Sointula—A Finnish word meaning "harmony."

Nigei Island—After the hereditary name of the principal chief of the Nahwitti tribe of Indians.

Port Alexander—By Captain Richards, 1861, after Lt. Alexander Fraser Boxer, R.N., master of the *Alert*.

Cape Caution—By Captain Vancouver, 1793, owing to the hazards of navigation in the vicinity. During the previous year, his ship *Discovery* was nearly lost here on a rock.

Rivers Inlet—By Captain Vancouver, 1792, following examination by Lt. Peter Puget, after George Pitt, first Baron Rivers of Strathfieldsaye.

Calvert Island—By Capt. Charles Duncan of the sloop *Princess Royal*, 1788, after the noble house of Baltimore, perhaps more specifically, Lord Cecil Calvert, second baron of Baltimore, who was first governor of Maryland.

Hecate Island, Bay, Channel, Cove, Strait, etc.—By Captain Richards, 1861-1862, after H.M. surveying vessel *Hecate*.

Bella Bella—An adaptation of the name of a tribe of Indians residing in the neighborhood.

Seaforth Channel—By officers of the Hudson's Bay Company, circa 1840, after Francis Humbertson Mackenzie, Baron Seaforth of the Seaforth Highlanders.

Milbanke Sound—By Capt. Charles Duncan, 1788, after Adm. Mark Milbanke who had a distinguished naval career, 1736-1793.

Nakwakto Rapids—By Captain Pender, 1865, after the Indian tribe residing there under Chief Siwiti.

Slingsby Channel—By Captain Pender, 1865, after Sir Charles Slingsby, tenth and last baronet of Scriven Park, Knaresborough, Yorkshire.

Safety Cove—Named Port Safety in 1788 by Capt. Charles Duncan of the *Princess Royal* who stayed here in the summer of that year after trading for some weeks between Queen Charlotte Islands and the continental shore. Vancouver, who adopted the name safety Cove, was at anchor here with his vessels August 10-19, 1792, while his boats examined the continental shoreline from Cape Caution to Menzies Point.

23

Narrow Channels
Between Wooded Islands

Early morning was beautiful. A bit of lingering night was still a dull gray along the shore and in the shadows of the tall evergreens. Higher up, the rounded hills were bathed in soft blues, purples and golds, all reflected on the glossy waters of Rescue Bay as the sun awoke.

Aboard the cruiser *Aukai*, in the predicted log race to Alaska, we prepared for another warm summer day cruising the famous Inland Passage to Alaska. This was definitely "flying bridge" weather. There was plenty of sun for tanning yet the morning air had a crisper feel to remind us we were truly getting to the north country.

Trading assignments with *Aukai*'s observer, we went aboard Thol Simonson's *Largo* for the day's run. Eventually, *Largo* was the overall winner.

Rescue Bay is almost a part of scenic Jackson Passage, lying at its eastern entrance in Mathieson Channel. We were hardly out of the bay before the bow poked into Jackson Narrows. Here is one of those spots where a skipper making the trip for the first time is torn between scenery watching and duty. There really isn't much choice, however, because the tricky, narrow channel requires full attention in order to stay off the rocks and reefs. Large-scale chart #3711 makes the job easier—and safer.

Jackson Passage itself is a five-and-a-half-mile east-west arm connecting Mathieson and Finlayson Channels. It can hardly be called spectacular but it is certainly one of the beauty highlights of the trip. The thickly wooded hills on the north are steeper and higher than those on the south, and at least half a dozen small bays, coves and islets invite closer inspection, while combining to produce an intimate, sylvan loveliness that isn't soon forgotten.

In contemplating a first-time trip to Alaska, it's easy to imagine waterways winding between high and steep purple

mountains with snow-capped peaks, as seen in travel folders. These will all be found well up in Alaska itself, but cruising the Inland Passage through British Columbia is very little different from a trip through the San Juan or Gulf Islands. It's an enchanting cruise in a labyrinth of channels between fairyland islands thrust up from the sea, with fir and cedar growing to the water's edge, neatly bobbed in a straight line by the high tide.

There's a certain sameness, yet an almost imperceptible difference, but for most it is never boring. An interesting game for the youngsters in the fleet—and some of the adults—was to see how many animal shapes or human faces could be traced in the imagination among the hills and outcroppings of rock. Such suggestions of shapes and faces in Jackson Passage are remarkable.

Crossing Finlayson Channel, we rounded the southern end of Cone Island to enter Klemtu Passage, which separates the sliver of Cone Island from the larger Swindle Island. This is a narrow but interesting channel, an extension of Milbanke Sound, and is the quickest way to get out of Finlayson Channel if it is rough. Larger ships go up Sarah Passage, where Klemtu Passage becomes Tolmie Channel.

There are several small coves in Klemtu Passage, and on Swindle Island, about two-thirds of the way up Cone Island, is the fishing and cannery village of Klemtu. Fuel and limited supplies are available here.

Around Split Head, at the top of Swindle Island, are two interesting waterways. Meyers Passage is a narrow arm connecting Tolmie Channel with the sea, via Laredo Sound. With a common entrance, Alexander Inlet takes off to the west and southwest for five miles, great for fascinating exploration. High peaks, steep walls, Bingham Narrows, a wealth of islands and islets, along with several coves, make

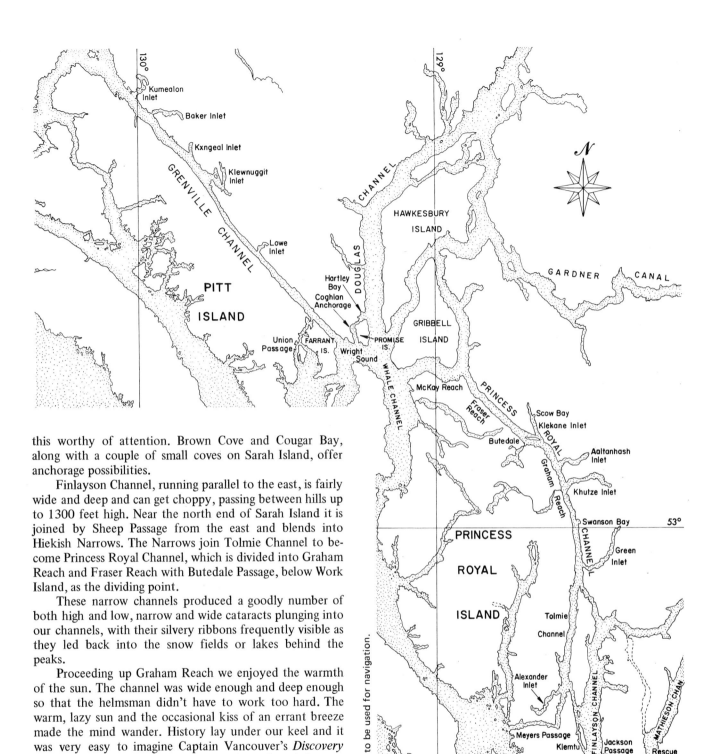

this worthy of attention. Brown Cove and Cougar Bay, along with a couple of small coves on Sarah Island, offer anchorage possibilities.

Finlayson Channel, running parallel to the east, is fairly wide and deep and can get choppy, passing between hills up to 1300 feet high. Near the north end of Sarah Island it is joined by Sheep Passage from the east and blends into Hiekish Narrows. The Narrows join Tolmie Channel to become Princess Royal Channel, which is divided into Graham Reach and Fraser Reach with Butedale Passage, below Work Island, as the dividing point.

These narrow channels produced a goodly number of both high and low, narrow and wide cataracts plunging into our channels, with their silvery ribbons frequently visible as they led back into the snow fields or lakes behind the peaks.

Proceeding up Graham Reach we enjoyed the warmth of the sun. The channel was wide enough and deep enough so that the helmsman didn't have to work too hard. The warm, lazy sun and the occasional kiss of an errant breeze made the mind wander. History lay under our keel and it was very easy to imagine Captain Vancouver's *Discovery* and *Chatham* working up this same channel, and the captains sending one of the small boats in to explore the four navigable miles of Green Inlet with its Horsefly Cove, islands and reversing tidal falls.

About five miles farther up is Swanson Bay, an anchorage favored by skippers of small boats. An abandoned sawmill and pulpmill on the north shore add to the romance of the bay. Its quiet is occasionally broken by the shrill scream of an eagle, questioning trespassers in his domain as he glides gracefully, high overhead, making his way from one shore to the other.

Graham Reach has two more inlets, both with Indian names. Khutze Inlet is four and a half miles north of Swanson Bay and runs eastward for about five miles between densely wooded, steep slopes with several sheer cliffs on the north side. A little more than two miles farther is four-mile-long Aaltanhash Inlet, also splitting the hills to the east. The depths in both of these inlets are too great for

Top: Light morning fog at Rescue Bay, eastern entrance to scenic Jackson Passage. Bottom: Mercer Girl ties up at float in front of the falls at Butedale, fishing settlement and usual stopping place along the route.

good anchorage although, at the very head of each, one can drop a hook in 10 to 20 fathoms—if he has the scope.

Princess Royal Channel turns northwest at Redcliff Point to become Fraser Reach, with Work Island in the middle and Klekane Inlet taking off to the north-northwest. As in the others, depths up to 100 fathoms preclude good anchoring, except in Scow Bay. This is sometimes a good crabbing spot, and the water is so clear that these delectable shellfish can easily be seen along the bottom walking on their awkward stilts.

The fishing settlement of Butedale is a usual stopping place on the route. Set in a small bay to the south of Work Island, it features a picturesque waterfall to the right of the main floats where Butedale Creek helps empty part of Butedale Lake into the saltchuck in a rocky splashing pattern of several streams. There are a post office, store, and fuel dock; however, radiotelephone service is undependable.

Fraser Reach continued northwest, parting the hills for us as they began to get higher and steeper. Rounding Kingcome Point, the route turns west into McKay Reach for an eight-mile run to cross Whale Channel and Wright Sound. Our objective for the nightly rendezvous was Coghlan Anchorage behind Promise Island near the entrance to Grenville Channel.

It was here that *Nothing More*, delayed by a broken high-pressure fuel line, caught up with the fleet.

Just north of Promise Island, off Douglas Channel, is Hartley Bay with its Indian village, mission, post office and government float. We stopped here on the return trip and our arrival seemed to signal at least half of the population of Indians to come down to investigate the ships. That night a tribe of teen-agers woke us up with whooping, banging, general noisemaking and yells of something about "palefaces." The scene reminded us of vivid stories of Indian encounters 100 years ago.

Douglas Channel continues north and then northwest from here to end at Kitimat, British Columbia's new aluminum town, site of the big Canadian plant. Gardner Canal, several channels, arms, inlets and bays in this area present an intriguing invitation for future exploring.

July 22 dawned with cloudy skies and rain starting at 0715, and we were back aboard our home ship, *Gala*. Since an extra leg had been run the previous day, it was decided to run the two remaining legs, totaling 68 miles, all the way through to Prince Rupert, thus arriving there a day early. We encountered several gill netters and purse seiners but managed to spot their nets in time to avoid them.

These are a frequent hazard in Northwest waters, and it is the responsibility of the yachtsman to keep clear. He is liable for any damage done by his yacht's propellers. The nets, hung below the surface of the water from a line usually marked by white or orange floats, stretch behind the fish boat up to 1000 or 1500 feet. In rippled or choppy seas, they can be hard to spot.

Almost two-thirds of the day's run was through 43-mile-long Grenville Channel, a straight and narrow passage connecting Wright Sound with Arthur Passage and the approaches to Prince Rupert. Hills along the shore are rounded, fairly low and wooded, backed with higher inland hills.

Those on the northerly side are higher, rising to barren rocky peaks with snow patches. Greens of the forest clothing vary from brilliant emerald to a grayish olive, and these fade abruptly to the browns, blacks and dirty whites of the rocky peaks.

Although this channel appears to be just a long, straight ribbon on the chart, it has several intriguing sideshows. A little over four miles beyond the southeast entrance, Union Passage joins it from the south. This interesting waterway, separating Pitt and Farrant Islands, connects with Squally Channel and features Peters Narrows and Hawkins Narrows, both with fast-running rapids, and several bays and little coves.

A favorite stopover for many is Lowe Inlet, poking its finger northeastward for nearly two miles. A highlight of Nettle Basin, at its head, is Verney Falls which forms the mouth of the Kumowdah River. A boat can be brought right up to the base of the falls, where fishing is usually excellent. Our effort to land a lunker proved fruitless.

Nettle Basin, the inner third of the inlet, offers secure anchorage in a captivating setting. The entrance to the basin in highlighted by a tree that seems to have been transplanted from a Japanese garden to the very tip of Pike Point. We saw its branches loaded with small white birds, probably terns, a picture scented with romance.

A delightful lake lies behind Nettle Basin; it can be reached by portaging the dinghy along the shelves of rock west of the falls, and again over rock beside a smaller waterfall. Swimming, fishing and exploring can be enjoyed in this large, warm, freshwater lake.

The next two inlets have fascinating names. Klewnuggit Inlet has several arms with at least half a dozen good anchorages. Unpronounceable Kxngeal Inlet is a mile-and-a-quarter-long northerly finger between high hills and offers anchorage in 17 fathoms near the head.

Baker Inlet extends eastward for about three and a half miles and is entered through Watts Narrows. The inlet is large enough to run a considerable volume of water through the narrows, producing a strong and fast current. Slack of around five minutes is about the same time as high and low tides at Prince Rupert. A cozy anchorage in 8 to 10 fathoms is found at the head of the inlet.

Probably the most beautiful of Grenville's various side attractions is Kumealon Inlet. About two miles in length, this inlet, lacking the steep walls of some of the others, has a quiet beauty that makes it a favorite anchorage, and it is only 30 miles below Prince Rupert. It had originally been scheduled for an overnight rendezvous and, since it lay at the end of a race leg, we went in to renew memories of a previous anchorage here.

The mirror-smooth surface of the water reflected *Gala*'s hull, like a white ornament on a lime-frosted cake. The rich, warm water showed green over the shoal areas, blending into midnight blue in the deeper parts, as dark fingers of our slow-moving wake scouted the shore.

An inner bay lies behind a scenic island and its group of satellite islets and rocks, with entrance to the left of the island. We predict this will be logged as a favorite anchorage. A shallow, tortuous narrows, generously scattered with

This enchanting waterfall in Graham Reach is just one of many to be seen splashing their way down the steep hillsides from lakes or snow fields behind and higher up.

Indian village of Hartley Bay has a picturesque setting just off Douglas Channel, and offers protected moorage.

rocks, leads to a tidal falls into Kumealon Lagoon and offers some excellent dinghy exploration possibilities. Anchorage also can be found in the little bay behind Kumealon Island, at the entrance to the inlet.

No Inland Passage trip should be made without a stopover, or a look into, at least a couple of these five appendages to Grenville Channel. You'll like what you see and, if time won't permit lingering, you surely will schedule more time here on a future trip.

Leaving Kumealon Inlet, we found a stiff southeasterly wind kicking the channel into a chop. Ahead of us was a fogbank. From the northwest end of Grenville Channel, we rounded Gibson Island to its left and headed up Arthur Passage. Fighting a following sea, and using the radar to help identify landmarks in poor visibility, we were busy enough when the port engine decided to add to these problems by quitting.

Taking time out from the race, we pulled into Chalmer's Anchorage, a protected little bay on the north end of Elliott Island. The problem involved the fuel feed system. We couldn't immediately remedy the trouble so continued the 19 miles to Prince Rupert on one engine. Although there was still a haze, visibility had improved, and our crossing of the southeast corner of open Chatham Sound presented no great difficulties.

Prince Rupert is on the northern end of Kaien Island, with Digby Island buffering it from the open ocean. The channel between them has several shoal areas which are well marked but require close attention to chart and position.

The small boat basin is just a bit northeast of the Prince Rupert Rowing and Yacht Club.

This northwesternmost port of Canada is almost a metropolis for the area with a population of better than 15,000. Known as the "Halibut Capital of the World," it is fishing and boating oriented. Some paved streets, traffic lights, theaters and stores make for a decided contrast, following days of cruising in these pristine waters that are practically unchanged since Vancouver first saw them nearly 200 years ago.

Here we enjoyed the hospitality of the yacht club members and of the city officials and held an awards banquet for race winners, as this marked the end of the first half of the race. It is a natural dividing point where the Inland Passage leaves British Columbia waters, crosses Dixon Entrance and enters the southeastern Alaska Panhandle.

Our cruise thus far had covered nearly 700 miles through some of the finest cruising waters in the world. Both long and short channels and straits provided calm and protected waters in which to traverse this magnificent country, with its wealth of evergreen-clad islands, forested hills, steep, rocky cliffs, frosted mountain peaks, and inviting bays and coves. There is a sameness to the awe-inspiring and spectacular scenes which continue to unfold in varied beauty with every mile, yet one never tires of it but continues to look eagerly for more.

The Inland Passage just has to be one of the most fascinating cruises a yachtsman can take!

128

GLOSSARY OF PLACE-NAMES

Finlayson Channel—By Capt. Charles Dodd of the Hudson's Bay Company steamer *Beaver,* 1845, after Roderick Finlayson, chief factor of Hudson's Bay Company, Victoria, 1859, formerly at Port Simpson.

Tolmie Channel—After William Fraser Tolmie, a medical officer in the service of the Hudson's Bay Company, who was stationed at Puget Sound and British Columbia posts, 1833-1836, and was later a member of the B.C. Legislature.

Grenville Channel—By Captain Vancouver, 1792-1793, after Baron Lord Grenville, William Wyndham Grenville, cousin of William Pitt.

Lowe Inlet—By Captain Dodd, 1844, after Thomas Lowe, whose early life was spent with the Hudson's Bay Company. He left the service in 1850 to establish firms in Oregon, San Francisco and Victoria.

Chatham Sound—By Vancouver, 1794, after John Pitt, second earl of Chatham, older brother of William Pitt, one-time prime minister of England. During the years of Vancouver's voyages, the earl of Chatham was first lord of the Admiralty and was responsible for signing the expedition's papers.

Kaien Island—Indian name adopted in 1892, meaning "foam" which frequently floats on the water at the south end of the island after a heavy rain.

Prince Rupert—After Prince Rupert, cousin of King Charles II of England, and the first governor of the Hudson's Bay Company. The name was submitted by Miss Eleanor M. Macdonald of Winnipeg in an open competition by the Grand Trunk Pacific Railway Company.

Digby Island—By Captain Pender, 1867, after Capt. Henry Almarue Digby, Royal Navy Pacific station, 1866-1868.

Graham Reach—After Sir James Robert Graham, baronet of Netherby, first lord of the Admiralty, 1852-1855.

Fraser Reach—By Captain Pender, 1866, after Donald Fraser, native of Scotland, well-known resident of Victoria for several years and one of the largest holders of real estate on Vancouver Island.

Coghlan Anchorage—After St. James Edmond Coghlan, R.N., assistant surveying officer, *Beaver.* He rose to captain, retired in 1897.

Princess Royal Island (and channel)—By Capt. Charles Duncan, 1785, after his sloop, *Princess Royal.*

Butedale—Probably by Vancouver, 1792, after John Stuart, third earl of Bute.

Swanson Bay (Graham Reach)—After Capt. John Swanson of the Hudson's Bay Service, who had charge of several of its vessels, including *Beaver,* 1858, and was witness in San Juan boundary dispute.

24
Cruising the Coastal Canyons

Alaska is becoming a magic cruising word to more Northwest yachtsmen each year. This is the great land of scenery, the most spectacular imaginable. And the people of this new state are very friendly.

Vistas of white-haired purple mountains with their feet in the sea form precipitous backdrops for blue green waterways, generously sprinkled with green-clad islands and winding between forested hills. Solitude is the word—a massive quietness that pervades the entire panhandle to produce a feeling of peace and remoteness not to be found in today's civilized areas.

But to a specific cruising day. We were about to cross Dixon Entrance, last of the three exposures to the open ocean on this inland passage. The skipper had scheduled an early start and rolled us out of warm bunks at 0500. First mate Anne had one of her always excellent hot breakfasts ready in no time, and we left Prince Rupert at 0605.

Digby Island forms a buffer across the outside of Prince Rupert Harbor to protect it from the wrath of the Pacific. A northbound skipper has the choice of two courses: the longer and easier one around the south end of Digby Island or the shorter, more tortuous, yet more beautiful Venn Passage to the north.

We chose the short route. This kept a pair of navigators as well as the skipper and a depth-sounder-watcher busy with a constant check on position, the multitude of lights, ranges and buoys, and the various points and turns. It's a lovely passage, one that certainly should be experienced. It is well marked, but, if it is to be enjoyed, a bit of concentrated study of the large-scale chart will eliminate some nervous moments.

Under an overcast sky, *Gala*, our sturdy Tollycraft, negotiated the passage without incident, left Tugwell Island to starboard and headed for Lucy Island in the open sea. We were lucky to be greeted by calm water. Chatham Sound was flat as we came into the protection of Dundas Island and her satellites to run through Oriflamme Passage into open ocean again.

Our luck held beautifully. A solid cloud cover broke into patches of blue which grew and grew until we crossed the international boundary under a dazzling summer sun. As we struck the Canadian flag from the starboard yardarm and raised the Alaskan flag with its eight golden stars on a blue field, we hoped the weather was a good omen for the balance of the trip.

The sea remained calm as we rounded Tree Point to enter Revillagigedo Channel and the protected waters of the Inland Passage. We were in Alaskan waters exactly two weeks after departure from Seattle, leaving behind leisurely passages through some of the best cruising waters in the world.

Although we had crossed the line and knew we were in the forty-ninth state, a look around us didn't show anything different. It looked like the same mountains, precipitous with deep green sides and snowy tops, stretching to the bright-blue, cotton-flecked sky. The same dark-green islands detached themselves from the round, lighter-green hills lining the same two-toned channels.

It was lunchtime. Skipper Harold decided we'd relax and eat in the bay at the north end of Mary Island. This was the perfect time to get up-to-date on pertinent facts about Alaska. The name itself comes from the Aleut word Alaysxaq, meaning "Great Land." Its 586,400 square miles make it more than twice the size of Texas.

Perhaps it could be said there are two Alaskas. One is the traditional Alaska of cartoons and old movies: a great icebox where grizzled prospectors stumble onto giant veins of gold or carouse in bawdy saloons. Then there's the real Alaska: a land of incredible beauty with a rich past and a fabulous future. It's America's last frontier where you can walk in minutes from modern city streets to rugged mountains, warm, lush valleys, or the magnificent hush of a forest. It is of interest to the yachtsman that Alaska has a general ocean coastline of 5770 nautical miles but boasts a tidal shoreline of more than 33,000 miles.

The southeastern, or panhandle, portion of the state is almost all a part of the Tongass National Forest. It consists of a 30-mile-wide strip of mainland bordered by an 80-mile-wide compact chain of islands. About 40,000 of Alaska's 260,000 people live in 16 organized communities in the panhandle area. Besides being one of our younger states, Alaska's people are young, with an average age of 23.3 compared to the U.S. average of 29.5.

It was only 23 more miles up the Revillagigedo Channel, past Annette Island, Bold Island and Pennock Island into Tongass Narrows and Ketchikan. Here, in the "Salmon Capital of the World," we were royally welcomed by officers and members of the Ketchikan Yacht Club who had moved their ships out of moorages so our fleet could be accommodated. A party at the dockside clubhouse was followed by a dinner and dance they had arranged at the Elks Club.

By evening we knew we were in Alaska. Not only had we been inducted officially into the Order of the Alaska Walrus with suitable certificates and pins, but our lovely, bright day had changed to rain.

This is something any visitor to Alaska should expect and learn to accept. While there can be warm, sunny days, clouds and rain (with totals from 60 to well over 100 inches a year) can be the rule on an average of 220 days. Maximums seem to be at Little Port Walter on the east side of Baranof Island, where 220 inches fall in 269 days of the year.

Alaskan weather can be a psychological thing. If the visitor accepts that certain amounts of fog, clouds and rain are an inevitable, and yet integral, part of the overall picture, outfits himself accordingly and makes up his mind to enjoy all of the many virtues in spite of the weather, he will have a pleasant trip. Otherwise he will find himself and his crew continually griping and fretting until they become unbearably grouchy and unpleasant.

The waters in the vicinity of Ketchikan and north to Skagway, like all of our great Northwest cruising waters, offer more channels, islands, bays, inlets and coves than could be explored in a lifetime. Our race and cruise course, after leaving Ketchikan, called for a trip up the Behm Canal to Yes Bay and Bell Island. This proved so fascinating we wanted to see more of it; so we made the entire Behm Canal circle on the return trip.

However, this is a separate chapter, and so we'll leave Ketchikan (after transferring to Thol Simonson's *Largo*), go out Tongass Narrows and head up Clarence Strait. Here a choice of four routes and several overnight stopping places forces a decision. Two of these courses continue up Clarence Strait, while the other two turn up Ernest Sound and

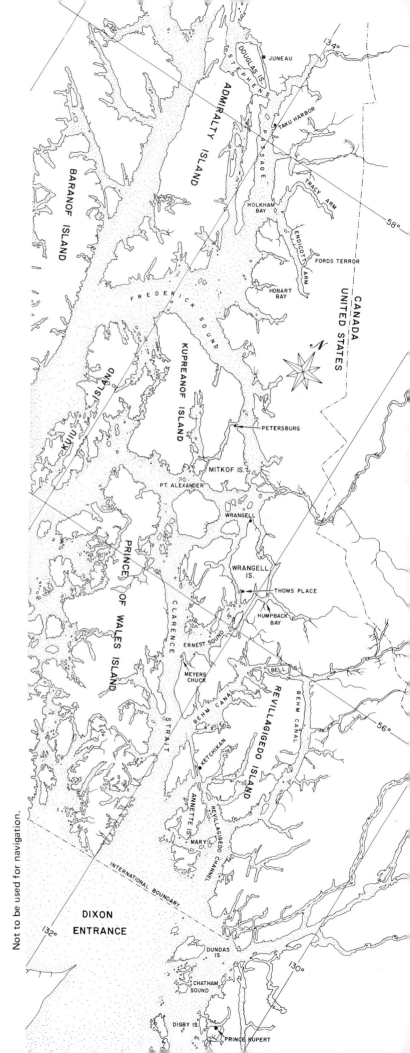

Not to be used for navigation.

then split to run on both sides of Wrangell Island, the westerly one through Zimovia Strait and the easterly one through Blake Channel and Eastern Passage.

The weather had cleared early in the morning to bring us a hot summer day as we cruised on the Simonsons' *Largo*. As always, it was a pleasure to cruise with these delightful Californians, and the heat of the day made their boat feel at home as she plowed through the glossy water. Mountains shimmered in the sun as reflections turned the shore upside down, and a huge white anvil of a cloud in a deep-blue sky waited for the armorer's hammer of thunder.

At the point of decision between Clarence Strait or Ernest Sound, we turned into one of the featured spots on any Alaska Cruise. A friendly little cove bearing the name Meyers Chuck has a couple of stores, a post office, a good public float and grids for emergency use. It lies in behind some islands on the west side of Lemesurier Point.

Thoms Place, near the southwestern tip of Wrangell Island, is a delightful anchorage on a protected bay for those planning on taking the Zimovia Strait route. The strait can be a bit tricky but it is well marked and, with a large-scale chart, presents no serious problems.

For those going up the eastern route, Humpback Bay (Anan Bay on some charts) is the natural anchorage as well as the starting point for an interesting hike. About a mile up, a delightful, rustic trail running alongside Anan Creek is an observatory shelter where hikers can sit and watch for black bear fishing in the creek or humpback salmon fighting their way up the falls to spawn.

Wrangell, on the northern tip of Wrangell Island, is the second oldest settlement in southeastern Alaska. It was founded by the Russians in an effort to forestall any hunting by the British Hudson's Bay Company up the Stikine River. It is both a fishing and lumber village with freezing and canning facilities for shrimp and crab, and a large sawmill.

A large modern supermarket makes this a good place to replenish ship's stores, while the principal visitors' attraction is a Tlingit Indian Community House and a collection of totem poles in all sizes, shapes and colors, located on Chief Shakes Island in the town's harbor.

From Wrangell it's about 20 miles to Point Alexander and the entrance to Wrangell Narrows. This interesting waterway runs for about 21 miles to separate Mitkof Island from the Lindenberg Peninsula of Kupreanof Island and leads to Petersburg on the northern end of Mitkof Island.

The channel is narrow, and intricate in places, with currents at some points averaging four to five knots and attaining six to seven knots on spring tides. An extensive system of lights, ranges, beacons and buoys, along with the chart of the narrows, makes for fairly easy navigation. It's a good idea, however, to keep a close check of the aids both in the waterway and on the chart. Numbers on these aids from the southern to northern entrances run from 1 to 63.

This was another clear, warm day. We were now cruising with Herb and Marge Schaefer on their *Margy M III*. Here are more pleasant visitors from Southern California making their second trip into these waters. We enjoyed hearing about and seeing the pictures of their restoration

Black bears find good fishing in foaming Anan Creek.

and lengthening of this lovely 1938 Matthews to its present mint condition.

Making the easterly turn to come into Petersburg, we came upon one of those Alaska postcard scenes. Sharp peaks of a tremendous range of mainland mountains poking through the extensive, glittering snow fields formed the background with the glistening, blue water of Frederick Sound below and a foreground of the Petersburg massed fishing fleet nestled in the arms of the harbor floats. Captain Meade of Vancouver's 1794 expedition called the scene "uncommonly awful and horribly magnificent." Devil's Thumb, a 9077-foot peak with an almost perpendicular shaft rising 1662 feet above the crest of the range, is most impressive.

The day wasn't serene for everyone, however. As *Largo* made the turn in the channel to approach Petersburg, her propeller picked up about 18 feet of one-inch-diameter polypropylene line. Skipper Simonson donned his wet suit and managed to clear the wheel and shaft, but he still had to put the boat on the grid and have the shaft straightened.

Petersburg, known as Little Norway, was settled by people of Norwegian ancestry and is built around the fishing industry, with shrimp, clam, crab, salmon and halibut processed there. The town also has a sawmill. It was here that we found an electronics expert who was able to get our ailing radiotelephone back on the air.

It's a little more than a hundred miles from Petersburg to Juneau. Although the fast boats can make it comfortably in a day's run, there are things to be seen along the way, so any one of several good anchorages is desirable. Hobart Bay, several coves in the vicinity of Holkham Bay, and Taku Harbor are some of the more popular ones.

From Petersburg the course enters Frederick Sound, turns north in Stephens Passage and Gastineau Channel. The itinerary called for an overnight rendezvous in a small cove northeast of Point Coke and a day of sightseeing in Tracy or Endicott Arms and Fords Terror. Icebergs become a common sight in all of these waters, and killer whales are frequently encountered.

Fords Terror, a sensationally beautiful inlet, has been covered previously. (*Northwest Passages, Volume 1.*) Icebergs and glaciers are the subject of another chapter in this volume, so we pass quickly over these attractions.

The whales didn't disappoint us. Several showed up in Frederick Sound and we saw a large pod heading south in Stephens Passage. These awesome mammals put on a fascinating show for us. Some merely rolled lazily, porpoise-fashion, then dove, later to surface and blow a geyser high into the air. Others, in a playful mood, would emerge from the water, seeming to stand on their tails momentarily before flipping to dive back in. Still others would jump clear of the water in a mighty leap and fall back in a resounding splash that set off what looked like a small tidal wave. The show offered a tremendous challenge to the shutterbugs.

The channels continued to part the mountains, so we could cruise between sheer cliffs, massed in bronze and forested in greens. North of Petersburg, the whole scene changed to the more typical Alaska mood as depicted in the travel folders, picture postcards and books. Colors became deeper with the browns of the mountains turning to a definite purple. The landscape became more rugged and an occasional glacier ground down from the ice and snow field. Streams tumbled down over dark rocks or sent a silvery pencil from the heights to cascade into the forest or water below.

As we approached the entrance to Holkham Bay, it started to rain and the wind increased in velocity as it turned colder. The scheduled anchorage behind Point Coke wasn't too desirable in this kind of weather, so it was decided to run a part of the next day's race and go on to Taku Harbor for the night.

The rain beat down cold and slanting on the decks and cabin sides. We could see the bow waves of the nearby boats, smiling and showing white teeth as they plunged into the growing seas. The storm didn't last long, however, and by 1900, as we entered the harbor, the wind had nearly died and only a light rain was falling.

We rafted out from others in the fleet tied to the small

Left: This whale, one of a large pod in Frederick Sound, seems to be enjoying life as it jumps clear of the water in a lively exhibition put on by the giant mammals. Right: Door to Tlingit Indian Community House on Chief Shakes Island in Wrangell's harbor. A collection of totem poles includes all shapes, sizes and colors.

float with *Doressa* providing us a friendly moorage. Taku Harbor, a protected bay, was home base for the late Father Hubbard, Alaska's famous flying priest.

With only 20 miles to go and a scheduled group finish and parade up Gastineau Channel to Juneau at 1400, we spent a leisurely morning cleaning and dressing ship. The rain had quit but the sky was still overcast. The fleet left Taku Harbor pretty much together and, after finishing the last leg of the race at Juneau Island Light, regrouped in alphabetical order for the parade.

Members of the Juneau Yacht Club had arranged moorages for us all and were on hand to direct us to them. Later they entertained at their clubhouse, and the next night the Grand Awards Banquet was held at the Baranof Hotel. The two top overall places went to California boats with *Largo* first and *Doressa* second, followed by *Nothing More* of Seattle.

It's called a race and participants do get experience and

fun in trying to match their predictions. Basically, though, it's a group cruise with racing rules so relaxed that the whole affair is a grand adventure. First-timers get the chance to make the trip through unfamiliar waters in company of those more experienced, and to be guided through some of the trickier passages.

In addition to the attractions in Juneau itself, the visitor should not miss a trip to 15-mile-distant Mendenhall Glacier and Visitor's Center for a better understanding of the spectacular glacial landscapes in the area and the mechanisms of this force of nature at work.

Another must in our book is a visit to the Chapel by the Lake at Auke Bay for the spectacular view of the lovely lake in the foreground and the glacier and snow field behind.

Juneau is one of Alaska's newer towns and the first to get its start under the American flag. Two gold seekers, Joe Juneau and Dick Harris, landed their canoe there in 1880 and made a rich strike, starting a rush to this beautiful and remote channel. Today it has progressed from a mining camp to a modern community.

Fishing is usually good throughout Alaskan waters with some spots especially favored. Remember, though, you must have a fishing license.

Alaska continues to intrigue West Coast Yachtsmen and will no doubt do so for years to come. The cool quietude of seemingly endless blue green channels and peaceful coves, the swirls of fast-running rapids in exciting narrows, the cedars, firs and hemlocks clothing the rounded hills or marching up the steep sides of mountains to the timber line, the magnificent majesty of snow-capped peaks, glaciers glistening in the sun, the crisp invigorating air and the friendliness of the people—all combine to produce a fascination not to be denied. Alaska is indeed the "Great Land."

Top: Meyers Chuck, a peaceful little settlement in behind some islands, is about halfway between Ketchikan and Wrangell. Bottom: Juneau, one of Alaska's newer towns, was end of the race and scene of the Grand Awards Banquet.

25
Nudging Around the Rivers of Ice

"Icy shingles on Alaska's steep roof," is an apt description of the thousands of glaciers which flow from the snow and ice fields in the mountains along our forty-ninth state's rugged coast.

Glaciers, and the icebergs which break off from them, are certainly feature attractions for the visitor to this north-land. While it isn't always feasible, safe, or sometimes even possible, to cruise to the face of a glacier, a skipper at least looks forward to cruising among the bergs.

Our preplanned itinerary had scheduled time out for trips up Tracy and Endicott Arms. Johnny Johnson, arriving in Petersburg early in his *Mercer Girl*, had flown over the entire area and reported almost no ice in either arm. LeConte Bay, however, had icebergs and so it was decided to spend a day sightseeing there.

The steel-hulled excursion boat *Blue Star* made regular and special trips to LeConte Bay from Petersburg, but the group voted to take four ships from our own fleet on a share-the-ride basis. *Nothing More, Doressa, High Cotton* and *Gala* made the 16-mile run down and across Frederick Sound.

The LeConte Glacier is the southernmost active tidewater glacier in North America. It is also one of the faster-moving glaciers, which accounts for a large amount of calving or breaking off of huge chunks of ice from its face.

Approaching the entrance to the bay, we saw the long marine parade of varicolored sculptured icebergs heading for Dry Strait. It seems the floating ice doesn't always head south. The harbor master at Petersburg told how wind and tide occasionally bring large bergs right into the harbor.

Nothing More led the way into the bay and soon disappeared in what appeared to be a solid ice field. Picking their way slowly among the bergs and smaller floes, the other

boats worked into the bay. Wind, sun and rain had all contributed to sculpturing the icebergs into fantastic shapes, many of them as beautiful as ice sculptures seen in fancy restaurants.

Colors of the fractured ice are as interesting and varied as the shapes. Some were dazzling white, while others ranged from a light blue to a deep indigo or ultramarine with some turquoise, and others had a glittering iridescence that both charmed and awed.

There was considerable speculation about the cause of the different colors. We were told later that the surfaces of the glaciers that have been longest exposed to the sun and atmosphere are always white or clear and glittering, while the ice from the inside, or unexposed, portions of the glacier is blue—the deeper the ice, the deeper the blue.

We had been warned about approaching too close to the face of the glacier. The admonition was unnecessary in our case for the farther into the bay we went, the thicker the ice became. We had also been told to stay clear of even the smaller ice floes and not to reverse the propellers, as the ice was extremely hard and could easily damage hull and wheels. We decided against going all the way in.

Another warning not to get too close to the bergs was dramatically emphasized when a huge chunk, easily the size of a small house, upended and, with a terrific splash, rolled over. Almost at once it rolled back to its original position and then repeated the action a half dozen times. It was an awesome performance.

Although it has been said that the smaller chunks of ice are soft and rotten, we didn't find this to be true. After the spectacular display of the overturning berg, we were wary about approaching the larger ones too close for some centuries-old cocktail ice. With the help of the pike pole and

Top: Seals find resting places on bergs and floes, and usually stay put for a photograph. Bottom: Cruiser moves in for a closer look at one of the icebergs.

fish-landing net, and some expert maneuvering by the skipper, we managed to get several smaller pieces into the cockpit ice chest. It seemed to be as hard and long lasting as that cut from the bigger bergs.

Usually the Holkham Bay area is just as dramatic. On previous trips we have enjoyed the cruise up Tracy Arm for a look at Sawyer and South Sawyer Glaciers or up Endicott Arm to see North Dawes and Dawes Glaciers. Fords Terror, a spectacular inlet off Endicott, is also a featured attraction of this area. (*Northwest Passages, Volume 1.*)

These arms are usually full of beautiful and dramatic icebergs which overflow through Holkham Bay into Stephens Passage. Here, too, it is sometimes almost impossible to get in far enough to see the glaciers because of packed icebergs and floes.

Just around the corner from Juneau, up Taku Inlet, is Taku Glacier, originating in the massive Juneau snow and ice fields which also spawn a host of other glaciers, including famous Mendenhall. Taku originally meant the "place where the geese sit down." In times past, most recently around 1750, the glacier extended across the head of the fjord, creating a 36-mile-long lake in the valley to the east. Telltale lines of the old lake can be seen today on the sides of the valley.

Taku is advancing again. In a few decades it could close off the fjord once more to form another lake "where geese can sit down."

Leaving Juneau, we headed for Glacier Bay, about 100 miles by water to the northwest. After a start down Gastineau Channel, we turned back for some engine repairs. It was midafternoon before we got away and, since the tide was right, we decided to try the very shallow Small Boat Pass which is Gastineau Channel's route around the north end of Douglas Island into Saginaw Channel.

Having seen from the land how this channel dries at low tide, we took it on a slow bell and kept a wary eye on the depth sounder. We had been told the channel was okay up to two hours after high tide, if we followed the markers carefully.

These markers, all red, are frequently placed. Some are the conventional type and others are merely anchored oil drums, painted red. We followed the channel as marked very carefully and experienced no trouble, although there were times when depths were down to three and four feet under the keel with bottom clearly visible.

It was an interesting experience and we were glad to have had the opportunity to cruise this waterway. Beside the shallow channel, highlights included the excellent views of Auke Bay and a particularly alluring scene of majestic Mendenhall Glacier.

Once past Entrance Point and in the deeper waters of Fritz Cove, we headed for Shelter Island. From here it's about 75 miles up Lynn Canal to Skagway. Our course took us up Saginaw Channel, nearly to Faust Rock, and around Point Retreat to head south to Funter Bay, our anchorage for the night. On the southerly run the hills on the islands ahead were noticeably lower, while to the west and northwest the mountain peaks were higher, sharper and more rugged.

Aerial view of LeConte Glacier. It was impossible to get a boat in close enough for a picture of the glacier face.

Funter Bay proved a cozy anchorage and by bedtime our crab trap had produced several good keepers.

Next morning the trap was again full but had only two legal-sized males. We trolled outside the bay for a half hour without a strike and then headed for Point Couverden and turned up Icy Strait for the 35-mile run to Point Gustavus and the entrance to Glacier Bay. The strait, which can be a nasty piece of water, was comfortably smooth.

It was a warm, sunny day as we cruised up Icy Strait. Hills of the smaller islands are low with some higher peaks, mantled with snow, behind. While these are beautiful and impressive, reminding us of the mountains around Knight

and Kingcome Inlets, they are dwarfed by the steep, jagged snow-covered peaks of true Alaskan grandeur in the background.

Glacier Bay, an extensive body of water, is really composed of a collection of bays and coves, most of them with glaciers at their heads. The entire area, 90 miles at its widest point and some 70 miles from north to south, was established as a national monument in 1925. It contains nearly 3600 square miles, and Glacier Bay itself is about 50 miles long.

The bay lies between two nearly parallel mountain ranges, which are loftier than any in the United States out-

John Hopkins Glacier flows like a slow-motion river from peaks of Fairweather range. Its ice face is 200 feet high.

side of Alaska. To the east are the ice-draped peaks of the St. Elias Range, largely unmapped and unexplored. This range reaches its climax 140 miles northwest of the bay in 18,000-foot-high Mount St. Elias, one of the world's most spectacular glaciated mountains. Muir, Cushing and associated glacers are fed from this range. Although its highest peak within the monument, Mount Barnard, is only 8214 feet high, its sheer rise from sea level lends grandeur.

The snowy Fairweather Range lies to the west of the bay with 14,320-foot-high Mount Fairweather highlighting its northwest boundary. John Hopkins, Brady, Lamplugh, Reid, Hugh Miller, Geikie Glaciers and others have their origin in this range. Grand Pacific Glacier, at the head of Tarr Inlet and originating in Canada between the St. Elias and Fairweather Ranges, is a product of both.

The monument contains more than 20 tremendous glaciers. These represent all stages from actively moving ice masses to those that are stagnant or slowly dying. It has been determined that today about 10 percent of the glaciers advance, 60 percent recede, and 30 percent hold their own. These glaciers are rivers of ice, hundreds, sometimes thousands, of feet deep, which flow slowly down the mountain valleys because of the great weight of the snow and ice constantly accumulating at their sources, high in the mountains.

Famous Muir Glacier, one of the most active on the Alaska Coast, has a sheer face rising some 265 feet above the water and is nearly two miles wide. Most of the eight fjordlike inlets of the bay have similar ice cliffs at their heads with great chunks continually calving or cracking off as the cliffs become undermined by the water.

The "flow" of these rivers of ice is extremely slow compared with rivers of water. A travel rate of an inch or two a day is common, a foot or two is comparatively fast, and 20 to 30 feet a day, as in the case of Muir Glacier, is rare. Because of warm lowland air and a slow accumulation of snow, some glaciers melt away at the lower end before reaching the sea. Hugh Miller, Cushing, Adams and Rendu Glaciers are of this type.

Glaciers in this area have been receding in recent years, some of them quite rapidly. About 1700, Glacier Bay as we know it today was completely covered with an ice cap some 3000 feet thick. When Captain Vancouver sailed out Icy Straits in 1794, the ice extended as far south as the Beardslee Islands just inside the entrance to the bay.

Nearly a hundred years later, in 1892, ice still covered most of Muir and Reid Inlets, while Tarr Inlet was invisible and unnamed. Between 1899 and 1913, Muir Glacier receded eight miles. By 1921, Tarr Inlet had emerged but Muir and Reid Inlets were considerably shorter than at present. Between 1913 and 1946, Muir Glacier receded an additional five miles, leaving John Muir's cabin, originally close to the terminus, more than 13 miles away.

After a common entrance which extends northerly for some 24 miles, the bay divides into two arms, with Muir Inlet continuing to the north while the other arm turns to the northwest. Navigation and piloting should have close attention. Reports are that the charts are not completely accurate. The depth sounder should be constantly watched and even small ice chunks should be avoided.

Berg Bay, North and South Sandy Coves, Hugh Miller Inlet, Bartlett Cove and a couple of almost hidden small coves offer the best anchorages. We headed north into Muir Inlet with *Nothing More* and *Doressa.* Once again a heavy concentration of icebergs and floes prevented our getting in far enough to see the glacier itself. We could see McBride Glacier on the right but Burroughs Glacier on the left had receded far enough that we couldn't see it from the main channel.

After picking up some more ice for the cockpit ice chest, we headed back to Bartlett Cove in behind the Beardslee Islands, site of the National Park Service's Glacier Bay Lodge. This picturesque resort, opened in 1966, nestles under towering spruce trees and offers a main lodge with a huge stone fireplace, dining room and private guest rooms, each with bath.

If you should be in Alaska other than in your own boat, a regularly scheduled flight of 30 minutes will bring you from Juneau. The Park Service conducts a nine-hour boat tour of the bay for a modest fee which includes a box lunch.

For a place to relax and forget the cares of the workaday world, Bartlett Cove and Glacier Bay provide the perfect answer. With appetite whetted by the crisp, clean air and stories to tell about the big ones that didn't get away, or about a fascinating cruise among iceberg-filled fjords, or about mountain goats spotted high among the lofty crags on Mount Wright, your day comes to a satisfying end.

Closely surrounded by the serene, isolated charm of a virgin wilderness with a background of lofty, ermine-trimmed mountain peaks, endless forests of a dozen hues of green, massive rivers of ice, sparkling waters and flaming sunsets, you'll agree that this is one of Alaska's most spectacular spots—and one that is well worth a visit.

26
A Visit to Sitka

Alaska smiled on the next portion of our trip. One of our objectives was to get to Sitka. While this can be accomplished via a protected route from the "inside" with very little exposure to the open Pacific, the morning dawned in Glacier Bay's Bartlett Cove so calm and peaceful we decided to take the outside course down the west coast of Chichagof Island to Salisbury Sound and thence inland to Sitka.

Although there was a thin morning overcast, the orange sun blushed as it pushed the broken clouds aside to promise a good day. To the west and northwest, the glistening snow-crowned peaks of the Fairweather Range reflected the kaleidoscopic reproduction of sunrise colors. Naked cliffs glowed in warm shades of rainbow colors, while forested slopes merged their varying tones of green. The placid waters of the bay mirrored all of this in one glorious giant-screen color show which set the mood for an excellent breakfast.

Glacier Bay was doing its utmost to keep us there another day or two, but our skipper's business commitments wouldn't allow deviating from the schedule. The pleasant mood of the morning continued as we left the protection of the bay to enter Icy Strait. Sometimes rough and frequently dotted with icebergs, this waterway greeted us with its best manners showing.

We chose North Inian Passage to Cross Sound, Cape Spencer and the open Pacific. By going down Lisianski Inlet and Strait, then ducking in behind a series of islands along the coast, one can almost have an "inland passage" nearly to Salisbury Sound and from there inside to Sitka. The day was so lovely and the sea so calm that we chose the outside course rather than the inner which, on the chart, appears to be studded with rocks and many narrow passages. A large variety of bays and coves invited future exploration and offered possible havens if the Pacific became restless.

Cruising at a comfortable 12 knots, *Gala* left the protection of the Inian Islands for the 68-mile run in open water through Cross Sound and the ocean. A gentle swell from the southwest was barely perceptible as we shed our jackets and shirts to enjoy the sun, which by now had chased the clouds to become a fluffy white feather-bed cover for the mountain tops to the east, and warmed the air to a comfortable summer day.

Although they received no encouragement from us, a convoy of sea gulls provided flight cover most of the way down the outside. We enjoyed watching their graceful flight maneuvers as they glided and swooped. It became a game as each of us would choose a bird and see which one would hold a glide the longest without moving a wing.

As the afternoon wore on, a southwest breeze became stronger and, as we approached Salisbury Sound, swells became higher with a chop added. The mountains had thrown off their covers to spread a blanket of clouds across the sky and hide the sun. Shirts and jackets became comfortable once more and, as the clouds began to spit rain, the flying bridge was deserted for the more comfortable main cabin.

Salisbury Sound lies across the top of Kruzof Island, below the bottom corner of Chichagof Island, and forms a common entrance to waterways leading southeast along Baranof Island to Sitka and northeast to Peril Strait which is the protected approach from Chatham Strait.

Between Baranof and Kruzof Islands is Partofshikof Island with Neva Strait on its east and Sukoi Inlet on its west. We had chosen Sukoi Inlet for an overnight anchorage. It had been a delightful cruise except for the last half

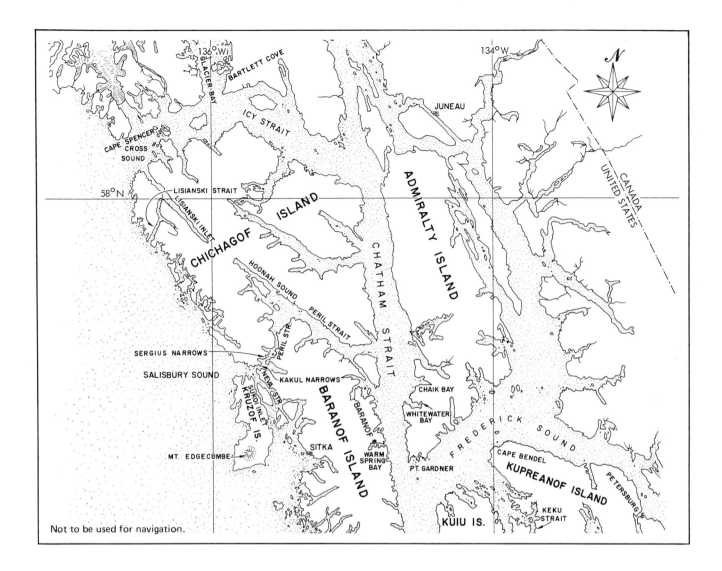

Not to be used for navigation.

hour, yet it was good to be snugged down in a protected, quiet haven.

Since none of us had been to Sitka before, there was a mood of anticipation as we set out next morning. Leaving Sukoi Inlet and rounding Hayward Point on the north end of Partofshikof Island, we gave wide berth to islets and rocks in center channel. St. John Baptist Bay shoots off to the southeast, but looked quite open and unprotected.

At Zeal Point we entered Neva Strait, a narrow waterway of about four miles ending in Whitestone Narrows. The narrows, scattered with rocks and reefs, are tricky but have plenty of markers, buoys and lights. With a large-scale chart, passage is fairly easy and safe. It's well to remember in these waters that "from seaward" means north from Sitka; so heading south red buoys are left to port and black to starboard.

One is hardly out of Neva Strait before an S turn opens up the entrance to Olga Strait, another narrow passage with a couple of hazards but much easier than Neva. Emerging from Olga Strait, several groups of islands and islets are all left to starboard on the eight-mile run to Sitka. Again,

buoys, lights and chart #8244 make for an easy approach. Heading for a moorage in Crescent Harbor, we toured the town's waterfront on our left with Japonski Island and the airport on our right.

The distinctive atmosphere of history which is Sitka's became apparent as we cruised slowly past piers standing on their long, spindly legs, some harboring fish boats, others a freighter, an ancient launch, an airplane float, or a ferry from the island across the channel. Rounding Old Russian Dock at the foot of Lincoln Street, Keekor, or Castle Hill, with its Russian cannon aimed through the rampart over the harbor, dominated the scene.

Sitka, a Tlingit Indian word meaning "in this place," is beautifully set with a backdrop of mountains and looking out across a harbor dotted with cupcake islands to Mount Edgecumbe, an extinct volcano wearing a crown of snow and looking like a twin to Japan's Fujiyama.

Established in 1799 by Alexander Baranof as a base for the Russian-American operation, Sitka (first called St. Michael, and later New Archangel) is the second oldest white settlement in Alaska and its past is loaded with interesting history. In spite of its remoteness, a lavish and glittering social life during much of the nineteenth century earned it the name "Paris of the Pacific."

For 119 years one of the town's outstanding features was St. Michael's Russian Orthodox Cathedral. Started in 1844 and finished in 1848, the church housed one of the finest collections of Russian Orthodox ecclesiastical pieces. Priceless icons, paintings, vestments, wedding crowns and other valuable treasures were in the collection.

On the icy morning of January 2, 1966, fire destroyed much of Sitka's business district, including St. Michael's Cathedral. Through the heroic efforts of many of the citizens, most of the church's treasures were saved from the fire. Insurance and donations provided for the building of a foundation and multipurpose basement where services are held. Plans are underway for a financial campaign for the building of an exact replica of the original building with its "onion dome and carrot spire."

In military ceremonies in front of Baranof's Castle atop Castle Hill on October 18, 1867, the Czarist Russian double-eagle flag was lowered and the 37-star United States flag was raised in its place, as Alaska was transferred officially from Russian to United States ownership. Sitka was proclaimed territorial capital and remained such until 1900, when Juneau was designated the capital, territorial offices moving there in 1906.

There are many other bits of history to learn and a host of interesting sites to visit in Sitka, with a couple of must items topping the visitor's list. These are the Sitka National Monument with its Visitor's Center and a fine collection of totem poles, and the Sheldon Jackson Museum with excellent displays of Indian, Eskimo and Russian artifacts and relics.

The modernistic Centennial Building is adjacent to the Crescent Harbor moorages and houses the Chamber of Commerce and general tourist information bureau. In the auditorium, a group of local housewives stages authentic Russian dances for visitors whenever a tour ship is in town.

On the lighter side, Sitka is the source of a couple of modern-day phrases. The word "hooch" is derived from a violent drink which local Indians distilled from molasses and called hoochinoo. The expression, "on the water wagon," is said to have originated in Sitka when U.S. Marines and Navy men had to haul the water delivery wagon around town as a punishment.

Sitka was a never-to-be-forgotten experience and is a highly recommended visit on any Alaskan itinerary. It's a bit off the beaten track but well worth the extra effort.

It was in Crescent Harbor that we again met Townley and Mazie Bayle in their beautiful *Blue Chip.* Their invitation to join them for a cruise down Keku Strait, between Kuiu and Kupreanof Islands, and down the west side of Prince of Wales Island was an intriguing idea, but again prior commitments dictated that we decline.

After fueling, we left Sitka in a light rain to head for Olga and Neva Straits. We felt like veterans as we negotiated the two straits and Whitestone Narrrows with complete confidence. We drifted near Kane Island for lunch then ran Kakul and Sergius Narrows without event about one hour

St. Michael's Cathedral as it looked before the 1966 fire.

after maximum flood. Progressing through Peril Strait, first on a northerly and northeasterly course until we passed the entrance to Hoonah Sound and then southeasterly to join Chatham Strait, the scenery once again reminded us of a quiet passage through the San Juan Islands. The green of the forest cover in the low islands was light. On the heavily wooded hills behind, the greens grew darker until they turned to a dark olive. Mountains in the background were snow crowned and became higher with more snow as we entered Chatham Strait.

This was another of those peaceful passages where the protected waters were mirror smooth, belying any peril suggested in the name of the strait. Many different waterfowl and shorebirds, gulls, sandpipers, plovers and arctic terns marked our passing, while several majestic bald eagles logged our progress from perches in the tops of stately Douglas firs, cedars or hemlocks. The morning rain had given way to a clearing sky about noon and we enjoyed another of those warm, sunny afternoons. Progressing down Chatham Strait the mountains grew higher, the snow-capped peaks brighter, and the overall picture was a typical Alaska postcard scene.

It didn't last too long, however. We were headed for Warm Springs Bay and Baranof for the night and the last few miles in Chatham Strait we experienced the beginning of a southeasterly front. The water became rougher as the wind increased, and we were glad to turn into the relative protection of the bay although the sea followed us clear to the Baranof floats.

Island-dotted harbor at Sitka, established in 1799 by Alexander Baranof and the second oldest white settlement in Alaska.

After a pleasant dinner we hiked up the float and the boardwalk to the store. Here, for a dollar, we obtained towels and soap for a bath in wooden tubs fed by the medicinal hot springs. The relaxing baths were the perfect prelude to a night's sound sleep in spite of a rather uncomfortable roll aboard the boat as the wind, accompanied by rain, grew stronger through the night.

It was still raining as we cast off next morning headed for Point Gardner, across Chatham Strait on the southern tip of Admiralty Island. Winds were piping up to around 30 knots and seas were short and steep from the southeast. It didn't take very many minutes to convince us that this wasn't the kind of a sea we wanted. The Tolly took it beautifully but we had no desire to fight it, so returned to Warm Springs Bay.

We went into the cove on the southern shore of the bay but the anchor dragged and so we anchored in a small bight on the north shore where we ate lunch. Another try after lunch got us uncomfortably across to Point Gardner but we weren't too anxious to go into Frederick Sound. A small cove above the point offered temporary shelter but, by now, we were looking for some place to spend the night.

Up the west coast of Admiralty Island, Wilson Cove looked like a possibility but it was too open. Six miles farther north Whitewater Bay, with Point Caution seeming to offer a buffer, looked good. The bay was aptly named, however, and there was no protection inside as rough, white capped waves prevailed clear into the head.

Another five miles north an arm of Chaik Bay offered a likely haven. We got a good bite on the anchor and, although we rolled a little, we spent a fairly comfortable night.

Winds abated somewhat by morning as we weighed anchor about 0645. Seas were comfortable to Point Gardner, grew rougher as swells came up the strait from the ocean and then flattened as we headed east-northeast in Frederick Sound. Crossing the entrance to Keku Strait as we headed for Cape Bendel, on the northwestern tip of Kupreanof Island, brought a pang of regret that we weren't turning to the southeast for what appeared to be a possibly exciting adventure. A date with a radio repairman in Petersburg and our skipper's appointment in Ketchikan with an eastern airline quelled any thoughts of changing course.

Once more Frederick Sound produced a fascinating show featuring both killer whales and dolphins. The latter produced an argument among the crew as to whether they were dolphins or porpoises. With Scrabble a favorite game aboard, there were several dictionaries which defined dolphin as a whalelike mammal with a beaklike snout and a porpoise, the same with a blunt snout. We decided these had to be dolphins.

The whales put on their customary exhibition including a game of tag in which the entire pod seemed to leap out of the water at once to fall back with a tremendous splash. The more artistically inclined were graceful as they rose out of the water to stand on their tails momentarily before making a quick turn and a headlong dive back into the waters of Frederick Sound.

Top: Totem Square on Sitka's waterfront, with Alaska Pioneer Home in background. Bottom: Reconstructed block-house of type used to guard the city's stockade walls.

We arrived in Petersburg in a driving rainstorm after one of the most scenic and interesting cruises it has ever been our privilege to enjoy. We say again that the trip off the beaten track to Sitka is well worth anyone's time. The wealth of bays and coves on both sides of Chatham Strait on the eastern shores of Chichagof and Baranof Islands and on the western shore of Admiralty Island are good for weeks of exploration.

While we didn't have the opportunity on this cruise to enjoy the deeply scalloped shore of Kuiu, Kupreanof and Prince of Wales Islands with their thousands of satellite islands, bays, coves, arms and inlets, this all holds a future promise of many months of fascinating cruising.

A couple of words of caution should certainly be inserted here. Alaska cruising is not difficult or more dangerous than any of our more well-known Northwest waters. However, if you must have civilization close by, if you dislike remoteness and isolation, Alaskan cruising isn't for you. If you are of a nature that can't accept a good bit of rain, cloudiness and fog as a natural part of this glorious "Great Land" without complaining and letting it spoil your enjoyment, Alaskan cruising isn't for you.

However, if you can button up your heavy-weather gear, let the rain course down your face as you breathe in the pure, pine-scented air and thrill to the peace and quiet of nature in a small cove where your staunch ship is the only bit of civilization for miles around, then you will enjoy cruising in Alaska and will return again and again.

27

Behm Canal:
Alaska's Scenic Circle

Only superlatives can describe the many attractions of Alaska's Behm Canal. Off the usual course of the Inland Passage, this 100-mile horseshoe waterway, winding around in back of Ketchikan, almost encircling Revillagigedo Island, offers the cruising yachtsman some of the loveliest bays and coves, some of the most scenic inlets and some of the best fishing to be found anywhere.

Leaving Ketchikan, we cruised up Tongass Narrows to the Guard Island Light. Instead of turning up the main channel of the canal, we chose the shortcut through Clover Passage in back of Betton, Hump and Back Islands. Running northerly for some 27 miles before it turns to the northeast, the canal has a number of bays on both sides. Some of them are too deep for good anchorage, but a close look at chart #8079 will turn up a host of cozy places to snug down for a night or more.

The itinerary for Harold Hovland's *Gala* called for a lay day and a choice of Yes Bay or Bell Island for moorage.

Yes Bay is not large but is inexpressibly charming and lovely. Nature has painted and draped everything with a soft and quiet harmony. Moss covering the huge boulders and slabs of brown and gray rocks, glows with varying shades of gold and amber and green. Lithe and straight cedars grow impenetrably close together, their feather foliage making a gloomy shade.

Mountains rise straight up from the shoreline, their bases sometimes as high as 100 or 200 feet straight up from the water with an ascent so steep there is no foothold. From every crevice cedars grow with an apparent uniformity of height so that the mountainside looks like a newly mown lawn.

The domes and spires of the mountains with their snow peaks look down on an exact timberline, seeming to command the crouching trees marching up the sides to come no farther. Some of the tops are bare black stone, which stands out in the glittering snow to form a variety of imaginary shapes of animals and birds and heads of gnomes and demons.

With all its beauty, Yes Bay is steeped in history. The modern lodge, on a point jutting out into the bay, surveys the entrance and seems to deny the prior existence of a saltery erected in 1886. This and a fish-canning business operated under different firms until dismantled after the 1931 season. The U.S. Bureau of Fisheries established salmon hatcheries here in 1905.

The unusual name of this bay comes from the Tlinget Indian word yaas or yas meaning "mussel." It was first called McDonald Bay by Dall in 1879.

The lodge offers a variety of rate packages from straight room and meals to six days with room, meals, boat, motor, fuel, tackle, bait, rain gear, cleaning, icing, packaging or smoking of fish, and a guide if desired. In addition to restful vacationing and excellent fishing, there is fall hunting for mountain goats and black bear. The lodge is open from May 15 to October 1.

Up behind the lodge is McDonald Lake, feeding McDonald River which joins the saltchuck beside the lodge. Here is good fishing for rainbow, Dolly Varden and cutthroat trout. Steelhead to 18 pounds are not uncommon and the average is over 10 pounds. During July, humpback salmon enter the river by the thousands to offer exciting sport for the angler, especially on light tackle.

This area has some of the best fishing in southeastern Alaska. Past experience has contributed to a fishing calendar which shows, generally, the best dates for particular fish. Peak periods are: sea-run cutthroat trout, May 15-June

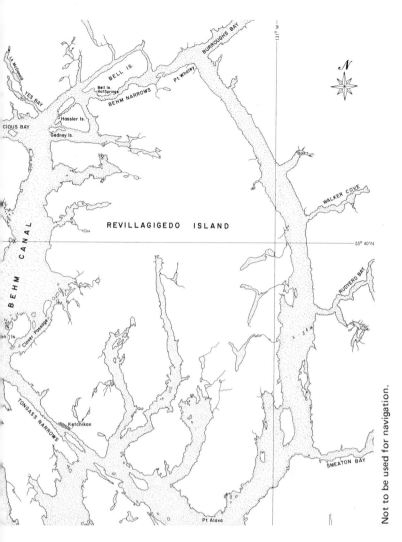

gers of our wake poked among the rocks and pebbles along the shore and, after the small wrinkles in the water had flattened again, everything on shore was seen upside down.

We drifted for a few moments with engines stilled, soaking up the sunshine and the peace and beauty of our surroundings, and attempting to relate the reflection of our modern 40-foot Tollycraft cruiser, which had brought us from a life of tense civilization, to the past of this lovely bay with its history of Indians, pioneers, Chinese workers in the fish cannery, and rugged fishermen. There was almost a sad, unheard music, grieving for this past, with its evidences now almost entirely covered by moss and the luxurious growth of bush and tree.

Doressa, anchored behind *Northwest* at the mouth of the McDonald River where it enters the bay beside the lodge, had sent her small boat out to set the crab traps in a cove of Spacious Bay, around Bluff Point from Yes Bay. Next morning the trap was brought back almost half full of those luscious shellfish. They were nearly all large and a good percentage was male keepers. During the day various members of our "fleet" managed to connect with some nice salmon.

The Behm Canal turns northeastward near the entrance to Yes Bay. At the bend are Black, Hassler and Gedney Islands. Between and behind them are several interesting passes with a half dozen coves and bights. A little farther up the channel, Bell Island splits the canal into Bell Arm and Behm Narrows with Anchor Pass joining them together farther on.

Snuggled in behind Bell Island's Snipe Point is a picturesque little cove and the Bell Island Hot Springs Resort. A long boardwalk leads from the floats to a central lodge, both modern and rustic cabins and an Olympic-size pool of hot mineral water. Captain Vancouver was here and named the island after a member of his crew.

Indians first, and later traders and fishermen, enjoyed the mineral hot springs. Shortly after the turn of the century the resort was started and grew to enjoy a good patronage by visitors seeking a cure for their ills from the warm springs. Presumably it looked much as it does today with cabins along the boardwalk bordering the rushing stream.

In addition to the pool there is a bathhouse with tubs, and oversized tubs are in the cabins. Accommodations and services similar to those of Yes Bay are offered at Bell Island at matching prices. A fascinating trail winds through the mossy woods to a couple of small lakes above the resort.

Although salmon is king in the area, there are also clams, shrimp and crabs. The only access is by boat or plane. Charter planes fly to both resorts from the airfield on Annette Island or from Ketchikan. Planes also are available for fishing trips to inland lakes and streams.

Whether the visitor is a cruising yachtsman, a fly-in vacationer, or fisherman, he will find a variety of interesting pursuits to enjoy in this upper part of the Behm Canal.

It was another clear morning in the bay as powerboat exhausts gargled their throats in preparation for a day of cruising or fishing. The canal continues northeasterly for

15; steelhead trout, May 20-June 15; king salmon (spring run), May 20-June 30; rainbow, Dolly Varden and cutthroat trout, June 1-October 1; humpback and chum salmon, July 1-August 20; silver salmon and fall kings, August 10-October 1; rockfish, halibut, cod, all season. King salmon can be caught from May 20 to October 1.

Alaska requires a sport fishing license on salt water as well as fresh. A 10-day nonresident license is $5; a season license is $10.

Just around a small peninsula across from the lodge is a cozy little cove which offers quiet, protected anchorage. Caution is called for to avoid a drying reef and rocks lying off the peninsula on the outside.

Yes Bay continues for a couple of miles with a group of small islands marking the entrance to an inner bay. The preferred channel is to the right of the islands, with a slow bell and favoring the right-hand shore.

In the quietness of a sunny Sunday morning, our excursion to the inner bay produced a quiet, almost worshipful mood. The bright blue of the still water mirrored the small white feathers of clouds and the green of the trees framing the golden moss on the islands. The exploring fin-

another five miles to Burroughs Bay where it turns south-easterly and then south. This stretch of our cruise reminded us of Desolation Sound with fairly low hills rising straight up from the water. The wide and deep channel runs like a noble river between these mountainous hills, densely timbered from the line of rock at the shoreline. Trees are a dark green and are vigorous, covering the hills uniformly, except where bare rock faces, 50 to 100 feet high and wide, are too smooth to permit growth of any kind to gain foothold.

Wisps of white fog or low clouds lie in little valleys. Close behind the hills rise higher green mountains and behind these still higher snow-crowned peaks. From these great domes lovely waterfalls leap down, some of them shooting straight down like a long pencil while others curve in and out, hiding and displaying themselves like flashes of silver among the shadows of the trees.

Occasionally a large stream dashes over a rocky parapet near the top of a mountain. It falls, leaping and foaming throughout its course, with beautiful cascades before it hides its buoyant life in the quiet cloisters of the sea.

Now the sunshine fades as a leaden cloud covers the sky and occasional light showers dimple the placid water. No matter where we cruise, whether in sunshine or clouds, the fascination of the northern scenery is so absorbing that we try to see it all. True, much of it is similar; yet there is always a difference and it never becomes monotonous.

After rounding Point Whaley, the hills and mountains rise higher, some to 4300 feet. There are more snow patches and the white peaks appear sharper and more jagged in the background. Cruising sometimes close to the shore and observing what appears to be solid rock faces on the hills, we wonder how so many sizable trees can find footholds among the few scattered fissures.

Our next objectives are Walker Cove and Rudyerd Bay, the first some 20 miles down the canal after the turn at Burroughs Bay. The water was an almost glacial pearly gray. As the skies alternately clear and cloud over, we note the everchanging pattern of colors. The play of sunshine and shadows upon the hills and mountainsides is capricious and constantly changes their aspect as we cruise between them.

The same applies to the water which changes from gray green to the blue of the sky above, to cold and steely gray, or to ebony black with a purplish gleam fitfully flashing from its dark depths. Several small coves and the mouth of a river offer some temporary protection, although most of them are either too deep or too shallow to be considered good anchorages.

Suddenly the Channel Islands detach themselves from the eastern shoreline. Two and a half miles beyond, the mountains part to reveal a dark and romantic fjord sitting between them which is Walker Cove. This seven-and-a-half-mile-long inlet, poking its watery finger into the steep hills, forms a canyon with all of the spectacular aspects of Princess Louisa Inlet except for a falls at its head.

The fluted, rocky walls rise almost vertically from the water to heights of 4480 feet. Water depths approach the 1000-foot mark at lower low tide. The high cliffs, with overlapping and interlocking bases, seemed to greet each

Double waterfall in Walker Cove is dwarfed by rock walls, which rise almost vertically to 4000-foot heights.

other in friendly grasp as we looked toward the head of the cove. This is an immense mass of volcanic rock and granite boulders welded together into firm, hard walls. Some portions are clothed in green hemlock, fir and cedar, standing straight and proud in silent splendor, while others are barren, varicolored with several shades of gray and brown mixed with a dash of green. Some look like giant chunks of fondant with melted chocolate poured on top and running down the sides. Walker Cove is a spectacular and awesome sight to be carefully savored and enjoyed.

Rudyerd Bay, about nine miles down the canal, also

Top: Part of the fleet ties up at Bell Island Hot Springs Resort. Bottom: Walker Cove, running between steep hills, forms a canyon that is spectacular and awesome.

splits the mountains to the east for some seven miles before it divides into two arms, each running about three miles to the north and south. Punchbowl Cove takes off to the south about two miles inside the entrance.

Although mountain heights in Rudyerd Bay do not quite equal those of Walker Cove, still a top of 3680 feet can be most impressive, especially when it rises from the water as a sheer rock wall. Depths here equal those in Walker Cove and there are only a couple of spots offering good anchorage.

Punchbowl Cove, so named because its precipitous walls remind one of a gigantic bowl, has a stream flowing into its head from Punchbowl Lake. We found good anchorage at the head near the southwest shore and slept soundly, as on a bay of balm. Rudyerd Bay and its Punchbowl are most scenic and impressive, although perhaps not quite as spectacular as Walker Cove.

The Behm Canal continues southward for another 14 miles before turning southwest for another 12 miles to join Revillagigedo Channel at Point Alava, the southeastern tip of Revillagigedo Island. At the turn Smeaton Bay runs eastward for seven miles to divide into Wilson Arm and Bakewell Arm. Here again depths are too great for good anchoring, although there are a few small coves which can be used. There are a couple of high peaks north of Smeaton Bay but generally the mountains are not as high as farther north.

From Walker Cove south in Behm Canal there is a variety of small bays, coves and bights offering protection and anchorage possibilities. Almost four miles below the entrance to Rudyerd Bay in mid channel is New Eddystone Rock, a remarkable shaft which rises 234 feet from a sand shoal. This can be passed on either side, keeping a half mile off to avoid the shoal and a small pinnacle rock at the eastern extremity which uncovers at about four feet.

Cruising among the mountains as we did on this portion of our trip, and anchoring with a high barrier to the west, sunsets were lost to our view. Their reflected counterparts on the peaks, however, sometimes were as striking and colorful as the real thing.

As the night came down and the twilight settled deeper, the shapes grew black upon the silent waters. We could catch a gleam of brightness along the upper edge of western peaks with the sunset on their opposite sides. By turning to the higher peaks in the east we could see them lighted like flaming beacons. Peaks and domes of all the white mountain tops which inclined to the west reflected the glory of the sunset, bathing the lesser mountains and hills below in a golden glow of radiant beauty. It was a thoroughly enjoyable reversed sunset.

The Behm Canal with its appendages, though off the direct routes, is well worth a visit by any yachtsman in the vicinity who can spare the time to investigate its charms.

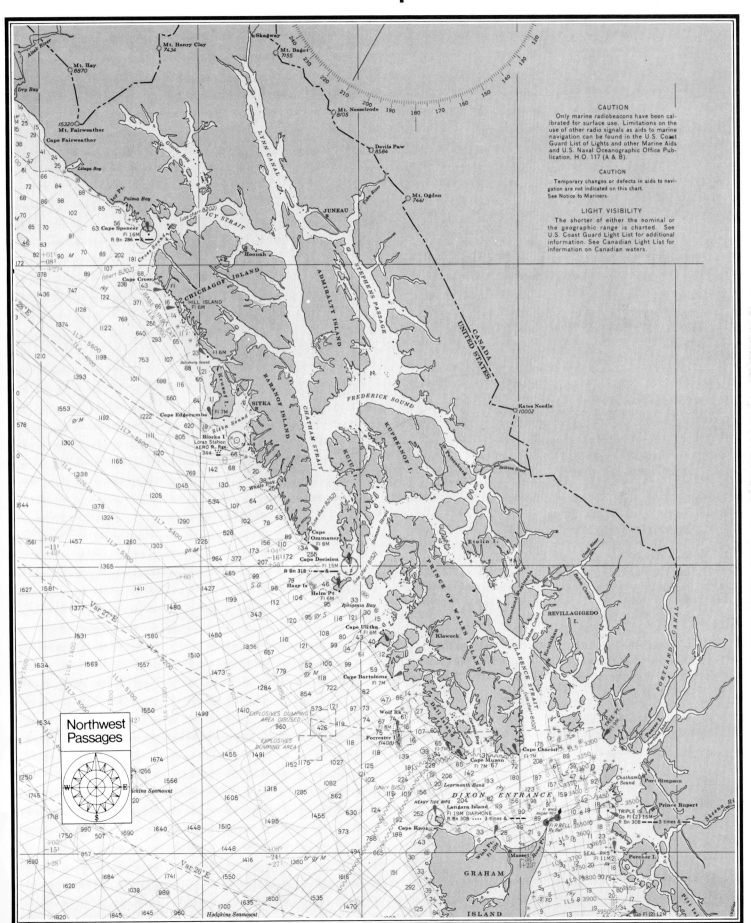

28

Home Cruiser to Alaska

by Ruth Baird

As we left our home in Southern California and headed for Seattle by auto, ours was to be far more than a highway trip—58 days of cruising from Seattle to Skagway, Alaska, and back in a houseboat. For the trip it was Captain Wynn Baird, First Mate Ruth and Second Mate Ricky Baird, our 11-year-old grandson.

"Houseboat" is a generalized term and does not detail our 47-foot *Miss Westerner*, which is a seaworthy "home cruiser" with a Veed bow and the general lines of a monohull beneath. *Miss Westerner* had arrived in Seattle a month earlier, by train, and we had flown up to discuss the preparation for the trip with Jim McGinnis at Marina Mart.

We have shown these yachtlike home cruisers at three Southern California boat shows and stressed their advantages as blue-water cruisers, pointing out that they perform beautifully in the rough water crossing to Catalina Island. Part of the purpose of our trip to Alaska, besides the pleasure of the adventure itself, was to demonstrate the advantages of *Miss Westerner* on a long cruise, where water and currents vary and are not always easy. We had made the trip before and knew that photographs of her passage to Glacier Bay and across Icy Strait to Sitka would be proof of her ability to perform well in rough water.

We arrived in Seattle on July 12, inspected *Miss Westerner,* and went out for a dinner of fresh salmon. The salmon made us want to hurry on and catch our own, cooking it over an open fire on some island all to ourselves.

Dinner over, we returned to the boat to make up our bunks. Somehow it doesn't seem right to call our luxurious queen-size innerspring bed a bunk.) How heavenly it was to be up north where the evenings are so long. I felt like singing nature's praises, but decided to refrain until we found the island.

We spent three days checking out the boat and getting supplies aboard. On July 16, a beautiful sunny day, we untied *Miss Westerner* and headed her out into Lake Union on her maiden voyage. We went through the locks and were really on our way—a wonderful feeling after all our months of planning.

In 1960 we had made this trip in a 24-footer and our crew comprised four adults and a dog. This time we had room to spare and such luxuries as an electric stove with rotisserie, refrigerator and freezer.

We went through Deception Pass at 3:00 P.M. just as the tide changed. The water was smooth as glass, a change from our first trip this way when we encountered rips and whirlpools. At 4:15 P.M. we pulled into Blakely Island for our first gas stop. An hour later we cruised into Fossil Bay on Sucia Island where we tied up for the night at a small dock.

We followed inviting paths through the woods, then returned to the beach to show Ricky how to dig for clams and pry oysters off the rocks. The sun set at 9:30 and we returned to *Miss Westerner* for dinner.

The next morning began another beautiful sunny day with just a few drifting clouds overhead. Awakening on the water, enclosed on two sides by trees, birds calling, gulls diving for fish, we were happy just to be alive. At 8:45 we made our way out of Fossil Bay, heading for Bedwell Harbor and Canadian waters.

For those from Southern California who haven't been through Canadian Customs, Bedwell is a good port of entry. Ricky and I stayed aboard while Wynn went ashore with our papers. Within a few minutes Customs gave us clearance and we all headed for the store. Even if one doesn't need supplies, it's always fun to see what the stores have to offer.

Back aboard *Miss Westerner*, we shoved off for the gas dock. We've learned *never* to pass up a gas dock, on the better-safe-than-sorry principle. At 10:30 we raised our Canadian flag and were on our way. It was slack water on the flood, so we took a shortcut through Shark Cove, then into Plumper Sound and through Navy Channel.

Coming into Trincomali Channel, we were cruising around 20 knots, and couldn't have asked for better water as we approached Dodd Narrows. At 1:15 we came around Protection Island and entered Nanaimo Harbor on Vancouver Island to gas up. We navigated out of the harbor along Newcastle Island, past the old Indian village, and around Horswell Bluff.

We carefully stayed to the port side as we passed Five Fingers Islands, as the water is only a few feet deep between these islands. Ballenas Channel was unbelievably calm as we started the five-hour run to Campbell River, our destination for the night. The weather seemed too good to last as we passed Cape Lazo with never a wave, and continued on through Discovery Passage.

We anchored at 6:30 P.M. at April Point Yacht Club, a favorite port on Quadra Island. This resort, owned by Mr. and Mrs. Phil Peterson, has a lovely lodge with a dining room overlooking the narrows. At April Point we like to tie up in the bay by the cannery, where it's quiet and comparatively warm.

After dinner we trolled back and forth with the other boats until 9:30, but with no luck. Ricky got a fish head at the cannery for our crab net, and in the morning we were rewarded by four specimens of our favorite seafood.

We stocked up on meat, frozen food and ship supplies as Campbell River would be our last large town. The shopping center is only a block from the marina's guest moorage. We visited the government liquor store, the grocery, bakery and the hardware store. We stowed the supplies, topped up the gas and water tanks, checked our tide chart and hurried to make Seymour Narrows.

Cruising up Discovery Passage, we felt truly on our own at last. Fleecy clouds started to form. Close to the steep, rocky shores killer whales were surfacing and blowing. To prove to Ricky that this is the land of salmon, we went around to Stuart Island where we've always had luck. Ricky and I put the deck chairs topside, leaned back comfortably, propped our feet on the deck rail and were ready to fish.

It was peaceful and quiet as we trolled from the bay along the steep shore, then partway up the Hole in the Wall Passage. The tide was running softly as we turned and repeated our course. The captain, who only put his pole in the water to please Ricky and me, got a bite, and I climbed down to take the wheel while he reeled in a 10-pound silver—our first salmon, and a beauty.

On the nineteenth we woke to a cold and cloudy day. I made French toast and bacon for breakfast to keep the second mate happy. Breakfast over, dishes put away and bunks made, we were ready to start. The tide was just starting to run as we approached Yaculta Rapids.

Small whirlpools formed all around the boat, and it was starting to rain. As we retraced our course to Chatham

Miss Westerner puts her nose right into an ice flow in Glacier Bay.

Point, the rain became harder and we suspected that the good weather was over for a while. We passed Rock Bay around Ripple Point, crossed Johnstone Strait to Kelsey Bay for fuel. At 11:45 A.M. the tide was running and there was a two-foot chop. It was still misty and cold and whitecaps were forming.

On our last trip through Johnstone Strait, we had stopped in three different coves waiting for the tide to change and the wind to die down. This time with *Miss Westerner* we decided to fight it out. In Campbell River we had taken on four six-gallon cans of spare gas—an ample reserve to get us into Alert Bay on Cormorant Island. We arrived at 5:00 P.M. and tied up at the government wharf by the schoolhouse. Alert Bay is an old Indian fishing and trading post, and its large Indian population is still made up of fishermen.

On Saturday, we shopped and visited and showed people over the boat, which always aroused considerable interest. On Sunday we walked to the Totem Pole Park, the old Indian burial ground west of town. Ricky fished off the back of the boat and caught a rock cod, which made his day happy.

Monday, we made an early start along with the fishing fleet. No other pleasure boats were up this early. We cruised past Fort Rupert with its Indian village and airport for the small seaplanes which hop from one island to another. In this area seaplanes are as prevalent as boats.

Approaching Hardy Bay, we turned north through Christie Pass to God's Pocket, a small safe bay used by the fishing boats when the weather is rough outside in Queen

Charlotte Strait. The water had been kind to us so far, so we decided to go on, leaving the northwestern tip of Vancouver Island and following our compass course across the strait.

At 12:30 the tide changed and the swells grew larger. We were in the open Pacific, riding the breakers. As the breakers grew larger, we headed starboard of Pine Island which brought us closer to land. We were across by 1:30 and pulled into Kinn Bay for lunch. The sun came out as we headed for Namu Harbor and Ricky and I sunbathed topside.

Namu is a pretty little fishing village with woods coming down to the water's edge. Attractive walkways lead to the cannery and the general store. As we stopped at the gas dock, an Indian boy in his outboard motorboat headed our way to warn us that we could not stay overnight at the dock which is dry when the tide goes out. His mission accomplished, he sped away.

Our tanks full again, we started up Fisher Channel to Lama Pass. This pass is very narrow, with small reefs and floating logs adding to the hazards. We slowed down and kept a sharp watch until we came out into Hunter Channel. At 6:00 P.M. we started looking for a place to anchor for the night, and found a beautiful bay just eight miles north of Bella Bella. The tide was low, so we went in far enough to run our bow up on the beach. We jumped ashore to investigate the old, abandoned boat repair yard, with some of its buildings still standing.

Ricky put on his bathing suit and waded out for starfish. Then we dug clams and gathered driftwood for a campfire. As the sun set, the peace of the evening was broken only by the calling of the gulls and crows. This little bay is an ideal place to anchor. It's the first bay on the port side, as one enters Raymond Passage from the north.

Just before turning in, Ricky thanked us for a wonderful day and all the fun he had. Can there be any greater reward in family boating? We wanted him to enjoy his month with us, and to see as much of the Northwest as possible.

We were up at 6:00 next morning, and it was so warm that I put on a sunsuit. We followed the course past Lake Island and up to Jackson Passage, another of those narrow waterways with an S-turn at the east entrance. Rounding Begg Point, we followed Finlayson Channel. Between Jane and Sarah Islands, we found a small cove where we could pull in for a coffee break while Ricky hunted for more starfish, which fascinate him.

We followed Tolmie Channel to Butedale. Arriving at noon, we found the whole town closed down for lunch, and so we went exploring. Butedale is on a lovely bay with a large waterfall at the entrance. On our last trip there had been a cannery, but we were told that this had been washed away in a flood. Now one of the town's chief diversions is the visiting yachts which come in for gas. We walked up the wooden stairs behind the store, past all the company houses. Then the path turned and went straight up via a wooden ramp. Picking berries as we went, we reached the top and were rewarded by the sight of a beautiful lake at the top of the waterfall.

By 1:30 we had filled our tanks, replenished our supply of milk and were again underway. Continuing our course up Fraser Reach, we passed one waterfall after another. Drifting clouds covered the snow peaks as we rounded Kingcome Point, turned into McKay Reach and crossed Wright Sound to Grenville Channel. It was still too early to anchor so we decided to pass by Lowe Inlet and continue on to Baker Inlet, where we anchored just off the beach. The captain got the dinghy down for the first time, put on the outboard, and Ricky took off across the bay at full speed on his own private cruise.

We made an early start the next morning as we had Dixon Entrance to cross. It turned cold as we headed out of Baker Inlet, which had proved to be an ideal overnight anchorage. By 10:00 A.M. we were slowing down to enter Prince Rupert Harbor, which is narrow, shallow, and has many sandbars.

Prince Rupert, the last town in Canada, is at the end of the highway, and many people drive here, then put their cars on the ferry to Alaska. It's a pretty little town with flowers everywhere. Ricky and I stayed aboard while Wynn went in search of the Canadian Customs Officer to turn in our papers and get clearance.

At 1:30, as we headed out to Chatham Sound, it was still cloudy. We were going against the tide, but the cruiser rode the large swells like a surfboard, to Ricky's great enjoyment. Past Dundas Island, we crossed the line into Alaskan waters. The water was good up through Revillagigedo Channel, and by 4:30 we were entering Ketchikan Harbor. We tied up at Thomas Basin while the captain visited the customshouse.

Then on to Bar Harbor, two miles farther down. Here we tied up for the night at the guest mooring. We walked the two miles to town and had dinner at the Fireside Inn, an excellent place to eat. The servings were generous and we decided that Alaskans must have bigger appetites than the rest of us. It rained hard during the night and was still raining the next morning—not surprising in a land which averages 278 inches a year.

Now that we had reached Alaska, we meant to slow down and start fishing. We headed out for Naha Bay at Loring, a U.S. Forest Service observatory for bear watchers who come to study the animals' fish-catching technique. We tied up at the float in Naha Bay, put on our rain gear and walked up the path through dense woods to a lake at the head of a waterfall. We found salmonberries and blueberries along the trail, but no bears.

Back aboard *Miss Westerner*, we got out our fishing lines and started trolling along the shore, but all we caught was a collection of rock cod. Ricky caught six. At 4:30 we headed across Behm Canal. The water was so rough, with the sea building with the tide, that Wynn headed across to Helm Bay to wait for the tide to change. But the Helm was a poor place to stay with the wind blowing right up the bay. Smugglers Cove looked like a promising place to anchor, but it was not deep enough for overnight, so we selected a deeper bay.

The next morning was again rainy, foggy and cold. The water was still rough, although better than the day before.

As we rounded Caamano Point, we were going with the tide, still riding the waves. The water was calmer in Clarence Strait on our way to Humpback Bay and Wrangell. We took a shortcut through Seward Passage, Ricky and I at the bow to watch for rocks.

At noon we pulled into Humpback Bay and anchored offshore in 40 feet of water. The sun came out after lunch and Wynn got the dinghy down for an expedition upstream to see the bears, and fish for salmon. It's worth a trip to Alaska just to visit Humpback Bay, one of the most beautiful primitive areas we've ever seen. We rowed the dinghy to the head of the stream and then started hiking.

We saw bald-headed eagles on almost every tree top, and heard ravens calling. The stream was black with salmon fighting their way up. We stopped to rest atop a large boulder while Ricky fished. Across the stream we saw a bear lying on his side to fish. Ricky and the bear both kept on fishing, each on his own side of the stream.

The next morning promised a beautiful, warm, sunny, lazy day. We cleaned house in the morning while Ricky went fishing. After a lunch of fresh-caught crab we all took to the dinghy and again headed upstream. We pulled the dinghy ashore and tied it to an old log, then started for the trail, hoping to explore further. The well-defined path followed the bank above Anan Creek, taking advantage of tree roots for stepping stones. Logs bridged the gulleys of small tributary streams. The wild ferns were thick and there were wild berries to eat along the way. The mountain slopes were covered with forests of spruce, cedar and pine.

We paused on a ledge above a waterfall to watch the salmon. Hundreds of them were working their way upstream, leaping high, falling against the rocks, resting a while in a quiet pool at the water's edge, then trying again. Farther along the trail, we came upon a large quiet pool which appeared to be the spawning ground of those salmon lucky enough to reach it. Bald-headed eagles circled overhead; ravens called raucously and an occasional bluebird darted through the tree tops. As we watched, a black bear came from the forest, balanced along a log, then waded into the stream. He batted a salmon with his paw, picked it up in his mouth and ambled off into the woods for lunch. Ricky, too, did well with his fishing.

On the twenty-seventh, we navigated Blake Channel, the Narrows and Eastern Passage to Wrangell. What a gorgeous harbor! We pulled into the gas dock with only two gallons to spare—a little close for comfort. The dock attendant told us that, if we had run out of gas, we could have radioed to Wrangell and they would have sent gas out.

A brief stop at Wrangell, then out Sumner Strait and through Wrangell Narrows to Petersburg where we tied up at the public wharf and went shopping. Petersburg is a pleasant town. We found a good-sized grocery store and an excellent bakery. In the meantime, Ricky was back at the wharf fishing for herring to use for bait.

We left for Tracy Arm to sleep among the icebergs. There were Frederick Sound, Thomas Bay, Baird Glacier, Farragut Bay, Cape Fanshaw. There was a whole school of gray whales in Stephens Passage, surfacing and blowing. Icebergs, large and small, presented a display of modern free-

form sculpture for our pleasure—and navigational problems for the skipper. As we entered Tracy Arm at 6:30 bergs swirled all around us. We chipped some ice for our cocktails. Glacier ice is beautifully clear and lasts much longer than commercial ice. At the end of the arm we nestled down with the bergs for the night.

Weaving our way through icebergs, whales and porpoises, we reached Taku Harbor at noon and tied up at the

Ricky Baird with the big fish he caught in Glacier Bay.

dock to make lunch. A girl on a neighboring boat invited Ricky aboard and taught him the best way to clean salmon. We walked up the ramp to explore an old, abandoned cannery which was once the headquarters of the glacier priest, Father Hubbard. The cabins where he lived and taught are still standing. Then underway again and through the Gastineau Channel to Juneau.

We tied *Miss Westerner* and walked into town, one mile up the side of the hill. We visited the new post office and the gift shops. Back at the dock, we had dinner at the new Breakwater Inn, then visited with the fishermen.

Thursday, we shoved off for Glacier Bay. Four miles through the narrows we hit a sandbar and were stuck for two hours. At 5:30 the tide came in and we started to move, weaving our way out of the narrows. Out in Favorite Channel we had heavy going against the tide and were glad to reach Bartlett Cove. At Glacier Bay Lodge we were invited to tie alongside the *Mercer Girl*, C. H. Johnson's cruiser from Seattle Yacht Club with Jack and Carolyn West of San Pedro, California, aboard.

August 1 was our day for seeing the large glaciers, and we headed out into Glacier Bay early. We went up Muir Inlet, then on to John Hopkins Inlet. We anchored for the night at Gilbert Island in a beautiful spot between Hugh Miller and Skidmore glaciers, and fell asleep to dream of the ice age.

In the morning, we ate breakfast on the fantail and watched the seals swimming by. A whale was blowing in the distance. We returned to Glacier Bay by late afternoon. In the evening a ranger presented a picture-lecture about the glaciers, and we were disappointed to learn that they have a relatively short life and are receding rapidly.

The next day was salmon-fishing day, so off we went with a fishing guide. We crossed the bay to Rush Point where Ricky caught a huge 125-pound halibut, the largest ever caught at Glacier Bay. On Sunday we went fishing on our own. Drifting back and forth along the shoreline, we caught a lot of halibut. Just south of Rush Point, we anchored and went ashore to explore the dense forest. The tide was out and we followed large bear tracks in the wet sand, but did not catch up with the bear. We collected shells and gathered driftwood for a beach fire. We cooked our halibut over the open fire and it surely tasted good.

On Monday, the thermometer registered 70°—sunsuit weather again. We cruised down Icy Strait to Hoonah, a typical Indian fishing village which we particularly wanted Ricky to see. The town had changed very little since our previous visit.

Leaving Hoonah, we headed for Skagway. The wind started to blow hard in Icy Strait and the rollers seemed ten feet high. We cut across Chatham Strait to find a cove to wait out the wind. We rounded the point into Hawk Inlet in midafternoon to find the water swarming with fishing boats, also waiting out the wind.

By morning, the water had subsided to a small chop as we again headed out into Chatham Strait. We took a short-cut to Auke Bay, taking the port side of Coghlan Island—a mistake which cost us new props. We were told at Taylors Marina that many yachtsmen hit those submerged rocks. Wynn changed props while I baked a cake.

On our way out, we carefully went the recommended side of Coghlan Island and back up Favorite. At Lynn Channel, we hit the tide run and a northerly, and pulled into Amalga Harbor to await the tide change. Lynn Channel is a long waterway ending in Skagway, and it's always better to go with the tide. This is spectacular scenery. We cruised up fjord inlets with 7000-foot Mount Sinclair in the background and countless waterfalls along the way. We reached Skagway, Gateway to the Yukon, in midafternoon and rushed into town to make arrangements for a train trip to Lake Bennett the next morning. The town was crowded with tourists, some arriving by ferry, others by train. We dined, shopped and attended a show at the Town Hall.

In the morning we boarded the narrow-gauge train, one of the original trains used during the gold rush period. At Lake Bennett we had moose meat for lunch in the old station house. Looking straight down into the deep gorge below, one can still see the old trail of the sourdoughs. Lake Bennett was the site of a boatbuilding operation in gold rush days, and the boats sailed north to Dawson and the gold creeks of the Klondike.

Back in Skagway, we visited the Trail of '98 Museum where we enjoyed reading old court records and legal papers of the pioneers. An odd item in the museum was a blanket of small skins, with small bags of pepper sewed behind each skin to preserve it from moths.

Early on August 8, we pulled out of Skagway Harbor just in front of the 22-knot cruise ship *Wickersham,* and we barely managed to stay ahead of her. In Haines, we stopped for gas and Ricky and I went shopping for a deerskin. Every time we make a town stopover it's expensive.

We pulled into Juneau at 2:30 and asked Ricky how he would like to spend his last night on the cruise. He chose dinner cooked ashore, a big fire and some target shooting. Accordingly we cruised around Douglas Island to Admiralty Cove to anchor for the night. The weather was balmy and warm, perfect for eating ashore. Ricky wished he didn't have to leave and his grandfather hated to see him go. He had enjoyed teaching the boy to fish, boat, shoot and explore. They comforted each other with promises of summers to come.

Friday, we saw Ricky off on the plane then drove to the Baranof Hotel in Juneau for our wedding anniversary dinner. On Saturday, missing Ricky very much, we headed *Miss Westerner* south to Sitka. This time the sea was smooth as we cruised down Chatham Strait to Sitkoh Bay and the town of Chatham, home of the New England Fish Company and very much a company town. We refueled and, since the evening was lovely, decided to cruise a few more hours before anchoring for the night. Peril Strait was very scenic with good-sized bays all along the way. After a startling encounter with a large ferry boat at Rapids Point, we reached Fish Bay and tied up to an old log float. We've marked this place on our chart for good overnight staying.

In the morning, we continued through Peril Strait, which might be called an inside passage to Sitka. This was our first trip to Sitka, and I was looking forward to seeing the town. I had just read *Sitka* by Louis l'Amour, a historical novel set in this country.

The passage through Neva Strait is narrow and tricky; Krestof Sound and Olga Strait are narrow and shallow. It was a magnificent scene as we cruised into the sound with Mount Edgecumbe across the water, and the sound dotted with small islands. We threaded our way through the small fishing boats and at noon entered Sitka's harbor, well protected by its rock breakwater.

Anxious to explore the town, we docked quickly and set out. Business has been conducted on Sitka's Lincoln Street since the early nineteenth century when Sitka was known as the "Paris of the Pacific." Men from all over the world walked these streets while their ships were in port, and, as we retraced their steps, we tried to visualize those days under the rule of the czar.

On Monday, we got out our Avanti fold-up bikes with

motors and went forth to see the town and countryside. Six miles out of town, we stopped at the Alaska Lumber and Pulp Company, a Japanese-owned corporation which produces 500 tons of pulp daily and employs some 500 people, and an additional 500 for logging contractors. Exploring the back streets of Sitka, we visited the Sheldon Jackson Museum, the National Cemetery and other beautiful and interesting points.

Tuesday evening, we were back at Fish Bay off Peril Strait. When we stopped at Chatham Cannery for gas on Wednesday, a fisherman told us to go to the end of the bay, where the river flows in, to see the salmon. They were going upstream by the thousands. It's always a thrill to see the salmon jump, and we went ashore and hiked upstream to see them better. Our anchorage that night was at Hidden Falls in Kasnyku Bay. Thursday morning, we explored the bay, going into the abandoned cannery and sawmill. The woods were wet with rain, and our boots filled with water as we crossed the stream and clambered over old log pilings and slippery rocks.

In the afternoon, we headed down to Warm Springs and Baranof. This beautiful deep bay has a large waterfall at the head. We tied up to the dock, took out our trout poles and hiked a mile up to Baranof Lake at the top of the falls. No trout, but the walk was lovely.

Rain is an integral part of an Alaskan trip, but I noted in the log entry for August 16 that this was the wettest day to date. Rain, rain and more rain! We really appreciated the spaciousness of our quarters. And on such a day food becomes more important than ever. I went to the freezer for meat, which went into a big pot of chili. With cheese, bread and wine, our lunch was a change from the Alaska seafood menu. Wynn kept busy fixing things.

Mr. and Mrs. Peterson from Petersburg invited us to their cabin, along with friends, to see home movies of crabbing, skin diving and cruising taken by Wayne and Barbara Short. The Shorts live year-round at Warm Springs. During the spring and summer Wayne tends his crab pots and during the harsh winter months he writes books. Two which have been recently published are *The Cheechakoes* and *This Raw Land*. These are Alaska adventure stories based on the Shorts' experiences and hardships; however they both love the country.

The next day it was kicking up outside the bay, but we decided to leave anyway and found ourselves going against it. It was slow going, but the seas smoothed down some in Frederick Sound. At noon we pulled into Kake on Kupreanof Island, where we waited among the fishing boats to buy gasoline.

We checked the charts and decided on a different course through Keku Strait. One always has to be watchful. The charts show that passage through should be on a rising tide. Some of the fishermen assured us we would make it. There had been some dredging; so they warned us to move slowly and watch the markers closely.

It is that feeling of adventure that makes cruising so intriguing in this country. On this passage there were so many small islands that we had trouble identifying them. And the markers weren't as well defined as we had hoped.

Small craft and float planes tied up close together, as seen here, are commonplace in Alaska.

We felt as though we were wandering through channels in the Everglades. I took a position on the bow, watching for foul ground. It was beautiful, but we wouldn't advise this passage.

And then we rounded Devils Elbow. "He" must have had a sore one! The charts say "dredged to 5 ft.," but don't believe it. Wynn was busy kicking up the outdrive units as we floated over dangerous rocks. Approaching Sumner Strait, we went from the frying pan into the fire. The wind was blowing a gale and we soon found it was too rough to cross. We searched out a friendly hold in a bay near a logging camp just inside Point Barrie. The log boom, as usual in this north country, became our tie-up float, though tying wasn't easy in the heavy wind.

Sunday, the rain and wind were gone but it was still cloudy. As anyone knows who has spent a night under similar circumstances, it wasn't a restful one for us with the wind slapping us against the boom.

We headed across Sumner Strait over to Prince of Wales Island. After a choppy crossing, we put into Baker Point to refuel. The fishermen were helpful in making a place for us to tie and they filled the air with questions about our craft as they don't see many pleasure boats in this area. Rain is a blessing to them at times, and they were glad to have had the heavy rains of the previous day as the streams had fallen so low that the fish weren't coming in.

Back into Sumner Strait, I called it "My kind of cruising water." Fishing boats were everywhere. The skipper remarked, "I don't see that fishing boat's net. Guess he isn't fishing." Then we looked again and saw white floats ahead. It was too late to turn so Wynn cut the engines, tilted the units and we slipped over the net, pleased that we weren't sitting out there fouled up. Those nets can become nightmares at times. And it's costly if one cuts them up with the props.

Screen Island offered refuge, and we pulled around in back of it for lunch. Many things made the balance of our day another of those enjoyable days in a primitive setting. We'd tried trolling for salmon, but with no luck. We entered McHenry Inlet and anchored near the stream at the head. Fish were jumping all around. After dinner we started out in the dinghy and went up the stream as far as we could go. Here was a bear crossing the stream, obviously after a salmon dinner. The salmon were thick in the shallow waters.

Then we explored some more, going over to another stream that I can best describe as boiling with salmon. Some seals had come in and were having a feast. We pulled the dinghy onto some rocks as it was too shallow for further cruising. But the overgrowth and the narrow stream prevented further exploration on foot. We watched the salmon for a while, then put the dinghy back in the water. Just then a large black bear walked out of the woods to stand on the spot we had just vacated. He didn't seem to see us right away. He sniffed our tracks, looked up as we pushed off, then walked across the stream and into the woods on the other side. We saw another bear as we returned to *Miss Westerner*, and also three seals fishing for dinner. We'd had our associations with Alaska wildlife for the day.

On Monday we spent the morning doing "lazy day" puttering around the boat. A doe and her fawn came down to the water's edge to eat grass. We marked McHenry Inlet as a beautiful stop worthy of any yachtsman's visit. As we got underway a small seaplane came in close above us, apparently looking the boat over.

We cruised down Clarence Strait, through Skowl Arm and into Saltery Bay for another log boom tie-up. Here we met a young couple and their two-year-old son. The parents teach school during the winter and fish commercially in the summer.

On Tuesday, we headed for Ketchikan, about 25 miles distant. We filled the gas tanks and picked up some detailed charts, planning to double back and explore more little bays and coves. By early Wednesday morning, however, the wind made up, rain squalls came in, and exploring beautiful bays lost its attraction. We spent the day quietly reading aboard *Miss Westerner,* venturing forth in the evening for supper in uptown Ketchikan.

By Thursday morning, the winds were gone and the sun came out. The radio reported that the previous day's winds had been blowing up to 60 knots right at the entrance. Three salmon seining boats had stayed out too long —"fish hungry" they call it in some areas—and capsized in the gale. Their nets were out and they were unable to come about. We were glad we had stayed in port.

Our next visit was to another of those places which add so much to a trip like this—the Haida Indian Village at Old Kasaan on Skowl Arm. The lovely old totem poles were almost hidden by grass and trees. We cruised on to Polk Inlet and dropped anchor. Another wonderful bay. The sun was out bright and warm.

That evening we got into a complicated series of radio-telephone calls between *Miss Westerner,* Ketchikan, Seattle and Southern California. Our son Bob was calling up. With the help of the U.S. Coast Guard, the call was finally completed and we learned that Wynn's father had died.

By 11:00 the next morning, *Miss Westerner* was tied up in Ketchikan and we were on a seaplane enroute to Annette Island where we were to board the jet plane for Los Angeles.

Two weeks later, on September 6, we were back in Alaska, our son with us to do some fishing and hunting. The Alaskan fall had set in. Our first cruising was up Behm Canal with a stop in Shrimp Bay, a lovely spot with a wide stream at the head of the bay. Bob set out to do some bear hunting and saw several at a lake at the top of a waterfall.

Sunday morning started off great. Bob brought back a string of trout for breakfast. Then we went to the Bell Island Fishing Resort to pick up some additional foul weather clothing. We enjoyed the visit with the people there and learned a lot about where to fish. As we stood visiting in front of the lodge, a bear casually strolled out of the woods and began to fish in the stream. This is a lovely place and we hope to come back.

We followed the advice and went up Behm Narrows where we cut the engine and drifted with the tide while the men fished. One of Bob's salmon was a 28-pounder. At the end of the day we pulled into Anchor Bay. We went ashore in the dinghy, then went hiking. We had salmon for dinner and went to bed early. It had been a long day.

The next morning we had trouble with the dinghy and finally, after everything was straightened out, we returned to Shrimp Bay. Though it was late, Bob rowed ashore to go bear hunting. An hour later he was back. He had got his bear. To shorten a long story, we all went out next day to help skin the bear and bring it aboard. By early afternoon as we were returning to *Miss Westerner,* presumably at anchor, we came around the last bend—and couldn't see her. We were concerned, no doubt about it.

The tide was high as we rowed out in the dinghy. We rounded the bend, and still no boat. Bob rowed faster and faster—only one more bend before Behm Narrows. And then we sighted her. When we finally rowed alongside, we found she had dragged her anchor and was slowly drifting along the bay.

And this is the way September cruising went for us in this part of Alaska. Now it was Ketchikan, here we come. Then the long run back to Seattle. Then the government locks where we entered to tie up at Lake Union.

We had lived aboard *Miss Westerner* for 58 days, and we covered 3300 nautical miles. Now we are enthused for the coming year, and it is our plan to explore all of Prince of Wales Island, including the west coast side. If all goes through, we will start in June and return by August.

29

Skookum Maru Goes North

by Gordon and Blanche Rogers

A long time ago at one of those dinner parties where everyone swaps stories of yachting experiences, some friends from Vancouver said, "If you are really interested in cruising you should come to British Columbia. We could find you a boat to rent." We took them up on the offer and this was the open sesame to our 30 years' cruising in British Columbia and Alaska.

There were no regularly chartered boats then as there are today. But our friends found us the *Mabel C*, a 35-foot cruiser powered by a four-cylinder Cadillac engine. The galley had a coal cook stove. The bare boat charter was $8 per day.

What is it that takes us from Berkeley, California, to spend our summers exploring this vast region year after year? Obviously, it is the fun we have in every aspect of boating—the boat itself, the work, the play and every facet of nature which we find in the sea, beaches and forests. My wife and I are mutually blessed by this love of boating.

After four bare boat charters out of Vancouver, B.C., we decided to part with our sailboat on San Francisco Bay and build a cruiser for the Northwest. We sketched our specific needs and took them to Ed Monk in Seattle, asking him to design our boat. The result is our *Skookum Maru.*

Our last trip up the coast from San Francisco was in 1960 and we now winter the boat in Seattle.

Skookum is a Siwash Indian word meaning "strong," or "husky." Maru means "circle" in Japanese, and since the boat was built in Japan, we added this name which is used for Japanese merchant ships, because they say a ship is a complete independent entity, like a circle. And *Skookum Maru* is truly a husky and complete little ship, dependable and successful as a cruising yacht.

Her hull is from a 40-foot displacement trawler design,

much like the fishing boats of this area. The layout, with sleeping cabins and heads forward and aft, provides complete privacy for two couples, with bunks made up at all times, and ample storage in drawers and closets. The oil stove with oven—a necessity in this country—not only turns out good food, but keeps the boat dry and the people warm. There's an electric heater in the captain's cabin, and for the occasional warm day we use two Primus kerosene single-burner stoves.

After years of uncertainty with a gasoline engine in our sailboat, the dependability of our three-cylinder GMC-71 diesel engine is a joy. In 13 years and 27,000 miles of cruising, it has never failed us.

We enjoy cruising alone as well as with guests and we alternate these pleasures. We particularly enjoy guests who are friends of some years and who are able to entertain themselves. Preferably they are boating people, familiar with living aboard and a boat's operation. We try to give our guests a sampling of about everything that Northwest cruising has to offer.

In scheduling a summer cruise, we try to fit the area and the tempo to the individual needs of our guests. Some prefer runs on the open coast or around the west side of Vancouver Island, while others take greater pleasure in inland cruising. In the past nine summers in British Columbia and Alaska waters, we have regulated our rough passages so that no one has been scared or sick.

After a day's run or on a lay day, we get off the boat and stretch our muscles. Our guests pursue varied interests —bird watching, shell gathering, beachcombing or photography. *Skookum Maru* carries two Canadian Davidson nine-foot dinghies, and we arrange shore expeditions and rowing trips in these.

Heavy windlass and bow roller make anchoring a pleasure.

Yachtsmen cruising these waters should condition themselves for rain, and a certain amount of heavy clothing should be provided. Summers vary. There are good years, filled with sunshine. And sometimes it seems to rain 50 percent of the time.

On a cruise from Seattle to Alaska, one can drop the hook in a different beautiful anchorage for lunch and dinner every day. There are some places of special scenic interest that should not be missed. The trip up the fjords from Pender Harbor to Princess Louisa Inlet is outstanding. This beautiful spot belongs to the yachtsmen of the world. Although it is under the care of the Canadian Park system, it was given to us by "Mac" Macdonald who continued for many summers to be the host of Princess Louisa living on his houseboat by Chatterbox Falls.

Farther north, between Milbanke Sound and Dixon Entrance, the Gardner Canal and its approaches wind 60 miles into the interior, providing beautiful fjords guarded by snow-covered peaks. East of Ketchikan is the Rudyerd Bay-Walker Cove scenic area. Sheer rock walls rise to 4500 feet above the water, a wilderness in an ocean setting. There are good anchorages in each inlet.

South of Juneau, Tracy Arm is a 30-mile-long fjord with two glaciers calving icebergs at the head. The inlet may be filled more or less with icebergs and here, as in Glacier Bay National Monument, we proceed with caution. We stay a half mile away from any glacier face, for there is real hazard from very large waves created by the calving glacier face.

On one visit to Glacier Bay, we were fortunate to have a clear day; so we started our adventure at 4:00 A.M. Ahead of us was the spectacular 15,000-foot Mount Fairweather Range with ice flowing down the sides. We traveled slowly from one glacier to another for 40 miles until at last the sea ahead of us was choked with icebergs. We anchored in Sandy Cove that night and woke in the morning to find a big blue iceberg stranded near us. The clouds were down to a 100-foot ceiling and the scenery was gone but we had had the finest day in 30 years of boating.

The Mendenhall Glacier recreation area, 15 miles from Juneau, is well worth the trip and, in addition to the glacier, the Visitor's Center with guides is very informative. There are innumerable possibilities for short plane trips into the interior of Alaska or a five-day circle tour from Juneau to Fairbanks, Nome, Kotzebue and Point Barrow. One flying trip we recommend is an hour's flight over the Juneau Ice Field. Here is a frozen mountain area of 1500 square miles, the source of 16 glaciers and a most spectacular sight.

But to us this cruising land offers much more than a spectacular scenic boat ride. We like to go on the beaches, up the rivers and into the forests. Fifty feet inland from the beach one is in a dense rain forest, a different world.

We have fished a tide rip at Point Baker where the upwelling of the ocean currents brought food to the surface. Schools of herring were pursued by the salmon. Seals and two whales were in on the kill and the air was full of seabirds picking up the scraps.

We have seen salmon so densely packed in a bay—as they waited for high water—that they looked like a rock reef. In such places it is impossible to get bottom soundings with an echo sounder. At Anan Creek, the forest service has built a little shelter high above the stream where one can watch the bears scooping the salmon from the stream.

Fisheries experts try to calculate the number of spawning salmon that each stream can support. They then regulate the number of days for commercial fishing and close critical areas. In the gravel beds of the streams, we see those salmon which have surmounted all these obstacles, spawning and thus ending their life cycle.

Many animals are curious about us, as we are about them. One evening, looking out through our cabin rear window, we saw the little face of a raccoon who was watching us. He ran as we opened the door but returned to the float for a fillet of fresh salmon. Sea otters are curious too, and have followed us for hours as we trolled from a dinghy.

Once a large wolf, looking much like a German shepherd dog, appeared across the stream while we were trout fishing, unafraid and interested in the strange creatures with fish poles. A little black bear was fascinated by our fly casting, his little head twisting back and forth as he watched the casts of the fly line.

These black bears are harmless but the brown or grizzly bear can be very dangerous. These bears are found on the mainland of British Columbia and Alaska and on the three large Alaskan islands, Admiralty, Baranof and Chichagof. The Tongass National Forest recommends, "When traveling in brown bear country, make it a practice to travel with others and to carry a .30-06 or larger rifle." We carry a 35-calibre rifle but the first mate sees to it that we don't see even a chipmunk. Her system is to make a lot of noise. Sometimes she ties a tin can containing a couple of rocks to her belt. More often she makes the canyons echo by blowing a foghorn. We hiked a mile up a remote stream in Alaska with regular blasts from this horn. At the outlet from the lake, we were surprised to find a camp with three young scientists doing a summer research project on the Dolly Varden trout. Imagine their bewilderment at the sound of this horn coming up the canyon!

It is difficult to hike any distance inland due to the dense growth and fallen, rotting timber, so that a trail or logging road is almost a necessity to get up these streams and to the many lakes. In Alaska the Tongass National Forest comprises most of the area of Southeast Alaska including the islands. A map shows more than 100 fishing and hunting areas accessible by boat or plane. Cabins are provided which give the small cruiser a place to camp and dry out. At many of the lakes, free boats are provided. Using this map we have been able to locate anchorages with trails leading to "out of this world" stream and lake fishing. It is available by writing to Tongass National Forest, P.O. Box 2278, Ketchikan, Alaska 99901.

Our own charts are scribbled with notes made over the past 30 years. Some of these notes are from an experienced cruising man who, having sold his boat, said, "Now I will tell you all of my secret fishing holes." Typical examples: abalone at Fog Rocks, prawns in Pendrell Sound, Dungeness crabs at Cascade Inlet, Alaska king crab in Red Bay, halibut at the head of the Dean Canal, a hole for red snapper on Cortez Island, an abandoned apple orchard in Evans Bay, and of course salmon holes on every chart.

Onshore there are summer runs of big steelhead on the Dean River, excellent rainbow and cutthroat fishing in the Karta River near Ketchikan, wild strawberries at Glacier Bay, blueberries at Kakushtish Harbor, red huckleberries at Quathaski Cove by Campbell River, and wild blackberries at Lund.

Our modern civilization with its highly processed and frozen foods denies most people the chance to enjoy the delicious flavors of truly freshly caught seafood or freshly picked fruits. Here in the north country is a culinary treat completely unavailable even to the gourmets in the city. Our habit is to take only the amount we can use fresh and never never to freeze it. The one exception to the rule is salmon. We have it smoked and canned at different places along the coast. There is a sportsman's cannery at April Point on Quadra Island, near Campbell River, B.C., and Rick Kapus has a little cannery at Point Baker, Alaska. Several times we have caught salmon at other locations and sent them to the cannery by float plane at a modest cost, and picked up the canned salmon on our way south. There is a new and very fine little resort at Yes Bay near Ketchikan. There Hazel, the cook, will smoke or can the fish for the guests.

Many times we are asked where one can find these epicurean delights and learn how to prepare them. We find abalone on the rocks among the kelp at a very low tide in areas swept by water fresh from the sea, as in Queen Charlotte Sound. They are small but delicious when cleaned,

Skookum Maru in Queen's Reach, British Columbia, on her shakedown cruise.

sliced, pounded lightly and cooked fast. We find crabs at the head of most of the inlets north of Seymour Narrows. We try to set the traps in 20 to 30 feet on a sandy stream delta. Bait the trap with a fish head or a perforated can of sardines or dog food and you will catch all the crabs needed. Our method of preparation is not standard. We stab the crab in the belly to kill it and then clean it before boiling.

Setting and pulling prawn traps is too much work to do blindly. Better ask the local people for the best locations and depth. We set our traps in 40 fathoms. Prawns seem to prefer an oily fish bait like salmon or dogfish (the older the better), rather than cod. We also use lean meat scraps, and we are told that smashed clams in a perforated can will work. Prawns should not be cooked until they have been dead for two hours.

In recent years the clams have at times and in certain areas been toxic due to red tide. It is wise to check locally before eating clams. We make a delicacy from the ugly big horse clam. We split the neck and peel off the outer heavy skin, then pound it paper thin and fry it along with the mantle for one minute in hot butter. It's a lot of work but worth it. Our most popular hors d'oeuvre is barbecued oysters which we cook on the hibachi. We fasten one half strip of very thin bacon around each small oyster with a toothpick, place the oyster on the grill and cook until the bacon is completely crisp. These are delectable.

A different activity from the garnering of seafoods is exploring the underwater life on certain reefs at low tide. An excellent area for this is the reef in Malaspina Inlet, on the left just after entering. The offshore islands at Beaver Harbor near Port Hardy are another favorite. For this exploration, a minus tide is required.

Most of the place-names which we have given are familiar places on the charts but we like to get away from the standard cruising pattern, sometimes seeing no other boat or dwelling for several days. On a two-week trip from Ketchikan to the west coast of Prince of Wales Island, we saw just one other yacht. We stopped at charming little harbors like Meyers Chuck, Point Baker, Point Protection, and then south through the beautiful 70-foot-wide dredged channel, El Capitan Passage, to another little gem of a harbor called Tokeen. Here we bought shrimp from a little one-man-and-wife shrimp business and traded three cans of beer for a six-pound chicken halibut. There are clean, free, hot showers at the fish-packing plant here.

Being off of the regular traveled channels, it is important for us to be self-sufficient and to take all possible precautions. The rocks are not so well charted in those areas, and it is wise to travel well offshore. We have reported several rocks to the Coast and Geodetic Survey in Washington. We try to go through almost all of the rapids at slack water on the theory that we have plenty of excitement in our boating without looking for more. With the current tables, it is no problem to navigate any of the rapids at slack water.

Although we like to explore these remote areas, we realize it is important for us and our guests to be in contact with home. Before we leave for the summer we provide our family and guests and our business with a schedule of the dates on which we will cruise certain areas and the time of day at which we will listen to the radiotelephone. The marine telephone operators regularly call the names of ships for which they hold delayed telephone calls, after the weather broadcast three times a day. We carry the ship-to-shore crystals for Seattle, Vancouver, Prince Rupert, Ketchikan and Juneau so that we are daily available by telephone. The ship-to-shore also makes it possible for us to charter a float plane in case of need. Since they can land in any inlet or bay, help in case of accident or illness is only minutes away. Only last year we were moored way off in Kingcome Inlet when an emergency call came from home at 7:30 A.M. Within an hour and a half, the float plane picked up the captain and he was in San Francisco that same night.

During these years of cruising, we have seen many changes: in the coves the houses used by the hand loggers are still standing, but the loggers vanished 20 years ago; the forests are full of rotting timber tramways and huge rusting steam donkey engines. Today the logging is being done by large organizations using expensive machinery; fish are caught by modern boats using modern equipment.

Pleasure yachts are traveling farther north in greater numbers each year as enthusiasm for these waters grows. But in spite of "progress" this primitive country will remain, in our lifetime at least, the world's most rewarding.

30

Glacier Cruise in a Trailerboat

by Mona Green

We decided long in advance on our cruise through the Inland Passage to Alaska, so we spent much of the winter and spring in preparation for it. Among other items, Thornton enrolled in and passed a correspondence course in coastal navigation, and I studied it along with him so I could be helpful.

Along with this was a major construction job on the boat. The convertible top was eliminated and Thornton built a hardtop cabin, increased the headroom, raised the seats and increased the windshield height. He built in a compact galley, installed an electric refrigerator, a depth finder and other instrumentation. All in all, our 23-foot *Gadabout III,* an Arenacraft with 210-horsepower OMC conversion V-8 Chevrolet 287-cubic-inch engine, is a snug little craft. We lived on her for five and a half weeks and proved her snugness, because there was rain most of the last four of those.

Before beginning the Alaska trip, we had a week in March for shakedown on the Gulf of California. Next, we made trips to Lake Powell in April, May and June. The last one was our annual week of cruising with two grandchildren, selected for the cruise upon reaching 12 years of age. We traveled more than 300 miles on Lake Powell in that week, explored many canyons, enjoyed lots of swimming and some fishing. When we returned to Tucson to put the children on a plane for their homes, it was June 26 and there were 10 days left to complete our preparations and packing for the big trip.

On July 7, we left home trailing *Gadabout.* We were accompanied by our friends, George and Mary Alida Corneveaux, trailing *New Horizons,* a 23-foot Fiberform with the same engine as ours.

We drove to Anacortes, Washington, for the launching and began the voyage on July 13. The weather was beautiful for the first week, but after we crossed Queen Charlotte Sound, the clouds moved in and stayed with us. We had rain and drizzle almost constantly, with occasional glimpses of the sun. In spite of the weather, it was a wonderful trip and a great experience. One of the nicest parts was meeting fine people along the way. In every port, there were friendly pleasure boating groups, commercial fishermen and local residents.

Our stay in Namu, B.C., was enlightened, and prolonged, because of a group of Canadian Japanese children and their families who live there during the season of salmon cannery activity. The older boys showed us how to use our crab pot and how to handle crabs. They also took us clam digging. We all paddled dinghies to a gravel beach at low tide, and scraped and dug as the two boys taught us to find butter clams and littlenecks; and hastily to throw away horse clams. When our questions became too much for them, they loaned us a book on marine life in British Columbia.

Their relatives gave us fish for cooking and salmon lures of their own make. We tried the lures, but had no luck in catching any salmon. One of the mothers asked us to her home for tea and fish cakes on our last evening in Namu, a truly delightful evening.

We met those on other pleasure boats in Butedale who had been farther north and they reported continuing rain, but we thought it had to clear so kept moving north to our destination port of Juneau. We reached it on August 1.

We stayed a week to see that part of Alaska. First we took a run down to Taku Inlet, hoping to see some glacier activity, but there was no calving at that time, and no floating ice or bergs in the inlet. On the way back, the shaft on

Glacial masses, such as Taku Glacier, at left, offer dazzling spectacles to Alaska's boating visitors. Above: Thornton and Mona Green take Gadabout III right up to the face.

Corneveaux' *New Horizons* snapped; so we towed them from Bishop Point up Gastineau Channel to our moorings in Juneau.

While repairs were being made on the boat, we took a trip to Skagway by ferry and over the narrow-gauge Yukon and White Pass railroad to Lake Bennett. The scenery up Lynn Canal was gorgeous, and the railroad trip most interesting and a change of pace. But after weeks of living aboard *Gadabout III*, we found difficulty sleeping in beds at the Klondike Hotel in Skagway.

Once back at Juneau, we found that repairs were incomplete, so we rented a car and drove to Mendenhall Glacier. In crossing Steep Creek, we watched hundreds of salmon making their spawning run, fighting over the gravel bars and shallows. It was fascinating, but sad to see the dead and dying salmon as nature ended their life cycle.

And then came the spectacular part: A wonderful Alaskan couple whom we had met on the way up, Carl and Gennie Rusher on *The 4 EEEs*, escorted us to Dawes Glacier at the end of Endicott Arm. Many tours are made into Tracy Arm, the northerly branch of Holkham Bay, but very few attempt Endicott because of the great amount of ice. Our host suggested that we anchor our smaller boats near Sanford Cove, opposite Sumdum Glacier, and get aboard his 34-foot Tollycraft Plicor for the trip.

For four hours, he pushed and wove a course through the many miles of floating ice. We saw the blue beauty of the icebergs, the myriad seals, and that never-to-be-forgot-

ten glacier that snapped and growled and spilled off ice, as it towered above us. We were dazzled by the spectacle. Another four hours of careful return put us aboard our boats, where we planned to ride out the night, and then continue our southerly course toward home. But next morning the weather turned us back.

We poked out into Stephens Passage to find 20-knot headwinds. We anchored again back in the same spot which seemed so well protected. In less than an hour, the wind swung to the one direction that could reach us, and we began to roll and pitch, and we had to set two anchors. We stayed there all that day and the next night, with the wind sweeping over the ice, and cakes of ice floating by. It took two of us to hold the pots steady on our stove. It was cold and raw and we now refer to that cove as "Ice Cube Bay."

After the hours of constant rolling and pitching, we were on the radio to Ketchikan for another weather report and concluded that we should return to Juneau and postpone Petersburg. On the way, we had to duck into Doty Cove for four hours before we could cross Taku Inlet into Gastineau Channel. Into smoother water, we were tired and cold but a distress signal from a 20-foot boat brought us around. Four teen-age boys needed a tow. Their main engine and an auxiliary outboard had both failed.

We made our way south for two very stormy days, as far as Wrangell, and there, for a variety of reasons, mainly weather, we loaded our boats and ourselves on a ferry for Seattle. Tucson weather felt good when we got home.

31

The Littoral and Glaciers of Lituya Bay

by Margaret Ellis

In front of Lituya Glacier we shut down *Chilton*'s engines and drifted among the icebergs. It is awesome to see such stark, primitive grandeur.

Nor were we alone in this world. Those dark spots on the icebergs were hair seals. It was siesta time and the adult seals were all conformists. There were 20 or 30 of them on the big ice floes, 10 or so on the medium bergs, and one or two on the small ones. We were entertained because they looked as relaxed as if they were in airy mattress ads.

They lay in a variety of positions and, if we'd been a bit nearer, we surely would have heard a variety of snores. True to form, the younger and smaller seals were swimming and diving like any group of human animals on a beach holiday. Now and then they'd climb out and shake water all over their sleeping parents. Unconcerned, Mom and Pop would drowsily go on enjoying their "sun-and-ice" rest period.

This scene even had its orchestra—the accompaniment of glacial music: loud rumblings, crackings and sloshings. The noises didn't bother the seals at all, but it would take us some time to share their complacency. There were hundreds of these seals in this small bay, and we are glad that this is part of Glacier National Monument and presume that the seals are safe there from trigger-happy fishermen. Whether the seals commute for their livelihood or summer there, the source of their food is abundant, because they were sleek and fat.

The *Chilton* is truly a home afloat; whether we are cruising, lying at anchor, or moored to a float—life goes on. We seldom miss a meal, nor do we often lose any sleep. We can carry enough gasoline for 600 miles of cruising at nine knots; water tanks hold 350 gallons. We stock our deep freeze with fine things to eat: purchased food ashore and shrimp, crab, abalone, clams and a variety of fish caught at sea. Our little oil stove keeps *Chilton* warm, and there is always plenty of hot water for dishes, baths or the washing machine. *Chilton* has bunks for six people, two heads, a bath tub, two Chrysler Crown engines, a 110-volt Kohler plant and other accessories. She was designed by Edwin Monk and built in Bellingham by Pete Lind. She flies the Ketchikan Yacht Club burgee and the Ellis Airlines twin-goose house flag. Between cruises she rests at Ellis Island near Ketchikan. *Chilton* is 53 feet of the happiest yacht in the Pacific Northwest.

When I first became the wife of an aviator, it took awhile to learn to welcome and expect the unexpected. Then we were deeply involved in Ellis Airlines, and the unexpected became routine. I had grown accustomed to the occasional disappearance of husband, perhaps 30 minutes before guests were due to arrive for dinner.

"Well," I'd explain as cheerfully as I could, "Mrs. Jones, in Klawock, had a few pains and decided she'd better fly in to the hospital so Bob went out to retrieve her. He'll be along about eight—or nine—or ten . . ." It all depended on the weather and time of year.

My two crowning achievements arrived not with managing the frequent VIP dinner guests but with a donkey (huge) and a baby seal (untrained). The first arrived to spend the night because it was too cold for the mail boat to make the run to Craig and because the donkey was too large to ride in our Bellanca. So into the basement went donkey, amid the cheers of our children and all their friends, none of whom had ever seen a donkey before.

The weather then deteriorated, while the donkey remained as a houseguest and soon I was reminded of a peasant household in Europe in the Middle Ages. Day One:

Chilton finds Glacier Bay a scenic refuge from bad weather.

basement acquired a different odor; Day Two: first floor smelled a bit odd; Day Three: bedrooms on third floor began to get that way too. Fortunately then, the weather moderated and our guest departed via mail boat.

The baby seal arrived just 10 minutes before a dinner party.

"Hello dear," was my friend's greeting, "would you take care of this seal for the night? I don't know what to do with it." Neither did I, but when a live seal is plunked in one's arms, a decision comes naturally. Into the bathtub went seal, and from then on all night we had a steady, plaintive, noisy cry which sounded like, "Mah! mah! mah!"

I dug out a baby bottle and warmed some milk but seal just splashed, cried and was very noisy. Came the guests and I airily said, "Oh, do come and see our new baby having his bath!" We all spent the evening in the bathroom trying to get the seal to take the bottle. Finally, one guest who was truly a genius, added some cod-liver oil to the milk, and we had it made. That is, aside from spending most of the next day cleaning the bathroom. The seal departed for the zoo it should have gone to the day before, and things returned to the normal state of organized confusion. But that dinner party was a great success: Ellis was home in time and remained all evening.

A fun game we play near Ketchikan, is "Getting a Free Meal from the Sea." The bays and inlets adjacent to the Gulf of Alaska are bountiful with seafood but we had spectacular failures to detract from our score, until we acquired the so-necessary, local knowledge.

Our favorite three-day trip is to leave Ketchikan for Cleveland Peninsula, stop underway at "four fathom rock" and fish for what we call red snapper, but which is actually, scarlet rockfish. The fish here bite as if they are starving to death and, in an hour, we have all that we can use. We go on to Helm Bay and set a couple of crab traps, baiting them

with what remains of our fish after we've enjoyed the choice fillets for dinner.

The next night we dine on the large, fresh, Dungeness crabs while we're moving to another bay to set our shrimp traps. We have the best luck setting them in 40 fathoms, but shrimp are restless souls who migrate, so this takes a bit of prospecting. While the shrimp traps are soaking with the fish heads as bait, we fish for king salmon in the Bell Island area.

Once again, a winning point comes from knowing the time and places to fish for the fighting king. I recall a spot on the west coast of Prince of Wales Island, Cruz Pass, where we saw herring literally "boiling up" to the surface in order to escape the salmon. Anchoring as fast as we could, we launched the skiff and, in no time at all, there was a happy shout, "Fish on!" This king was true to form and put up a real battle, but Bob won and we had a beautiful, 42-pound white king aboard. Many more fish were there for the taking but this was all we needed.

While Bob took our prize to the beach for cleaning, I rowed idly along the shore looking down into the clear, shallow water. Suddenly I bumped into something. Looking around, I saw a huge king salmon beating a hasty retreat. Intent on chasing the herring, he'd come almost to the beach and collided with my skiff. Surprise, was the name of that game!

When Bob retired our long-planned cruise to Lituya Bay became a reality. We left Ketchikan on July 7, and had aboard with us Mary and Bill Royce of Seattle. They left us at Petersburg to fly home after spending a week of cruising in typical, but unwelcome, July weather, featuring wind, rain and low visibility. They are good sports and know Alaska well, so we were not reduced to constant apologies about the lack of sunshine.

Heading up Frederick Sound and then Chatham Straits,

Angoon and Kilisnoo Inlet on Admiralty Island was on our route from Petersburg. Angoon is a Tlinget village and we stopped there to visit before spending a couple of days at the head of the inlet, in Mitchell Bay.

To get there with *Chilton*, we had to wait for slack water before we could navigate the Skookum Chuck. We had a great guide in Rod Darnell, a retired Juneau sportsman, but even with his help, we had an interesting ride because the whirlpools were very active and *Chilton* danced her way up instead of proceeding in her usual sedate fashion. We anchored in a protected cove near the end of Mitchell Bay, about eight miles in from Chatham Straits.

A little beyond our anchorage is a salt lagoon, separated from the bay by a waterfall. At high tide the falls disappear, and we entered the lagoon very easily with our outboard and skiff. Happily we explored the lagoon and caught some cutthroat trout. Suddenly we realized that if we didn't want to pack the outboard and dinghy on our backs through the brush beside the falls, we'd better start down the inlet. By the time we got to the falls, the tide had started to flow rapidly out, and we had an exciting fast-water descent.

We made it in great style with our little dinghy, accompanied by a family of otters. They were soon so busy fishing below the falls, they paid no attention to us. In a matter of minutes, we discovered that we were not in their class at all and stopped our fishing to watch their sport. Disappearing beneath the turbulent current, first one and then another otter would bob up to the surface, stick his head above the waves, a trout dangling crosswise in his mouth, and steady himself for the feast. A few frantic wiggles while the otter chomped methodically, and the fish disappeared. Our grandstand seat was perfect and the show was great.

Exiting from Mitchell Bay, a tail wind from the sou' east gave us a fast ride up Chatham Straits until we anchored in tranquil Pavlov Harbor, on the east side of Chichagof Island. In a small cove near where *Chilton* lay at anchor, there was a waterfall descending from a lake situated about 20 feet above salt water. We saw thousands of Dolly Varden trout hurling themselves up the falls. We rowed into the cove at high tide, slung a line over a convenient rock at the base of the falls, slid the skiff into a deep pool, and in a few minutes caught our full share of "dollies." We kept on fishing and released the rest of them, unhurt and eager to resume their journey. They would only bite on a bare spinner but they attacked that with fury.

We were so engrossed that we almost became marooned by the receding tide. As it was, we had to laboriously haul the skiff for several hundred feet, wading in a couple of inches of water over slippery rocks before we could row back.

The next morning, we rounded Chichagof Island, heading west out Icy Straits and arrived at Hoonah at five o'clock on a Saturday afternoon. It was a madhouse of seine boats, all trying to get fuel and supplies. It was too busy for us, so we did our shopping and then went on into Glacier Bay in rain, wind and low visibility once more. We did get a glimpse of a few mountain goats high up on the slopes of Mount Wright, but that and some drifting icebergs

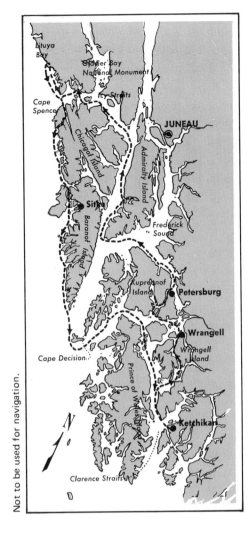

Not to be used for navigation.

was about all we saw. The National Park Department has an attractive lodge at Bartlett Cove, near the entrance to Glacier Bay. Presumably the tourists were content to stay inside, warm and comfortable.

After waiting out the storm in Glacier Bay for a couple of days, we headed out into Icy Straits again, past the Inian Islands, across Cross Sound, and rounded Cape Spencer. We kept well out to sea in this area, as the cape is notorious for its violent tide rips and we were rewarded by the absence of those sharp peaks and square holes that make life afloat a bit uncomfortable. But soon the low southwesterly swell we were enjoying out there in the Gulf of Alaska, acquired a sea that rapidly became more and more confused. But it didn't confuse us and we were happy to change course for Graves Harbor with its quiet anchorage.

There were only a couple of trolling boats in the bay, but soon some 50 others arrived and, by dusk, we were in the center of a small village of people and lights and boats. The surest sign of an approaching storm, is when the fishing fleet shows up en masse. During fine weather, many of the trollers remain out all night in the open ocean and at those times we found ourselves alone in the isolated harbors; the contrast was always interesting. We were the only pleasure boat among them, but they are good neighbors.

Stormbound for two days in Graves Harbor, we donned rain gear and explored the bay and beaches. Then clear weather and our "outside" trip to Lituya was delightful: sunshine, a gentle ocean swell and fabulous scenery. It is surprising and fascinating to cruise by La Perouse Glacier and see it ending directly into the gulf, with the big waves breaking against the 200 feet of blue, icy cliffs. Glacier faces look so primitive — and impenetrable. Traversing one on foot would not be for me!

All along our course we could see miles of sandy beaches, which looked like Utopia for beachcombers. Alas, we were unable to explore them because the heavy surf prevented us from rowing ashore. This stretch of coastline contrasts sharply with the rocky islands of southeastern Alaska. Here the beaches, the glaciers and the huge, snow-covered peaks give one an impression of a land undiscovered by man, yet it has been extensively explored.

We entered Lituya Bay with ease on the flood tide,

which conceals the fact that the tidal action is swift and the bar treacherous. The calm waters of the bay were delightful, and we were elated to have arrived in clear weather. To live for a few days among these tall mountains, rising right up from the salt water, is a very rewarding experience. We had, from our anchorage, superlative views of the Mountains Fairweather (15,320), Quincy Adams (12,500), Salisbury (12,080), Lituya (11,910), three unnamed peaks (9,350, 10,842, and 9,750 — where but in Alaska would such giants lack titles?), and Crillon (12,727) — in our opinion, the most beautiful.

Cascade Glacier was visible but we wanted to see the others; so we cruised up to Crillon and Gilbert Inlets, which lie at the end of Lituya Bay. There were Crillon and Lituya Glaciers, one at each end of the inlets, and we were privileged to be alone when we viewed them. No other boats were in the bay, and not even the sound of an airplane was there to disturb the tranquility of the scene. But we were forcibly reminded that violence lived here, too, as we could plainly see the devastation caused by the 1958 earthquake.

Rounding Cenotaph Island, which lies in the center of Lituya Bay, we first heard and then saw thousands of kittiwakes all intent on laying and hatching their eggs. They were nesting on a steep cliff, 300 feet high, and although it did have narrow ledges, it looked like the world's worst spot for a nursery. Kittiwakes are smaller and trimmer than the harbor gull but they were just as noisy. While great numbers circled overhead, countless couples sat cosily side by side and indulged in much open-beak caressing.

As the tide ebbed, we were treated to a parade of small icebergs drifting by *Chilton*, where we lay at anchor. The littlest icebergs look as if they'd been sculptured by some avant-garde artist. Many of them were adorned with a pair of the little gulls, sitting cosily with their heads together, creating just the right finishing touch to the exhibition of natural art. Several times we scooped up a couple of the tiniest bergs in our salmon-landing net, put them in our deep freeze and now we have glacial ice for our cocktail hour, aged and very long lasting.

A few days of fine weather, and the trolling boats appeared. First just one or two, but soon there was a steady procession and the bay was filled with the sound of anchor

Chilton is a home afloat for Bob and Margaret Ellis, with such comforts as oil stove, bath tub, deep freeze.

chains running out. Sure enough: another storm. Soon the weather cleared again, and we joined the outbound procession of boats.

The procedure is to await slack water, line up with the two markers ashore, get in the traffic pattern and head for the bar. It was like Lake Washington Ship Canal on a weekend. Waves were breaking on both sides of our path, but we were committed and there was no turning back. The boat ahead pitched violently as she hit the swells, but *Chilton* rode it through with style and we were back out in the gulf, starting our journey down the coast to Pelican and Sitka.

We had a fast, rough ride for the 60 miles in the Pacific before we could enjoy the calm waters of Lisianski Inlet, which separates Yakobi and Chichagof Islands. Here, too, the scenery is spectacularly beautiful. We spent the night at the busy fishing village of Pelican, surrounded by trollers, seiners and halibuters. Next we went out to the ocean again, via Lisianski Straits, and headed for Sitka to pick up mail and supplies. Sitka Sound is a great place for cruising but so is the outside of Baranof Island, and in spite of the fact that we had made this part of our trip several times previously, we still had bays to explore.

The outer coast of Baranof Island has one bay after another indenting its rocky shoreline. Rising steeply 4000 to 6000 feet from the various fjords, the mountains march down the center of the island. We spent several days fishing and exploring some of the bays: Whale, Red Fish, Little Branch and Big Branch. Each one is different, yet all are delightful wilderness playgrounds. Several times, we watched a doe feeding on the beach with her fawn, always a very special treat. Hunting on the few outer beaches for driftwood and Japanese glass floats is a fun activity, too.

We bounced around Cape Ommaney, with the boisterous tide rips keeping us busy holding our sou'easterly

Lituya Glacier eases into the ocean at the head of an inlet.

course. But the wind was astern, the sun was shining, and it made for an exuberant passage. In fact, we rather hated leaving that wild, uninhabited coast.

Encountering violent winds whistling over Coronation Island, we did not linger, but rounded Cape Decision and turned into Sumner Straits. With a stop at Point Baker for fuel and an overnight stay at Red Bay on Prince of Wales Island, we headed down Clarence Strait for the home stretch to Ketchikan.

Seven times we've cruised south from Alaska, through the delightful inland waters of British Columbia to Seattle and return. With *Chilton* we've rounded Cape Chacon and enjoyed the west coast of Prince of Wales Island. We found our Lituya Bay trip the most memorable of all.

32

Five Months and Six Thousand Miles

by Marge Schaefer

In 1965 Herb and I bought the *Moana Mele*. We cruised her up the coast to San Francisco to see her reaction in rough seas.

We had been searching for a seaworthy boat to remodel for extended coastal cruising; and after five weeks of various types of weather and seas, we decided *Moana Mele* would make a comfortable cruising boat and warranted a change of her gasoline engines to diesel power. Herb had her delivered to our backyard and, after 20 months, the *Margy M III* was launched in July of 1967.

It is a long list, but in that 20 months Herb rebuilt her forward staterooms, added a transom step, rebuilt a flybridge, repowered her with two GM 3-53N diesels, modernized the galley with electrical appliances, changed the head and added a shower, and removed one forward bunk to set in a spinet-sized organ. There were reupholstering, carpeting, painting and delays, but now we were ready for our cruise to Alaska from Long Beach.

The cruise began through miles of boiling bait, past half acres of feeding sharks and hundreds of sea gulls too gorged to do more than swim out of our path. Then the first coastline to be seen through the fog was Point Mugu. We followed the smooth ribbon of the offshore kelp line and enjoyed the antics of the sea life as we proceeded. We saw two herds of seals with their young feeding from the

---

It can take a qualified skipper up to 20 months of backyard boatbuilding to repower, refurbish and modernize a sound 46-foot Matthews cruiser; and it took 4000 gallons of diesel oil to move her across more than 6000 miles of ocean from Long Beach, California, to Skagway, Alaska. Here are excerpts from a 30,000-word log of the Schaefers' five-month tour.

boiling bait and watched hundreds of gooney birds (velvety appearing brown birds similar to sea gulls). A school of porpoise played back and forth close under our bow and surfed up and down our wake.

We passed Port Hueneme, the coastline dotted with all sizes of Sunday sailboats and sport fishing boats, and entered busy Channel Islands Harbor. June 3, we left the slip and toured the marina in hazy sunlight, noting the large restaurants, numerous well-maintained slips, and decided it is good for the finish of a predicted log race. Outside, another school of porpoise joined us, sunfish flipped and we saw sharks outside a wide kelp bed, perhaps a breeding ground for 8 or 10 young at a time. The afternoon wind came up, 25 knots of warm air, the smell of fresh-mown hay came from the dry hillsides. Later, we were anchored at Cojo Anchorage behind the wide kelp line in a relatively calm sea.

A large blue heron attempted to settle his long legs on the moving kelp, while we enjoyed a peaceful dinner. Herb remarked that the day's cruise had been so pleasant, it could become boring day after day all the way to Alaska. But "unboring" experiences lay ahead. The June 4 morning breeze turned to 35- to 40-knot winds, we took water over the flybridge, and the boat took a pounding in the confused seas and shuddered as she hit the bottoms of breaking swells.

One motor suddenly slowed; Herb turned it off and eased her to Morro Bay and anchored offshore in water less cluttered with Morro's usual floating sea grasses and debris. Herb found a clogged oil filter. I marveled at the numerous types of seabirds along the sandspit: snipes, plovers, gulls, large white pelicans and many types of herons. One heron made many trips to her nest in the top of a tall tree, balancing on small branches and feeding her young. Captain Herb announced cleanup time. Later he lowered the dinghy and asked, "Your chariot awaits, Madam, may I have the pleasure of taking you to dinner?"—a mile in the wind and cold to a delicious seafood dinner.

A week into June had now gone by and we waited for small craft warnings to come down. We made one try at leaving but the motor wouldn't purr properly and we returned to the Morro Bay Yacht Club dock. However, all seemed well and we headed out again, choppy water blowing completely over the flybridge. We decided to stop at San Simeon. Even behind the bluffs, the wind was blowing whitecaps. Once safely settled, we did relax and enjoy the sight of the shrub-clad bluffs and the red-tiled roofs of buildings along the coastline. Herb used steak for bait and caught a good-sized crab for a cocktail with our steak. And, surprise, *Margy M III* was on her way at daybreak in smooth-water, no-wind conditions.

I was particularly impressed by Point Sur, which resembled a long mound of sand that a youngster had left on the beach for the surf to level out. The coastline was a deep green above the dark, irregular cliffs, and the water-washed, jagged rocks increased as we cruised north. And so we watched the antics of the sea lions on the breakwater entering Monterey Harbor. An undesirable slip was picturesque, as pigeons, nesting on the cross beams, cooed and strutted for the attention of young lady pigeons. One favorite spot was a sign reading, "Seven Day Metered Parking"—pigeon love by the penny.

On the tenth, leaving for San Francisco, we viewed starfish, abalone, mussels and many forms of sea life. We had intermittent fogs up the coast and then that thrill—San Francisco, welcoming us as we passed under the Golden Gate Bridge, bright sunshine on the hillsides and homes. We cruised the south shore and into the Golden Gate Yacht Club moorings to a slip assigned by the harbor master. We spent three days there visited by our younger son Chris, who had just completed law school finals.

Our tours around the bay came next, Sausalito, Raccoon Strait, Angel Island and its busy park, beautiful, secluded, yet so close to glamorous San Francisco. It was June 14 when we headed out under the Golden Gate Bridge and into the turbulent waters of the unpredictable Pacific. Sunny, but rough, we cruised with 15 charter fishing boats in a fishing derby, bright flags aflying.

The water was still very bumpy off Point Reyes, with short breaking swells coming from all directions. We bumped and bounced to Bodega Harbor, where we followed salmon fish boats past 50 channel markers before we realized that they intended to unload their catches and nets at the fisheries with the salmon fleet. We retraced our way to marker #41 and entered a tiny marina called Shaw's Landing. Our day had been rough on *Margy M III*. We mopped up where we had been certain water could never come in. The forward stateroom looked as though buckets of water had been dumped on the bunks. We spent two days resting. Shaw's Landing is in a small bight in the harbor. Across from it, weekenders spend hours digging for long-neck clams, frantically for a few minutes, and, with

luck, come up with a sizable clam. Small boats were fishing near the mud flats, while larger boats and salmon-fishing boats were constantly on the move. The Coast Guard was busy and towed in several fishing boats.

Fathers' Day was the sixteenth, and the following morning we cleared the 41 channel markers, cruised between the two breakwaters and out to a smooth sea with long comfortable swells. Visibility was about a half mile through the haze and fog. We arrived at Point Arena, where the water was choppy and rough and, in the foggy haze, we could barely make out the conical lighthouse on the low, bare cliff of the point. As we rounded the point, we could see the charted, submerged rocks a mile and a half from shore. They looked odd so far from shore, with breakers crashing and spraying water high into the air. We had rough water and fog until we cruised under the bridge at Noyo Anchorage.

As we rounded the small breakwater, two young coast guardsmen met us in a skiff and escorted us up the river, around a bend and into fishery row, where we nested next to an odoriferous fish boat. The scenic, narrow river lined with canneries and fish boats, the tall trees climbing the steep hillsides, the pleasantries exchanged with the fishermen made up for the strong aroma of fish. We spent the afternoon watching small boys play on rickety rafts, like typical Huck Finns. In the evening, we watched families line the shore and fish. Even tiny youngsters could flick lines up and down, and fill the buckets with herring. The Huck Finns joined the adults and flicked the three or four small hooks fastened to short lines on the long bamboo poles, catching dozens of fish from the schools of jumping herring and frying them as we would grunion. We left calm Noyo fishing village on the eighteenth, through the narrow river crowded with sleeping fish boats four abreast on either bank and close to the fisheries, small restaurants and private docks. We made the jog in the river just as daybreak was tinting the sky pale blues, pastel pinks and yellows. We passed the natural breakwater and entered the deep, blue, boiling sea.

As we bounced along in *Margy M III* off the twinkling lights of Fort Bragg, we soon slowed to a pounding crawl in fog too thick for seeing. Herb considered returning to Shelter Cove but, after reading of the submerged rocks (Coast Pilot), continued on. We later went back to this cove, after seeing Punta Gorda, riding even rougher water, and noting the breakers on the coastline and the riptides. The fog lifted for our entry past the dangerous rocks. Overnight, we were once again on our way to Punta Gorda to retrace 20 miles. The silhouettes of tall pine trees made a beautiful picture in the sunrise. A patch of wild flowers shone bright gold. We were taking water over the bow as soon as we headed north. Spume was already blowing from the tops of the deep swells. We tacked to make the ride more comfortable.

We spotted the marker for Reynolds Rock, and the sea was no longer blue, but a blowing, white foaming sea. Buckets (no, barrels) of water poured over the flybridge and made a pool in the cockpit. The water couldn't run out or off the boat as fast as we were taking it on, although the bilge held little. It took us 40 minutes to run four miles to

The Schaefers found icebergs of every size in Glacier Bay, where Margy M III is shown at ease (top). Skipper Herb (center) turns to remark on the size of one of the bergs. Bottom: Lowe Inlet in Grenville Channel, below Prince Rupert, where salmon fight their way over the waterfalls.

Punta Gorda marker. The winds ripped our new burgee to shreds. We reached Relief Lightship, relieving Blunts off Blunts Reef near Cape Mendocino, and were out of the frothing water.

An hour off Humboldt Bay entrance, the water smoothed out and looked like a gray lake. We entered the bay and cruised past stacks of giant redwood logs and lumber, acres of sawdust and wood chips in piles as high as a four-storied building, and watched several foreign freighters loading lumber. We passed floats filled with the fishing fleet. We looked for a small boat harbor in Eureka, but the depth indicator was rapidly decreasing. We headed back to the Enco fuel dock. It was time to mop up seawater. We rinsed 20 dripping bath towels that had been placed around "water tight hatches." It was late; so it was dinner at the wharf-side Lazio's restaurant, a dinner that far surpassed our expectations.

June 21: We passed hundreds of idle fishing boats, watched a porpoise play in the wake of a passenger ferry loaded with mill workers, and enjoyed the morning activities for the 40 minutes it took us to reach open sea. We saw cut lumber being loaded aboard a German freighter, giant redwood logs being loaded aboard Japanese ships, and boxcars being filled. Lastly we passed the four-storied Coast Guard station, white and stately as a southern mansion, with the American flag flying. A pretty sight!

We had been told, as we progressed up the coast, that the thick foggy area ended at Humboldt Bay, but the fog increased. We passed numerous large rocks that looked like mountains with rolling swells breaking around them. Every few miles we'd pass a lumber camp, with the inevitable inverted-funnel incinerator pouring out smoke. The sea was calm and several large whales blew beside us as they followed between the coast and Redding Rock, situated four and a half miles offshore. The first whitecaps of the day ruffled the water, an hour before we reached Crescent City. We anchored in Crescent Bay, swinging on our bow anchor, surrounded by tall rugged rocks, a breakwater, docks and more salmon-fishing boats waiting for a price increase. One island rock on the sea side of the bay held a group of buildings and a lighthouse no longer in use. The island can only be reached at low tide, and the buildings house a nautical museum.

It was now June 22 and impossible to believe we had been cruising the California coast for three weeks. We quickened the pace to meet Thol and Lillian Simonson at the Bellingham Yacht Club, our exchange observers for, first, the International Cruiser Race, and then the Alaska Race. We neared Oregon and it was chill, almost like a weather border line.

Mack Arch is the most spectacular rock and I was for cruising through, but Herb issued an emphatic, "No!" because of small rocks nearby. Suddenly, Oregon's rain that keeps it so green. We hoped for enough to wash off the sawdust, soot and salt accumulated from lumber camps and sea spray.

It was still raining as we cruised between Island Rock and the group of Six Redfish Rocks, a mile offshore. These rocks were more than 100 feet high, the tops were obscured, and gave the feeling of cruising through immense tunnels. We entered the tiny harbor of Port Orford in a torrential rain that washed the boat spotless.

We spent the night listening to the rain, and our bow anchor chain noisily echoed the fact that we were over a bed of rocks. We were glad to head up the coast once more. The water was gray and choppy, but the rain stopped. We cruised through the reef area between Port Orford and Cape Blanco by using a large-scale local chart. Cape Blanco looked barren. We cruised right past Coquille River, noting that it was well marked with buoys and a breakwater, and headed for Coos Bay. As we approached Coos Bay, we could see the swells breaking high and white as they crashed into the breakwater. A large freighter was steaming out of the bay, so laden that her name on the bow was barely visible above the breaking water. We entered, dodging the many outboards speeding in every direction, having their Sunday fun bouncing over the rough water, and tied up at the Charleston Small Boat Basin, our first marina since Bodega Bay and reasonable at $1.50 per night, including utilities. The weather was uncooperative and we couldn't leave because of fog that was so heavy we could barely see the bow of our boat. But on the twenty-fifth, we joined the parade of fish boats leaving the harbor, and headed north on a smooth sea.

For several hours, we followed a straight coastline dotted with small clumps of trees and high sand dunes. Rolling hills dotted with homes took the place of the desolate sand dunes, and we saw the first rocks of the day, then the numerous lumber mills. We followed the buoys into Yaquina Bay and tied at the public dock at Newport; around us were fishboats of every vintage and size from small outboards to large seiners.

We were held up at Newport while Herb made some repairs and checked over the cruiser after the hard going. He located a corroded cast-iron fitting on the generator and fixed that.

Out of Newport on the twenty-seventh, we rode the breakers on the bar for 10 minutes, then cruised "hang-onto-the-wheel" water for 12 hours, enroute to the Columbia. Slowed, we arrived off the big river with an ebbing tide. Oooh, those swirling breakers. And we surfed from marker #4 to #10 before reaching the welcome smooth of Hendrickson's Marina at the old mill town of Warrenton. We acquired local knowledge, tried the "go" signal from a CG patrol boat, and later turned back to cruise and sightsee the area around Astoria and the long, new bridge between Oregon and Washington.

The last day of June, after two rough-water experiences on the Columbia bar, I wished for a back exit. We hit the morning slack at 0420, the first spray on the windshield at 0510 at #10 marker, ground swells short and from every angle; and we were across the bar, an easy ride. We turned north at #3 marker with the sun edging the black rain clouds with gold and the Pacific a smooth, deep blue. Later we hit a large, submerged log, circled to see the damage to the log so we could estimate the damage to the now-vibrating starboard propeller. It showed a deep gash; so our next stop would require going on the ways at Gray's Harbor. We

milled with the fleet of Sunday fishermen, hovering around the Coast Guard vessel, waiting for the signal for a safe bar crossing. I counted 76 small boats in the cluster, and more coming from every direction. I didn't think I'd ever wait for three hours for a bar to open, but it wasn't until 1345 that the water, which had been breaking high, leveled out and the boats crossed on smooth water.

We were fortunate to find a boat yard open on a Sunday at Westport on Gray's Harbor and *Margy M III* was hoisted out of the water. Herb removed the bent propeller and shaft, and we spent the night aboard the boat, swinging on the two slings. Our wish to quicken our pace to meet the Simonsons had come to a sudden halt. The bent propeller and shaft were sent to Aberdeen to be straightened. Herb spent the next several days scraping and cleaning the boat's bottom. On July 2, the straightened propeller and shaft were returned, and Herb had them back in place by midnight. On July 3, we crossed the bar with ease, rounded #2 marker, and headed north for La Push, Washington. Haze hung over the coastline and whitecapped low swells broke over the bow and sprayed high over the flybridge. The windshield wipers were busy as we kept a sharp lookout for logs.

Sea Lion Rock loomed to starboard through an increasing fog; so we slowed to a safer speed. Herb refigured his predicted time in order to change course at Destruction Island. He turned off the motors, and we could hear the friendly foghorn; by 2030 we were close to the Giants Graveyard, an eerie place to be at that time of night in a heavy fog, because of the tombstone rocks, 200 feet high, and others barely awash. Herb moved to the flybridge to watch for the Quillayute Needle group, near the La Push entrance. In that blanket we eased away from the coast, knowing that these rocks jut out a mile, but by now our predicted time said that we should have seen them; so we worried that we had passed La Push.

In our more than 30 years of boating, we have never felt the need to call for assistance, but subscribing to the oft-heard theory that the CG would rather lead a boat in than tow it in, Herb gave them a relative position and the required information. The reply came that they had us on their radar screen; so we cruised *Margy M III* in large circles. It was 2245 when the Coast Guard suggested we anchor at sea and wait for clearing weather, as their vessel suffered from a failing radio. We anchored in the lumps and swells, and Herb stretched right out on the rolling deck and slept, he was that tired from having painted 46 feet of boat bottom in the early morning and cruised through heavy fog all day.

Happy Fourth of July! We could see the breakers on the beach and the rocks near the La Push entrance all around us. We eased out, realizing we had been that close and yet that far from the safe harbor. It was a pleasant cruise, past Cape Flattery, crowded with holiday fishermen and their bobbing boats, and the 28 logs (by actual count) we also saw bobbing about. We entered the famous Strait of Juan de Fuca and anchored in picturesque Neah Bay. We cruised the shoreline after lunch and marveled at the beauty of the rolling hills and tall trees growing right down to the

During their long cruise, the Schaefers passed many ports and enjoyed a variety of scenic attractions. Here from top are: Skagway, with its wooden store fronts, La Push, Washington, harbor, where fishing boats found protection from a gale; and famed Mendenhall Glacier, which moves three feet a day, dropping bergs.

water's edge. Little Crescent Bay was next, but it was filled with a Power Squadron cruise and there was no place for our boat. The smell of burning logs and barbecuing steaks was overwhelming at the dinner hour and they waved and invited us in, but we went on to Port Angeles.

It was July 5, and on to Bellingham to meet our friends who were waiting for us. Thol and Lillian helped us tie up at the yacht club. They were accompanied by Fred Woodward and Bob Guhl, well-known to Southern California predicted log racers. They were there to compete for the Barusch Trophy.

On July 14, I was awakened from my nice, warm bunk with the starting of the diesel engines and the rasp of the anchor chain being weighed. There was a patter of early morning rain and a thrill all around that we were into the first day of the two-week predicted log race to Alaska, 27 legs, a course of approximately 1000 miles, and free run cruising between many of the legs. It was on to lovely Refuge Cove on the edge of beautiful Desolation Sound, where Thol rejoined us after having been an observer on another cruiser for the day. We began the second day of the race on July 15. We encountered our race master's cruiser, down with engine trouble, and we towed her back to Refuge Cove, the details being duly noted in our log, an accepted procedure in the lengthy Alaskan race. Now underway, the 70-mile day was picturesque as we passed through those beautiful pine-and-cedar-covered islands. Through the control points, we were aware that we had negotiated three small rapids among other interesting maneuvers, and finally it was Minstrel Island, a famous area for Dungeness crabs. Herb and Thol rowed out with a newly purchased trap to bring back our dinner. They had the instructions and they had the bait but they came back in the dinghy with nothing but excuses, and Lillian and I went ahead with our alternative dinner plans.

We pulled away from the dock at Minstrel Island on the sixteenth, with the water as beautiful as a large pane of variegated rippled glass. The tall trees reflected a deep-green tone, spiraling toward mid channel, and the beige hues of the rocky sections added to the beauty of the reflected contrasts. There were dozens of tiny islands the size of Ship Rock at Catalina. We saw small seals diving for fish and spotted many whales ablowing, while golden and sea eagles soared across the inlets and ravens noisily objected to our intrusion. By noon, we were slowly cruising along the shoreline of famous Alert Bay, the small city with many-colored roofs, a hospital, drugstore and other services, and at the extreme end, an Indian graveyard with colorful carved totem poles. We called our next control point, then spent several hours in Hardy Bay and waited, with two other boats, for the plane bringing our race master and his wife, who left their boat rather than wait for the motor parts. Another racer radioed he had hit a log and was coming into Alert Bay to check the damage. We entered a choppy Queen Charlotte Strait and rendezvoused with the racing fleet at Port Alexander. July 17 was something else called "gill-net-dodging day," 100 miles of working our way through the 1000- to 1500-foot gill nets and their salmon-fishing boats with no time allowances. Our day ended at

Bella Bella. We took on fuel and water while we were there.

The little things are so memorable when cruising. We were visited by a lonely Canadian boy from a survey vessel. This was his first time away from home, but he was obviously enjoying the work of surveying and charting. Then there were the four small Indian girls who rowed a paintless boat across the bay from an Indian village and begged trick-or-treat fashion from boat to boat. They were given candy and cookies. Thol bought a delicious salmon from a nearby fisherman. The Alaska racers exchanged observers in the morning. On the eighteenth, we left Bella Bella, one by one. It was a sunny day on the flybridge, one of needlelike waterfalls, snow-capped mountains, the very narrow channel through Jackson Passage where only local boatmen go, and finally into Scow Bay, where Thol and Herb again filled their crab trap with pounds of starfish. Next day, we left the rickety dock at Scow Bay and went into tiny Butedale before the race started. We saw many things in the warmth and sunshine of the day—more whales, loggers felling trees, plus a unique way of lowering the trimmed log to a boom. We saw the boisterous and wide Lowe Inlet Falls, where hundreds of silvery salmon were attempting to jump the boiling water on their way to spawn. We rendezvoused at Kumealon Inlet. We would finish the first week on the twentieth with the big affair at the Prince Rupert Yacht Club where trophies were presented for the first big leg of the race, *Margy M III* taking fourth.

On July 21, we were off for the second big part of the race, this to Ketchikan. It was a Sunday morning and we had another encounter with the gill-net fleets.

At noon, we crossed the British Columbia border into Alaska, and it was a thrill just knowing we were there, this far and long out of Southern California. Nine hours later, we pulled into our slip in Ketchikan, which is every bit as picturesque, with its stilt homes, as you have undoubtedly heard it described. And you have probably read in previous stories about the big Welcome to Alaska party at the Ketchikan Elks Lodge, where dinner was a delight.

Next we nested with the rest of the Alaska Cruiser Race boats in Humpback Bay, near the mouth of the Anan River. Herb and I rowed up the river in the dinghy to a spot known as a place where bears feed on the spawning salmon. We became stranded on the shallow sand and rock bed and didn't even see a bear. We eased out of the shallow area and returned to the boat as Lillian and Thol Simonson returned from their hike, warm and muddy. There was a try at swimming but only Thol stuck it out in the icy water.

The next day some of the gasoline-powered cruisers fueled at Wrangell, and we headed across the wide expanse of mirror-smooth water rippled only by sea gulls. We finished that race day at Petersburg and went shopping for vegetables and fruit. Thol came aboard with freshly packed cans of crab and tiny shrimp, the results of a cannery tour back at Wrangell.

Next we had a 47-mile race to Entrance Island and our first glimpses of glaciers. The mountains were spotted with snow fields but the glaciers were unbelievably solid. Others, we were told, had disappeared completely within the past 20 years, leaving scarred rock roadways. We all had a lot of fun at Entrance and apparently frightened some of the small children and women who were spending the summer there while the husbands were fishing for salmon. But when they saw what it was, one mother asked us to mail letters for her, since few boats put in there.

We decided to race the next 24-mile leg. As we turned into Endicott Arm, the air suddenly turned frigid. As we slipped into jackets, we sighted the reason for the change in temperature. What we had thought were boats heading toward us were floating icebergs that had freshly calved from a glacier. There was so much beauty, it was a thrill to cruise one of nature's wonderlands.

Thol was determined to have iceberg ice to fill our bar box and had Herb pull alongside a bright blue iceberg. Herb was reluctant to pull in too close, so I handed Thol our stainless-steel long-handled marlin gaff hook. Thol stood on the bow and hacked at the ice. The hook bounced off of the astoundingly hard ice, but he hacked at it again and again, as Herb repeatedly yelled, "I have to back off!"

Suddenly Thol disappeared over the bow, one Topsider clinging to the bow railing and the other Topsider hanging over the pulpit. Thol kept yelling, "Forward, Herb, forward!" and he wouldn't turn loose of the now bent gaff hook which was embedded in the ice. We were afraid that we would lose Thol overboard or that the large iceberg would unexpectedly flip over, but he came up with a big, pleased grin, bent gaff hook in one hand, and hugging two large melon-sized pieces of compressed blue ice crystals. We were finally all together at the end of July 25.

The next day, we awakened to the sound of rain. Sumdum Glacier and the tree-clad hills were hidden by heavy, white fog. It was a dismal day for our planned sightseeing tour of Tracy Arms, two inlets noted for their numerous icebergs. It was 22 miles to Bay of Taku where we visited the Father Hubbard Museum.

July 27, we were to dress ship for the finale of the 27-leg, two-week race. Our race boats converged in the rain at the finish line, looking as though they had a bright, bedraggled washing hanging from stem to stern. The congenial committeemen of the Juneau Yacht Club greeted us and later returned to transport us to the Baranof Hotel for the festivities of the evening.

We lunched and held our last visit with the Simonsons, who had an afternoon plane to catch for Los Angeles. The race group presented Thol with a gift—the thing he had been searching for, a replica of his "desired" Indian maiden with the big parka. The final affair at the Baranof Hotel was a big one. Thol and Lil were there also, as their plane's takeoff was delayed.

Margy M III came in fourth in total race with a percentage error of 3.8 for the 1000-mile event. There were many awards from the dignitaries.

Thol was called forward to make a speech which could be as long as he was able to hold the Iceberg Chronometer. When he opened the case before the large audience, he found himself ready to hold a 100-pound chunk of iceberg, an honor denoting his antics in procuring the bar ice from that iceberg. His speech was very short because his hands were rapidly freezing.

Fast moving LeConte Glacier produces many large icebergs.

So, on July 28, we were at the Juneau Yacht Club, entertaining many people who came to see the relatively small boat that cruised from Southern California to enter this race. Among them was the secretary of state of Alaska. So many visitors were interested in the organ aboard.

In the afternoon, we drove inland in a rented car to view the famous Mendenhall Glacier, which moves three feet each day and drops numerous bergs continually into the water. It is an unbelievably beautiful sight, surrounded by acres of colorful wild flowers. The next morning, the whole scene changed as we bade good-bye to the returning race boats and suddenly realized we were now alone to begin our cruise to the north.

Family cruising is what it says it is—with all the excitements that go on in a family. We were called to the phone for a call from San Francisco and were greeted by our son Chris' voice with, "Where have you been? I've been trying to reach you for two weeks to tell you that I'm engaged and would like you to return to San Francisco soon for the wedding."

I explained there was no definite time for our return, but that he was also being charged at the rate of $10 for the first three minutes and $2 thereafter and he better write us a letter. Our young attorney was engaged to Pamela, a young lady who had accompanied us on the tour of San Francisco Bay with Chris.

We left Juneau and cruised south under the span bridge and along the shoreline of Douglas, with its many new small homes. The air felt chilly from a light drizzle, combined with the heavily snow-capped mountains reaching to the timberline. As we rounded Douglas Island to head north toward Skagway, we had a last glimpse of Mendenhall Glacier, massive and permanent in all its icy magnificence. We pulled into a small cove and anchored for lunch. The tide was low and the rocky shoreline of the island was covered with a moss the color of goldenrod. The tall green trees sparkled with raindrops, and the birds were feeding. The only sound was the hum of the fishing reel as Herb cast a hook. We lazily absorbed the peace, quiet and beauty of the area as we finished our lunch, then headed north. We cruised along Lynn Canal for hours seeing only a cruise ship returning from Skagway. In Chilkoot Inlet, we inched our way through the fog and around another gill-netting salmon fleet.

A small, faded sign read, "Welcome to Skagway." We tied to a small boat gangway. A boat cruised up and a friendly voice asked if we could use some electricity. This was the harbor master and the town electrician, and he suggested we plug into his long-cord outlet curled on the dock. It would not be practical to plug into the outlet on the piling because, by morning, it would be 25 feet in the air at low tide. That was our introduction to the modern, small town that looked like a movie set of the gold rush days.

Herb hailed a cab, and we toured the town of one short main street, one slightly longer residential street and two short connecting streets with a sprinkling of buildings near the railroad track, running parallel with the nearby hillside. In 10 minutes, we had seen all of the landmarks of the past, present and future for the sum of $2, the standard fare.

In the 1890s, the museum had been a courthouse. Now it offers visitors the opportunity to acquaint themselves with the history of the town. The museum was crowded with tourists browsing among the abundance of mementos of the past, of the determined gold miners and of Eskimos. We especially admired the bone jewelry made by the Eskimos and marveled at the crude instruments used by the dentists and doctors on the miners. Down main street is an accumulation of authentic 1890 buildings, moved from their original sites and housing curio and gift shops, grocery stores and bakeries, bars, hotels and restaurants and a railroad station.

It was the first day of August and the morning was chilly. We set out for the narrow-gauge railroad and bought our $17.50-per-person tickets for the nostalgic 82-mile round-trip mountain ride used by the miners back in the late 1800s. The trip includes a dinner at Lake Bennett in British Columbia.

We boarded one of the old original chair cars with hard wooden seats, oil paintings depicting Alaska scenery painted overhead and on long end panels, and with a large pot-bellied stove burping smoke. The train jolted and began to move. As it increased in speed, the car creaked and rattled around the steep sides of the mountains across fragile-appearing wooden trestles and through long wooden snowsheds. We whizzed past a small station house, where the motorman leaned out and picked up mail from a clothespin attached to an extended pole. We reached the summit, crossed into British Columbia and stopped at the small station at Lake Bennett.

Everyone filed into the large dining hall for an old-fashioned dinner served home style on large platters and in huge bowls, a very filling miner-sized dinner. We walked beside the blue lake and up a short hill to an old wooden church once used by the miners. The walls had been braced in the deserted and crumbling church, but it still had the appearance of holiness and majesty, with its worn steps, tall, peaked roof and hand-carved cross.

Once more we boarded the train, but this time we entered a plush car with velvet-covered seats, more beautiful oil painted paneling, and a well-behaved potbellied stove. Then we began the jostling return trip down the steep grade. On the descent, we could see the worn paths used by the miners of 1898. They were very rugged men. During most of our return trip, we looked down on mountains of tall trees, we looked across ravines at waterfalls tumbling into rushing streams, where beavers had built substantial dams.

As we neared Skagway, the train stopped to couple on some freight cars and the jolt broke a coupling. The passengers waited patiently, and we were entertained by a troupe, moving from car to car, costumed for the playing of *The Shooting of Dan McGrew* in Skagway. Finally we hiked back into town.

August 2, we reluctantly left the movie set atmosphere of Skagway and cruised most of the day down Lynn Canal. We headed into Icy Strait and startled a large whale. It, in turn, startled us by blowing near our port side and flipping its large tail, which looked ten feet wide. We entered Bartlett Cove to spend the night and anchored near a pier lined with fishing boats. We watched the fishermen working with their nets and the activities at the attractive lodge of the National Park and Recreational buildings.

We breakfasted leisurely and headed next toward Glacier Bay to find glaciers and icebergs. For the first time in a week, the sun decided to spend the day with us. Hundreds of tiny ducks were feeding on the smooth waters and several blackfish broke water near us and flipped their large dorsal fins. A large iceberg floated by.

We were disappointed to find that many of the charted glaciers had receded to the mountain tops, leaving only grooved roadways to the edge of the water to show their paths. But as we entered Muir Inlet, we were gratified to find icebergs of every size, some as large as freighters, floating toward us, and we knew that a calving glacier was ahead. The bergs varied in color from snow white to turquoise to deep-blue purples. They were beautiful. The chart showed no depths to the deadend inlet, but our depth meter indicated a variance from 100 to 200 feet, too deep for anchoring to take pictures.

We cruised around the icebergs and then lowered the dinghy into the water and towed *Margy M III* through the icy slush to get within 150 feet of the 200-foot-high ice cliff at the lower edge of the glacier. We lost all concept of time, taking pictures and staring in awe at the magnitude of the icy spectacle. The wonder of the view left us with a feeling of insignificance; and it was dinner time before we finally towed our floating home to clear water, raised the dinghy and headed back to Bartlett Cove for the night.

On August 4, we began a two-day cruise to Sitka. We saw giant gray whales leap completely out of the water, seem to stand on their wide tails, and suddenly sound with a terrific splash. We followed Chatham Strait south until the snow-laden mountains and glaciers were behind and we were once again cruising between spruce, hemlock and cedar islands. During the day, we passed a tug towing one of San Francisco's ferries which will be used as a fishery.

We headed for an Indian village at Angoon, on the opposite side of Chatham Strait, and we were surprised to find the six-mile width was as rough as heading up the coast. Contrary to our chart, Angoon had no protected area to anchor; so we changed course southward.

We hesitatingly tied to a crumbling dock, no longer connected to the shore of the small Killisnoo Island. We could see several deserted buildings overgrown with vines and shrubbery, a desolate sight, but we were protected from the wind and spent the night.

After dinner, we dinghied ashore, tying to a piece of railroad track running out into the water for a one-time whaling station. We examined the remains of rendering vats, and the processing plant for whale oil. We saw small houses with two-storied fireplaces constructed in the main room, for cooking downstairs and for heating the tiny upstairs bedrooms; an old building labeled "Store" in faded black lettering, another with its steep roof caved in; a schoolhouse with old-fashioned desks scattered about. We collected sea-urchin and spiral shells, small pieces of driftwood and colorful rocks.

Peril Strait was next, then Rapid Point, with its turbulent waters swirling haphazardly around us. We cruised two eddying narrows, dodging giant logs and debris, and several straits and found it satisfying that we could cruise alone around the many small islands in these unfamiliar waters, and so thoroughly enjoy it. As we neared Sitka on August 5, we had our first peek at the blue Pacific in more than a month. We stopped at the fuel dock, took on fuel and water. We watched a group of teen-agers shoving one another from a pier into the chilly water. They were unconcerned for their clothes and glad to splash in the clear water, because the temperature was a very unusual 100 degrees.

We cruised into Crescent Harbor, the northward part of

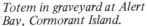

Totem in graveyard at Alert Bay, Cormorant Island.

our trip almost over. We could see the small brick museum on the college campus in Sitka, the whole of which seems to reflect the friendly populace. There are the tall totems, the beautiful brick church and Russian mission, and a seldom-seen combination of architecture, ranging from the ornate Russian to the false-front American and then the modern American. And, I might add, $4.50 haircuts which sent Herb fuming.

While I was at the laundromat, Herb visited with five tiny Eskimo girls who were helping mother with the washing. Even the three-year-old had a chore; the seven-year-old sister had her mind made up to live in Hollywood and said she was saving money from ironing clothes.

Some of the highlights we enjoyed around Sitka: The museum and its Russian, Indian and Eskimo artifacts; the Russian mission which is still in use and had many religious artifacts of the early 1800s; and the display of delicately painted artifacts from the old St. Michael's Cathedral, when these were saved from its fire. We went to Totem Pole Park and another interesting brush with the animals, tiny squirrels scurrying through ferns and around the spruce tree trunks; and a visit to the pioneer home, listening to mining tales told by elderly gentlemen. We visited an Indian and Eskimo district, then drove up a rocky road to a mountain top to again watch a bright red sunset as late as 2200, this time setting behind that beautiful group of small islands protecting Sitka from the Pacific Ocean, a breathtaking sight.

August 8 was an important day. We readied *Margy M III* for the next day's departure on the homeward cruise, which began by retracing our course around Baranof Island

Seen along the route were stilt houses at Prince Rupert (top) and Angoon Indian Village, near Chatham Strait (bottom).

instead of the shorter but rougher route through Sitka Sound and the open Pacific. Again such wonderful views of nature as the island bank and a young deer nibbling on yellow moss. Herb blew airhorns; the deer merely glanced up but birds shrieked from the thick shelter of the spruce trees. We were again in fog and went through Chatham Strait and south to Warm Springs Bay on Baranof Island, where there is a general store and other weathered buildings.

At the end of the inlet was a roaring waterfall, where we watched salmon attempting to jump the high falls. It was permissible to catch salmon at the base of the falls and youngsters in rowboats were using red beads as lures. I didn't consider this quite sporting; so I baited a hook with a piece of steak and fished from the dock to catch two nice bass for our dinner. While there we rowed around the tiny coves, watched fish swimming in the shallow water and seabirds diving after them. The tall trees cast shadows and the fish would attempt to hide in these watery shadow areas.

On our return to our cruiser home, a fisherman off a commercial boat gave us a large king salmon for dinner. He told us of the mineral baths nearby in a red-roofed building. He said the fishermen in the area always stopped for baths, so Herb, with the bathing essentials, climbed the steep ramp to the general store and along a wooden walk to the bathhouse. An hour later, when he returned very relaxed, he said my trip would be a treat, but I waited until dusk because he informed me the bathhouse lacked locks.

We had our wonderful king salmon dinner and then Herb escorted me to the bathhouse where I rebelled at the musty smell, but he insisted I hold my nose, if necessary, and enjoy the warmth of the mineral water in the king-size, worn wooden tubs situated in six small individual rooms, protected by doors too warped to close. Herb was right and, once I settled into the slimy-feeling tub, the warm mineral water was so relaxing that I also hated to terminate the bath. With a soft light coming only from the moon, this was luxury.

On August 10, we cruised away from the musical sound of the waterfall and entered Chatham Strait where we crossed into Frederick Sound. Near Cape Strait, we could see the deep grooves running down the mountainside, carved by the glaciers of the past. Dead ahead were the heavy ice fields of Patterson Glacier and floating toward us were two 70-foot icebergs. We entered Petersburg with its waterfront homes picturesquely built on stilts, then sauntered through a gift shop and small center, bringing back a hot loaf of good Scandinavian bread for our dinner. Afterward we went up a few unpaved streets to the museum. This small modern building features a large fountain, has an outside centerpiece constructed in copper in abstract depictions of the fish of Alaska. A unique piece of sculpture, incongruous in a town with boardwalks and few paved streets. I was interested in a large, crank-style music box inlaid with mother-of-pearl, which had been used up until recent years in a nearby skating rink.

Upon leaving, we met the husband of the lady curator and they were about to drive into the hills to dump their rubbish, as there is no collection service. He told us of the bears searching for food at the dump and, learning that we were newcomers, invited us to join up. This couple spent its honeymoon in Petersburg more than 55 years ago and now even has greatgrandchildren residing in the area. We reached the dumping grounds over a bumpy dirt road into the hills and we kept everything tight to avoid those little, biting "No-see-'ems." A dozen cars were on the scene, tourists with cameras patiently cruising around. We saw one large brown bear slowly come out of the thick growth of trees. He surveyed the cars and some of us who were now hiding behind a tree, and he ambled back into safety.

We were invited to our hosts' lovely little home on the waterfront, backed by gardens of flowers and wild blueberries and currants in abundance. They even grew orchids in the shelter of the enclosed back porch. They had a marvelous collection of glassware and hand-painted dishes from the brushes of local artists. It is a joy to meet such wonderful people. Interesting trips and visits like this add great dimension to cruising.

The eleventh was a most interesting day. We left Petersburg and headed up Frederick Sound for Le Conte Bay. On the way, we passed numerous blue-toned icebergs floating outward, each sculptured from the warmth of the sun.

Describing Le Conte Bay: It was low tide when we entered, and the rocky shore was covered with grounded icebergs, many of them with a definite waterline indicating where three-quarters of their vast depth and size was hidden beneath the surface of the water. It was a real experience aboard *Margy M III* as we slowly eased between the floating bergs toward the famous Le Conte Glacier. The ice flow became a hazard to the propellers; so we took to the dingy and tried to row to the face of the glacier, but the floe was too heavy even for that. We spotted a chunk of rock embedded in an iceberg and Herb pried it out for my collection. Pearls could not have pleased me more.

We used the dinghy to slowly tow the Matthews out of this bay of icy splendors and negotiated the eight miles of Dry Strait to deep, anchoring water. That tremendous run out was truly turning us into a dry strait and we had to hurry. Next it was Wrangell, and our noting of Shakes Island and the Indian community house and colorful totem poles. There were a large cannery and lumber yard and, beyond, a main street consisting of a few shops and restaurants, the streets were unpaved, most of the walkways were of boards. A new waterline was being laid, and we were intrigued with the removal of the old wooden pipe from another age and by two noisy street fights, a bit of the "rough and ready" of a frontier lumber town.

The next day was away from Zimovia Strait and down the narrows in rain to Whitetail Cove. The narrows were difficult and there was lots of "tacking" through tiny island channels and reefs and, finally, with difficulty, through the narrows and into the deep waters of Clarence Strait. By two in the afternoon, we stopped at quaint Meyers Chuck which is a beautiful bay and was being enjoyed by the vacationing cruisers and sports fishermen. Next it was Tongass Narrows and the small Guard Island, which is crowded with a lighthouse, many buildings and tall trees.

Thol Simonson gets ready to gaff a berg to provide some of the aged blue ice that tastes so good in drinks.

Once again, it was an enjoyment of the sheer beauty of this vast and rugged country We saw a tremendous rainbow whose bright colors lasted for 15 minutes and, as the sun appeared, faded into diamonds from the rain droplets. We passed a cruise ship on its way to Skagway, as we rounded our marker to enter Ketchikan at six in the evening, our last stop before leaving Alaska—such a sad thought at the time.

The free public docks are maintained at Ketchikan and, after dinner, we did walk up through the town and the stores. The following day was spent with boating chores, checking out fuel and oil and scanning our charts for places we wanted to revisit on our trip back through British Columbia.

Revillagigedo Channel was whitecapped and it was difficult to spot floating objects. In fact we bumped a submerged log with a thud, but could detect no damage. As we passed Lord Rock and its flashing light, which officially took us out of Alaska, we began plotting a return trip and making notes of numerous areas we had missed in our 24-day cruise. We were into Prince Rupert, B.C. at 1900.

On August 15, and another day of drizzle, we picked up our tourist habits again and visited a fish-packing plant, watched the whole process of filleting halibut that would run as high as 200 pounds. Thousands of salmon were being unloaded from trollers. There were individual freezing rooms that contained a half million pounds of fish ready for shipping.

Prince Rupert is a city of artfully arranged flowers, baskets from street signs and light posts, flowers in the yards. I enjoyed the colorful collections.

We started on our way again on the sixteenth and trolled for salmon off Kinahan Islands, where Herb did catch a 12-pounder and recorded numerous strikes. Chatham Sound began to whitecap as we wound in our lines and cruised through Arthur Passage into Grenville Channel and into the anchorage of Kumealon Cove. I caught two halibut while Herb steaked the salmon for dinner.

Top view dramatizes Columbia Bar conditions on many days. Margy M III encountered some of this rough water. Below are more of the icebergs seen in Glacier Bay.

It was now past the middle of August, as we cruised around a reef into Grenville Channel and encountered one of those famous B.C. flotillas of a dozen salmon trollers, grouped on each side of a lead boat. The lead boat does the steering while the others sleep. But we saw an interesting maneuver when the pilot spotted a large freighter. He gave a few toots on the horn and the fishermen all came to life, unlashed their boats and spread out in the narrow channel. Our trip down was an enjoyable repeat of the many places we visited coming up.

On the nineteenth we cruised down Klekan Inlet and into the long narrow Graham Reach, where we saw one of those Alaskan tugs with 20 boxcars on barges. Next, it was down Tolmie Passage, all the while dodging logs, and into Klemtu Passage; we stopped at the little village of Klemtu. We made our way down Klemtu Passage and to the end of Cone Island and, this time, we followed the tree-clad coastline of Swindle Island into Milbanke Sound. We could see the Pacific Ocean as we passed Ivory Island and a surf breaking high on the rocks near the lighthouse.

On the twentieth we left Bella Bella and went over for a better look at New Bella Bella and the various buildings. We had fog through Lama Pass, trolled for salmon in Fisher Channel, and went into Namu, that small town with bright green lawns and beautiful flower beds. On the way down, I enjoyed watching wild Canadian geese feeding along the shore.

It had been suggested that we fish Koeye Inlet off Fitzhugh Sound, but it was so congested with floating logs and kelp, and agitated by turbulent water, that we stayed near Koeye Point. I hooked a large salmon but failed to land it at the edge of the boat. It was after five o'clock off Safety Cove and we were slowly trolling when Herb told me to reel in my line, and during this action a salmon hit the lure. This time, I slowly and carefully eased in my catch. It was a creditable-size salmon and luck was on my side. We had a great salmon dinner.

We weighed anchor in sunny Safety Cove on August 21 and cruised into Fitzhugh Sound. A fog persisted through North and South Passages of Queen Charlotte Sound, and we dodged large trees coming in on the swells off the Pacific. Next, it was Christie Passage and a peek into that wonderful cove on Hurst Island known as God's Pocket. By the time we reached Malcolm Island, we were aware of a haze from a forest fire on Vancouver Island and we could smell the smoke from the burning timber.

At Port McNeill, we became the center of interest at the dock by a reception committee of young boys and dogs. Someone noticed "Los Angeles" on our transom and they had questions galore about Disneyland and Hollywood. And they explained to us that the fire was only one of burning off "slash" so that the area could be reseeded in the spring—an old logger custom. Both groups learned something.

We did take in the town at Alert Bay on Cormorant Island. Another day was spent working through the unpredictable tide rips of Pearse Passage, cruising through Knight Inlet, Chatham Channel again, Havannah Channel, the whitecaps of Johnstone Strait and a night's tie-up at Port

Neville. It was rather empty there, and the fuel dock is abandoned.

We headed for the renowned Yaculta Rapids on August 23. At Wellbore Channel, we had over a mile of whirlpool rapids; we hit more of the swirling waters in short Greene Rapids, then it was through Dent Rapids, where at one point the bow of *Margy* wanted to trade places with her stern. We dodged through Gillard Passage and tied to a government dock in Big Bay, at the top of Yaculta Rapids. When we had cruised all the way down to Jervis Inlet, we went inland through Prince of Wales Reach and Princess Royal Reach to the magnificent Princess Louisa Inlet, where we enjoyed fresh oysters off the beach.

After working our way down to Cowichan Bay, we used the twenty-eighth to go to Port Browning on North Pender Island and visit Mannie Shansby and wife, Emily, so well-known to the Power Squadron members. They have had a summer home there for several years now and keep a boat there. A few days with them were very memorable. We cruised around some interesting places.

We went on to Victoria and had a wonderful stay at this lovely city. On the day after Labor Day, we were back in the United States. We went all the way down to Seattle and in for a cruise of Lake Washington and the various areas.

It was September 13 when we left Neah Bay, rounded Cape Flattery, passed Umatilla Lightship, and were on our way down the Pacific Coast. We spent five days at the tiny Indian reservation town of La Push because of howling gale outside. During the third day of the storm, two Coast Guard vessels put out, a 36-footer and a 44-footer braving high seas to rescue six from a sunken tug. The crew waited on its tow, a barge loaded with drums of creosote.

We hopped from major harbor to major harbor down the Pacific Coast. It was September 24 when we left Coos Bay. We followed the 10-fathom curve between the rocks from Pyramid Point to Point St. George and finally entered Crescent Harbor. We were in California. We had some interesting times at the little harbors along the Northern California coast and cruised through the Golden Gate at 1400 on October 1. We spent some time with Chris and his fiancee, helping them with wedding plans, before we started down the coast to meet them at Carmel for the wedding on October 10. Not many parents arrive at the wedding by sea in a cruiser. We had a chance to entertain friends and relatives aboard the *Margy M III* which worked out very well. The wedding over, it was on the fourteenth that we inched our cruiser out of Monterey Bay.

We spent the night in Santa Barbara in beautiful weather. You would think that we had had enough cruising but no, before going to Long Beach, we went on over to Catalina Island. We spent two additional weeks fishing, exploring coves and planning our next cruise to Alaska, where we wish to extend our plans as far as Anchorage and the Gulf of Alaska.

On November 1, we reached the Long Beach Marina with five wonderful months, 6000 nautical miles under the keel, and Herb adding up courses across 99 charts for total of 150 daily runs. One last homey touch: I became more proficient at playing the organ. Practice makes perfect.

33
Washington State Parks for Boating Families

With civilization spreading out and the population explosion constantly bringing more people to the Northwest, it is indeed fortunate that the Washington State Parks and Recreation Commission has had the foresight to acquire property and establish state parks for public use. The boat owner is particularly fortunate in this program. Water is fine for boating and we have plenty of it, but the skipper, family and guests need and like to get ashore on occasion. An impressive list of state parks on the water offers a variety of facilities for the cruising family.

The program was given an added boost, several years ago, when the voters approved Initiative 215. The state imposes a gasoline tax which is for roads and highways, and is refundable to purchasers who use the gasoline in their boats. Many boat owners do not claim the refund, and the initiative specifies that this unrefunded money be used for the purchase of property for marine parks.

Help has also come from the Washington Interclub Association, an organization of yacht and boating clubs. Some years ago, through donations from the clubs and their members, Sucia Island in the San Juan Islands was purchased just as it was about to be sold for real estate development. They subsequently turned it over to the parks department to become one of the most popular marine parks in the area. A committee of the association is also active in searching out and recommending desirable sites for future marine parks.

For purposes of easy identification and location, we have divided the list into three categories. The first group includes those parks which are definitely marine oriented. The second group lists parks which are not exclusively for marine use but are located on the water and have some marine facilities.

The third group is a listing of islands, rocks and properties which have been acquired, but are either undeveloped or being held for future development. This list can be valuable to the pleasure boat owner because it tells him where he may go ashore, dig clams, take oysters or skin dive, secure in the knowledge that he isn't trespassing on private property.

Listings in each group are by geographic area: Southwest area, the general Puget Sound area, Northwest area, and the San Juan Island area. This list does not include

Boats at Blake Island, a popular Washington marine park.

182

lakes, many of which have good park facilities, or anything east of the Cascade Mountains. Information on these parks can be found in the state's *Outdoor Recreational Guide,* available from the Parks and Recreation Commission, P.O. Box 1128, Olympia, Washington 98501.

Washington State with some 5246 miles of saltwater shoreline, not including islands, has much to offer the boat owner. Puget Sound is known as the "Boating Capital of the World." State parks are an adjunct to all of this. Use them, enjoy them, and please help keep them as clean as nature did before we took over.

The listing appears in the accompanying box.

	Mooring Floats and/or buoys	Launching facilities	Tables and Stoves	Kitchens or Shelters	Campsites	Toilets	Showers	Swimming	Clamming	Fishing
MARINE PARKS										
Southwest Area										
1. Beacon Rock—Columbia River— 35 miles east of Vancouver	X	X	X	X	30	X	X	X		X
Puget Sound Area										
2. Blake Island—5 mi. W of Seattle	X		X		36	X		X	X	X
3. Fort Flagler—NW end of Marrowstone Island	X	X	X		82	X		X	X	X
4. Illahee—3 mi. NE of Bremerton	X	X	X	X	25	X	X	X	X	X
5. Jarrell Cove—N end of Hartstene Island	X		X	X	10	X		X	X	X
6. Penrose Point—Carr Inlet	X		X	X	100	X	X	X	X	X
7. Pleasant Harbor—Hood Canal	X					X		X		X
8. Squaxin Island—E of Shelton	X		X		13	X		X	X	X
9. Twanoh—5 mi. E of Union, Hood Canal	X	X	X	X	81	X		X	X	X
Northwest Area										
10. Deception Pass (incl. Cornet Bay)— N end of Whidbey Island	X	X	X	X	267	X	X	X	X	X
11. Mukilteo—5 mi. SW of Everett	X	X	X			X		X	X	X
12. Sequim Bay—4 mi. S of Sequim, Strait of Juan de Fuca	X	X	X	X	69	X	X	X	X	X
San Juan Islands Area										
13. Jones Island—W of Orcas Island	X		X		19	X		X	X	X
14. Matia Island—NE of Orcas Island	X		X		6	X		X	X	X
15. Posey Island—N of Pearl Island outside Roche Harbor			X		1	X		X	X	X
16. Prevost Harbor—Stuart Island	X		X		6	X		X	X	X
17. Reid Harbor—Stuart Island	X		X		7	X		X	X	X
18. Sucia Island—N of Orcas Island	X		X		33	X		X	X	X
19. Turn Island—1¾ mi. E of Friday Harbor			X		4	X		X	X	X
PARKS ON THE WATER WITH SOME MARINE FACILITIES										
Southwest Area										
20. Fort Canby—2 mi. W of Ilwaco	X	X				X		X		X
21. Ocean City—3 mi. SE of Ocean City		X			151	X	X	X	X	X
22. Twin Harbors—3 mi. S of Westport		X	X		370	X	X	X	X	X
23. Westhaven—W of Westport		X				X		X	X	X
Puget Sound Area										
24. Belfair—Hood Canal—3 mi. W of Belfair		X	X		147	X	X	X	X	X
25. Dash Point—5 mi. NE of Tacoma		X			110	X	X	X	X	X
26. Dosewallips—Hood Canal at Brinnon		X			75	X		X	X	X
27. Dungeness (Cline Spit) — 5 mi. NW of Sequim, Strait of Juan de Fuca	X					X		X	X	X
28. Fay-Bainbridge—NE end of Bainbridge Island	X	X	X		27	X	X	X	X	X
29. Fort Worden—1 mi. N of Port Townsend						X		X		X
30. Kitsap Memorial—Hood Canal S of Floating Bridge		X	X		25	X	X	X	X	X

	Launching facilities	Tables and Stoves	Kitchens or Shelters	Campsites	Toilets	Showers	Swimming	Clamming	Fishing
31. Kopachuck—Carr Inlet, 5 mi. W of Gig Harbor		X	X	41	X		X	X	X
32. Old Fort Townsend—3 mi. S of Port Townsend		X	X	28	X	X	X	X	X
33. Potlatch—Hood Canal, NW of Union		X		15	X	X	X	X	X
34. Saltwater—18 mi. S of Seattle	X	X	X	34	X	X	X	X	X
35. Scenic Beach—Hood Canal, 12 mi. NW of Bremerton		X		20	X		X		X
Northwest Area									
36. Birch Bay—10 mi. S of Blaine		X	X	179	X	X	X	X	X
37. Camano Island—On SW Camano Island	X	X	X	129	X	X	X	X	X
38. Fort Casey—3 mi. S of Coupeville	X	X		63	X		X		X
39. Larrabee—7 mi. S of Bellingham	X	X	X	75	X	X	X	X	X
40. South Whidbey—W side of Whidbey Island		X		55	X	X	X	X	X

PROPERTIES UNDEVELOPED OR HELD FOR FUTURE DEVELOPMENT

Southwest Area
41. Leadbetter Point—24 mi. N of Long Beach

Puget Sound Area
42. Cutt Island—Carr Inlet
43. Eagle Island—Between Anderson and McNeil Islands
44. Fort Ward—S end of Bainbridge Island
45. Graveyard Spit—Near Dungeness Spit
46. Jones Beach—8 mi. NE of Olympia
47. Stretch Island—Small acreage N end
48. Wolfe Property—N end Hood Canal Bridge behind Hood Head

Northwest Area
49. Deception Island—1 mi. W of Deception Pass
50. Hope Island—3 mi. ESE of Deception Pass
51. Northwest Island—N of Deception Island
52. Pass Island—Under Deception Pass Bridge
53. Skagit Island—1 mi. E of Hoypus Point
54. Strawberry Island—½ mi. E of Deception Pass Bridge
55. Everett Jetty—NW section of Everett
56. Fort Ebey—3 mi. W of Coupeville
57. Useless Bay—Tidelands only, SE corner of Whidbey Island

San Juan Island Area
58. Spencer Spit—E side of Lopez Island

59. Blind Island—Blind Bay, Shaw Island
60. Cemetery Island—Entrance to Reid Harbor, Stuart Island
61. Clark Island—1¾ mi. NE of Orcas Island
62. Danger Rock—1.2 mi. SW of Disney Point on Waldron Island
63. Doe Island—E of Orcas Island
64. Dot Rock—SE of Decatur Island
65. Ewing Island—Sucia Group
66. Ewing Point—Sucia Group
67. Freeman Island—Off NW Orcas Island
68. Gossip Island—Entrance to Reid Harbor, Stuart Island
69. Iceberg Island—4 mi. N of Iceberg Point, Lopez Island
70. James Island—E of Decatur Head, Decatur Island
71. Lopez Island (27 acres)
72. Rock Island—Near Johns Pass
73. Skull Island—West Sound, Orcas Island
74. Unnamed Island—Reef off S end of Yellow Island, Wasp Islands Group
75. Unnamed Island—Off SW corner of Fox Cove, Sucia Group
76. Victim Island—West Sound, Orcas Island
77. Guss Island in Garrison Bay—Part of San Juan Island National Historical Park.

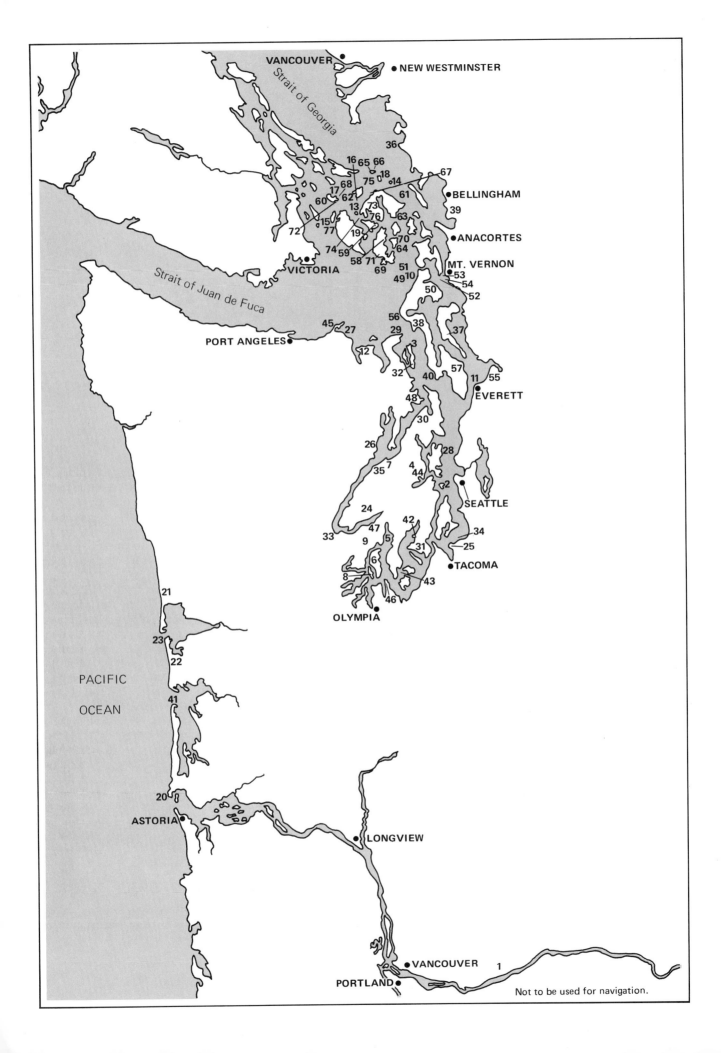

VANCOUVER •   • NEW WESTMINSTER

Strait of Georgia

36

16 65 66
75   18
68   14
17 62   61   • BELLINGHAM
60 13 73   39
15 76 63
72 77 19   70   • ANACORTES
74 59   64
58 71   51   • MT. VERNON
VICTORIA   69   49 10   53
54
50   52

45 27   56   38
29   37
PORT ANGELES •   12   3

32   57   11 55
40
48   • EVERETT

30

26   28
35   4
44   2   • SEATTLE

24
47   42   34
33 9 5   31   25
6   • TACOMA
8   43
46   OLYMPIA •

21

23
22

41

PACIFIC

OCEAN

20
ASTORIA •

• LONGVIEW

• VANCOUVER   1
PORTLAND •   Not to be used for navigation.

34
British Columbia Parks for Boating Families

The coastal waterways of British Columbia, which include a myriad of inlets, sheer-walled fjords, secluded anchorages, snug coves and innumerable islands in sheltered and open waters, present the yachtsman with an incomparable cruising paradise. Nearly 200 years ago the Spanish and English explorers were investigating both the Canadian outside western coast and the vast inland sea. They began the massive task of charting these unnamed areas and unlocking the tremendous storehouse of natural resources.

Today thousands of pleasure craft, in addition to the fishing and commercial vessels, ply the straits, sounds, passes, wind through the islands, past headlands bearing such names as Vancouver, Quadra, Georgia, Plumper, Porlier, Pender, Mayne, Galiano and hundreds more, given them by these early explorers or conferred later in commemoration of their exploits or positions.

Recognizing the recreational boating potential of its cruising waters, the government of British Columbia, through the Parks Branch of the Department of Recreation and Conservation began in 1957 the development of a system of provincial marine parks. The first to be established was Montague Harbor Provincial Marine Park on Galiano Island. Since then, more marine parks and marine park reserves have been added to an expanding system that now stretches from near the southernmost part of British Columbia waters to the remote areas north of Johnstone Strait.

These marine parks are designed to provide essential facilities for the enjoyment of the boating public and, at the same time, keep in mind the need to maintain the natural surroundings and beauty of the area. Most have safe anchorages and mooring buoys, some have landing floats, some have campgrounds and some have picnic facilities. If

possible, fresh water is available. Sanitary facilities are located at all developed parks and provision is made for the collection and disposal of refuse.

In some places fresh water is difficult to obtain and, in some of the marine parks, the water supply may be at a distance from the anchorage. It is recommended that skippers plan to replenish their supply at marinas and fueling stations.

As in the case of Washington State Marine Parks, the Parks Branch of the Department of Recreation and Conservation of the Province of British Columbia has received assistance in the establishment of marine parks by the donation of land or funds from individuals and organizations. Those giving such help include the Council of British Columbia Yacht Clubs, the Princess Louisa International Society, James F. Macdonald, Crown Zellerbach Canada Ltd., Capt. E. G. Beaumont and the Gibson family.

Following are the established provincial marine parks:

Beaumont Marine Park—In Bedwell Harbor on the west side of South Pender Island. Good mooring and anchorage. Gravel and sand beach. Camping and picnicking. Drinking water. Store, fuel, and Customs at Bedwell Harbor Resort.

Montague Harbor Marine Park—A landlocked bay on the southwest side of Galiano Island providing protected anchorage. Enter from Trincomali Channel either through the passage between Philmore Point and Julia Island or by the northern entrance between Parker Island and Galiano Island. Good beach, mooring buoys, floats, wharf, camping, picnicking, drinking water, and boat launching ramp. Accessible by road and car ferry from Swartz Bay via Montague Harbor or from Tsawwassen via Sturdies Bay.

Plumper Cove Marine Park—A snug anchorage, protected from most winds, on the northwest side of Keats Island

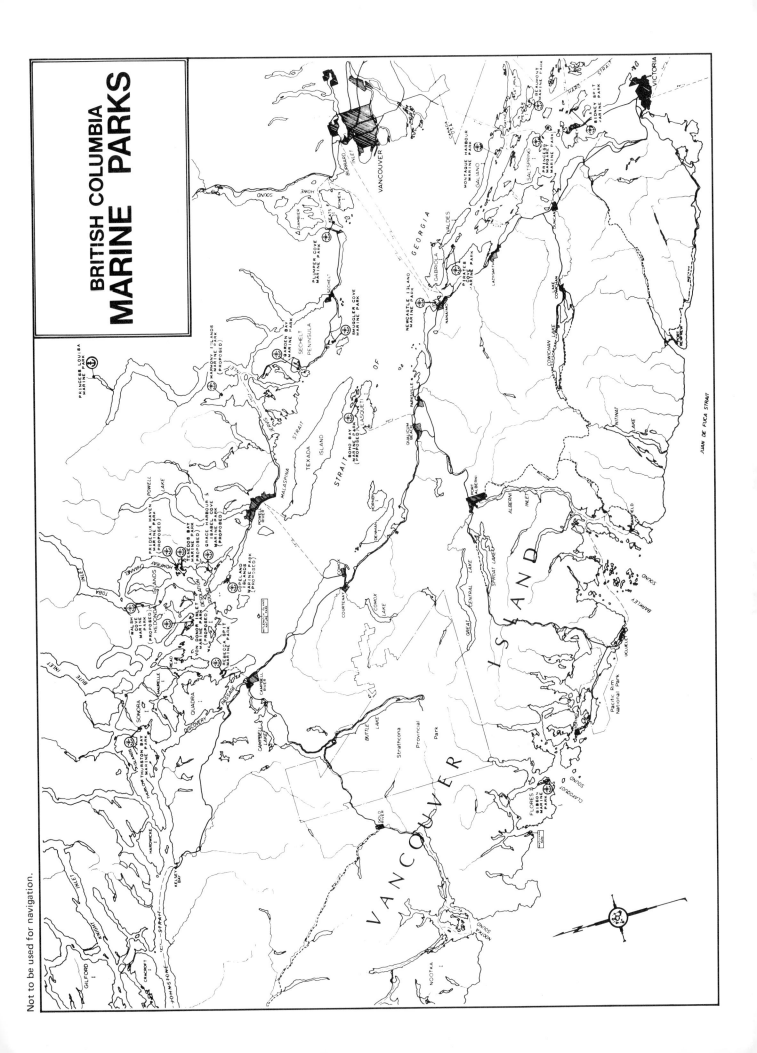

BRITISH COLUMBIA
MARINE PARKS

Not to be used for navigation.

in Howe Sound. Enter from Shoal Channel through passage between Observatory Point and Northern Shelter Islet. Good gravel beach, mooring buoys, floats, camping, picnicking, and drinking water.

Rebecca Spit Marine Park—On the east side of Quadra Island. Enter from Sutil Channel. Mooring and anchorage at northwestern tip of spit. Camping and picnicking, drinking water, and launching ramp. Road access by car and ferry from Campbell River via Quathiaski Cove.

Newcastle Island Marine Park—A 700-acre island in Nanaimo Harbor with several small attractive bays. Floats and mooring buoys on south side, camping, picnicking, drinking water, trails, view points, and historic sites. Passenger ferry operates between Nanaimo and Newcastle Island summers only.

Pirates Cove Marine Park—On southeast side of DeCourcy Island. Enter from Pylades Channel. Keep clear of kelp-covered reef extending north from the point at entrance to channel leading to cove. At low tide this channel must be negotiated with care. The best course is just right of center channel. Anchorage, mooring buoys. No shore facilities and no drinking water.

Princess Louisa Marine Park—At the head of Princess Louisa Inlet, off Queens Reach of Jervis Inlet. Entrance through Malibu Rapids is narrow and subject to tidal currents (see British Columbia Coast Pilot and Canadian Current Tables). Spectacular Chatterbox Falls at head of inlet. Anchorage at head of inlet near falls, mooring buoys, floats, picnicking, drinking water, trails.

Smugglers Cove Marine Park—Located at north end of Welcome Passage, this small scenic anchorage affords all-weather protection. On entering cove keep close to Isle Capri as reefs extend from southerly side of channel. Entering inner anchorage requires caution as reef extends from France Islet.

Sidney Spit Marine Park—At north end of Sidney Island. Anchor or moor on west side of spit. Mooring buoys, landing float for small boats. Camping, picnicking, no drinking water. Sandy beach and bottom, shallow. Enter from Haro Strait via Miners Channel or Sidney Channel.

There are also five provincial marine parks which are undeveloped and have no facilities but are available for use. These are:

Princess Margaret Marine Park—Portland Island at junction of Swanson Channel and Satellite Channel, southeast of Saltspring Island. Sandy beaches on northwest and southeast sides. Should be approached with extreme caution.

Garden Bay Marine Park—On north shore of Pender Harbor at Garden Bay. Enter Pender Harbor from Malaspina Strait.

Thurston Bay Marine Park—On northwest side of

Sonora Island. Enter from Nodales Channel. Park includes Block Island in Thurston Bay.

Echo Bay Marine Park—On northwest side of Gilford Island. Enter from Cramer Passage.

Gibson Marine Park—On Flores Island in Clayoquot Sound, west side of Vancouver Island. Sheltered anchorage in Matilda Inlet. Broad sandy beach at Whitesand Cove. Ahouset Hot Springs are in the park.

In addition to these provincial marine parks, the following locations are proposed for future development as marine parks:

Prideaux Haven—The most popular anchorage in Desolation Sound. Laura Cove, Melanie Cove and Prideaux Haven proper afford excellent anchorage and warm swimming waters. Entrance is from Homfray Channel to the east of Eveleigh Island. Use extreme caution on entering.

Tenedos Bay—East side of Mink Island in Desolation Sound. Enter from Homfray Channel. Anchorage behind the island is most secure and the bay at the mouth of the river is popular. Caution must be exercised in setting the anchor. Freshwater swimming in nearby Unwin Lake.

Grace Harbor—Off Malaspina Inlet. Safe anchorage at the head.

Isabel Cove—On Lancelot Inlet. Enter through Malaspina Inlet. Good shelter behind island.

Walsh Cove—On east side of West Redonda Island. Enter westward of Bluff Point on Gorges Islands from Waddington Channel.

Von Donop Inlet—Near northwestern end of Cortes Island. Enter from Sutil Channel. Good anchorage for small craft.

Copeland (Ragged) Islands—A chain of islands, islets and rocks at the northern end of Georgia Strait, north of Lund, separated from the mainland by Thulin Passage. Several scenic anchorages. Watch for rocks.

Harmony Islands—On east side of Hotham Sound. Enter from Jervis Inlet.

Boho Bay—On northeast side of Lasqueti Island. Enter from Sabine Channel or Bull Passage.

At this writing the exact status of Tent Island, just south of Kuper Island on Stuart Channel, is unsettled. It has been a provincial marine park for some years, the property on lease from a local Indian tribe. It is understood that it is still available for use by cruising yachtsmen.

Several areas around, and in the vicinity of Pruth Bay, at the top of Calvert Island in Queen Charlotte Sound, are parts of a recreational reserve.

The Parks Branch of the British Columbia Department of Recreation and Conservation has done, and is doing, an excellent job of providing for the ever increasing number of boats and people who are enjoying these "greatest cruising waters in the world."

35

Visiting Northwest Light Stations

Almost since man began sailing boats on the seven seas, some form of light has been used to help guide his ships through fog and the black of night. From a candle or lamp in a window in ancient times to the sophisticated high-intensity lights and prism lens of today, the guiding of mariners by sight and sound has been an important function.

In recent years this responsibility on this side of the international boundary line has been assigned to the United States Coast Guard. Along with buoys, markers, beacons and other types of navigational aids, light stations perform a necessary and appreciated service to those who go down to the sea in ships.

Here in the Northwest it was 1849, two years before the founding of Seattle, when Congress appropriated $15,000 for the establishment of two lighthouses and 12 buoys to mark the bar and treacherous entrance into the Columbia River. Thus was born the lighthouse service in this area.

It was in 1856 that the Cape Disappointment Lighthouse went into operation on the bluff at the north point of the mouth of the Columbia. The following year lighthouses were established at Cape Flattery, on Tatoosh Island at the entrance to the Strait of Juan de Fuca, and on the long sandspit at New Dungeness, on the south shore of the strait.

During the next 50 years new lights poked their fingers through the darkness all over the area's navigable waters, starting with the Willapa Bay Light in 1858 and ending with the Mukilteo and Burrows Island Lights, both established in 1906. Seattle's two light stations were built at West Point in 1881 and at Alki Point in 1887. Last station to be set up in local waters was at Lime Kiln in 1914, on the west side of San Juan Island.

Although there are now many lights in our area, modern technology has done away with the need for manning some of the stations. Automation and remote-control devices have taken over. Today only 15 lights on salt water in the state of Washington have resident personnel tending the stations.

In addition to the historical interest at the various lighthouses and the fascination of learning how the lights and fog signals operate, these stations generally offer spectacular panoramic views, much enjoyed by the camera fan when the weather is good. A visit to one or more of them is a worthy project, particularly during the winter months when cruising weather may not be suitable on certain weekends.

At the stations in Washington with resident personnel, in most cases, visitors are welcomed. Only three of these do not allow visitors: the Cape Flattery Light on Tatoosh Island, the Smith Island Light and the Burrows Island Light. The remaining 12, in order of their age, are:

Cape Disappointment Light—South of Ilwaco, Pacific County. White conical tower on north side of Columbia River mouth. Built in 1856. Available by automobile.

New Dungeness Light—On Dungeness Spit north of Dungeness. White conical tower on dwelling at outer end of spit. Built in 1857 and rebuilt in 1927. Available by boat.

Ediz Hook Light—White house on top of control tower at the Port Angeles Air Station on the sandspit at Port Angeles. Built in 1865 and rebuilt in 1946. Available by automobile.

Point No Point Light—On sandy point near Hansville in Kitsap County. White square tower on tip of point. Built in 1879 and rebuilt in 1900. Available by automobile.

Point Wilson Light—White octagonal tower on fog-signal building on end of spit at Port Townsend. Built in

1879 and rebuilt in 1914. It can be reached by automobile.

West Point Light—White square tower at end of point. Built in 1881 and rebuilt in 1901. Available by automobile through Fort Lawton in Seattle's Magnolia District.

Point Robinson Light—White octagonal tower on east end of Maury Island. Built in 1885 and rebuilt in 1915. Available by automobile.

Alki Point Light—White octagonal tower attached to a building at end of the point in West Seattle. Built in 1887 and rebuilt in 1918. Available by automobile.

Patos Island Light—White square tower on fog-signal house on northwest end of the island in the San Juans. Built in 1893 and rebuilt in 1908. Available by boat.

Turn Point Light—White concrete tower on northwest point of Stuart Island in the San Juans. Built in 1893 and rebuilt in 1936. Available by boat and by trail from state marine parks on island.

Slip Point Light—White square tower on pile structure on east side of Clallam Bay. Built in 1905. Available by automobile.

Mukilteo Light—White octagonal tower attached to building on Elliot Point. Built in 1906. Available by automobile.

All other lights are unmanned and not available to visitors. Remember, if you do visit lighthouses, you are guests of the resident personnel. Their homes are private, and access to the towers will be at the discretion of the officers in charge.

The extensive waters of British Columbia are generous-

A visit to a Northwest light station is an interesting experience. Pictured are Grays Harbor Light (top); open wooden frame structure containing old lens used at Point Robinson prior to 1915 (left); and (below) the more modern Point Robinson Light on Vashon Island.

ly dotted with hundreds of lights, 36 of them manned with resident personnel. Some of these are available by automobile but many are in rugged positions on remote waterways. Access by boat in some cases is hazardous. It would be best to check with government authorities as to which of these lighthouses permit visitors.

From the historical viewpoint, it's interesting to note that both the Race Rocks and Fisgard Lighthouses were constructed of granite blocks brought from England.

Of all the lights in the southeastern panhandle of Alaska, only five are manned. These are the Cape Decision Light, the Cape Spencer Light, the Five Finger Light in the Five Finger Islands, the Point Retreat Light in Saginaw Channel and the Eldred Rock Light in the Lynn Canal. Here, too, better check with local Coast Guard authorities about visitation privileges.

The men operating these lights do a yeoman job in providing these essential navigation beacons the year-around. If you are a yachtsman and visit any of these lighthouses, let them know of your appreciation for the service.

Despite its rugged setting here, Mukilteo Light is located near the ferry slip and has a neat lawn with picket fence.

36

The Grand Marine Pageant

It was May 6, 1945. "Gas rationing was still in effect. I was invited aboard the Calverts' cruiser *Starlight* to view a rather loosely made up Seattle Yacht Club Opening Day which, hopefully, would be the harbinger of bigger yacht parades at the war's end," recalls Bob Walters, who was editor of *Pacific Motor Boat* at that time. Realistically, about 150 powerboats and sailboats turned out, all preciously "metering hoarded fuel rations."

But the day itself was one of the most beautiful, hot May days on record. This gave special impetus to 1946, and its May 4 Saturday was another delightful weather day. Lawrence Calvert was Admiral of the Day. Other Puget Sound clubs joined with Seattle. Three hundred yachts, this time gaily decorated, were officially in the parade. Portland and San Francisco clubs also started mass parades on the same weekend.

By 1958, the actual count of participating Puget Sound and British Columbia yachts parading from the Seattle Yacht Club to Lake Washington, had reached 1412.

Opening Day of the Yachting Season, one of the most colorful yachting affairs in the country, is a misnomer. Sponsored and staged by the Seattle Yacht Club for Northwest yachtsmen on the first Saturday of May each year, Opening Day really can't "open" something that has never closed. Boating is a year-round activity in the Puget Sound area, as it is on most of the Pacific Coast.

With invitations to participate going to some 37 yacht and boating clubs in the vicinity this year and between 1200 and 1500 boats expected to converge on the waters of Portage Bay, Opening Day really becomes a festival in color. While Seattle Yacht Club is the principal host, other clubs add to the overall effort. There are breakfasts at several of the clubs as well as open houses and dinners.

The official program calls for boats to assemble in Portage Bay. A commissioning ceremony with a band, officials in dress uniforms, local VIPs, a lineup of visiting commodores and a host of skippers and their crews is staged on the club lawn. This is followed by a parade of gaily decorated and dressed yachts of all sizes, both sail and power, through the canal connecting the bay to Lake Washington. A sailboat race, a visit to Meydenbauer Bay Yacht Club's open house, dinner at Seattle Yacht Club, or one of the other clubs, sundown ceremonies and trophy awards on the lawn, and dancing finish out a memorable day of fun and beauty.

This isn't something that was dreamed up all of a sudden by some promoter. It has grown through the years. History is a little bit thin in spots but most old-timers are agreed that Opening Day probably got its start back in 1909. It seems that President Teddy Roosevelt was anxious to publicize the U.S. Navy and a fleet of seven round-the-world warships was in the Puget Sound region when something the yacht club called the Potlatch Regatta was scheduled. It's possible that there may have been as high as 60 spectators to watch a parade of the warships, a cross-sound ferry and about a dozen "dressed" yachts. It's believed these were all sailboats, racing hulls from Everett, Bellingham, Victoria and Vancouver, which joined annually with Seattle yachts in spirited competition. Of course this all took place at the old clubhouse at West Seattle.

The Potlatch Regatta grew into a May Regatta and by 1913, with the club still a relatively small organization, sailboats far outnumbered powerboats. In an effort to encourage the members to get the winter wraps off their boats, turn to with scrapers, sandpaper, paint and varnish and get other spring commissioning chores done, a group of enthusiastic club leaders came up with a plan to be called Opening Day.

Boats were to be dolled up, made ready for racing or cruising and put on display for the day. Open house at the club, sailboat races and an evening dance were scheduled.

Results were amazing. The first Opening Day engendered great enthusiasm. Boats came out of their winter covers and were shipshape and ready for the season when the day arrived. The desired ends had been accomplished. Both members and boats were prepared for the racing or cruising season; and they all had a good time celebrating the accomplishment.

After the club moved to its beautiful new site on Portage Bay across from the University of Washington campus, Opening Day activities began to expand. The parade through the cut to Lake Washington in 1925 had a good number of powerboats following the sailboats. A few years later, in 1927, many of the boats in the parade were fully decorated to celebrate the start of the new cruising season. The idea continued to grow with more and fancier decorations and exciting powerboat races to add further fun and color to the day's activities.

Then came World War II, with rationing and a shortage of gas and parts. Before long the white paint and varnish on pleasure craft turned to Navy gray as many boats took on patrol duty for the Coast Guard. Apparently some effort was made to continue Opening Day, for archives of the Queen City Yacht Club refer to it in 1944.

After war's end, Opening Day was revived in earnest. Yacht owners made an effort to erase the ravages of war, not only from their minds but from their boats. New paint and varnish were much in evidence, brilliant new flags and bunting appeared, and once more the canal was alive with beautifully decorated yachts.

As the festival grew in popularity, other yacht clubs on Puget Sound were invited to join in the celebration. Boats from British Columbia and members from Inland Empire clubs came in large numbers. They, too, were ready and wanted to join in this welcome to the new season.

Things really began rolling in 1946 when Lawrence Calvert, later to be the first Admiral of the Day, was chairman of arrangements and got things started toward making Opening Day the "Seattle Spectacular" it is today. Ceremonies were performed on the lawn and later a great mast with a tremendous yardarm was set up from which to fly burgees of visiting clubs. More than 300 boats participated.

In 1950 the tradition of Admiral of the Day was started, with Calvert the first Admiral and Con Knutson the Vice Admiral. In 1959 the Admiralette was added, with Jean Harthorn having the honor to be the first.

Commissioning ceremonies in 1955 were attended by several admirals and high ranking naval officers. A new tradition was started when club member John A. Soderberg included the individual raising of each visiting club's burgee and the official greeting of each visiting commodore as a part of the program.

It was 1956 when another attraction to the day's event was added with Meydenbauer Bay Yacht Club's inauguration of its open house. The clubhouse on the east side of

Lake Washington becomes a carnival of fun with members in appropriate costumes, plenty of food and refreshments, and afternoon dancing.

By evening, boats return to Seattle Yacht Club, which is decorated to the theme of the day. Dinner, sundown ceremonies and dancing end this salute to a new season of yachting in the Puget Sound region.

Some past winners are shown here (top to bottom):
Ta'aroa of the SYC, Comrade and Margarita, both of MBYC.

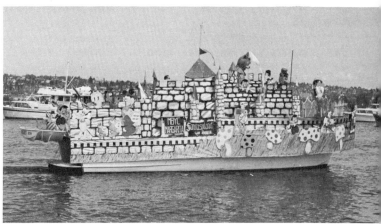

37

Miriam's Unusual Winter Cruise

by Al Molzan

One fall, I casually mentioned that it might be fun to see Princess Louisa Inlet in the winter and suggested that we cruise there for our New Year's Eve party. Skipperette Geneva was a little less than lukewarm to the idea, but after mentioning it a few more times, she agreed to go and we asked our good friends, Anita and Irv Shuman, to share the cruise with us.

Miriam is a 66x16x6-foot William Garden design, heavy displacement type yacht with sturdy 300-horsepower diesel engine and a 10-kilowatt diesel generator. We cruise at 10 knots. She is electrically heated, has a fireplace, and is very comfortable. *Miriam* is our home, and so a winter's cruise into interior British Columbia seemed very feasible.

We left the Tacoma Yacht Club basin at 1343 hours, on December 27, with Port Madison our destination for the first day's cruise. The five-day weather forecast was for 10° below normal temperature, with snow flurries and strong winds from the northeast. At the moment it was cloudy, with winds from the southwest gusting to 30 miles per hour.

This meant that we could have more than just an interesting adventure, but we had planned to take it from day-to-day and see how the weather developed. On the radio we kept hearing about impending snow conditions from the north, but so far, encountered only flurries. When we reached Point Sanford, however, the wind changed to north and whitecaps began to form on the water. It appeared that the radio forecasts were authentic.

There had been some very high tides recently and the water was full of debris—some of it quite heavy. This was one thing we were going to keep a sharp eye out for and, accordingly, charted our course through Rich Passage and around the west side of Bainbridge Island, since it was get-

ting darker, and the drift would be harder to see in the rougher water in the sound off Elliott Bay.

Port Orchard Channel was smooth, as expected. At 1640 we entered Port Madison inner harbor, tying up at the Seattle Yacht Club moorings where we had hoped to take on water, but the water pipes were frozen and so we would have to ration our supply somewhat.

This day's cruise had been beautiful as is often the case with our winter cruises, which we enjoy as much as our summer cruises.

At 0740 on December 28, we left Port Madison for the San Juan Islands. The weather was quite cold—there was ice on the mooring lines. The wind was blowing from the north and we were in for a cold day. As we cleared President Head, the water became very sloppy, with the north wind blowing at 35 knots and the temperature 12° above zero. Spray began flying over the bridge and freezing the second it hit the windshields.

The condensation inside the boat was freezing on the windows; we managed to keep it off, to some extent, in the area of the fan at the center windshield. The windshield swipe, at this point, managed to keep a small part of the windshield outside clear enough for the minimum visibility essential to keep us going until we could get out on deck to scrape the ice from the rest of the windshield. At this point, this was inadvisable because of the motion of the boat, and also the decks were a sheet of ice. Next the swipe became encrusted with heavy ice and reduced its efficiency almost to zero. We wondered if any other pleasure boats were out on this morning! At 0900 hours we received the weather forecast for 60 mile-per-hour winds from the northeast, north of Everett.

When we were in the lee of Whidbey Island, the sea was

smooth enough to get out on deck and scrape the ice from the windshield. The sun was now shining on the foothills of the snow-covered Cascades, and the view was grand. We hoped we would get out from under the cloud cover so we could get some good pictures of the scenery. Upon reaching Sandy Point, we again got the effects of the north wind and also encountered a low fog condition which was caused by the air being much colder than the water. It was only a few feet above the water—a rare phenomenon. Visibility was good for miles above the fog blanket, but very poor immediately ahead.

Suddenly the fog became higher, even though the wind was increasing and was freezing on the windshield in such a fine sheet that the swipe was not clearing it off. Reluctantly, about halfway between Sandy Point and East Point, we decided to turn our backs to the weather, and changed course for the Everett Yacht Club moorings.

We arrived at Everett at 1130 and found the floats covered with about six inches of snow and the temperature 6° above zero. Ken Tapert was on the floats and graciously offered to taxi us anywhere we wanted to go in Everett. We decided we should have some deicer spray and Ken drove us to the nearest service station, where we purchased their entire supply of three cans. Our boat was completely covered with ice, topsides and all.

In view of the conditions and forecasts, we decided to spend the rest of the day and night in Everett with the hope that the weather would break and allow us to continue on with our voyage.

Sunday morning, I went outside to clean off the windshields with the spray solution and found that, due to the zero temperature, it tended to freeze and so was not of too much help. The wind seemed to be down, but we were waiting to hear the weather forecast from Vancouver Radio at 0830, to decide whether to go north or south. The forecast was for gale winds in the Bellingham area, gusting at times to 60 miles per hour. We took a vote and decided, however, to head north for the Deception Pass area.

We left Everett at 1030, after purchasing four gallons of antifreeze for our engines. The sky was clear, the water smooth and the sun shining brightly. Under those conditions, one could not help but feel exhilarated and optimistic. It was bitterly cold outside which was evidenced by the fact that, although the temperature in the wheelhouse was very comfortable, condensation was freezing on the glass. To try to lick this problem, we placed a 110-volt portable heater close to the windshield, after removing the a.c. fan connection, hoping that the elements would stand the hotter d.c. current, and if so, we should have the ice on the windshield (inside) problem solved—which turned out to be the case. However, it did have a 15° effect on the compass which we had to keep in mind.

On clearing Rocky Point, Mount Baker and all the surrounding mountains came into view and it was a magnificent and majestic sight. In trying to locate the buoys marking the Skagit flats channel, we found all to be white instead of red, being covered with ice, and on Hope Island, we saw icicles up to 10 feet long.

It was our plan to take a quick look at conditions on

Miriam takes a rest during her cruise in sub-zero weather.

the other side of Deception Pass and decide whether to continue on or tie up for the night at Cornet Bay. At 1430 we were under Deception Pass bridge, and Rosario Strait looked smooth as a table top. Visibility was clear and sharp and the skyline was vivid with contrasting colors. The day's cruise so far had been beautiful—it would be hard to find a calmer day in the summertime. But at the Belle Rock light we met a heavy tide rip; the wind sprang up and again we had heavy spray on the windshields.

Our improvised heater kept the spray from freezing but the warm windshield caused the water to evaporate rapidly and the salt to dry hard, which presented a new hazard to good vision. We were soon down to a very small area of visibility, and navigation in narrow channels is something less than fun in these circumstances. We hoped to get into calm water inside Thatcher Pass, but this was not the case, as the gale winds, which had been forecast, suddenly struck us and, in the area south of East Sound, the water was about as rough as it had been off Elliott Bay. Also darkness was approaching.

We had hoped to reach our destination, Deer Harbor, before it became dark, but now knew we wouldn't. We had to slow our speed to make it possible for me to get out on deck, on its very slippery surface, to scrape ice and wash salt off the windshield so that we could keep going. The other members of the crew took their turns at this since it was too cold, around zero, to take it for more than a few minutes on deck.

Finally, we reached Harney Channel, and the change in direction of our course placed our backs to the weather and once again, for a short time, visibility was good. We did not want to chart our course through Pole Pass, however; so went around Crane Island to enter Deer Harbor. We arrived at the Deer Harbor floats at 1730 and had a hard time mooring *Miriam,* having to make three passes, on account of the strong wind, which was gusting to 45 knots.

At last we secured the boat but were uneasy about the construction of the floats on account of the size of *Miriam* and her weight. We had been assured in Everett that the floats had been rebuilt and were substantial. To ease our minds, we tied a bowline to a piling.

We had our dinner and settled back for relaxation when we suddenly heard a loud report and, on dashing to the deck, found that all the bowlines had broken off the tie rails on the float. We then tied a second bowline to the piling, hoping the stern lines would hold, but a short time later, these gave way too and we were hanging off the piling. The terrific surge caused by the sudden slackening of the lines, when the wind gusts passed, caused *Miriam* to spurt bow first into the floats, and we knew we must leave. We snubbed her close to the float and cut the lines, as there was no chance to get on the float for untying, and then anchored toward the north end of the harbor in 30 feet of water, with some 300 feet of chain and cable for scope, and very thankful that we had purchased a new 145-pound anchor several months ago.

After keeping an anchor watch for about an hour, we decided we would stay put—and so to our bunks at 0145 for a badly needed rest. Before retiring, Irv felt a tingling sensation in his kneecaps. He had done quite a bit of kneeling on the float and also on the decks, to keep his balance but thought he was suffering only from some exposure. In the morning, though, his knees were very painful and had ugly looking splotches in addition to being badly swollen, and we knew he had gotten frostbitten and would need medical attention. The temperature was 5° below zero. So, reluctantly, we decided to go back home, and let the Princess Louisa trip remain among the things to dream about when one needs a little time for relaxation from daily chores. We heard later that Princess Louisa Inlet was frozen solid and we couldn't have got in anyway.

Thirty minutes after leaving Deer Harbor, we noticed that the muffler on *Miriam* was heating up, which was an indication that the saltwater pump impeller was failing; so we changed course for Friday Harbor, both for medical attention to Irv and to install the spare impeller.

Dr. Heath, who treated Irv's knees, wanted him to stay in Friday Harbor for two or three days for observation, and so instead of New Year's Eve in Princess Louisa, it was New Year's Eve in Friday Harbor. Friday Harbor is a quaint little town in the heart of the San Juan Islands, and had the appearance of a cluster of jewels, especially at night, with its lights sparkling on an eight-inch blanket of clean, white snow. Also, many of the lighted Christmas trees and decorations were still up and created a real holiday atmosphere.

On the morning of January 2, Dr. Heath gave Irv clearance to leave. With the weather moderating rapidly and all ice gone from *Miriam,* we started for home and had a very smooth, uneventful cruise to Port Madison, where we arrived at 1800 hours. We traveled in the dark for the last hour, but the water was smooth and we were easily able to see the large amount of previously mentioned drift.

We arrived at the Tacoma Yacht Club moorings at 1300 on January 3, and our winter cruise was at an end. We saw no other pleasure boats under way on this cruise. Our faith in people was stimulated as both at Everett and at Friday Harbor, everyone was more than friendly and helpful, especially Dr. Heath, who came from the other side of the island that snowy morning to treat Irv's knees. Too, we had proven to ourselves that we could navigate in sub-zero weather in gale winds, which gave us a lot of satisfaction, and we are looking forward to other adventure-type cruises.

38

Queen Charlotte Can Be Tough

by Captain Ray Tarr

One October I flew up to Sandspit in the Queen Charlotte Islands and then 70 miles back toward the southern end of the islands to join the *Norango* and bring her back to Vancouver. There was a skipper aboard, and a darn good one, too. But he was the only one on board who could run the ship and he needed some relief. As it turned out, however, neither he nor I left the bridge for 26 hours running, once we got started south and caught in a storm. And I do mean storm!

The Shell Oil drilling rig, which is standing on bottom (so I am told) in 800 feet of water near the north side of Queen Charlotte Sound, recorded 90-mile winds and 75-foot swells. I guess they would be in a position to get a fairly accurate reading on the height of the waves, all right. The first thing anybody asks is, "What were you doing out in that kind of weather?" Well, we listened to the weather forecasts and the weather bulletins and believed them, that's why.

The two previous days it had been blowing 60 to 70 knots and we were holed up. Even in the bay where we were anchored, the wind-speed indicator registered 60 knots, but not much of a sea, as only about half a mile reach from shore. Even then we dragged anchor half a mile. We kept watching it on the radar and finally had to haul up the anchor, at 3:00 A.M., and steam ahead, back to the

Crossing Queen Charlotte Sound between the north tip of Vancouver Island and the Queen Charlotte Islands can be a comfortable cruise or an adventure to tax both man and boat. Capt. Ray Tarr of Vancouver, B.C., describes a recent crossing in which he helped a friend bring a 160-foot North Sea trawler yacht back to the islands.

16-fathom patch we had been on, and then let out about 600 feet of scope, and that time she stayed put.

The day we left for the crossing, the report said, "Gale warning over" and the bulletin had 10 knots at Cape St. James and 15 knots at Cape Scott. The forecast was for winds southeast at 15 knots. What more could you want for a 160-foot steel North Sea trawler built as a yacht? Well, we got started south and, as soon as we got out from behind a few points of land, we began running into some pretty big swells, but only about 15-knot winds. We figured the swells would naturally be there after two days of 60-knot winds, and the 15-knot breeze was just what the weather forecast called for.

The wind kept freshening and the waves building up; we slammed along at 11 knots and figured we'd be in the lee of the north tip of Vancouver Island in about 10 hours. It was getting dark, and we had the oil drilling rig on radar 12 miles inside of us to the east. Visibility was lousy and getting worse.

It must have been around 6:30 when we started taking solid seas over the forecastle, and soon after that a sea wiped the top clean off the 23-foot *Norangal* that was sitting in its cradle on the foredeck. Then one smashed an armor-plated window on the starboard side of the main salon. So we put her at half speed ahead.

The wind went up over 50 knots, then over 60 and stayed there all night, with many gusts to 70 and above. We couldn't see a thing. The ship took it okay, but it was the worst I've ever seen. The skipper has been all over the world and said that, even in the Bay of Biscay, the China Sea and the Indian Ocean, he'd never seen anything like this. Of course the reason was the current, plus the shallow water.

197

It is over 110 miles across this opening, and we took until the next noon to get across. The wind never stopped, or even slowed down the whole time. The roll indicator on this ship is one that registers the maximum roll the ship takes and keeps it marked. It went clear to the end both ways. I think the thing that bothered me most was not knowing whether or not we were making any headway. Too far for radar, nothing to sight on, and me wondering if we were maybe just sitting out there making no headway, and would have to just sit there until she blew herself out. And she wasn't blowing herself out a bit.

As it turned out, from the time we set her down to half ahead we were making three knots over the bottom. We ran on autopilot. If we had had to steer by wheel, I doubt if we could have done it and held a course. On the foredeck were five aluminum boats which had been rented from a marina in Horseshoe Bay. They all looked like paper bags that had been stepped on by the next day when it grew light enough to see anything. Water got into the main salon and other places, and we figured that about $12,000 would cover the damage. I know the swells were big, all right, because we climbed way up one side and way down the other side with a 160-footer. The owners were not aboard; there were just eight of us, all but three in the sack, hanging on tight!

39
Washington Ports of Call

As a rule cruising yachtsmen are primarily interested in getting away from the city to find a quiet little cove where they can forget the pressures of civilization and commune with nature. There are times, however, when, for a variety of reasons, skipper and crew find themselves moored at some city float or in a municipal yacht basin.

When this happens, depending, of course, upon the length of stay, there are usually certain things ashore to see and do which are of interest. Highlighting some of the feature attractions in cities and towns situated on the water in the Puget Sound area, the following list may help in the enjoyment of a shoreside visit.

OLYMPIA—Washington State's capital city is located in a beautiful setting at the southern extremity of Puget Sound and has a population of 22,000. It was originally called New Market, then Smithter or Smithfield. Its present name comes from the Olympic Mountains. The Olympic Yacht Club has a guest float and is almost in the center of the downtown area with a wide variety of stores, shops, restaurants and amusement centers. The Capitol and Legislative Buildings, set in beautifully landscaped grounds and flower gardens, are worth a visit. Guides are available in summer only. Tours of the State Historical Museum, the Olympia Oyster Company, the Olympia Brewing Company, and several industrial plants are available. Oyster harvesting can be observed at three nearby places. The many lovely parks include Capitol Lake Park, Priest Point, Tumwater Falls, Sylvester, Maple, Woodruff, Bigelow, Lions and Millersylvania State Park. Christmas Island, in Capitol Lake, is rated as one of the top attractions in the United States when, during December, it depicts the Nativity Scene in a spectacle of color. Olympia has six marinas to serve the cruising family.

SHELTON—Named for its founder, David Shelton, in 1853, the town's population is 6225. The Simpson Timber Company, founded in 1890, manages local tree farms which supply logs for several wood-processing plants in the town. ITT Rayonier's Olympic Research Division delves into all phases of wood chemistry. Tours through these plants are conducted from June through August. Shelton is also the site of the Washington Correction Center, a reception center for male adults and treatment center for youthful first offenders. In Shelton Park can be seen a retired logging steam locomotive. The Mason County Forest Festival is held in Shelton the latter part of each May with giant logs on display, an old-fashioned log-bucking contest and demonstrations of tree-falling from a springboard. The Shelton Yacht Club is located on the waterfront.

TACOMA—This third largest city in the state has a population of 156,000 and is the county seat of Pierce County. Old Tacoma was first settled in 1864 as Commencement City. In addition to the many stores, shops, restaurants and entertainment centers, some of the principal attractions are: the nations' tallest totem pole, carved from a single tree 105 feet high by Alaskan Indians; Wright Park with one of the finest arboretums in the Pacific Northwest, containing 800 trees of 111 varieties; the Tacoma Smelter; Point Defiance Park with 638 acres, rose and flower gardens, a zoo, and breathtaking view points; a municipal boathouse with 200 rental boats; an aquarium with 2246 live specimens of 211 species of Puget Sound and Pacific Ocean marine life; the Job Carr home and first post office, built in 1865; a bathing beach; Never-Never Land, a five-acre storybook land with lifelike figures of Mother Goose and other fables; Camp Six, Western Washington Forest Industrial Museum; Old Fort Nisqually; the Tacoma Narrows Suspen-

Entrance to Gig Harbor, a village with a 104-year history.

sion Bridge; State Historical Museum; and the Escalade, moving sidewalks in the downtown area. The annual Daffodil Festival is held the first part of April each year. The Tacoma Yacht Club, with new clubhouse and moorages and guest float, is near the Tacoma Smelter on Commencement Bay, and the Day Island Yacht Club is across town on the Tacoma Narrows.

GIG HARBOR—The quaint little village on the shores of a landlocked harbor has been gradually changed during its 104-year history from a bawdy fishing and logging town to a delightful cultural center. Its population, including many Scandinavians and Yugoslavians, totals 1666, but this is augmented by some 200 more across the bay and 400 in the Shore Acres development above the town. The visiting yachtsman will be intrigued by a wide variety of specialty establishments, some of which have taken over old hotels, store buildings, saloons, and farms. Much of the charm of yesteryear will be found in places such as the White Whale Art Shop, Candles of Gig Harbor (also selling rare wines), the Poggie Bait Ice Creamery, Three Fingered Jack's Tavern, Harbor Inn, Century 19 Millwork (nautical artifacts), the Galleries Kenady, Cellar Arts, Bonneville Weaving, the Corridor, Mostly Books, the Beach Basket, Slaughter's Decor, the Little Showcase, the Hobby Hut, Helena's Upholstery and the Fabric Fair. Then there is the well-known Scandia Gaard, a collection of buildings housing Swedish, Norwegian, Indian and Pacific Northwest museums, gift shop, and restaurant featuring Norwegian pastries. Fishing boats always add color to a harbor, and Gig Harbor is home port for a fair-sized fleet of them. The Shoreline Restaurant not only serves excellent food but has floats to accommodate those coming by boat. The Gig Harbor K O A Campground is on the outskirts of town, and just a bit out of town are Hedstrom's Floral Gardens and Dominex Imports. The Gig Harbor Yacht Club has quarters in the bay and there are several marinas.

DES MOINES—A new breakwater and small boat basin now give ready access to this community on East Passage, midway between Seattle and Tacoma. The Des Moines Yacht Club, formerly the Vagabond Yacht Club, is based here, and there are stores and restaurants adjacent.

BREMERTON—With the Puget Sound Naval Shipyard situated here, this can almost be called a navy town. Its population varies from 35,000 to 40,000, depending on the number of naval personnel stationed there. It was named for William Bremer, a territorial pioneer from Germany, who is regarded as the city founder. The shipyard, founded in 1891, has the greatest capabilities of any shipyard, public or private, in the United States and boasts the worlds largest drydock. Ships of the mothball fleet are anchored in the bay. Tours of the shipyard and aboard the Japanese surrender ship U.S.S. *Missouri* are conducted daily. There are the Naval Shipyard Museum and the Kitsap County Historical Museum. Historical points include the Wyckoff Marker, and the Bremer Marker. Gun enthusiasts will enjoy a visit to Western Stocks Inc., in East Bremerton. The Bremerton Yacht Club is located behind the town in Phinney Bay and municipal floats are located next to the ferry slip.

PORT ORCHARD—This was the last section of Kitsap County to be settled and developed. First named Sidney after its founder, Sidney Stevens, in 1885, the name was changed to Port Orchard in 1895. Mail to the Puget Sound Naval Shipyard came by way of the Sidney post office, and the town's inhabitants thought the name Port Orchard carried more potential benefit as a popular designation for a great naval base. Population is 3700. The county seat for Kitsap County was moved here from Port Madison in 1892. Just east of town at Retsil is the Washington Veteran's Home. The Kitsap County Historical Museum is in Port Orchard, and there are stores, restaurants and boat yards. The Port Orchard Yacht Club has quarters on the waterfront.

POULSBO—Called a "Little Bit of Norway," this is home port for a fleet of fishing boats, and docks are a beehive of activity in the spring as fishermen ready their boats and gear for the season's work. During the summer many pleasure boats use the city floats. The Viking House Restaurant is at dockside, and there are public showers, restaurants, ice, water and electricity. Poulsbo proves its friendliness to visitors with a large "Velkommen" sign at the waterfront. On a fill along the waterfront is Anderson Parkway, affording parking for shoppers and benches from which to watch the ships and marine activity. In addition to a number of stores, specialty shops include David's Variety

Store with imported Scandinavian items and Bauer's Bakery featuring Scandinavian "goodies." Out of town a bit is the famous Yarn Barn with sweaters and patterns of Norwegian design, looms, and craft kits. Poulsbo is also the home of Ole Berg's Auto Clinic. Ole is a yachtsman and sports fisherman (when he can find time) but he is famous as the "best gol-durned mechanic" in the area. An Arts and Crafts Festival, held in town each May, attracts artists and craftsmen from all over the Northwest. The Poulsbo Yacht Club and a launching ramp are adjacent to the public floats.

SUQUAMISH—This was the tribal home of Chief Sealth, for whom Seattle was named. The visitor will find a totem pole carved by Joe Hillaire, late chief of the Kitsap tribe; the remains of Old Man House, an Indian-type condominium residence for many families; and Chief Sealth's grave. In late July or early August each year Chief Seattle days are held, featuring Indian games, boat races and salmon barbecues.

SEATTLE—The "Queen City of the Pacific Coast," as a major metropolis, has far too many attractions to list them all. Just a few of the highlights include the Municipal Shilshole Bay Marina with moorages for 1600 boats; the Hiram Chittenden Locks connecting freshwater Lakes Washington and Union with Puget Sound; the downtown waterfront with its seafood restaurants, import shops, aquarium and performing whale and seals, harbor tour boats, the ferry dock, restored lightships and tugboat, and Ye Olde Curiosity Shop; the Space Needle, Food Circus, Science Center, and other attractions on the site of the 1962 World's Fair; two Lake Washington floating bridges; the floating house community; Underground Tours, and a host of others. Yacht clubs in the Seattle area include the Corinthian, Elk, Lakeside, Maydenbauer Bay, Puget Sound, Queen City, Rainier, Seattle, Shilshole Bay, Tyee, University of Washington, Wave Toppers, West Seattle, Yarrow Bay.

EDMONDS—Just north of Seattle, this community was incorporated in 1890 and has a city park, beach parks, several other parks and recreation areas. The Edmonds Yacht Club is located at the excellent small boat harbor and moorage.

MUKILTEO—The name is an Indian word meaning "good camping place." Here was the state's first salmon-salting works, first brewery, first salmon canning north of the Columbia River, and first seat of Snohomish County. The oldest continuously operated boathouse is next to the public launching ramp, where many hundreds of boats are put into the water every weekend. Governor Isaac Stevens met here with Indian leaders on January 22, 1855, for the signing of treaties. Mukilteo is the gateway to Whidbey Island, where thousands of cars and people board the ferry to the island. The Mukilteo Lighthouse on Point Elliott is a point of interest to visitors.

EVERETT—Named after Everett Colby, this town with a population of 65,000 was platted in 1891. Interesting tours are available to the Boeing 747 facility, the *Everett Herald,* Scott Paper Company, Simpson Lee Paper Company, and the Weyerhaeuser Company plant. There are the Historical Museum and the Snohomish County Museum. Several parks include Grand Avenue Park, site of Vancouver's landing here, and Forest Park. The long sandspit across part of the waterfront is an interesting place to visit and picnic. A ferry to the spit runs from the Port of Everett's Fourteenth Street Boat Basin, and the Everett Yacht Club is also located here.

LANGLEY—The community on the east side of Whidbey Island has public floats with adjacent marina, stores, library, movie theater, Arts and Crafts shops, and the Doghouse, featuring the glowering head of a one-ton Cape Buffalo shot in Kenya, Africa, by a Whidbey Island sea captain.

COUPEVILLE—Joseph Whidbey, master of Vancouver's H.M.S. *Discovery* landed at Penn Cove in 1792, and proved that this was an island, not part of the mainland. Thomas Glasgow took up a claim near here in 1848 and Isaac Ebey, in 1850. Thomas Coupe, a sea captain, settled in 1852 on what is now Coupeville. By 1856 other families had arrived and seven blockhouses had been built, one of which still stands near the waterfront. Several pioneer houses, built over a hundred years ago, are still in use today. The Coupeville Methodist Church was built in 1893 and the Catholic Church, formerly Old Academy and Congregational Church, in 1853. There is a city park with picnic and camping facilities and the Island County Historical Society Museum. The annual Coupeville Festival in mid-August features arts and crafts, performing arts, a salmon derby, an Indian salmon barbecue, and other events. The Port of Coupeville has recently expanded and has renewed the old wharf and floats and added a fuel wharf.

OAK HARBOR—The first settler arrived here in 1849 and for nearly a century it was a quiet little island village. Today with its nearby navy base, it boasts complete modern shopping centers, but its 100-year-old buildings hold a fascination for artists. The Flintstone Freeway is a man-made street through the tideflats, complete with a stone-age car.

LA CONNER—A trading post was established here in 1867 and called Swinomish. In 1869 John S. Conner bought it and named it after his wife, Louise A. Conner. The post office was established in 1870. With sternwheel boats for transportation, the town became a hub of shipping for grain and farm products. Some of the present docks are remnants of the old days. The charm of La Conner is that it has preserved much of its colorful past, lovely old buildings and homes, while adding interesting shops. Historic points of interest include: Pioneer Monument, depicting scenes from pioneer days, and a time capsule to be opened in 1986; Tillinghast Seed Company, founded in 1885, oldest operating retail seed house in the Northwest; canoe display of two ancient Nooksack dugout canoes; an early fire wagon, built in New York in 1850 and used in the San Francisco fire after the earthquake; logging wheels; log display with an 11-foot block from a Douglas fir which began growth in the thirteenth century; the *Puget Sound Mail,* the oldest weekly in Washington, established in 1873, and an interesting museum of early Americana; City Hall, built in 1886, Territorial County Court House; pioneer log cabin, built in 1869 by Magnus Anderson with hand tools and lumber he brought from Utsalady by rowboat; the Skagit County Historical Museum; and the Scenic Arch

Aerial view of the Sand Spit, Bainbridge Island, with Port Madison Bay in the background.

Rainbow Bridge across Swinomish Channel and to the Swinomish Indian Reservation. The Port of Skagit County recently completed a marina and small boat haven with covered moorage and transient guest floats.

ANACORTES—This town on Fidalgo Island, called the "Gateway to the San Juan Islands," was incorporated in 1890, has a population of 9000, and was named by its founder, Amos Bowman, for his wife, Anna Curtis. The island is connected to the mainland by the Swinomish Channel Bridge and to Whidbey Island by the Deception Pass Bridge. The town's several parks include Cap Sante Park, with a splendid vista point view of the Cascade Mountains, Mount Baker, Puget Sound, and many of the San Juan Islands; Washington Park, 100 acres with camping, picnicking and boat launching facilities; and Causland Memorial Park. One of the most unusual parks in the Northwest, Causland is an artistry in native stone with walls designed after those in an old Austrian city park. Many beaches nearby attract rock hounds for vesuvianite, some jasper, a few agates and serpentine, a stone locally known as

Whidbey Island Jade. Local rock shops will provide information on collecting areas. Sunset Beach is a good spot to view some spectacularly beautiful sunsets. Tours can be arranged through the several oil refineries, chemical, wood pulp, plywood and hardboard plants. An Arts and Crafts Festival is held the first weekend in August. The Anacortes Yacht Club and several good marinas are on the waterfront and Skyline Marina in Flounder Bay has complete boating facilities, moorage, restaurant, store and swimming pool. Ferries run through the San Juan Islands to Sidney, British Columbia, from Anacortes.

BELLINGHAM—This town on Bellingham Bay has a population of 37,000. The bay was named by Vancouver for Sir William Bellingham, who assisted in providing stores for his voyage. The town is the site of Western Washington State College and has an outstanding museum in the imposing red brick former city hall. There are numerous parks and industrial areas including the Uniflite Inc. boat plant where Uniflite pleasure cruisers as well as boats for the navy are built. The town is a hub for many short trips to nearby interesting places. The Bellingham Yacht Club is located in the Port of Bellingham's excellent boat harbor.

BLAINE—With a population of 1800, this town is on the United States-Canadian International Boundry with its beautiful Peace Arch Park, featuring the massive arch 67 feet high, built in 1921. This is the only monument of its kind in the world and it commemorates over 100 years of peace between two great countries with a common border. The park has lovely lawns and colorful flower gardens. Blaine has one of the finest small craft harbors in the Northwest with complete facilities, launching, marine railway for boats up to 100 feet, repair service, marine supplies and fuel station, all enclosed by a sturdy breakwater. It is home port for many fishing boats and site of a nylon net and web factory. Camera fans like the concrete sidewalk floats at water level. Complete supplies and services are available in town.

PORT GAMBLE—On September 1, 1853, Andrew J. Pope, William C. Talbot and Cyrus Walker arrived to found this mill town. From these pre-Civil War days to the present, it has remained basically a mill town. In 1953 a centennial plaque was dedicated commemorating its founding. Today the tiny mill which sawed Port Gamble's first log has been replaced by a modern plant surrounded by stacks of lumber on four acres of docks and yard space. One of the most historic cemeteries in the state dates back over 100 years and is the burial place for early white settlers and sea captains. One of the oldest graves is that of a German boy killed in the Indian War of 1856. Port Gamble also boasts the second oldest Masonic Hall in Washington, established in 1876.

PORT LUDLOW—The former mill town, closed in 1936, is now completely gone, replaced by a modern community recreation and residential development.

PORT TOWNSEND—Named by Vancouver after the marquis of Townshend, the town was actually founded in 1851, six months before Seattle's birth. The flags of every nation at one time flew from the gaffs of sailing ships in the harbor. All types of boats have known her harbor. During early days the men from these ships made the waterfront a place too wild for the respectable people. Today Port Townsend, with a population of 5600, is noted for its historic charm, picturesque buildings and old homes, and scenic surroundings. The Victorian architecture of business buildings constructed in the boom days of the late 1800s can be seen in the Leader Building, 1874, oldest standing two-story stone structure in the state, the Mount Baker Block, Customs House, 1892, Old German Consulate and the Court House, 1891. Stately old homes also attract much interest, with architects coming from all over the world to view these remainders of a past era. Over 200 homes have signs with the date of construction and the name of the original owner. A tour of the city includes 33 points of interest. Crown Zellerbach Corporation's kraft paper mill is the largest single industry. Fort Warden is now the state treatment center for youth. There is a variety of parks and beaches, and the Rhododendron Festival the third weekend in May and the Jefferson County Fair in early August draw many people from the surrounding area. There are a museum, an art gallery, Summer School of the Arts, and the Key City Players and Port Townsend Festival Theater provide live entertainment. John Ashby Conway's "The Farmhouse," on the outskirts of town, offers an exciting gourmet dining experience. The Point Hudson Boat Basin and the recently enlarged Port Townsend Boat Haven provide good moorage and services for the visiting yachtsman. The Port Townsend Yacht Club is based here.

PORT ANGELES—In 1791 Don Francisco Eliza sailed his ship into the protected harbor formed by the Ediz Hook sandspit and called it, Puerto de Nuestra Senora de los Angeles or "Port of Our Lady of the Angels." Organized as a town in 1890, it has a population today of 15,800. It has several parks; numerous freshwater and saltwater launching facilities nearby; the Pioneer Memorial Museum, Visitor's Center, community swimming pool; nearby clamming, crabbing, rock hounding and a skin-diving club; a symphony orchestra and community players. Industry includes pulp, paper and allied products, logging, lumber and wood products. Tours are available through the Rayonier Inc., Crown Zellerbach and Peninsula Plywood plants and the Coast Guard Air Station. The Puget Sound Pilot Station is on Ediz Hook, next to the Coast Guard station. Port Angeles is headquarters for fishing in the area and is a base for many short trips to places of interest. The Clallam County Fair is held here the latter part of August, and there is an annual Labor Day Weekend Salmon Derby. The Port Angeles Yacht Club is located in the public boat basin. A car and passenger ferry runs from here across the Strait of Juan de Fuca to Victoria, British Columbia.

FRIDAY HARBOR—This historic town on San Juan Island still has many old buildings and some of those more recently built have been designed to match the older architecture. This is Customs port of entry and boasts two canning companies and two shipyards, as well as stores and an antique shop. A few miles away are the University of Washington Friday Harbor Laboratories, founded in 1904 when the original laboratory was built south of town. The present site was obtained in 1921 and construction started in 1923. Visitor's tours are conducted Wednesdays and Saturdays at 2:00 and 4:00 P.M. The American and British Camps of the Pig War boundary dispute are on the island and now a part of the San Juan National Historical Park. There is a public boat basin and moorage, and the San Juan Island Yacht Club is based at Friday Harbor.

40

British Columbia Ports of Call

As in Washington, when the yachtsman finds himself "in port" with time on his hands, there is much of interest to be found in British Columbia cities situated on cruising waters. The larger cities—Vancouver, Victoria, Nanaimo and Prince Rupert—have a wealth of attractions for the visitor. Most of the smaller towns with their marine facilities and services are well-known to Northwest cruising families.

Here are some of the highlights at these larger British Columbia saltwater ports of call.

VANCOUVER—It is unfortunate that the man who did so much discovering, exploring and charting of our Northwest waters, and for whom this city was named, never knew of the honor. Few great cities of the world can boast a more beautiful setting with protected harbor, miles of scenic sandy beaches and a background of snow-crowned mountains.

Incorporated in 1886, Vancouver has a population of over 410,000 to make it Canada's third largest city. It is a major manufacturing, shipping and transportation hub for all of the province. Known as the "Gateway to the Orient" and "Canada's Evergreen Playground," it has an area of 44 square miles.

It was a stroke of genius when, sometime in the past, farsighted planners set aside the 1000 acres for beautiful Stanley Park. Located on the peninsula projecting into English Bay to form the protection for the inner harbor, this delightful park has enough attractions (including a zoo and aquarium) to keep a visitor busy for days.

Vancouver's Chinatown, second only to San Francisco's, has many interesting stores, shops, and restaurants. There is much to see on a stroll along the docks and commercial waterfront, where ships from all over the world load and unload their cargo. Queen Elizabeth Park with its arboretum, sunken gardens and Little Mountain, affording a magnificent panoramic view, is one of the lovliest of the many parks scattered throughout the city.

If time permits, yachtsmen will particularly enjoy a visit to the British Columbia Building at Exhibition Park to see and study the huge topographical relief map of the province. Looking down on it, as if from an airplane, a new perspective is obtained as you mentally cruise up the inlets and are able to relate the waters to the surrounding hills and mountains.

A spectacular panorama of Coast Range Mountains, the Strait of Georgia, the Gulf Islands, Burrard Inlet, and the mouth of Howe Sound, dominates the beautiful setting of the University of British Columbia. The campus, located on the tip of Point Grey, consists of 982 acres.

The City Museum, the Vancouver Maritime Museum, several art galleries, the Queen Elizabeth Theater and Playhouse, the Ann Hathaway District, the First Iron Horse, and the Old Hastings Mill, together with all kinds of entertainment spots, stores and restaurants, are just a few of Vancouver's many attractions. The city's environs, West and North Vancouver, Burnaby, New Westminster, and Richmond, also have much to interest and entertain the visitor. The Royal Vancouver, Burrard, Kitsilano, West Vancouver, Eagle Harbor, Richmond and Royal City Yacht Clubs, and the Vancouver Cruising Club are the principal boating organizations with headquarters and clubhouses in the Greater Vancouver area.

VICTORIA—Known as "A Little Bit of Old England," this provincial capital of British Columbia is a paradise for the visitor. Tying up at the Inner Harbor floats in front of the Empress Hotel, one immediately has the feeling of arriving in a foreign country. Scenically situated on the southeastern tip of Vancouver Island, its rugged rocky shores with protecting islands, its downtown hanging flower baskets, the many lovely parks and the exquisite private home lawns and flower gardens (designed and tended with typical English talent)—all blend to make a city of incomparable beauty.

With both a pioneer and a maritime background, Victoria's history is a fascinating study. Growing out of the Hudson's Bay Company's Fort Victoria, established in 1843, it was incorporated in 1862. Probably the best way to see some of the points of interest and, at the same time, enjoy a ride from out of the past, is to take one of the tours in the horse-drawn surreys, which leave regularly from the Inner Harbor area. A ride can also be taken on a genuine London double-decker bus.

Some of the town's most interesting attractions include the Parliament Buildings, museums, provincial library and archives; totem poles in Thunderbird Park; the Empress Hotel, with tea served each afternoon in the large lounge lobby; Crystal Gardens; the Royal London Wax Museum; the Undersea Gardens; old, historic houses, such as Helmcken House and Point Ellise House; and Fort Victoria with Bastion jail, cannons and museum. Children will enjoy the Land of Little People with Model Village and the Wooded Wonderland, a children's park.

At least one visit to Victoria should include the short trip to Butchart Gardens, as magnificent a display of outstanding landscaping and exotically beautiful floriculture in artistic arrangements as can be found.

In addition to the Inner Harbor, Oak Bay has an excellent marina complex with moorage, all services and a fine restaurant. Victoria has the Royal Victoria Yacht Club with clubhouses on Cadboro Bay, the Capital City Yacht Club, and the Victoria Cruising Club.

NANAIMO—This picturesque city is frequently visited by yachtsmen and frequently time is available while awaiting suitable weather for crossing the gulf. Lt. Comdr. Francisco Eliza named the place Bocas de Wintuhuyscn in 1791. Five Indian bands in the area had formed a confederacy which they called Sne-ny-mo, meaning "the whole group meeting together" or "a big strong tribe." From that evolved the name, Nanaimo. It had also been previously called Colvilletown. For many years a huge harvest of coal was taken but that has fallen off now and been replaced by logging, lumbering and sea products. High points of interest include Georgia Park, overlooking the harbor, with its totem poles and Indian war canoes; Bowen Park with Millstream Falls, picnicking and tennis; and the Bastion, old Hudson's Bay Company Fort established in 1853 and now a museum. South of the city is Petroglyph Park. Stores, shops, theaters and restaurants are close to the public small boat harbor. The Nanaimo Yacht Club, located north of the city's downtown section, has a clubhouse and floats.

CAMPBELL RIVER—Located on Discovery Passage just below Seymour Narrows, this town is perhaps best known as a sports and commercial fishing center. With modern shopping center, stores and markets, a variety of services and other facilities, it serves as a center for a huge surrounding area of islands and remote settlements. Largest industry is the Elk Falls Mill, and tours can be taken during the summer to see the conversion of logs to paper. The Campbell River Museum has a large well-known collection of early history and Indian artifacts. Indian carvings, pottery, soapstone carvings, shell and bead work, paintings, jade work, Indian sweaters, and rag rugs can be seen and purchased at specialty shops. A favorite pastime for young and old is casting for salmon off the government wharf, where fish up to 34 pounds have been caught. Canada's oldest Tyee Club, dedicated to the conservation and propagation of tyee salmon, is here. Annual events are the Salmon Festival, July 1-4; the Campbell River Courier Salmon Derby, the second Sunday in August; the Lion's Club Trout Derby in late May, and a Scuba Diving Meet, on the same weekend.

POWELL RIVER, WESTVIEW—Although Powell River is the town, yachtsmen are better acquainted with its residential suburb, Westview. As the last town of any size for many miles in a vast cruising area, it is a popular place to stop for provisioning and replenishing ship's stores before heading into the more remote regions. Two good small boat harbors are next to each other behind rock breakwaters. Most needs can be found in Westview but Powell River is a mill town and tours can be arranged through this huge plant.

KITIMAT—This town, with an Indian name meaning "People of the Snow," is a brand new city. It was 1948 when an Alcan survey crew found the area at the head of Douglas Channel and Kitimat area to be suitable for the establishment of a giant aluminum smelter. Work started in 1951 and now Kitimat is a well-planned community of 11,000 people. Over $470,000,000 has been invested to date. Tours are available through the plant as well as through the Eurocan Pulp and Paper Mill.

PRINCE RUPERT—Known as the "Halibut Capital of the World," this northernmost British Columbia port city has the third largest natural harbor in the world. There is a good small boat harbor and several moorages for the many fishing boats. During July and August the salmon canneries are open to visitors, and the Museum of Northern British Columbia, with its three historic totem poles, can provide hours of interesting pastime. Prince Rupert has a variety of stores, markets, restaurants and theaters. There are several parks and another attraction is the Butze Rapids, a reversing tidal stream. The Prince Rupert Rowing and Yacht Club is on the waterfront, just below the small boat harbor.

41

Alaskan Ports of Call

Although there are only a half dozen cities, as such, in the southeastern panhandle of Alaska, the yachtsman cruising in these waters no doubt will be more interested in spending some time in them than he might be in the cities closer to home.

There is an aura of romance about the pioneer towns of the north, hard to explain but making an exploring tour ashore an exciting event. The historical lore of the north, gold-rush days, Indians, fishing, and plenty of the frontier life still in evidence—all lure the visitor.

KETCHIKAN—This "First City in Alaska" is known as the "Salmon Capital of the World" although, with precipitation up to 156 inches per year, it is sometimes jokingly referred to as the "Rain Capital." With a population of about 7000, the town's name is derived from a Tlingit Indian name for the place, Kach-kanna. As the gateway to Alaska on the Inside Passage, the town with its friendly inhabitants does an excellent job of welcoming visitors to the forty-ninth state.

As in any seaport, the waterfront is always full of interest, and Ketchikan's waterfront is a long one. There are totem poles downtown, at the ball park, at the fish hatchery and two out-of-town displays, one 11 miles north at Totem Bight and the other a bit south at Saxman Indian Village. A new museum overlooks a famous salmon spawning stream. The replica of old Fort Tongass, standing high on a hillside, affords a sweeping view of the town, its waterfront and the channel upon which it is situated. With the pulp industry now an important part of Alaska's industry, a tour through the pulp mill at nearby Ward Cove is an interesting and educational trip.

Both the old and new Alaska will be found in the stores, and you can choose between a supermarket or a trading post. Good restaurants offer a variety of specialties with seafood, of course, high on the list. Being an Elk or friend of an Elk will get you into the Ketchikan Elk's Club, where the food is excellent. Thomas Boat Basin has plenty of moorage and the Ketchikan Yacht Club welcomes visitors from stateside.

WRANGELL—Informality highlights the charm of this small town. With some 2000 residents, it is situated on a natural harbor near the northern tip of Wrangell Island. Named for Baron Von Wrangell, a Russian governor of Alaska, it has an interesting past under the flags of three nations—Russia, England and the United States. The Russians originally built their fort, Redoubt St. Dionysius, at the mouth of the Stikine River to keep the British out of this rich fur-trading area. Later, when the British and the Hudson's Bay Company took over, they called it Fort Stikine and, still later, the United States named it Wrangell.

First as a supply point for fur traders and gold prospectors and more recently as a lumbering and seafood-processing center, it is an important hub in the area's economy. There has been no large "expansion" and life flows along on a comfortable day-to-day basis.

Visiting yachts can tie up at the floats in the outer harbor or go around the island to the inner harbor. The Chief Shakes community tribal house and large collection of totem poles are the main attraction of the park on the little island. Totem poles can also be seen on the short walk from the harbor to the center of town. A large modern supermarket, the Thunderbird Hotel, and Winnie's Restaurant are some of the more modern additions to the town.

If timing is right, it's possible to purchase a five-pound can of dry-pack shrimp at the cannery, and it's almost an even bet that these succulent little tidbits will be gone before you get back to the boat.

A spectacular four-day river cruise up the Stikine River,

past innumerable glaciers and historic landmarks, is available in a typical river boat for those who have the time. It is best to inquire in advance and make reservations at the Stikine Transportation Company in Wrangell.

PETERSBURG—Founded on fishing by hardy Norwegian fishermen in the late 1800s, this town, like Wrangell, has a population of about 2000. Unlike Wrangell, however, its people came to fish, and so almost everything is fishing oriented. Named for Peter Buschmann, one of its founders, Petersburg has that solid Norwegian look, with neat substantial homes.

The waterfront and boat harbor are a beehive of activity. One of the principal pastimes of young and old alike seems to be fishing or jigging for herring off the floats; grandpas and grandsons pick up a pailful in just a short time. There is a good tidal grid for work on boat bottoms or damaged propellers. Seafood, fish or the tasty little local shrimp, are readily available from the processing plants, at the stores or, sometimes, direct from the fisherman.

The downtown section has much the appearance of a frontier town with false-front buildings, although the stores and markets are completely modern. A museum is filled with items from the town's Norwegian past and the previous Indian culture. Dominating the displays is a stuffed and mounted record 126½-pound salmon. The Fiske Memorial (fiske for "fish") is an artistic fountain with salmon, halibut and herring fashioned in copper by Carson Boysen, who taught art at the high school for a time.

It's been said that Peterburg's World Champion Salmon Derby is in progress the year-around. Special holidays are the Fourth of July and Norwegian Independence Day on May 17. As in most Alaskan towns, much of the social life centers around the Elks Club.

There are at least three hotels, two restaurants downtown and one, the Beachcomber, famous for its smorgasbord, just out of town a few miles.

Icebergs are sometimes a part of life in Petersburg. The 15-mile-distant LeConte Bay, with LeConte Glacier at its head, is always spewing huge chunks of ice into Frederick Sound. At times some of these float into the harbor, occasionally they are big enough to cause trouble by endangering the boats, floats and shore buildings. Yachtsmen can take their own boats down to the bay to view the colorful icebergs and glaciers or take the *Blue Star,* a steel boat which runs regular excursion trip to LeConte Bay from Petersburg.

JUNEAU—This third largest city in Alaska and state capital has been correctly called a "cliff hanger." Situated on a shelf between a near straight-up mountain and an inland arm of the Pacific Ocean, it achieves an atmosphere of friendly togetherness that is unique. In addition, there's enough of the old pioneer and gold-rush mood to make it truly fascinating to the visitor.

Although the fixed price of gold has made mining the yellow metal unprofitable in this area, the aura of gold still hangs over the city, along with the busy business of state government. Steep narrow streets in the downtown area wind between a hodgepodge of old buildings and gleaming new structures. Stores, specialty shops, supermarkets, and business firms are strictly modern and progressive, and the people are typically western—friendly.

History and the old culture of the town and state are well documented in several places, highlighted by a museum, the Capitol Building, the Governor's Mansion and the library. Totem poles are much in evidence and the original Abe Lincoln totem is properly preserved in the museum. A must for the visitor interested in the lore and history of Alaska is a visit to the House of Wickersham, where you'll see artifacts and treasures from the past, get a palatable history lesson along with a serving of "flaming sourdough," all served up by this famous pioneer judge's niece.

A visit to the Alaska-Juneau Gold Mine is a never-to-be-forgotten experience which shouldn't be missed. The ride in an ore car through one of the tunnels ends with a breathtaking view of Juneau, next-door-neighbor Douglas, and the Gastineau Channel. A stop at the famed Red Dog Saloon with its sawdust-covered floor gives a taste of frontier life, although it lacks some of the old flavor since modern rebuilding forced it to move from its original quarters.

Another attraction is the Mendenhall Glacier, just a few miles out of town. Here you can meet a real Alaskan glacier intimately in a face-to-face confrontation and learn about these "shapers of the earth" in the Visitor's Center. This trip should also include a look at spawning salmon in the stream on the way, a visit to Auke Bay and a stop at the Chapel by the Lake, where the congregation looks out through a picture window across the blue lake to the glacier and the background of mountains.

There are many other things to see in this interesting town, and the Chamber of Commerce in the Gastineau Hotel or the Alaskan Airlines office in the Baranof Hotel will be happy to tell you about them and make any necessary arrangements or reservations. The Juneau Yacht Club has moorages and a clubhouse on one of the two excellent small boat harbors.

HAINES, PORT CHILKOOT, SKAGWAY—These towns, near the head of deep, fjordlike Lynn Canal, are each different although set amid the same spectacular scenery. For the yachtsman, they are the end-of-the-line for cruising in the southeastern panhandle, but for other travelers they can be the gateway to the north.

Although Haines and Port Chilkoot are sometimes called twin cities because they are located side by side, any twin-like similarity ends there. Their characters are entirely different. Haines, founded in 1881, has an economy founded on lumber and fishing. It is also today, as in the past, a source of supplies with well-stocked stores. A recent additional business activity is the tank farm on nearby Lutak Inlet, providing storage for the Haines-Fairbanks pipeline.

Port Chilkoot, ex-Fort William Seward, was sold as surplus after World War II to five war veterans and is still a typical army base in appearance. Local residents are proud of their town and happy to tell you about it or direct you to the places of interest.

Both towns have adequate hotels and restaurants, with Halsingland Hotel in Port Chilkoot a place to see, even if it is not patronized. The Dalton Trail Bar in Port Chilkoot with its "iceworm" is a popular social spot.

SKAGWAY—Looking much like a setting for a wild-west or ghost-town movie, this town maintains much of its turn-of-the-century atmosphere as a jumping-off place for the fabled gold fields of the Klondike. Unpaved streets, boardwalks, and false-front buildings all add to the frontier mood, yet there are modern buildings mixed in. Although the residents may work at keeping the ghost-town and gold-rush atmosphere, they are very active and alive. There in an interesting museum with a good collection of historical relics.

If you happen to be in town when a cruise ship arrives, you can enjoy a nightly performance of the *Shooting of Dan McGrew* and other acts put on for the fun of it by the local residents.

Skagway may be the end-of-the-line for the cruising yachtsman, but he can, and should, take the "Escape Hatch" train ride on the White Pass and Yukon Railroad to Lake Bennett and Whitehorse. Although the railroad has, of necessity, been modernized to some extent, there are still parlor cars with those old reversible plush seats, a water cooler with cone-shaped paper cups and a potbelly stove. The scenery over the pass at the lake is spectacular and magnificent.

SITKA—This former capital of Alaska takes its name from a Tlingit Indian word meaning "in this place." Steeped in history, the town has a wealth of interesting attractions. The Visitor's Center is a good place to get information on where to go and what to see, as well as to view several exhibits and perhaps, if you're lucky, catch a performance by the Russian Dancers, actually local housewives. The Sitka National Monument, the Sheldon Jackson Museum, Castle Hill, Totem Square, the Alaska Pioneer Home, two ancient cemeteries, and the reconstructed blockhouse are just a few of the many points of interest.

For years the Russian Orthodox St. Michael's Cathedral with its "carrot spire and onion dome" was a major attraction. Built in 1848, it was a treasure-house of valuable works of art, icons, embroidered altar cloths, old and rare Bibles, jeweled chalices and other historical and religious items. In January, 1966, it burned to the ground but, through the heroic efforts of the townspeople, most of the treasures were saved. The cathedral is to be reconstructed exactly as it was but raising the necessary money is a slow process. In the meantime, the foundation and basement houses the treasures, and visitors may view them.

There is plenty of interest along the busy waterfront, and a fine small boat harbor has plenty of moorage. Most of the town's attractions are within walking distance but guided bus tours are available. Sitka's setting is beautiful, with a harbor full of scenic little cupcake islands and Fujiyama-like Mount Edgecumbe dominating the background.

Southeastern Alaska's towns are all different but all fascinating, and the visiting yachtsman will want to plan his cruising itinerary to allow plenty of time to enjoy and savor them. We can only hope that the steady encroachment of more and more "civilization" will not reach them too soon and that, when it does, residents can somehow maintain a fair share of the charm with which they are now endowed.